Psychophysiological
Disorders

Psychophysiological
Disorders

**Research and
Clinical Applications**

Edited by Robert J. Gatchel and Edward B. Blanchard
American Psychological Association, Washington, DC

First printing December 1993
Second printing October 1994
Third printing April 1998

Published by
American Psychological Association
750 First Street, NE
Washington, DC 20002

Copies may be ordered from
APA Order Department
P.O. Box 92984
Washington, DC 20090-2984

In the UK and Europe, copies may be ordered from
American Psychological Association
3 Henrietta Street
Covent Garden, London
WC2E 8LU England

Typeset in Palatino by Techna Type, Inc., York, PA

Printer: Braun-Brumfield, Inc., Ann Arbor, MI
Cover and Jacket Designer: Ethel Kessler Design, Inc., Bethesda, MD
Technical/Production Editor: Mark A. Meschter

Library of Congress Cataloging-in-Publication Data

Psychophysiological disorders : research and clinical applications /
    edited by Robert J. Gatchel and Edward B. Blanchard.
        p.   cm.
    Includes bibliographical references and index.
    ISBN 1-55798-217-1 (acid-free paper)
    1. Medicine, Psychosomatic. 2. Psychophysiology. I. Gatchel
    Robert J., 1947–   . II. Blanchard, Edward B.
    RC49.P75   1993
    616.08—dc20   93-35621
                                                                       CIP

British Library Cataloguing-in-Publication Data
A CIP record is available from the British Library

Printed in the United States of America

Contents

Contributors

Bruce G. Bender, National Jewish Center for Immunology and Respiratory Medicine, Denver, Colorado

Edward B. Blanchard, Department of Psychology, State University of New York at Albany

Elizabeth Brondolo, Department of Psychology, St. John's University

Thomas L. Creer, Department of Psychology, Ohio University

Robert R. Freedman, Department of Psychology, Wayne State University

Steven Friedman, Department of Psychiatry, State University of New York Health Science Center at Brooklyn

Sheryle J. Gallant, Department of Medical Psychology, Uniformed Services University of the Health Sciences, Bethesda, Maryland

Robert J. Gatchel, Department of Psychiatry, University of Texas Southwestern Medical Center, Dallas

Alan G. Glaros, Department of Behavioral Science, University of Missouri–Kansas City

Ernest G. Glass, Department of Oral Diagnosis, University of Missouri–Kansas City

Jean A. Hamilton, Department of Psychology: Social and Health Sciences, Duke University

John P. Hatch, Department of Psychiatry, University of Texas Health Science Center at San Antonio

Marjorie Hatch, Department of Psychiatry, State University of New York Health Science Center at Brooklyn

John B. Kostis, Department of Medicine, Robert Wood Johnson Medical School, University of Medicine and Dentistry of New Jersey, Piscataway

Cheryl Paradis, Department of Psychiatry, State University of New York Health Science Center at Brooklyn

William H. Polonsky, Department of Psychiatry, Harvard Medical School

Raymond C. Rosen, Departments of Psychiatry and Medicine, Robert Wood Johnson Medical School, University of Medicine and Dentistry of New Jersey, Piscataway

Larry D. Young, Department of Anesthesia, Bowman-Gray School of Medicine, Wake Forest University

Foreword: Application and Practice in Health Psychology

The Division of Health Psychology (Division 38) of the American Psychological Association is pleased to announce the first volume in a new series that will highlight the application and practice of health psychology. One of the driving forces behind the establishment of the division was interest in health promotion and disease prevention and treatment through the application of principles and procedures that were emerging in the research arena. The vitality of health psychology depends on an active dialogue between its researchers and practitioners. One of the important goals of the series is to further expand this dialogue. Attempts to translate research findings into applications and interventions, to test and evaluate the efficacy of these interventions, and to denote important clinical experiences and research needs of the practice of health psychology will be the focus of these volumes. Transfer of knowledge; feedback to researchers regarding needs, failures, and successes of clinical interventions; and facilitation and expansion of necessary dialogue between scientist and practitioner are the objectives.

In service of these aims, the volumes in this series will function as vehicles for translating research into practice with an analysis of issues that are related to the evaluation, prevention, and treatment of health behaviors and health problems. These goals will be met by treating clinical or applied health psychology as broadly as possible, including community and public health assessment and intervention methods and problems of health care utilization. Issues will be considered across a variety of settings, including hospitals, the practitioner's office, community clinics, work-site settings, schools, and managed care settings. Each volume will provide direction in areas of need and populations to be served by health psychology intervention; critically examine issues and problems involved in clinical evaluation, prevention, and treatment of specific disorders; and illustrate the effectiveness of novel clinical approaches to diagnosis and treatment that may guide future research and innovation. Each volume will focus on a topic, such as this inaugural book's emphasis on psychophysiological disorders, and will synthesize research on a range of topics to reinforce the theoretical and scientific rationale for the practice of health psychology and to identify critical issues in the prevention, assessment, and management of health problems.

Andrew Baum
Bethesda, Maryland

Margaret Chesney
San Francisco, California

Preface

Over the past decade, health psychology has emerged as an important subdiscipline of psychology. It represents an amalgam of a wide array of diverse areas, from basic biomedical research concerns to health care–provider issues. As such, this field is expanding at a dizzying pace and is continuing to attract a growing number of researchers and clinicians. During its early years of development, the field was primarily "driven" by research-oriented psychologists who were intent on demonstrating in a scientifically rigorous manner the important links between health and behavior. Within the American Psychological Association, Division 38 (Health Psychology) was formed, and the journal *Health Psychology* began publication to lure more clinically oriented psychologists who were intrigued by the great many applied implications of this research. These clinicians joined an already substantial group of psychologists who were involved in health services. As a consequence, there has been a growing demand by these practitioners for the dissemination of more information that directly relates to applied clinical concerns such as health care–provider issues and service applications.

In an attempt to respond to this demand and the need for more clinically relevant materials being requested by practitioners, an edited series of volumes was proposed that would publish material that has greater relevance and interest to clinical health psychologists. The content of this book focuses on psychophysiological disorders. The combined topic of assessment and treatment of these disorders has provided a traditional interface between psychology and health and, therefore, was viewed as an appropriate lead volume in this series.

The chapter authors were challenged with the following goal: Provide up-to-date summaries and critical evaluations of the recent treatment and assessment literature on various psychophysiological disorders, as well as simultaneously present clinically useful information and advice for the health psychology practitioner who may be called on to provide clinical services to patients with one of these disorders. We believe that the authors of the chapters in this book have successfully accomplished this task.

The authors were specifically requested to address four principal topics in their chapters: (a) epidemiology, or the magnitude of the problem that the disorder represents; (b) etiology, especially what is known about the role of psychological and behavioral factors; (c) assessment issues; and (d) treatment issues. In covering the last two topics, the contributors were asked, as research clinicians, to draw on their own clinical experience and on summaries of the literature to make recommendations for clinical practice, especially for the practice of the clinical health psychologist. Although—as one would expect—the presentation styles of the authors differ, we feel that they all "did their job" and that the resulting product will be an invaluable resource to clinical health psychologists who regularly deal with psychophysiological disorders. Not only is there an up-to-date review of the topic concerning etiology, or what is known about etiology, but there is also a very thoughtful consideration of important assessment and treatment issues that will be of pragmatic use to clinicians. We hope that this book will serve as a stimulus for both researchers and clinicians who are involved in issues of etiology, assessment, and treatment of these challenging biopsychological disorders.

Robert J. Gatchel
Edward B. Blanchard

Chapter 1

Psychophysiological Disorders: Past and Present Perspectives

Robert J. Gatchel

> As you ought not to attempt to cure the eyes without the head, or the head without the body, then neither ought you to attempt to cure the body without the soul . . . for the part will never be well unless the whole is well.
>
> —Plato

Psychophysiological disorders, traditionally called psychosomatic disorders, are characterized by physical symptoms or dysfunctions in various bodily organs and systems that are intimately linked with psychosocial factors. The just-mentioned epigraph from Plato (cited by Lipowski, 1986), highlights the early Greek philosophers' holistic view of man. The mind (or soul) and the body were perceived as an interactive whole. Through the ages, perspectives on how closely these physical and psychosocial dimensions of disease and illness are interrelated have greatly changed and have significantly altered the manner in which such disorders have been perceived and treated. In this chapter, I review these changing perspectives to provide a foundation for better understanding current approaches to assessment and strategies for treatment in this important area of behavioral medicine.

Historical Overview of the Mind–Body Relationship

The relationship between the mind and body has long been controversial among philosophers, physiologists, and psychologists. Are experiences purely mental, purely physical, or an interaction of the physical and the mental? The view that there are delicate interrelationships between the mind and body can be found in ancient literary documents from Babylonia and Greece, in which dry mouth and racing heart are associated with fear or anger and in which headaches are triggered by emotional stress (Gentry & Matarazzo, 1981). Indeed, the ancient Greek physician Hippocrates (400–300 BC) proposed one of the earliest temperamental theories of personality. He suggested that four bodily fluids, called *humors*, were responsible for personality or temperament, as well as for physical or mental illness. The four proposed humors were blood, black bile, yellow bile, and phlegm. Subsequently, Galen (AD 130–200) elaborated on this four-humor theory. An excess of yellow bile was linked to a *choleric* temperament. It was assumed that yellow bile prompted an individual to become chronically angry and irritable, hence the word *choleric* (angry), which literally means bile. The *melancholic* personality type, which is characterized by dejection, sadness, and pessimism, was viewed as resulting from a preponderance of black bile. In direct contrast, the *sanguine* personality type resulted from a predominance of blood, which caused a buoyant, hopeful personality. Finally, the *phlegmatic* personality type resulted from a predominance of phlegm and was characterized by sluggishness and apathy. For all of its obvious shortcomings, the four-humor theory remained popular until only a few centuries ago. It illustrates how physical or biological factors have been seen through the ages as significantly interacting with and affecting the personality or psychological state of an individual. It implies the belief that psychological factors may cause bodily diseases. Indeed, the ancient works asserted that emotions, or *passions* as they were frequently called, not only could influence bodily functions but could also cause disease (Lipowski, 1986).

However, the traditional view of the interrelationship between mind and body lost favor in the 17th century. With the advent of physical medicine during the Renaissance, the belief that the mind (or the soul) influences the body came to be regarded as unscientific. Understanding of the mind and soul was relegated to religion and philosophy, whereas understanding of the body was considered to be in the separate realm of physical medicine. A new wave or approach to the investigation of physical phenomena emerged during this period. The seminal textbook on anatomy *De Humani Corporis Fabrica* (*"On the Make Up of the Human Body"*) was published in 1543 by the Dutch physician and teacher Andreas Vesalius. His work was based on the dissection of the human body and associated experimentation. It highlighted the revolution in methods of gaining knowledge through careful observation, experimentation, and instrumentation rather than relying on common sense, outdated dogma, or mythology. Vesalius's work marked the origin of the science of anatomy and paved the way for subsequent advances in anatomy and physiology. In 1628, the English physician William Harvey used this objective scientific method to make the monumental deduction that blood circulates in the body and is propelled by the heart. This discovery was especially important because it replaced the older theory of humors, which was based purely on conjecture rather than scientific experimentation, as the principal means of explaining physical functioning.

These revolutionary works marked the advancement of the view that the body can be explained by its own mechanisms. This *biomedical reductionism* gradually led to the belief that concepts such as the mind or soul were not needed to explain physical functioning or behavior. It stimulated a revolution of knowledge, with sciences such as physics, anatomy, and physiology evolving simultaneously, all of which are based on the principles of scientific investigation. This new mechanistic approach to the study of human anatomy and physiology also, unfortunately, fostered a dualistic viewpoint that mind and body function separately and independently. Before this time, civilization's physicians, in the multiple roles of philosopher–teacher, priest, and healer, had approached the understanding of mind–body interactions in a more holistic way.

The individual who is usually credited with developing and initially popularizing the dualistic viewpoint is the 17th century French philosopher René Descartes (1596–1650). Descartes argued that the mind or soul was a separate entity parallel to and incapable of affecting physical matter or somatic processes in any direct way. This *Cartesian dualism* of mind and body became the predominant philosophical basis for medicine. Descartes suggested that the mind and body could interact, with the pineal gland located in the midbrain being the vital connection between the mind and the body. However, his basic tenet of dualism moved the newly independent field of medicine away from a holistic approach to *psyche–soma* interactions and toward the mechanistic pathophysiological approach that has dominated the field of Western medicine until relatively recently. Indeed, traditionally in Western culture it has been hard to view the mind and body as one, as evidenced by the lack of an English word adequately denoting the union of the mind and the body.

The discovery in the 19th century that microorganisms caused certain diseases produced even further acceptance of this dualistic viewpoint. In the new scientific era of medicine, mechanical laws and physiological principles became the only acceptable basis for explaining disease.

Emergence of Psychiatry and Psychology

Strict dualism, however, mellowed during the mid-19th century, primarily because of the work of physicians such as Claude Bernard (1813–1878). Bernard was one of the first prominent physicians to emphasize the role of psychological factors in physical ailments. Subsequently, as discussed later, Sigmund Freud (1856–1939) became influential in stressing the interaction of psychological and physical factors in various disorders. In the United States, Benjamin Rush (1745–1813), who wrote the first U.S. textbook on psychiatry in 1812, argued that "actions of the mind" were possible causes of many diseases and that treatment of these actions might be medically beneficial. Although the emphasis was still on the role that the body, microorganisms, and biological factors had in determining illness, medicine gradually became aware of other significant influences. The concept of *psychogenesis* (i.e., the belief that psychological factors can affect bodily processes) was gradually revived.

The 20th century evidenced a great deal of growth in an integrated, holistic approach to health and illness, especially because of the advent of modern psychiatry and psychology. The concept of holism, as Lipowski (1986) notes, is derived from the Greek *holos*, or "whole." It was first introduced by Jan Christiaan Smuts (1870–1950) in 1926 and refers to a view of man and nature (Smuts, 1926). This concept dates back to the Greek philosophers Hippocrates, Plato, Aristotle, and others. It views the mind and body as an indivisible whole, and requires study of the whole person rather than isolated parts. The Cartesian dualism first expounded in the 17th century was a significant obstacle to this holistic view of humans as something other than machinelike bodies. However, the pendulum began to swing back to more integrated approaches.

The principal arena for this integration has traditionally been psychosomatic medicine, which has also gone through a transition in recent years. The basic belief of psychosomatic medicine was that social and psychological factors are important in the etiology, development, and maintenance of many illnesses, as well as in the treatment of these illnesses. This was based on increased reports of illnesses that did not fit the solely biomedical view of health and disease. The initial discoveries of the importance of psychological factors in health-relevant matters were made largely by psychiatrists and psychodynamically oriented psychologists. Their work stemmed directly from the psychoanalytic work of Sigmund Freud (cf. Freud, 1959), who described in detailed case studies the occurrence of many physical symptoms that were seemingly caused by psychological factors (e.g., in his classic studies of conversion hysteria). Even before Freud's influential writings, however, there were other reports of hysterical states. For example, Franz Mesmer (1734–1815), an Austrian physician practicing in Vienna and Paris in the late 18th century, reported many cases of hysterical conditions, such as blindness, deafness, and paralysis, in which the physical incapacities made no biomedical sense. Likewise, the well-known Parisian neurologist Jean Martin Charcot (1825–1893) also studied hysterical states and observed how hypnosis could be used to produce and remove such symptoms.

The first formal psychological formulation of psychosomatic disorders, however, was Freud's elaboration of conversion hysteria. Although conversion hysteria was not considered a psychosomatic disorder per se, because there is no actual organic dysfunction, the basic psychological mechanisms in both were considered similar. According to his psychoanalytic theory, when socially unacceptable and forbidden impulses cannot be expressed, they are repressed and alternative channels for discharging them are sought. If appropriate alternative channels cannot be found, more drastic methods, such as those that occur in hysterical conversion reactions, are used. For example, an individual's wish to strike a significant other may be unacceptable because of the threat of severe punishment. If repression cannot adequately defend against the expression of this impulse, then the individual might develop paralysis of the arm. This would be a compromise coping method that allowed the simultaneous discharge of energy in a defense against the action. Repressed instinctual impulses were assumed to be expressed at a somatic level, through the production of a somatic symptom that has a meaningful symbolic relationship to the psychic event. Psychophysiological disorders were interpreted in a similar fashion within this psychoanalytic perspective.

Subsequent Psychodynamic Formulations

Even many psychoanalysts, however, regarded this psychodynamic formulation as highly speculative, and little evidence supports it. However, Alexander (1950) elaborated the notion that specific illnesses are caused by an individual's internal conflicts, and such a theory of psychogenesis actually dominated the field of psychosomatic medicine until the 1960s. Unlike Freud, Alexander emphasized the association of specific personality patterns, rather than a single conflict, with particular illnesses. He rejected the view that conversion could account for any physical illness. For example, Alexander suggested that each of the psychosomatic disorders has its own specific dynamic constellation, or *nuclear conflicts,* and personality characteristics. His formulation was based largely on clinical observation of patients undergoing psychoanalysis. He believed that repressed psychic energy could be discharged directly into the autonomic nervous system, which would lead to impairment of visceral functioning. He assumed that specific unconscious emotional conflicts were associated with specific psychosomatic disturbances. Thus, repressed rage was the primary emotional conflict underlying essential hypertension, and unresolved dependency needs were significant in ulcer patients. Alexander's formulation has not been supported by much research, however, except in the case of essential hypertension, for which there has been some support for the association of certain personality characteristics with the expression of rage. The assumption of a simple, linear, causal chain between unconscious conflicts and the expression of physiological symptoms is no longer accepted.

A more recent psychodynamic formulation of psychosomatic disorders centered around the concept of *alexithymia*. Sifneos (1967) and Nemiah (1973, 1975) contended that the psychosomatic process is often characterized by alexithymia, which refers to a cluster of cognitive traits that are marked mainly by an inability of patients to describe their feelings. According to Nemiah (1975), the alexithymic personality displays the following: (a) an inability to describe feelings verbally, (b) a significant paucity of fantasy, and (c) an inability to make any significant internal psychological changes in the course of psychodynamically oriented psychotherapy. It is this emotionality deficit that is assumed to be the principal underpinning of psychosomatic disorders.

Another variation, although not strictly psychodynamic, was the *specific attitudes theory* that was proposed by Graham and colleagues (Graham, 1972; Graham, Stern, & Winokur, 1958). These investigators conducted a series of experiments that examined the relationship between specific attitudes toward a distressing life situation and the occurrence of particular psychophysiological disorders. These attitudes, which related to what individuals felt was happening to them on a chronic basis and what they wanted to do about it, were originally obtained in clinical interviews with patients who suffered from various psychophysiological disorders. These attitudes were initially assessed in a study by Grace and Graham (1952) in which 128 patients with 12 different psychosomatic disorders or symptoms were evaluated. This evaluation indicated that patients with the same disorder similarly described their attitudes toward events that occurred just before the appearance or worsening of their symptoms. Subsequent and better controlled studies by Graham and colleagues (cf. Graham, 1972) further validated the presence of these attitudes. Some of the associations found were hypertension (the person feels threatened by an ever-present danger and as a result must be on guard, watchful, and prepared), ulcers (the person feels deprived of what is due him or her and seeks revenge and to get even), and migraines (the person feels that something has to be achieved and then relaxes after the effort).

A significant advantage of the Graham formulation over previous approaches was its more precise operational definition of constructs, availability of independent variables that could be experimentally manipulated (the specific attitudes), and dependent measures that could be reliably and objectively measured (physiological responding). According to the Graham formulation, one should be able to predict the type of psychosomatic illness an individual is likely to get by assessing his or her attitudes toward life. However, support for these associations has not been consistently found.

Emergence of Psychosomatic Medicine

Lipowski (1986) provided a thorough historical overview of the field of psychosomatic medicine, which had its beginnings in the early 1930s and was greatly influenced by the concepts of psychogenesis and holism reviewed earlier. Two trends stimulated this movement. The first was that toward psychoanalysis, discussed earlier, which revived the concept of psychogenesis. The second was the articulation of holistic concepts by the U.S. psychiatrist Adolff Meyer (1866–1950) who labeled this field of study as *psychobiology* (Meyer, 1957). He proposed psychobiology as the scientific study of a human as a whole person, in both health and disease. The mind and body were viewed as two distinct but integrated parts of the human organism, constituting a whole or psychobiological unit. According to Meyer, to understand health and illness one had to evaluate both the psychological and biological features of their dynamic and interactive processes.

As Lipowski (1986) pointed out, this psychobiological approach was largely responsible for the development of general hospital psychiatry, the psychobiological research on mental illness, and the holistic viewpoint in psychiatric practice. One of Meyer's followers, Helen Flanders Dunbar (1902–1959), promulgated this approach and advanced its popularity by authoring an influential book on this holistic perspective on patient care (Dunbar, 1935). She stimulated clinical research on the correlation between personality types and various physical illnesses and popularized the field of psychosomatic medicine, which emphasized mind–body unity. She was the founder of the American Psychosomatic Society and the first journal in the field in 1939.

Later Changes in the Field of Psychosomatic Medicine

In the late 1950s, the field of psychosomatic medicine underwent a major crisis because of the growing reaction against the psychoanalytic approach (which had great influence in the field because of the work of clinical investigators such as Alexander). The psychoanalytic approach was viewed as unscientific because of the methodological weaknesses of the clinical data on which it was developed, as well as the often circular theoretical reasoning it used to explain various clinical phenomena. It was this unfortunate association with the concepts of psychoanalysis, which were seriously questioned by the more scientifically oriented behavioral approaches to maladaptive behavior, that caused many to challenge the scientific rigor of the field of psychosomatic medicine.

Harold G. Wolff (1898–1962) helped to save the field of psychosomatic medicine from the total decline to which criticisms of the psychoanalytic approach to the study of mind–body interactions threatened to bring it. Wolff's publication in 1953 of the work *Stress and Disease* made significant contributions to the field. On the theoretical level, he was much more rigorous, and his research was highlighted by careful description and measurement of both the psychological and physiological factors investigated. He strongly adhered to the scientific method. Moreover, he focused on conscious rather than unconscious emotions, in marked contrast to the then-dominant psychoanalytic approach. For example, in a well-known experimental study of gastric functioning in a fistula patient, "Tom," Wolf and Wolff (1947) systematically evaluated changes in gastric secretion and motor activity under different emotional stress conditions. In aggressive states of anger and resentment, Tom displayed an increase in gastric secretion and motor activity; the emotional states of fright and depression, on the other hand, led to corresponding decreases in gastric functioning. Studies such as these marked the move away from psychoanalytic attempts to deal with complex hypothetical constructs such as the unconscious to the direct assessment of quantifiable emotional states.

Wolff also cautioned against overly generalizing from clinical and experimental data, again a major "sin" of psychoanalytic approaches. Actually, his approach became known as the *psychophysiological approach* because of its concerted departure from the then-dominant psychoanalytic perspective. At that time, many clinical researchers began to use the term *psychophysiological disorders* rather than *psychosomatic disorders* because of the perceived need to disassociate themselves from the earlier and much criticized psychodynamic orientations and to associate themselves with the much more scientifically rigorous and more widely accepted behavioral (now cognitive–behavioral) approaches to these disorders. Today, there is still a strong adherence to the term *psychophysiological disorders* to emphasize this orientation (hence the title of this book). However, the terms *psychophysiological disorders* and *psychosomatic disorders* are used interchangeably.

Current Trends in the Field

Dissatisfied with the earlier psychodynamic formulations, many investigators interested in the role of psychological factors in psychophysiological disorders also began to shift their attention to the role of more easily and reliably quantified situational variables such as bereavement and separation as precipitating events (see Engel, 1967; Schmale, 1972). This research established that behavioral and physiological responses to separation and other environmental stressors may be correlated with an important intervening psychological variable—coping mechanisms (Weiner, 1977). Indeed, in the growing area of stress research, it has been demonstrated that the impact of any potentially stressful event can be significantly influenced by how a person appraises or copes with it (Gatchel, Baum, & Krantz, 1988). Cohen and Lazarus (1979), for example, classified such coping strategies into five general categories: direct action responses, information seeking, inhibition of action, intrapsychic or palliative coping, and turning to others. The psychophysiological consequences of stress can be modified by such coping mechanisms. Thus, coping-style processes may prove to be important variables to consider in any comprehensive model of psychophysiological disorders. However, not enough systematic research has yet been conducted to determine the predictive validity and utility of such psychological constructs.

One of the unfortunate consequences of the emergence of these psychological formulations of psychosomatic disorders was the paradoxical embrace of a somewhat dualistic viewpoint, which resulted from the preeminence these theoretical orientations gave to psychological factors as causes of physical symptomatology. Thus, there was a swing to the opposite view that the psychological component has a dominant impact on the physical component of human functioning. This was in striking contrast to mechanistic biological views, which gave preeminence to physiological factors.

Role of Physiological Factors in Psychophysiological Disorders

Paralleling these psychological formulations was a growing literature on the importance of physiological factors. A relatively broad theoretical model was initially used to conceptualize the physiological contribution to psychosomatic disorders. Such disorders were assumed to occur because of a bodily weakness, either a weak organ such as the stomach (ulcers) or a weak physiological system such as the cardiovascular system (essential hypertension). Furthermore, it was assumed that this bodily weakness could be inherited or could develop as a result of disease (e.g., respiratory infection predisposing an individual to asthma).

An extension of this weak organ–system theory was the idea that specific physiological response patterns to situations, including stressful ones, are inherited. The term *specific-response pattern approach* was used to convey the assumption that individuals tend to respond physiologically to stressful situations in their own idiosyncratic ways. It has often been shown that individuals differ in physiological response to situations (see Lacey, 1967). One person may demonstrate an increase in heart rate and blood pressure level but little increase in muscle tension, whereas another person in the same situation may display very little increase in heart rate and blood pressure but a great increase in muscle tension. This difference in response patterns is known as *individual response stereotypy* (i.e., individual differences in the stereotypic way of responding to situations). In an early study of these individual differences in an actual clinical population, Malmo and Shagass (1949) demonstrated that, under stress, patients with cardiovascular symptoms showed greater cardiovascular response than increase in muscle tension, whereas patients with muscle tension headaches showed the opposite pattern.

It was generally assumed that the particular physiological symptom or organ most constantly activated, and therefore most stressed, might be susceptible to a breakdown and the resultant development of a psychophysiological disorder. That is, the person who persistently responds to situations with a greatly elevated blood pressure level may stress the cardiovascular system, causing a disruption of its homeostatic mechanism and, as a result, rendering it more susceptible to hypertension. An important shortcoming of this general model, however, was its lack of predictive validity. It cannot explain why all individuals who respond with a significant degree of cardiovascular activation do not eventually develop a cardiovascular disease such as hypertension. Psychological factors were assumed to play some role in determining who does or does not develop a disease.

Role of Genetic Factors in Psychophysiological Disorders

Another missing piece of the puzzle was the parallel tendency during this period to assume that a specific physiological or genetic factor accounted for the majority of variance in the development of psychophysiological disorders. It is generally accepted that genetic factors likely play an important role in predisposing individuals to various psychophysiological disorders (Weiner, 1977). For example, Mirsky (1958) demonstrated that pepsinogen levels of ulcer patients are significantly higher than those of patients without ulcers. Pepsinogen level is a good measure of gastric secretion activity. In the stomach, it is converted to the enzyme pepsin, which digests proteins and which, together with hydrochloric acid, is the primary active agent in gastric digestive juices. Many investigators view an excess of pepsinogen as a cause of ulcers. In an initial study, Mirsky assessed significant individual differences in pepsinogen levels in newborn infants. Infants with high pepsinogen levels were likely to be members of families in which there was a high pepsinogen level. In addition, twin studies showed that pepsinogen levels for identical twins are very similar (Mirsky, Fritterman, & Kaplan, 1952; Pilot, Lenkoski, Spiro, & Schaeffer, 1957). This provided some early evidence that pepsinogen level, which is viewed as an important contributing factor in the development of ulcers, is an inherited characteristic.

In another study, Weiner, Thaler, Reiser, and Mirsky (1957) sought to evaluate whether oversecretors of pepsinogen were more prone to develop ulcers than were undersecretors. From a group of newly inducted soldiers, a subgroup of oversecretors was selected on the basis of a gastrointestinal examination conducted before basic training. Only soldiers who did not have ulcers at the time were chosen for the study. At the end of basic training (approximately 4 months later), the men were reexamined. It was found that 14% of the oversecretors had developed ulcers, whereas none of the undersecretors had. A similar study by Mirsky (1958), which was conducted with a population of children and adult civilians, showed a comparable tendency for ulcers to develop in individuals with a high pepsinogen level. Thus, the evidence indicates that individuals who develop ulcers may be genetically predisposed to do so because of excessive secretion of gastric acid, which in turn produces stomach lesions and ulcerations.

A great deal of additional research, using better methodology such as twin studies, is needed to delineate more clearly the importance of genetic predispositions in many psychophysiological disorders. Again, not all individuals with a predisposition develop a psychophysiological disorder. Moreover, although numerous family studies have shown that patients with a psychophysiological disorder come from families in which there is a high incidence of the same disorder, such findings could be attributed to common factors in learning and experience rather than to a genetic factor. A number of early studies, for example, indicated that certain patterns of disturbed parent–child relationships are common in cases of childhood asthma (see Purcell et al., 1969). Such common family relationship experiences could partly or totally explain the high family incidence findings. Future research will have to determine the relative contributions of such factors to each specific psychophysiological disorder. Moreover, as Weiner (1977) indicated, more is known about factors that predispose an individual to a disease than is known about factors that initiate or sustain it. Research is needed to isolate these latter factors.

Diathesis–Stress Model of Psychophysiological Disorders

Obviously, there are physiological, genetic, and psychological variables that need to be considered in comprehensively understanding psychophysiological disorders. In an attempt to include some psychosocial contributions to disease in the etiology of illness, researchers have devised the *diathesis–stress* model of illness (Levi, 1974). This model is a relatively simple statement of the ways in which psychosocial, environmental, genetic, and physiological elements should be considered in the description of disease. All elements continually interact with one another. Physiological predispositions toward a certain illness (such as genetic weakness or biochemical imbalance), psychosocial stimuli (e.g., stress and how a person responds to and copes with it), and previously experienced environmental conditions jointly determine many disease states. Biological factors are important, but other factors, including psychological variables, are also critical.

Using this model specifically with psychophysiological disorders, Sternbach (1966) emphasized the importance of considering all factors in any attempt to understand a particular disorder (Table 1). Even today, the diathesis–stress model serves as a helpful conceptual model for understanding psychophysiological disorders. The diathesis portion of the model postulates the presence of two principal factors: (a) individual response stereotypy, which Sternbach viewed as a constitutional predisposition to respond physiologically in a particular way to various situations with consistent activation of certain physiological systems or organs, and (b) inadequate homeostatic restraints, which may be caused by stress-induced breakdown, previous accident or infection, or genetic predisposition. The stress portion of the model refers to the persistent exposure of the individual to stressful, activating situations. Situational determinants are also important and

Table 1

Sternbach's (1966) Diathesis–Stress Model of Psychosomatic Disorders

IF	Individual response stereotypy (Constitutional predisposition to respond physiologically to a situation in a particular way)
AND	Inadequate homeostatic restraints (May be due to stress-induced breakdown, previous accident or infection, or genetic predisposition)
AND	Exposure to activating situations (Either exposure to actual external activating/stressful situations or misperception of an ordinary situation or event as stressful)
THEN	Psychosomatic episodes

Note. From *Principles of Psychophysiology: An Introductory Text and Readings* (p. 146) by R. A. Sternbach, 1966, San Diego, CA: Academic Press. Copyright 1966 by Academic Press. Reprinted by permission.

must be taken into account. For example, an individual exposed to an emotional stressor in a work situation may respond quite differently than if he or she were at home. Socially accepted methods of dealing with stressors differ from situation to situation, and thus the physiological consequences must be expected to differ. Indeed, early investigators in the field paid little attention to the social environment as an important factor contributing to health and disease in individuals. In 1948, James Halliday, a Scottish public health physician, published an influential book, titled *Psychosocial Medicine: A Study of the Sick Society*. This work was one of the first to examine the important role that the social environment can play in the study of human morbidity.

Along with exposure to actual external activating or stressful situations, Sternbach included in his model the possibility that, in the absence of objective real-life stressors, an individual may perceive ordinary situations and events as stressors and so react to them with heightened physiological response. These misperceptions are due to chronic attitudes (e.g., specific attitudes) or personality characteristics that significantly affect a person's perception and interpretation of stimuli.

Animal research has supported a diathesis–stress model of various psychophysiological disorders (Gatchel, Baum, & Krantz, 1988). Clearly, however, the investigation of psychophysiological disorders is complex. Many variables—genetic, physiological, situational, and behavioral or personality—must be taken into account in any comprehensive understanding of these disorders. As noted earlier, significant progress is also being made in biomedical research on the pathogenesis of these disorders. Unfortunately, parallel progress has not yet been made in research on psychological factors. Such research in the past has been sorely inadequate. However, more recent evaluations of specific behavioral characteristics (such as Type A behavior and coping styles) may provide useful avenues for future investigation.

Classification of Psychophysiological Disorders

Just as there has been a shift in the conceptualization of psychophysiological disorders, a parallel change in approaches to their classification has occurred during the past few decades. The *Diagnostic and*

Statistical Manual of Mental Disorders (DSM) was adopted by the American Psychiatric Association in 1952 as its official classification schema of mental disorders. In the original version, there was a category called *psychosomatic disorders*. Nine primary categories of disorders were delineated according to the affected part or system of the body. Disorders were classified as psychosomatic illnesses if a clear medical etiology could not be delineated. For example, in the case of hypertension, renal hypertension is a systemic disease caused by kidney malfunction. Essential hypertension has traditionally been classified as a psychosomatic disorder because it has no known medical cause. In other words, it is usually classified as *idiopathic*. This attempt to classify a disease as either functional or idiopathic, in a way, perpetuated the dualistic approach to medical disorders. The tendency to classify a disorder for which there is clear medical or biological understanding differently from a disorder for which there is not one was inherent in this system. The problem with this scheme is now readily apparent. With the increasing recognition that psychological or emotional factors are important in the precipitation or exacerbation of most organic illnesses, a change was needed in the classification system. Research has implicated psychological factors in the etiology and development of a number of illnesses not considered psychosomatic, ranging from neurological diseases such as multiple sclerosis to infectious diseases and malignancies such as tuberculosis and leukemia, respectively. The early *DSM* did not account for this. In 1968, a modified version of the *DSM*, the *DSM-II*, which was developed in collaboration with the World Health Organization, was adopted. In this new edition, the term *psychophysiological disorder* replaced *psychosomatic disorder* in an attempt to disassociate the terminology from the older view that psychological and somatic indices could be differentiated. This was also in keeping with the movement away from the psychoanalytic influence on the field, which I discussed earlier. A newer and considerably revised edition of the *DSM*, the *DSM-III*, was published in 1980. This was followed by the *DSM-III-R*, which was published in 1987. In these recent editions, the category *psychological factors affecting physical conditions* (PFAPC) has replaced the earlier category of *psychophysiological disorders* in another attempt to emphasize the degree to which psychosocial factors can affect any physical disorder. Table 2 lists the diagnostic criteria for this PFAPC category in *DSM-III-R*.

Table 2

DSM-III-R Diagnostic Criteria for the Category "Psychological Factors Affecting Physical Condition"

A. Psychologically meaningful environmental stimuli are temporally related to the initiation or exacerbation of a specific physical condition or disorder (recorded on Axis III).
B. The physical condition involves either demonstrable organic pathology (e.g., rheumatoid arthritis) or a known pathophysiologic process (e.g., migraine headache).
C. The condition does not meet the criteria for a somatoform disorder.

Note. DSM-III-R = revised third edition of the *Diagnostic and Statistical Manual of Mental Disorders* (American Psychiatric Association, 1987).

Lipp, Looney, and Spitzer (1977) first pointed out that the newer versions of this classification system *(DSM-III)* would have to take into account the degree to which psychosocial factors can influence any physical condition. In their proposal, which was subsequently adopted and incorporated into the newer editions of the manual, they recommended that the separate section on psychophysiological disorders be deleted and that a section titled "Psychological Factors and Physical Conditions" be substituted (the title was subsequently changed to "Psychological Factors Affecting Physical Conditions"). This section encompassed not only the traditional psychophysiological disorders but also any physical condition in which psychological factors were found to be significant in precipitating, exacerbating, or prolonging the disorder. This newer system allowed clinicians to avoid considering a given condition exclusively in psychological or organic terms. Most professionals in the field of psychosomatic medicine currently take such a multicause etiological approach to disease. In describing psychophysiological disorders, they refer not to a distinct group of illnesses but to any physical condition that is affected by psychological factors. Thus, *DSM-III-R* embraces the notion that psychological factors are potentially important in all disorders.

The American Psychiatric Association is currently in the process of producing the most recent revision of the *DSM*—the *DSM-IV*, which is due to be off press in late 1993 or early 1994. In an overview of possible changes in this new edition, Stoudemire and Hales (1991) noted that there is little evidence to indicate that the PFAPC category of *DSM-III-R* has received widespread clinical or research use. They state that the term *PFAPC* was used in the title or as a significant component of the content of fewer than 10 articles published in the past 10 years. They uncovered no articles that used it as the basis for empirical research.

In spite of its limited use, the *DSM-IV* PFAPC subcommittee decided to retain the category, its section now to be titled "Psychological or Behavioral Factors Affecting Nonpsychiatric Medical Condition." In this new edition, there will be a requirement by the clinician to specify the types of factors affecting a medical condition. Moreover, the category has been broadened to include behavioral factors of public health concern, in addition to the effects of psychiatric comorbidity on medical outcome. Table 3 presents the proposed diagnostic criteria, as presented by Stoudemire and Hales (1991). These criteria again reinforce the viewpoint that psychosocial factors are intimately linked with physical functioning and illness.

Summary

In this chapter, I have reviewed the changing perspectives on the relationship between the mind and body through the ages. These perspectives greatly affected the manner in which psychophysiological disorders were evaluated and treated. After a number of centuries during which biomedical reductionism dominated medicine, there was a gradual reemergence during the mid-19th and 20th centuries of the concept of psychogenesis (i.e., the belief that psychological factors may cause bodily disease), as well as a holistic approach to conceptualizing certain disease states. Today, it is generally accepted that the relationship between psychological factors and physical illness is quite complex and may be influenced by numerous biological and psychosocial factors. A diathesis–stress model, which serves as a meaningful conceptual framework highlighting the potentially complex interaction of such variables, was presented. The recent versions of the *DSM* further testify to the broad acceptance of the viewpoint that psychosocial factors are closely linked to physical functioning and illness. Throughout this book, there will be repeated

Table 3

Proposed Diagnostic Criteria for the Category "Psychological or Behavioral Factors Affecting Nonpsychiatric Medical Condition"

A. Psychological or behavioral factors adversely affect a medical condition (coded on Axis III) in one of the following ways:
   1. The factors influence the course of the medical condition (e.g., there is a close temporal association between the development, exacerbation recovery, or stabilization of the medical condition and the psychological factors).
   2. The factors lead to noncompliance with treatment recommendations (e.g., individual with denial of illness refusing to take medication).
   3. The factors lead to ignoring risk factors known to cause or exacerbate the medical condition.
B. The designated factors in A do not meet the criteria for any Axis I or Axis II disorder.
   Specify nature of psychological or behavioral factor (if more than one factor is present, indicate the most predominant).
   Psychological symptoms affecting medical condition (e.g., subthreshold Axis I conditions, e.g., depression, anxiety)
   Personality trait affecting medical condition (e.g., *DSM-IV* personality disorder traits)
   Defense or coping style affecting medical condition (e.g., denial of illness, Type A personality)
   Physiologic stress reaction affecting medical condition (e.g., exacerbation of ulcer)
   Lifestyle factors affecting medical condition (e.g., overeating, unsafe sex)
   Noncompliance with treatment regimen affecting medical condition (e.g., refusal to take medication, inability to understand nature of illness)
   Cultural factors affecting medical condition (e.g., cultural values leading to refusal to seek treatment)
   Interpersonal disturbance affecting medical condition (e.g., marital conflict)
   Unspecified psychological or behavioral factors affecting medical condition

demonstrations of this linkage when considering the broad array of psychophysiological disorders that require comprehensive assessment and treatment approaches for their effective management.

REFERENCES

Alexander, F. (1950). *Psychosomatic medicine.* New York: Norton.
American Psychiatric Association. (1952). *Diagnostic and statistical manual of mental disorders.* Washington, DC: Author.

American Psychiatric Association. (1968). *Diagnostic and statistical manual of mental disorders* (2nd ed.). Washington, DC: Author.

American Psychiatric Association. (1980). *Diagnostic and statistical manual of mental disorders* (3rd ed.). Washington, DC: Author.

American Psychiatric Association. (1987). *Diagnostic and statistical manual of mental disorders* (3rd ed., rev.). Washington, DC: Author.

Cohen, F., & Lazarus, R. (1979). Coping with the stresses of illness. In G. C. Stone, F. Cohen, & N. E. Ader (Eds.), *Health psychology—A handbook.* San Francisco: Jossey-Bass.

Dunbar, H. (1935). *Emotions and bodily changes: A survey of literature on psychosomatic relationships: 1910–1933.* New York: Columbia University Press.

Engel, G. L. (1967). A psychological setting of somatic disease: The giving up–given up complex. *Proceedings of the Royal Society of Medicine, 60,* 553–563.

Freud, S. (1959). *Collected papers* (Vols. I–V). New York: Basic Books.

Gatchel, R. J., Baum, A., & Krantz, D. S. (1988). *An introduction to health psychology* (2nd ed.). New York: McGraw-Hill.

Gentry, W. D., & Matarazzo, J. D. (1981). Medical psychology: Three decades of growth and development. In L. A. Bradley & C. K. Prokop (Eds.), *Medical psychology: Contributions to behavioral medicine* (pp. 6–15). San Diego, CA: Academic Press.

Grace, W. J., & Graham, D. T. (1952). Relationship of specific attitudes and emotions to certain bodily diseases. *Psychosomatic Medicine, 14,* 242–251.

Graham, D. T. (1972). Psychosomatic medicine. In N. S. Greenfield & R. A. Sternbach (Eds.), *Handbook of psychophysiology* (pp. 839–924). New York: Holt, Rinehart & Winston.

Graham, D. T., Stern, J. A., & Winokur, G. (1958). Experimental investigation of the specificity hypothesis in psychosomatic disease. *Psychosomatic Medicine, 20,* 446–457.

Halliday, J. L. (1948). *Psychosocial medicine: A study of the sick society.* New York: Norton.

Lacey, J. I. (1967). Somatic response patterning and stress: Some revisions of activation theory. In M. H. Appley & R. Trumbull (Eds.), *Psychological stress* (pp. 14–36). New York: McGraw-Hill.

Levi, L. (1974). Psychosocial stress and disease: A conceptual model. In E. K. Gunderson & R. H. Rahe (Eds.), *Life stress and illness.* Springfield, IL: Charles C Thomas.

Lipowski, Z. J. (1986). Psychosomatic medicine: Past and present, Part 1. Historical background. *Canadian Journal of Psychiatry, 31,* 2–7.

Lipp, M. R., Looney, J. G., & Spitzer, R. L. (1977). Classifying psychophysiologic disorders: A new idea. *Psychosomatic Medicine, 39,* 285–287.

Malmo, R. B., & Shagass, C. (1949). Physiologic study of symptom mechanisms in psychiatry patients under stress. *Psychosomatic Medicine, 11,* 25–29.

Meyer, A. (1957). *Psychobiology: A science of man.* Springfield, IL: Charles C Thomas.

Mirsky, I. A. (1958). Physiologic, psychologic, and social determinants in the etiology of duodenal ulcer. *American Journal of Digestive Diseases, 3,* 285–314.

Mirsky, I. A., Fritterman, P., & Kaplan, S. (1952). Blood plasma pepsinogen: II. The activity of the plasma from "normal" subjects, patients with duodenal ulcer and patients with pernicious anemia. *Journal of Laboratory and Clinical Medicine, 40,* 188–195.

Nemiah, J. C. (1973). Psychology and psychosomatic illness: Reflections in theory and research methodology. In J. Freyberger (Ed.), *Topics of psychosomatic research: Proceedings of the 9th European Conference on Psychosomatic Research.* Basel, Switzerland: Karger.

Nemiah, J. C. (1975). Denial revisited: Reflections on psychosomatic theory. *Psychotherapy and Psychosomatics, 26,* 140–147.

Pilot, M. L., Lenkoski, L. D., Spiro, H. M., & Schaeffer, R. (1957). Duodenal ulcer in one of identical twins. *Psychosomatic Medicine, 19,* 221–229.

Purcell, K., Brady, K., Chai, H., Muser, J., Molk, L., Gordon, U., & Means, J. (1969). The effect on asthma in children of experimental separation from the family. *Psychosomatic Medicine, 31,* 144–164.

Schmale, A. H., Jr. (1972). Giving up as a final common pathway to changes in health. *Advances in Psychosomatic Medicine, 8,* 20–40.

Sifneos, P. E. (1967). Clinical observations in some patients suffering from a variety of psychosomatic diseases. *Proceedings of the 7th European Conference on Psychosomatic Research.* Basel, Switzerland: Karger.

Smuts, J. C. (1926). *Holism and evolution.* New York: Macmillan.

Sternbach, R. A. (1966). *Principles of psychophysiology: An introductory text and readings.* San Diego, CA: Academic Press.

Stoudemire, A., & Hales, R. E. (1991). Psychological and behavioral factors affecting medical conditions and DSM-IV: An overview. *Psychosomatics, 32,* 5–12.

Weiner, H. (1977). *Psychobiology and human disease.* New York: Elsevier Science.

Weiner, H., Thaler, M. F., Reiser, M. F., & Mirsky, I. A. (1957). Etiology of duodenal ulcer: 1. Relation of specific psychological characteristics to rate of gastric secretion (serum pepsinogen). *Psychosomatic Medicine, 19,* 1–10.

Wolf, S., & Wolff, H. G. (1947). *Human gastric function: A experimental study of a man and his stomach.* New York: Oxford University Press.

Wolff, H. G. (1953). *Stress and disease.* Springfield, IL: Charles C Thomas.

Irritable Bowel Syndrome

Edward B. Blanchard

Irritable bowel syndrome (IBS) is a widespread functional disorder of the lower gastrointestinal (GI) tract. Research over the past decade seems to indicate a potentially prominent role for clinical health psychologists in its assessment and treatment. In this chapter, I selectively summarize what is known about IBS from the psychologist's perspective and describe in some detail well-validated approaches to assessment and psychological treatment that are based on 10 years of research from the Center for Stress and Anxiety Disorders (University at Albany, State University of New York).

Epidemiology: Magnitude of the Problem

Epidemiological research indicates that the lifetime prevalence of IBS is between 8% (Whitehead, Winget, Fedoravicius, Wooley, & Blackwell, 1982) and 17% (Drossman, Sandler, McKee, & Lovitz, 1982) among the adult population in the United States. A recent, carefully conducted epidemiologic survey of adults 30–64 years old in the upper Midwest also found a prevalence of 17% (Talley, Zinsmeister, VanDyke, & Melton, 1991). Thus, although IBS is a relatively minor health problem (in terms of severity) compared with disorders such as schizophrenia or cancer, it is a major (in terms of prevalence) source of everyday distress.

Other evidence of the potential impact of IBS comes from surveys of physicians specializing in GI disorders—gastroenterologists. Estimates of the number of new patient visits to gastroenterologists because of IBS range from 13% (Switz, 1976) to 50% (Ferguson, Sircus, & Eastwood, 1977).

My own experience over 10 years of clinical research on assessment and treatment of this problem is that many gastroenterologists welcome a responsible referral source for the psychological treatment of this disorder, in part because there seem to be no well-established and reliable pharmacological treatments. For example, a former chairman of medicine at the local medical school, a gastroenterologist, was supportive of early efforts of my clinic because of the results with one of his "problem" IBS patients whom he referred to us: although her GI symptoms were reduced only slightly, he considered her treatment a success because she ceased calling him on a weekly basis.

All IBS Sufferers Are Not IBS Patients

Given the epidemiologic estimates just described, one might wonder why such a potentially large-scale disorder has not been perceived as crushing or drowning the American health care system. Two recent studies (Drossman et al., 1988; Whitehead, Bosmajian, Zonderman, Costa, & Schuster, 1988), although independently conducted, provide converging answers to this question. Drossman et al. (1988) compared 72 IBS patients, 82 persons with diagnosable IBS who had not sought medical treatment and 84 normal subjects, on a number of psychosocial measures. The samples were predominantly White (88%) and female (89%). The two IBS groups differed on 3 of 20 GI symptoms: the IBS patients were more likely to complain of diarrhea (82%), abdominal pain (97%), and nausea or vomiting (50%) than the non-treatment-seeking IBS subjects. (One may question the diagnosis of IBS in a sizable portion of the latter group.) As a whole the IBS patients were more ($p < .001$) distressed on various psychological measures

(Minnesota Multiphasic Personality Inventory [MMPI], Profile of Mood States, etc.) than the normal or the non-treatment-seeking IBS subjects. The latter two groups did not differ ($p = .207$). For example, 20% to 30% of the IBS patients showed significant (i.e., with a t score > 70) elevations on various MMPI scales, whereas 5% to 17% of non-treatment-seeking IBS subjects showed elevations, as did zero to 4% of normal subjects.

Whitehead et al. (1988) studied 149 middle-class female community volunteers (98% White) and 54 patients with various GI disorders (IBS, lactose malabsorption [IMA], or function bowel disorder [FBD]). Among female volunteers, 28 had results suggestive of IMA, whereas 16 had IBS, 26 had FBD, and 46 were free of diagnoses. All were compared on the Hopkins Symptom Checklist (Derogatis, 1983). Patients as a group were more distressed ($p < .01$) than individuals with the same disorders who had not sought help. Interestingly, non-treatment-seeking individuals with (narrowly defined) IBS were not different from normal subjects, whereas the IBS clinic attendees were generally more distressed.

One of the most interesting of the Whitehead et al. (1988) results was the discovery that the vast majority of individuals with IBS or FBD had never sought medical attention for it. Of their community sample, 26% had IBS as defined by clinical criteria. Among the 329 individuals with current IBS in the study by Talley et al. (1991), only 14% had seen a physician for pain or bowel problems. Thus, it appears that most people with IBS suffer in silence and cope with it on their own, never seeking help for it.

When non-help-seeking IBS sufferers are compared with IBS patients attending GI clinics and with the non-IBS sufferers, non-help-seeking IBS sufferers appear relatively normal psychologically and do not differ from those without IBS. On the other hand, IBS sufferers who seek medical attention, as a group, are significantly more psychologically distressed, showing elevations on all measures used.[1]

It thus appears that the treatment-seeking IBS sufferers are psychologically distressed (more will be said on this point in the following

---

[1] In fact, in my experience with a number of groups of psychophysiologically disordered patients (e.g., chronic headache, hypertension, tinnitus, etc.), IBS sufferers as a group are more psychologically distressed than any other class of patients, as indicated by standard measures (e.g., see Blanchard, Radnitz, Evans, et al., 1986, for a comparison of IBS patients with chronic headache sufferers).

section). Whether this co-occurrence is causal is not currently known. Thus, it could be that it takes the combination of IBS symptoms in a somewhat psychologically distressed individual (usually anxious or depressed, or neurotic in the classical sense) to lead an individual to become an IBS patient (someone seeking medical attention). Alternatively, IBS could be a somatopsychic disorder; that is, sufficient severity and duration of the IBS symptoms lead both to psychological distress and eventually to the individual's seeking medical attention.

Some support for this latter viewpoint comes from a study (Blanchard, Radnitz, Schwarz, Neff, & Gerardi, 1987) that assessed anxiety and depression before and after (approximately 4 months apart) brief behavioral treatment (more details on treatment are given in the section titled Treatment). Those IBS patients whose GI symptoms were substantially relieved showed significant reductions in anxiety and depression (e.g., pretreatment Beck Depression Inventory [BDI; Beck, Ward, Mendelson, Mock, & Erbaugh, 1961] score of 14.3 vs. posttreatment BDI score of 7.1, $p < .001$), with posttreatment scores in the normal range. For IBS patients who did not show clinically meaningful reductions in GI symptoms, the psychological test scores were unchanged for the most part.

Finally, a sizable percentage of treatment-seeking IBS sufferers do not show noticeable elevations on standard tests (see norms on BDI and State–Trait Anxiety Inventory [STAI; Spielberger, Gorsuch, & Lushene, 1970] for IBS sufferers in the Psychological Assessment section).

Henceforth in this chapter, the term *IBS* refers to characteristics and responses of treatment-seeking patients with IBS. Obviously, clinicians are interested in this portion of the total potential population with IBS symptoms, for it is this portion that they see.

Clinical Hint

> A clinical hint, or tip, to take away from this discussion: Many, but not all, IBS patients have accompanying psychological distress; the use of standard psychological tests such as BDI, STAI, and MMPI are recommended as part of the initial assessment.

Assessment

Diagnosis: Changing Criteria

IBS has traditionally been a diagnosis of exclusion. Many disorders can lead to the same presenting symptoms as those of IBS. Thus, one must exclude those patients whose GI symptoms stem from various established organic diseases. Those patients with the symptom complex, or syndrome, who cannot be excluded are by default diagnosed as having IBS. (This form of diagnostic practice effectively means that health psychologists, as nonphysicians, cannot fully diagnose IBS because they cannot order the various tests needed to confirm the exclusionary conditions.)

The traditional diagnostic criteria (sometimes referred to as clinical criteria in recent articles) are taken from Latimer (1983) and are as follows.

1. Abdominal pain or cramping or severe abdominal tenderness.
2. Altered bowel habits (either diarrhea, constipation, or alternating diarrhea and constipation).
3. Symptoms present more or less continuously for 3 months (some would suggest a 6-month duration).
4. Inflammatory bowel disease (IBD), intestinal parasites, lactose intolerance or malabsorption syndrome, and other GI diseases have been ruled out.

Among biomedical investigators working with IBS, there has been growing recognition of the need for a more positive approach to the diagnosis of IBS, such that IBS can be "ruled in" on the basis of a set of symptomatic criteria rather than being the residual after other disorders are ruled out. A set of criteria that have gained fairly widespread acceptance among those specializing in IBS are those adopted by an international conference in Rome in 1988 (Thompson, Creed, Drossman, Heaton, & Mazacca, 1992).

The Rome criteria for IBS are as follows. At least 3 months continuous or recurrent symptoms of

1. Abdominal pain or discomfort which is
   a. relieved with defecation,
   b. and/or associated with a change in frequency of stool,
   c. and/or associated with a change in consistency of stool; and
2. Two or more of the following, at least a quarter of occasions or days:
   a. altered stool frequency (either more than 3 bowel movements per day or fewer than 3 bowel movements per week).
   b. altered stool form (lumpy/hard or loose/watery stool).
   c. altered stool passage (straining, urgency, or feeling of incomplete evacuation).

    d. passage of mucus.
    e. bloating or feeling of abdominal distension.

Validational studies (Talley et al., 1990; Thompson, 1984) have shown these Rome criteria to be useful (Thompson et al., 1992). A structured interview developed for assessing GI symptoms is helpful in making this diagnosis.[2] Talley, Phillips, Melton, Wiltgen, & Zinsmeister (1989) have developed a patient questionnaire to identify IBS cases using these criteria.

Clinical Hint

> Despite the growing adoption of the Rome criteria and the consequent positive diagnosis of IBS, I urge the clinical health psychologist to work in close collaboration with a gastroenterologist so that the latter professional can perform the tests that help rule out other potential diseases and disorders whose symptoms can mimic IBS.

GI Symptom Diary

A useful step in establishing the diagnosis of IBS, and one which is essential to both good clinical practice and good clinical research, is to have the prospective patient complete a GI symptom diary. This diary can help subcategorize the IBS patient into one of three main subtypes: diarrhea predominant, constipation predominant, and mixed. One can establish a working subcategorization on the basis of the clinical interview, but this should be confirmed by the daily diary. (The subcategorization is sometimes related to psychological differences among patients.)

We routinely ask patients to rate the severity and degree of distress caused by the following eight GI symptoms: abdominal pain or cramping, abdominal tenderness, diarrhea, constipation, bloating, belching, flatulence, and nausea. The ratings are requested once per day using the following 5-point scale: absent, not a problem (0), mild severity and distress (1), moderate severity and distress (2), severe severity and distress (3), debilitating severity and distress (4). We also ask patients to record numbers of bowel movements, as well as any food

---

[2] This structured interview is available from the author.

and activities avoided because of IBS symptoms and any medicines taken for IBS.

Weekly average scores from this diary have adequate test–retest reliability over a 1-week interval (abdominal pain and tenderness = 0.77, diarrhea = 0.83, constipation = 0.76, flatulence = 0.94, belching = 0.93, nausea = 0.46; all correlations $p < .05$).

Clinical Hint

I strongly advise having the patient complete the GI symptom diary throughout a pretreatment assessment phase and then throughout treatment. Such information provides the basis for discussing progress with the patient as well as for quantifying degree of improvement. If one adds the requirement that the patient note severe life stressors as they occur, the diary provides the basis for a good functional analysis with the patient.

Assessment for Comorbid Psychiatric Disorders

One of the most consistent findings from assessment studies of IBS patients is that they show a high level of psychiatric comorbidity. Beginning with the early studies of Alpers and his colleagues (Liss, Alpers, & Woodruff, 1973; Young, Alpers, Norland, & Woodruff, 1976) careful psychiatric assessments of samples of IBS patients have revealed that 50–100% of the sample meet the criteria for some psychiatric disorder. The bulk of the psychiatric comorbidity is in mood disorders or anxiety disorders. Most of the recent studies have used structured or semistructured interviews, of demonstrated reliability and validity (for a recent summary see Walker, Roy-Byrne, & Katon, 1990).

In recent research in my laboratory, we administered the *Anxiety Disorders Interview Schedule–Revised* (*ADIS-R*; DiNardo & Barlow, 1988) to all of our IBS patients. All of the assessors were advanced doctoral students in clinical psychology or doctoral level psychologists. Each had been thoroughly trained in administering and scoring the *ADIS-R* and had shown adequate interrater agreement on primary and secondary diagnoses during at least five training interviews with mental health outpatients.

Blanchard, Scharff, Schwarz, Suls, and Barlow (1990) compared the results of the *ADIS-R* evaluations for 68 IBS patients with those of 44 patients with IBD who were seeking stress management training at our center and with those of 38 age- and sex-matched, paid controls who were free of recent GI disorders. Comparisons of the three groups in terms of fractions positive for psychiatric comorbidity revealed that a significantly greater portion of the IBS sample were positive (met criteria for some revised third edition *Diagnostic and Statistical Manual of Mental Disorders* [DSM-III-R, American Psychiatric Association, 1988] Axis I diagnosis) than for the other two groups, which did not differ.

Table 1 presents comorbidity data on an enlarged sample of IBS patients applying to our center. In Table 1, one finds that 56% of IBS patients meet the criteria for at least one Axis I disorder. The vast bulk of those with a diagnosable condition are seen as suffering from

Table 1

Psychiatric Comorbidity of Irritable Bowel Syndrome Patients

Diagnosis	Frequency	Percentage of total sample	Percentage of those with any Axis I disorder
Anxiety disorders	(60)	(42.6)	(82.5)
Panic with agoraphobia	6	4.3	7.5
Agoraphobia without panic	3	2.1	3.8
Obsessive compulsive disorder	1	0.7	1.3
Social phobia	7	5.0	8.8
Simple phobia	5	3.5	6.3
Generalized anxiety disorder	40	28.4	50.0
Posttraumatic stress disorder	3	2.1	3.8
Atypical anxiety disorder	2	1.4	2.5
Mood disorders	(9)	(6.4)	(11.3)
Dysthymia	8	5.7	10.0
Major depression	1	0.7	1.3
Bipolar	0		
Somatoform disorder	2	1.4	2.5
Alcohol abuse	1	0.7	1.3
Borderline personality disorder	1	0.7	1.3
No mental disorder	61	43.3	
Total	141		
History of major depression	(29)	(20.6)	(36.3)

some anxiety disorder (71% of those with diagnoses and 40% of the total sample). Among those IBS patients with anxiety disorders, the most common diagnosis is generalized anxiety disorder (GAD). It should be remembered that the essential feature of GAD is worry or apprehension about 2 or more different life circumstances along with at least 6 of 18 psychophysiological symptoms.

Clinical Hint

The prevalence of GAD among IBS patients suggests a strategy of designing IBS treatments by adapting what has been found effective with GAD. Many things seem to work well with GAD with treatment to manage worry (Borkovec & Mathews, 1988) and treatment to manage overall high levels of arousal, including arousal reduction techniques such as relaxation and perhaps biofeedback. Conducting a thorough psychiatric evaluation of the IBS patient is more than an interesting intellectual exercise, however. It can provide valuable predictive information, as described later in this chapter.

Psychological Assessment

There is a rich literature, dating back over 20 years, on the assessment of IBS patients with various psychological tests. As mentioned earlier, a consistent finding has been that patients with IBS show elevations on almost every dimension or measure of psychological distress.

A recent study from our laboratory illustrates these points (Schwarz et al., 1993). One hundred twenty-one patients with IBS, 46 patients with IBD (as controls for having a chronic illness with GI symptoms) and 45 age- and sex-matched controls with no illness (who were paid for participation) were the populations. Comparisons across the three groups on the tests administered, as well as the group mean scores, are presented in Table 2.

Clinical Hint

To provide information with more clinical utility, norms for IBS patients on two of the commonly used measures (BDI and STAI) are presented for IBS patients in Table 3. It is hoped that this information will enable clinical health psychologists to evaluate individual IBS patients more readily.

Table 2

Comparison of Psychological Test Scores

	Group		
Test	IBS	IBD	Normals
Beck Depression Inventory	11.3[a]	9.1[a]	5.1[b]
State Anxiety	50.7[a]	43.2[b]	39.6[b]
Trait Anxiety	47.2[a]	41.6[b]	36.0[c]
Rathus Assertiveness Scale	−2.6[a]	5.4[a,b]	15.2[b]
Psychosomatic Symptom Checklist Summary	41.3[a]	35.7[a]	10.4[b]
Life Events Scale, 12 months	276.2[a,b]	269.1[b]	298.8[a]
MMPI			
1 Hypochondriasis	68.4[a]	68.2[a]	52.8[b]
2 Depression	70.1[a]	66.8[a]	56.6[b]
3 Hysteria	65.8[a]	65.0[a]	58.6[b]
4 Psychopathic Deviate	63.7	61.7	63.1
6 Paranoia	60.7	58.9	57.6
7 Psychasthenia	66.7[a]	60.7[b]	57.0[c]
8 Schizophrenia	63.4	61.4	60.6
9 Hypomania	55.0	55.8	58.1
10 Social Introversion	59.6[a]	55.9[a]	50.8[b]

Note. Numbers within rows that have the same superscript are not statistically different at the $p < .05$ level. IBS = irritable bowel syndrome; IBD = irritable bowel disease; MMPI = Minnesota Multiphasic Personality Inventory. From "Psychological Aspects of Irritable Bowel Syndrome: Comparisons With Inflammatory Bowel Disease and Nonpatient Controls" by Schwarz et al., 1993, *Behavior Research and Therapy, 31*, p. 299. Copyright 1993 by Pergamon Press. Reprinted by permission.

Treatment

The discussion that follows, possibly the most important section in this chapter for the clinical health psychologist, consists of five parts: (a) a summary and critique of controlled trials of psychological treatment for IBS; (b) a detailed description of the IBS treatment procedures

Table 3

Psychological Test Norms for Irritable Bowel Syndrome Patients

Beck Depression Inventory		Trait Anxiety		State Anxiety	
Score	Percentile	Score	Percentile	Score	Percentile
0–3	16	20–25	2	20–25	2
4–6	32	26–30	5	26–30	4
7–9	48	31–35	10	31–35	11
10–12	62	36–40	28	36–40	24
13–15	71	41–45	46	41–45	45
16–18	78	46–50	64	46–50	55
19–21	87	51–55	78	51–55	70
22–24	94	56–60	90	56–60	83
25–27	98	61–65	94	61–65	91
28–30	99	66–70	98	66–70	95
≥31		≥71		≥71	
Median = 10		Median = 46		Median = 48	

that we have used and evaluated at Albany; (c) a similar summary of the several controlled trials from my laboratory (Albany studies) over the past 8 years; (d) a summary of empirical data on long-term follow-up of IBS patients treated with psychological therapies; and (e) a summary of the limited literature on the prediction of treatment.

Controlled Evaluations of Psychological Treatment of IBS

Although there were several earlier uncontrolled trials of psychological treatment of IBS, I focus on the six published, controlled trials of which I am aware.

In Tables 4 and 5 are summaries of these six controlled trials. Table 4 summarizes methodological details, including synopses of the treatment and control conditions; Table 5 summarizes results and follow-up data.

Several things are apparent from reviewing these tables. In terms of subject selection, most studies have used the so-called clinical cri-

Table 4

Controlled Trials of Psychological Treatment of Irritable Bowel Syndrome Methodological Details

Study	Diagnostic criteria	Methods of assessment (dependent variables)	Treatment parameters		Treatment conditions and sample size	Dropouts
			Duration	No. sessions		
1. Svedlund et al., 1983	Clinical criteria, 1-year minimum duration	Clinician ratings of GI and mental symptoms; same rater, but not of own patients; pretreatment, end of treatment, patient global ratings at end of treatment and follow-up	3 months	10 1-hr (7.4 actual)	A. Conventional medical care: bulk agents, anticholinergics, minor tranquilizer ($n = 51$) B. Conventional medical care and psychotherapy: modification of maladaptive behavior, new solutions to problems, teaching means to cope with stress, showing connection of stressful events and GI symptoms; "dynamically-oriented but mainly supportive," "at a conscious level"; patients set goals and work toward them ($n = 50$)	18 refused to participate, 2 dropouts

continued

Study	Diagnostic criteria	Assessment	Timeframe	Sessions	Treatment conditions	Attrition
2. Whorwell et al., 1984	Clinical criteria, plus distention 1-year minimum duration; had not responded to other treatments (avg. of 6 per patient)	1 week of patient diary before and after treatment; patient rated pain and distention; bowel habit abnormality, well-being	3 months	7 30-min	A. Hypnotherapy for relaxation and control of bowel motility; education on bowel physiology; ego-strengthening exercises; daily autohypnosis with tape ($n = 15$) B. Placebo medication plus supportive psychotherapy, attention to life and symptom ($n = 15$)	Not relevant
3. Bennett & Wilkinson, 1985	Not reported, newly diagnosed	1 week of patient diary at T1, T2 (after 6 weeks), and T3 (after treatment): pain, discomfort, restriction of activity, fatigue, number of bowel movements; spouse ratings of verbal complaints and behaviors; STAI	14 weeks: 6 weeks pretreatment, 8 weeks treatment	8 1-hr	A. Education about normal bowel functioning; PMR; cognitive therapy (instruction to change self-talk); homework ($n = 12$) B. 1/month medical visits with combination of 3 drugs: antidepressant/anxiolytic; smooth muscle relaxant, bulking agent ($n = 12$)	5 from baseline, 2 from each treatment condition
4. Lynch & Zamble, 1989	Clinical criteria, at least 6-month duration	Daily GI symptoms diary for 4 weeks before and after treatment or waiting period, BDI, STAI, Queens Stress Index	8 weeks	8 2-hr	A. Relaxation (PMR); cognitive therapy (Meichenbaum) (change in self-talk); analysis of reactions to stressful situations; assertiveness training; homework ($n = 10$) B. Waiting list ($n = 10$) (unclear if they received medical care), later crossed over to treat-	7 (2 from each treatment condition plus 3 in baseline)

Table 4 (*continued*)

Study	Diagnostic criteria	Methods of assessment (dependent variables)	Treatment parameters		Treatment conditions and sample size	Dropouts
			Duration	No. sessions		
5. Harvey et al., 1989	Clinical criteria plus abdominal distention	Daily GI symptoms diary and of well-being (0–3)	8 weeks	5	ment A A. Hypnotherapy: general relaxation, warmth and relaxation of abdominal area, imagery of smooth flowing GI tract; practice of autohypnosis 2/day for 10 min Individual ($n = 17$), group ($n = 16$) (also group support)	3 (condition not specified)
6. Guthrie et al., 1991	Clinical criteria plus abdominal distention; at least 6-month	Physician global rating of abdominal pain, distention, diar-	3 months	7 total, initial 2-hr then 6 1-hr	A. Standard medical care; dynamic psychotherapy: feelings about illness and other emotional problems;	7

continued

treatment at GI clinic on bulking agents and antispasmodics with no improvement; at least 1 year total duration	rhea and constipation; patient global rating of overall severity of all symptoms plus ratings of pain, distention, diarrhea, constipation, and interference in life; patient daily diary of pain, bloating, bowel movement frequency; Hamilton Depression Scale and clinical anxiety scale by psychiatrist; at 1-yr follow-up, patient global rating of change in overall symptoms	relaxation tape for home practice (*n* = 53) B. Standard medical care; 2-hr interview for assessment; 3 brief visits to discuss bowel diary (*n* = 44)	6

Note. STAI = State–Trait Anxiety Inventory; PMR = Progressive Muscle Relaxation; BDI = Beck Depression Inventory; GI = gastrointestinal tract.

Table 5

Controlled Trials of Psychological Treatment of Irritable Bowel Syndrome: Results and Follow-up

Results	Percentage of sample improved	Collateral changes (psychological state, etc.)	Follow-up		Results at follow-up
			Length	Conditions	
1. Both groups improved on somatic and mental symptoms; treatment superior to control on abdominal pain at 3 months and 15 months; treatment superior to control on bowel dysfunction at 15 month; patient ratings show more improvement in somatic symptoms and ability to cope in treatment vs. control	Not reported	Similar improvement in both groups on anxiety and depression	12 months	None	Treatment gains maintained; further reduction in abdominal pain
2. Significantly greater improvement on abdominal pain, abdominal distention, bowel habit dysfunction, and general well-being for hypnotherapy vs. control; control improved significantly on pain, distention,	Not reported	Improvement in patient ratings of well-being	Not reported		

continued

well-being, but not bowel dysfunction 3. No change for T1 to T2; no significant interactions on GI symptoms, main effect from T2 to T3 on pain, discomfort, number of abnormal bowel movements; spouse reports showed reduced verbal report of pain		STAI scores reduced in Treatment A from T2 to T3 but unchanged in Treatment B			None
4. Treatment was superior to wait list in reduction of abdominal discomfort and constipation; treatment A did not show any significant reductions; when both groups combined after cross-over, significant reduction on abdominal pain, discomfort, diarrhea, constipation, flatulence, nausea, and bloating	7 of 11 for A, 0 of 10 for B, when B is crossed over 4 of 10; total: 11 of 21	Significant reduction with combined groups on depression (BDI) and trait anxiety and Queens Stress Index	4 months	None	Pain, discomfort, flatulence, nausea are still significantly reduced, but diarrhea, constipation, bloating are not; depression and anxiety still reduced
5. For individual therapy, no improvement in 8 (50%), improvement in 3 (19%), 5 (31%) symptom free; for group therapy, no improvement in 5 (29%), improvement in 6 (35%), 6 (35%) symptom free; overall, no symptom free; no	Not reported	Not reported	3 months	Continuing practice of autohypnosis 1 booster session at follow-up visit	11 most improved, continued to improve; others showed slight loss of benefit

Table 5 (*continued*)

Results	Percentage of sample improved	Collateral changes (psychological state, etc.)	Follow-up		Results at follow-up
			Length	Conditions	
improvement in 39%, improvement in 27%, 33% symptom free; no difference by method of treatment 6. On gastroenterologist global ratings, treatment was superior to control on overall severity, abdominal discomfort, and diarrhea; on patient global ratings treatment was superior to control on pain, diarrhea, and constipation; on daily diary, treatment improved more than controls on pain, diarrhea, and bloating	31 of 53 (58%) treatment, 10 of 43 (23%) controls, 21 of 33 (64%) controls improved when treated	Significant reduction in depression and anxiety in Treatment A relative to controls	12 months	None	57 of 83 (69%) treated patients gave global ratings (mail-in) of improvement at 1-year follow-up

Note.   STAI = State–Trait Anxiety Inventory; BDI = Beck Depression Inventory; GI = gastrointestinal tract.

teria (or Latimer criteria) with some additions, primarily the presence of abdominal distention. Two studies (Guthrie, Creed, Dawson, & Tomenson, 1991; Whorwell, Prior, & Faragher, 1984) added a requirement that the patients' symptoms had been refractory to standard medical care.

Treatment duration is relatively brief, lasting from 8 to 13 weeks. Moreover, the number of treatment sessions tend to be small, from 7 to 10. Evaluation has been by physician global rating alone (Svedlund, Sjodin, Ottosson, & Dotevall, 1983), patient symptom diaries alone (Bennett & Wilkinson, 1985; Harvey, Hinton, Gunary, & Barry, 1989; Lynch & Zamble, 1989; Whorwell et al., 1984), or the two combined (Guthrie et al., 1991).

Interestingly, relaxation training was a part of five of six studies (it was omitted only by Svedlund et al., 1983) and elements of cognitive therapy were present in three of five studies. Dynamic psychotherapy was an active part of treatment in two studies (Guthrie et al., 1991, and perhaps Svedlund et al., 1983), and supportive psychotherapy was a control condition (combined with medication placebo) in Whorwell et al.'s (1984) study of hypnotherapy.

Considering the results presented in Table 5, active treatment was superior to the control condition on some aspect of GI symptoms in four of five studies in which it was evaluated: only Bennett and Wilkinson (1985) had no differential effects of active treatment on these symptoms. (Harvey et al., 1989, included no control condition.) Later studies (Guthrie et al., 1991; Harvey et al., 1989; Lynch & Zamble, 1989) have begun to indicate the proportion of the treated cases that can be viewed as clinically improved. Almost invariably there are reductions in anxiety and depression accompanying the reductions of GI symptoms.

Two studies (Guthrie et al., 1991; Svedlund et al., 1983) present 1-year follow-up data, and Lynch and Zamble (1989) present a 4-month follow-up. For the most part, treatment effects were well maintained. In fact, only 3 of 31 patients found by Guthrie et al. (1991) to be improved at posttreatment appeared to have deteriorated by the 12-month follow-up. Caution must be observed in interpreting their follow-up data, however, because the method of assessing continued improvement versus relapse was markedly different at follow-up (patient global rating on mail-back card) than at posttreatment (physician global rating, patient global rating, patient diary). The change in measurement technique is unfortunate.

Among the most important findings among these six studies is the apparent replicability of the benefits of brief hypnotherapy with IBS. Harvey et al. (1989) presented a systematic replication of the original work on hypnotherapy by Whorwell et al. (1984). Using the same treatment techniques and evaluation procedures, Harvey et al. compared individually administered with group-administered brief hypnotherapy for 33 relatively refractory IBS patients. The results from both treatment delivery methods were essentially identical: overall 33% were essentially symptom free at 3 months and 27% more were improved. Although the results are not as strong as those of Whorwell et al. (1984), the positive results from an independent replication are impressive.

Whorwell, Prior, and Colgan (1987) presented additional data on the efficacy of hypnotherapy in a report on 50 cases of refractory IBS. Good maintenance was found for 13 of 15 of the original sample. Overall, 42 of 50 (84%) had a positive response to treatment. Potential predictors of response are discussed in a later section.

Overall, it is clear that several different brief psychological therapies, most of which include relaxation, lead to significant improvement in IBS symptoms and to improvement over control conditions. Hypnotherapy is especially promising, given its replicability. Concomitant improvement in psychological state is usually found, and limited results indicate good maintenance at 1-year posttreatment.[3]

The Albany Multicomponent Behavioral Treatment Program for IBS

Neff and Blanchard (1987) developed the initial treatment program, which was heavily influenced by the writing and conceptualizations of Latimer (1983). In essence, Latimer held that IBS sufferers are neurotic individuals who focus on bowel symptoms. As such, he believed that they are chronically overaroused and anxious, that they are maladaptive problem solvers, and that they have misinformation

---

[3] As best as I can determine, Brenda Toner in Toronto was, at the time of this writing, conducting a large scale trial evaluating a cognitive–behavioral treatment package. No results are yet available.

about normal bowel function that leads them to label themselves as sick and in need of help.

Latimer's (1983) views are in sharp contrast to those of most gastroenterologists, who believe IBS is primarily a disorder of bowel motility. (This is apparently still the dominant view, as of the 1992 National Institute of Diabetes, Digestive Disorders, and Kidney Disorders (NIDDK) Conference on IBS.) Unfortunately, the nature of this motility disorder, and very importantly, how to measure it reliably, are not yet agreed on by differing groups of gastroenterologists. Given the knowledge deficits, it is not surprising that there are no universally accepted medical regimens for IBS.

The Albany program thus had four components:

1. *Information and education* about normal bowel functioning, designed to correct misconceptions and to allay some concerns. As part of this, patients were also assured that we believed their symptoms were real and a source of great distress to them. (Some portion felt that their physicians doubted their veracity and had conveyed an opinion that the IBS sufferers were neurotic and that the problems were "all in their head." Thus, a number had been turned off by the regular medical community and reacted in a hypochondriacal fashion by doctor shopping or frequent requests for services.)

2. *Training in abbreviated progressive muscle relaxation* (PMR) was given over the first six sessions. Our relaxation regimen was adapted from that of Blanchard and Andrasik (1985), which had been successfully used with chronic headache patients. It in turn is an adaptation of many of the procedures described by Bernstein and Borkovec (1973) and was derived in part from the seminal research of Jacobson (1976).

Training starts with 16 muscle groups with attention to several things: (a) developing a muscle sense, or being able to discriminate differing levels of muscle tension; (b) deep, diaphragmatic breathing as an integral part of a deeply relaxed state; (c) incorporation of many suggestions of bodily sensations of warmth, heaviness, and relaxation; and (d) incorporation of calming and relaxing mental imagery as a part of total relaxation.

Regular home practice is stressed, and an audiotape to guide home practice was given to all participants. (We asked patients to keep track of their home practice on their GI symptom diaries, and these reports were checked at early sessions.)

The relaxation induction was next shortened to eight muscle groups and then to four muscle groups. We explained that we were interested in the patient's being able (a) to become deeply relaxed in a brief period of time (the initial relaxation induction takes about 22–23 minutes) and (b) to use their new relaxation skills in everyday situations as a way of countering stress and arousal.

Simultaneously, we introduced a more passive and mental form of relaxation, termed *relaxation-by-recall* by Bernstein and Borkovec (1973). Instead of tensing and releasing muscle groups, patients were asked to relax the same muscles passively by releasing any tension and by trying to match their bodily sensations to their memory (recall) of what it felt like when that muscle group was relaxed. The same progressive pattern was followed. A tape for passive relaxation-by-recall was also given to participants. Thus, we took patients through the four-muscle group relaxation induction using tension and release cycles, re-alerted them, and then had them repeat the induction using the passive relaxation-by-recall procedures.

The final step was to introduce what Bernstein and Borkovec (1973) termed *cue-controlled relaxation*. In this procedure, the patient is asked to become relaxed, and then attention is focused on his or her breathing. Finally, the patient is asked to subvocalize the word *relax* as he or she exhales. Thus, the sequence is deep inhalation and exhalation with simultaneous subvocalization of the word *relax*. This is practiced several times. (A shoulder shrug should probably accompany the subvocalization.) The patient is then urged to practice this procedure several times per day and to institute it when he or she feels tense or stressed, such as when caught in traffic, and so on. We thus stressed using this brief relaxation technique as an active coping strategy.

Patients were encouraged to continue practicing the full relaxation induction at least every other day once we progressed beyond the first six sessions. They were also urged to try relaxing without the audiotape but to return to it periodically to ensure deep relaxation.

The rationale for the PMR training was that it could serve, at a tonic level, as an antiarousal procedure through its regular use and, at a phasic level, as a coping strategy for dealing with everyday life stressors.

3. *Training in thermal biofeedback* (TBF) for hand warming was given in Sessions 7–12. The rationale for the inclusion of the biofeedback training was twofold. (a) It was included as a second, and somewhat

different, form of relaxation. Being able to engage in peripheral vasodilation requires the individual to be deeply relaxed and probably results in a reduction in peripheral sympathetic nervous system activity. We sought primarily the latter effect. (b) At a more psychological level, we believed that, if the patient could demonstrate to herself that she could gain voluntary control of some aspect of her physiology (i.e., hand temperature), she could then be led to believe that she should also gain control of another aspect of her physiology, her bowels. Thus, we hoped that the positive experience with the TBF would generalize at a cognitive–attributional level.

Only the first part of the rationale was presented to the patient at the beginning of Session 7. The second part was suggested during the latter half of the TBF training.

The actual TBF training occupied about 30–35 min and was always the first part of the session. The components were: (a) adaptation, about 5 min, patient sitting quietly; (b) in-session baseline, 5 min, patient continuing to sit quietly; (c) self-control, 4 min, patient asked to warm hand without the assistance of the feedback signal; and (d) feedback training, 16 or 20 min (depending on the study), patient warming hand with assistance of feedback.

Patients were usually allowed to sample both auditory and visual feedback and select their preference. A vast majority chose visual feedback. (In Blanchard & Schwarz's, 1987, group treatment study, no choice was offered—all feedback was visual.)

Several points were emphasized in the introduction to the TBF: (a) Patients were introduced to the idea of *passive volition,* or allowing the response to occur rather than trying to force it to occur; (b) patients were told no single strategy works for everyone, and that they should experiment with what worked for them; they were told that imagery works for some people, whereas others focus just on the meter display and others on bodily sensations; and (c) the need to stay relaxed and to breathe slowly from the diaphragm was emphasized. These points were repeated periodically.

Home practice was stressed. Patients were given alcohol-in-glass thermometers and asked to practice for at least 20 min per day, either in two 10-min blocks or one 20-min block. They were to record starting and ending temperatures for each practice. They were also asked to continue regular practice of the briefer forms of relaxation.

4. *Training in cognitive stress coping therapy* was the fourth component of treatment. It was introduced in Session 2 and was a portion of each session, receiving more emphasis in Sessions 4, 6, and 8 during the first 4 weeks of treatment (twice-per-week sessions). The therapy was modeled after procedures described by Holroyd and Andrasik (1982) for tension headache. It represents an amalgam of procedures from Meichenbaum (1977), Beck and Emery (1979), and Ellis (1962). The rationale was to teach IBS patients more effective ways to deal with stressful events in their daily lives and to try to counteract cognitive distortions and attributions that might be contributing to their overall arousal and distress.

The initial portion of the training focused on teaching the patients to become astute observers of their own behavior and subjective reactions. They were asked to note on diary sheets the antecedents and consequences of stressful events as well as their behavior and thoughts during the events.

Special attention was paid to their subjective feelings, to the possible onset of IBS symptoms such as pain or the urge to defecate, and to their thoughts or "self-talk" in Meichenbaum's (1977) terminology.

After patients became more proficient observers and recorders, more attention was paid in the therapy sessions to negative or self-defeating self-talk and to the affective consequences of it (feeling bad as a result of saying self-derogatory things to oneself about a situation). Patients searched for patterns, or regularities, in subjective reactions to stressful events.

As patients became sensitized to their internal dialogue and aware of negative self-talk, they were asked to explicitly substitute positive self-talk such as "I can master this problem" or "this situation is not worth developing a stomachache over," and so on. Checks on their ability to do this were made through the diary records.

As a final step, we attempted to discover negative schema (in the sense of Beck & Emery, 1979) and cognitive fallacies that led to anxiety or depression. At this point treatment became fairly idiosyncratic and reactive to the thoughts or attributions of the individual. Cognitive fallacies ("all-or-none thinking," etc.) were dealt with through direct challenge and explicit instruction to try reversing these automatic thoughts as they came to mind around stressful situations and at other times.

Summary of Albany Controlled Treatment Trials for IBS

Over the past 8 years, we have completed four controlled evaluations of the same set of treatment procedures for IBS patients. Subsequent to the last, and largest, trial, we have completed two other small-scale controlled evaluations of components of the initial treatment package. There were certain methodological commonalities across all six of these studies.

1. The GI symptom diary, described earlier, was completed by patients for 2 weeks before and after treatment, as well as throughout treatment. Data from the diary from those 2-week periods were the primary basis for evaluation. (In one instance [Blanchard, Schwarz, et al., 1992, Study 2], the pre- and posttreatment symptom monitoring phases were extended to 4 weeks each.)

2. The formal treatment program was scheduled to be 8 weeks in length; thus, the normal length of time for which the patient was involved with the research was approximately 3 months. (In some instances it took as long as 12 weeks to complete all of the treatment sessions.)

3. Patients were all diagnosed on the basis of the clinical criteria described earlier. Determination of whether patients met the inclusion criteria was made by doctoral students in my laboratory on the basis of structured interviews and examination of GI symptom diary data. A second evaluation was provided by the patient's own physician (in a great majority of cases this was a gastroenterologist or internist). Diagnostic tests that had been used were described in reports by the physicians sent to our center. In one study (Blanchard, Schwarz, et al., 1992, Study 2), all patients were evaluated by one of two board-certified academic gastroenterologists on the basis of review of patient records and a personal physical examination and history taken by those physicians. Sigmoidoscopies and other basic laboratory work were repeated on members of this sample if they had not been done within 1–2 years of the examination. (In only 1 case out of about 100 was a patient who had been diagnosed by her personal physician as having IBS found to have a different disorder, in this instance IBD. Thus, the combination of personal physician screening plus careful history taking by the psychologist yielded correct diagnoses in 99% of the cases.)

4. Most of the therapists were advanced doctoral students in clinical psychology with 2–3 years of previous clinical experience. In two cases postdoctoral fellows, again with experience in the procedures, were therapists. In one study (Blanchard, Schwarz, et al., 1992, Study 2) doctoral students with only 6 months of previous experience were used as therapists. (There were nonsignificant trends in Blanchard, Schwarz, et al. [1992, Study 2], indicating that less experienced therapists [especially one individual] achieved poorer results.)

Because IBS is a disorder with multiple GI symptoms, only a portion of which tend to be present in any individual patient, we adopted certain conventions in analyzing the outcome data derived from the GI symptom diary. We had certain biases in our approach to data analysis.

1. We believed that global ratings of degree of improvement (or deterioration) by the patient were subject to an overestimation bias due to such things as social desirability, and so on. Research from our center on the behavioral treatment of headaches has shown that patient global ratings overestimate improvement detected by daily symptom diary by about 35% (Blanchard, Andrasik, Neff, Jurish, & O'Keefe, 1981.) Likewise, we believe that therapist global ratings would also overestimate improvement.

2. We believed that the patient's daily diary of symptom ratings would be the most conservative and nearly valid measure of improvement.

3. Because IBS is a polysymptomatic disorder, with few patients complaining of all of the symptoms, we sought to develop a single composite measure from the diary data. A second reason for this development was to simplify analyses and diminish the possibility of capitalizing on chance inherent in analyzing multiple, potentially related measures on the same subjects. Thus, we developed a measure we have termed the *composite primary symptom reduction,* or CPSR, score. Our primary conclusions are drawn from CPSR scores.

4. In addition to comparing group mean CPSR scores to test for statistical significance, we also believe data on the proportion of the sample who individually show clinically significant change should be presented (see Blanchard & Schwarz, 1988, for a discussion of this topic).

The CPSR score was calculated as follows: for each of the primary symptoms of IBS, abdominal pain or tenderness, diarrhea, and constipation (which define the disorder), we first calculated a symptom reduction score:

Diarrhea Symptom Reduction Score $= 100$
$$\times \frac{\text{Pretreatment Diarrhea Score} - \text{Posttreatment Diarrhea Score}}{\text{Pretreatment Diarrhea Score}}$$

The CPSR score represents the average of the two (or three) symptom reduction scores:

$$\text{CPSR Score} = \frac{\begin{array}{l}\text{Pain and Tenderness Symptom Reduction Score} + \\ \text{Diarrhea Symptom Reduction Score} + \text{Constipation} \\ \text{Symptom Reduction Score}\end{array}}{\begin{array}{l}2 \text{ (or 3, depending on number of} \\ \text{primary symptoms the patient presents)}\end{array}}$$

The CPSR score thus assigns equal weight to improvement across each primary symptom. (A similar approach has been used by Whorwell et al., 1984, and Harvey et al., 1989.) Whether this matches each individual patient's perceptions has not been systematically examined.

5. We do, in fact, analyze the individual GI symptom scores but attach less importance to these results.

As a quick overall summary of the Albany studies, the mean CPSR score for each condition in these studies plus the percentages of the samples who reached our criteria for clinically significant improvement (a CPSR score of 0.50 or greater, i.e., an average reduction in primary GI symptoms of 50% or greater), are tabulated in Table 6.

Neff and Blanchard (1987) randomly assigned 20 IBS patients who met Latimer's (1983) criteria for IBS, and who received a diagnosis of IBS by their personal physician, to the 12-session Albany treatment program ($n = 10$) or continued GI symptom monitoring($n = 9$). One patient dropped out of symptom monitoring. Mean CPSR scores showed an advantage for treatment ($M = 50.4$) over symptom monitoring ($M = 15.4$; $t(17) = 2.31$, $p = .04$). Six of 10 (60%) treated patients reached the criterion for clinical improvement, whereas only 1 of 9 (11%) symptom monitoring patients did ($p = .04$, Fisher's Exact test).

Table 6

Summary of Results of the Albany Irritable Bowel Syndrome Studies

Study	Conditions	Sample size	CPSR score	Percentage of sample improved	
Neff & Blanchard (1987)	Multicomponent	10	50.4	6/10	(60%)
	Symptom monitoring	9	15.4	1/9	(11%)
	Treatment of symptom monitoring (multicomponent)	7	N/R	3/7	(43%)
Blanchard & Schwarz (1987)	12 weeks of symptom monitoring	14	N/R	0/14	(0%)
	Multicomponent	14	47.5	9/14	(64%)
Blanchard, Schwarz, et al. (1992), Study 1	Multicomponent	10	45.2	6/10	(60%)
	Attention placebo	10	38.0	5/10	(50%)
	Symptom monitoring	10	9.5	2/10	(20%)
Blanchard, Schwarz, et al. (1992), Study 2	Multicomponent	31	32.4	16/31	(52%)
	Attention placebo	30	30.4	14/30	(47%)
	Symptom monitoring	31	6.4	10/31	(32%)
	Treatment of symptom monitoring (multicomponent)	29	N/R	12/29	(41%)
Blanchard et al. (1993)	Relaxation	8	51.6	4/8	(50%)
	Symptom monitoring	8	−1.4	1/8	(13%)
Greene & Blanchard (in press)	Cognitive therapy	10	66.2	8/10	(80%)
	Symptom monitoring	10	2.1	1/10	(10%)
	Treatment of symptom monitoring (Cognitive therapy)	6	63.8	4/6	(67%)

Note. CPSR = composite primary symptom reduction; N/R = not reported.

On individual GI symptoms, there was a significant differential effect (p = .05) of treatment versus symptom monitoring only on flatulence; treated patients improved significantly (p < .025), whereas symptom monitoring patients were unchanged. The treated patients also showed significant reduction on diarrhea (p < .01).

Seven of the symptom monitoring patients were crossed over to active treatment. Even with this small sample, treatment resulted in significant reduction in pain (p < .04), constipation (p < .02), and flatulence (p < .025). Three of 7 participants had posttreatment CPSR scores that indicated clinically significant improvement.

All treated patients were followed up, prospectively, for 2 years (Blanchard, Schwarz, & Neff, 1988). For the 14 for whom diary data were available, 8 showed CPSR scores of 0.5 or greater and 2 others had CPSR scores greater than 0.4. As a group, there were statistically significant (p < .05 or better) reductions on abdominal pain and tenderness, diarrhea, constipation, flatulence, and nausea.

Blanchard and Schwarz (1987) completed the next study using a within-subjects design. Sixteen patients completed 12 weeks of symptom monitoring before starting treatment in small groups of 3–6. The same treatment protocol was followed with some adaptations for the small group format.

Two patients (both males) declined treatment after they completed symptom monitoring when they learned that treatment was in small groups. This left a total of 14 patients. No patient improved significantly during symptom monitoring (overall, diarrhea ratings from the diary were significantly higher after symptom monitoring). At the conclusion of treatment, 9 of 14 (64%) of patients had CPSR scores of 0.5 or greater. The group mean CPSR score was 0.475. Among individual symptoms, there were significant reductions in abdominal pain and in diarrhea at the end of treatment, with the improvements in flatulence and constipation reaching significance at 6-week follow-up. These results essentially replicated those of Neff and Blanchard (1987).

Clinical Hint

> It was our impression that the cognitive therapy component was not as intensive as in individual treatment. However, social support from group members seemed to compensate for this.

Study 1 of Blanchard, Schwarz, et al. (1992) was completed in 1987 by Maryrose Acerra-Gerardi for her dissertation, but her research was never submitted separately for publication. It served as a preliminary study for the larger study (Blanchard, Schwarz, et al., 1992, Study 2, is described later) and was published as part of the overall report. In this study, the Albany treatment program ($n = 10$) was repeated and compared with a symptom monitoring control condition ($n = 10$). There were no dropouts.

An ostensible attention-placebo control condition ($n = 10$), consisting of training in pseudomeditation (adapted from Holroyd, Andrasik, & Noble, 1980) and in biofeedback for suppression of the alpha activity in the EEG, was added. Patients in the control condition were also seen for 12 sessions. The training was presented as a multicomponent treatment involving biofeedback to try to give it equal credibility.

In the pseudomeditation condition, patients were asked to scan the body mentally in a systematic fashion while sitting upright. They were also asked to rehearse mental images of everyday activities. They were specifically asked not to relax, because that would interfere with the meditation. This condition continued for 6 sessions, with instructions for regular home practice.

In the biofeedback condition, EEGs were recorded from 0_z to the right mastoid with a forehead ground, a good site for detecting alpha activity. Patients were told to produce beta waves, which would be indicated by a decreasing feedback signal. A Biofeedback Systems, Incorporated, Model AT-2 device, with a digital quantifier, was used. Subjects were verbally given a numerical value from their baseline. Every 2 min thereafter, the therapist gave them a new numerical value that represented a 2% increase in the value, regardless of the actual value. Thus, patients were led to believe they were progressively succeeding at the task. (This condition was adapted from study by Plotkin & Rice, 1981, who showed it to be highly credible and that it led to reports of reduced anxiety in anxious college students.)

It is relatively easy to block alpha waves in the EEG by engaging in focused mental activity. Thus, patients had a genuine task that could be readily mastered and were given false verbal feedback indicating success at the task. Patients were asked to practice this activity, but without the aid of a home practice device.

Measures of treatment credibility were equivalent at pretreatment (multicomponent, M = 8.5 [on a 0–9 scale]; attention placebo, M = 7.9) and at posttreatment (multicomponent, M = 8.6; attention placebo, M = 7.8).

The mean CPSR scores were not different between the two treatment conditions (multicomponent, −0.45; attention placebo, −0.38), but did surpass those of the symptom monitoring controls (symptom monitoring, −0.095). Six of 10 patients from the multicomponent treatment had CPSR scores that indicated clinically significant improvement (with 4 exceeding scores of 0.75), whereas 5 of 10 patients from the attention-placebo condition were improved, as were 2 of 10 from the symptom monitoring condition.

Analyses of individual GI symptoms showed no significant change for the symptom monitoring group, whereas the multicomponent group improved on abdominal pain, abdominal tenderness, diarrhea, constipation, belching, and flatulence. The attention placebo condition improved on abdominal pain, constipation, and belching.

Given the superiority of results from the multicomponent condition over those from the attention-placebo control condition, a larger study replicating these conditions was initiated.

Under a grant from NIDDK, Blanchard, Schwarz, et al. (1992, Study 2) sought to extend the results of Study 1 through several changes: (a) Sample sizes were increased to 30 per condition; (b) all patients were assessed by the same two academic gastroenterologists, based on history, physical examination, and appropriate laboratory studies, as well as by the psychologist, again using the Latimer (1983) criteria; and (c) eight different therapists participated (7 were doctoral students in clinical psychology with from one semester to 3 years of experience; the 8th was a PhD in clinical psychology with experience). There were 23 dropouts during treatment, or 20% overall, equally distributed across conditions.

The treatment conditions were identical. Treatment credibility measures were again high and not different (multicomponent, M = 7.7; attention placebo, M = 8.0). The mean CPSR scores were noticeably lower for the two treated groups: multicomponent, M = 0.324; attention placebo, M = 0.302; symptom monitoring, M = 0.064). Fractions of the sample who met the criteria for clinically significant improvement were (multicomponent, 16/31 = 51.6%; attention placebo, 14/30 = 46.6%; symptom monitoring, 10/31 = 32.2%). Both treatment conditions led to significant reductions in abdominal pain and tenderness, diarrhea, flatulence, nausea, and bloating; constipation was reduced by the multicomponent treatment but not by the attention placebo; the reverse held for belching.

Twelve of 29 (41.4%) of the symptom monitoring controls who subsequently received the multicomponent treatment met the criteria for clinically significant improvement. On all individual symptoms but diarrhea they showed significant reductions after treatment.

These results were, of course, disappointing in several ways. The average CPSR results from the multicomponent treatment were noticeably lower than had been achieved previously (0.324 vs. 0.477), although the fraction of clinically improved patients (51.6%) was comparable with that from the other three studies (61.3%). Second, the symptom monitoring patients had better results (32% improved vs. 15% from the other studies). The principal procedural differences involved the use of much less experienced therapists. This might not have been important for the PMR or TBF, but it could have been crucial for the cognitive therapy component.

Later Albany Studies

We then examined components of the Albany multicomponent treatment program. In one study we examined PMR alone, and in a second we examined cognitive therapy alone.

Relaxation alone.   Given that five of the six other controlled treatment trials of IBS (see Table 4) included relaxation training in the treatment packages, and given our own results, we examined the effects of relaxation alone. In Blanchard, Greene, Scharff, and Schwarz-McMorris (1993), we compared a 10-session (over 8 weeks) relaxation training program with symptom monitoring. All of the components of the relaxation training were the same as described earlier; they were merely spread over a longer time.

Regular home practice was stressed, and an audiotape was again given to the patients to assist with the practice. Eight patients in each condition, again diagnosed by Latimer's criteria, completed the regimen. There were seven dropouts, six from the relaxation condition.

Clinical Hint

The high (6/14 = 43%) dropout rate may reflect the relative lack of attention to the individual's problems, which had been an integral part of the cognitive therapy component of the multicomponent treatment.

Patients in the relaxation condition had a significantly higher mean CPSR score than those in the symptom monitoring condition (relaxation, 0.516; symptom monitoring, −0.014). Four of 8 (50%) relaxation patients were clinically improved, compared with 1 of 8 (12.5%) in symptom monitoring. The small relaxation group showed significant reductions in abdominal pain and tenderness, constipation, and nausea. All three therapists were experienced (at least 2 full years or more of experience with this population).

Cognitive therapy alone.   Our most recent study (Greene & Blanchard, in press) was a comparison of a purely cognitive therapy treatment regimen with symptom monitoring. The therapist conducted the study as her dissertation and had 3 years of previous relevant experience. Ten patients, who were diagnosed according to Latimer's criteria, were randomly assigned to the cognitive therapy condition, and 10 others were assigned to symptom monitoring. Treatment was for 10 sessions over 8 weeks. The aspects of the previously described cognitive therapy were used. In addition, there was a special focus on identifying one or two underlying themes or schemas that appeared to be core problem areas for the patient and which were subsequently related to the IBS symptoms.

Process measures showed significant changes in the treated patients on the Automatic Thoughts Questionnaire and Dysfunctional Attitude Scale as well as in reported frequency of negative and positive self-talk. (The negative self-talk decreased and positive increased over time.)

Results showed that 8 of 10 (80%) of those who received cognitive therapy were significantly improved, as evidenced by CPSR scores of 0.50 or better, and the other 2 showed some improvement. This is in contrast to 1 of 10 patients showing improvement in symptom monitoring. The mean CPSR score for the cognitive therapy condition was 0.662, whereas for symptom monitoring it was 0.021.

Subsequently, six of the unimproved patients from the symptom monitoring group received somewhat abbreviated cognitive therapy (8–10 sessions, an average of 9). Four of six (66.7%) then met the criteria for improvement, with a mean CPSR score of 0.638.

It appears, on the basis of this small sample, that a purely cognitive therapy approach may hold great promise for helping a substantial proportion of IBS patients. Certainly, these results are better than any others we have seen. A replication of this study is currently in progress.

Long-Term Follow-up

As noted in other sections of this chapter, some limited data on long-term follow-up of patients treated with psychological treatments are available. Svedlund et al. (1983) found good maintenance on a group mean basis at 12 months. In fact, ratings of abdominal pain and bowel dysfunction showed further improvement from the end of treatment to the 1-year follow-up.

Guthrie et al. (1991) also reported good maintenance at the 12-month follow-up, with 69% of treated patients rated (by themselves) as improved. Interestingly, 10% (3 of 31) of patients who were improved at the end of treatment had deteriorated at 1 year. As noted earlier, the method of assessing status at follow-up was radically different than those methods used at the end of treatment, making definitive statements on maintenance difficult.

Whorwell et al. (1987) presented long-term (range = 14–21 months, M = 18 months) follow-up data on the 15 patients originally treated (Whorwell et al., 1984) with brief hypnotherapy. Patients were seen every 3 months for booster treatment sessions.

In the Albany studies, we described 2-year follow-up, documented by 2 weeks of daily symptom diary entries: 14 of 17 treated patients provided data. Eight of 14 (57%) were still clinically improved based on CPSR scores and 2 others were somewhat improved, for reasonable maintenance in 71% of the subjects.

We also obtained 4-year follow-up data on 19 of 27 patients (70.3%) who had received the Albany multicomponent treatment program (Schwarz, Taylor, Scharff, & Blanchard, 1990). On global ratings, 17 of 19 (89.5%) rated themselves as better than 50% improved. Of 12 patients for whom GI symptom diaries were collected, 6 still met or exceeded the CPSR criterion score of 0.50. All individual GI symptoms, except constipation, were significantly lessened at the 4-year follow-up point than they had been at pretreatment. It thus appears that improvements from psychological treatments are well maintained.

Prediction of Treatment Outcome

There have been five reports of potential predictors of treatment outcome. Unfortunately, the results are somewhat conflicting.

Guthrie et al. (1991) claimed to have examined data on 70 (of the 79) of their patients who completed treatment for possible predictors of outcome. However, they presented data on only 43 cases. Variables associated with a good outcome (improved status) were (a) initial presence of anxiety or depression (65% of improved patients vs. 25% of unimproved); (b) abdominal pain exacerbated by stress (65% vs. 17%); (c) shorter duration of illness; and (d) absence of constant (vs. episodic) abdominal pain (67% vs. 23%).

Whorwell et al. (1987) examined data on 50 patients treated with brief hypnotherapy. Although 95% (36 of 38) of "so-called classical cases" of IBS improved, only 43% (3 of 7) of "atypical" cases (intractable abdominal pain with little or no abdominal distention or altered bowel habit) improved. Sixty percent (3 of 5) of classical cases with noticeable psychological disturbance (General Health Questionnaire [GHQ] scores greater than 5) improved. Finally, of 8 patients over 50 years of age, only 25% were improved.

In one report from our laboratory on 45 treated patients (Blanchard et al., 1988), we found 26 (57.8%) had CPSR scores of 0.5 or greater, which indicates clinically significant improvement. Three variables emerged as potential predictors (trait anxiety from the STAI) (r [with CPSR] $= -0.39$, frequency of symptom-free days in baseline, $r = 0.32$; and gender, $r = 0.24$, $p = .06$). Males had a 70% success rate and females only 48%). Patients with more episodic symptoms (more symptom-free days) were more likely to improve. Finally, lower initial levels of trait anxiety were associated with success. For example, 60% of patients with STAI trait scores of 51 or lower were clinical successes as compared with only 15% who were failures. For those with scores of 52 or higher, only 37% were successes and 39% were clear failures.

Harvey et al. (1989), in their replication of the hypnotherapy effects, found that patients with GHQ scores of 5 or greater (indicative of psychological disturbance) responded poorly (38% improved vs. 68% improved for those with lower scores). Age was not a significant predictor in this study.

In a more recent study (Blanchard, Scharff, et al., 1992) that analyzed data from Blanchard, Schwarz, et al. (1992, Study 2), we found that the trait anxiety score result was not replicated for the 90 patients studied, nor were gender or baseline symptom-free days. The only significant predictor was the presence or absence of an Axis-I diagnosis from the ADIS ($r = 0.301$, $p < .01$). For the 48 patients who had an Axis I disorder, only 29% (14 of 48) met the criteria for improvement. For the 42 patients with no Axis-I disorder, 64% (27 of 42) had CPSR scores of 0.50 or greater ($p < .0009$). Thus, absence of an Axis I disorder indicates more than twice the likelihood of successful outcome from treatment.

Both of the results from our laboratory are contradictory of the results of Guthrie et al. (1991). Although we found low trait anxiety and the absence of any psychiatric disorder to be indicative of good prognosis, Guthrie et al. found the presence of anxiety or depression to be associated with a good outcome. The results of Whorwell et al. (1987) and of Harvey et al. (1989) are consistent with those of our group in that patients with lower GHQ scores (i.e., absence of psychopathology) did significantly better. This discrepancy could be due to different forms of treatment (brief dynamic psychotherapy vs. cognitive behavioral therapy or hypnotherapy). Clearly, further research is needed.

Clinical Hint

We strongly recommend conducting a thorough psychiatric evaluation of the potential IBS patient. This appears to be one of the best predictors of outcome. It is my impression, unfortunately unsupported by sound empirical data, that the best way to handle the presence of a comorbid psychiatric disorder is to attend to that disorder concurrently with the treatment of IBS. Specific therapeutic regimens for major depression, panic disorder, GAD, and so on, are now available. One could, of course, treat the psychiatric disorder first and see what happens to the IBS symptoms. No one has taken that approach to the best of my knowledge.

Conclusion

My recommendation to clinical health psychologists who are called on to treat IBS patients are threefold.

1. Conduct a thorough psychiatric evaluation of the patient. The presence of any Axis I disorder indicates a potentially refractory patient. It is probably necessary to plan for longer treatment

and to address the psychiatric disorder to get good results with the IBS.
2. Use a GI symptom diary to help evaluate progress.
3. Probably the best approach to treatment emphasizes cognitive therapy, and serious thought should be given to adjunctive relaxation training.

Fortunately, almost any treatment that is systematic and logical to the patient is likely to help at least 50% of IBS patients and possibly a higher percentage.

REFERENCES

Beck, A. T., & Emery, G. (1979). *Cognitive therapy of anxiety and phobic disorders.* Philadelphia: Center for Cognitive Therapy.

Beck, A. T., Ward, C. H., Mendelson, M., Mock, J., & Erbaugh, J. (1961). An inventory for measuring depression. *Archives of General Psychiatry, 5,* 561–571.

Bennett, P., & Wilkinson, S. (1985). Comparison of psychological and medical treatment of the irritable bowel syndrome. *British Journal of Clinical Psychology, 24,* 215–216.

Bernstein, D. A., & Borkovec, T. D. (1973). *Progressive relaxation training.* Champaign, IL: Research Press.

Blanchard, E. B., & Andrasik, F. (1985). *Management of chronic headache: A psychological approach.* Elmsford, NY: Pergamon Press.

Blanchard, E. B., Andrasik, F., Neff, D. F., Jurish, S. E., & O'Keefe, D. M. (1981). Social validation of the headache diary. *Behavior Therapy, 12,* 711–715.

Blanchard, E. B., Greene, B., Scharff, L., & Schwarz-McMorris, S. P. (1993). Relaxation training as a treatment for irritable bowel syndrome. *Biofeedback and Self-Regulation, 18,* 125–132.

Blanchard, E. B., Radnitz, C., Evans, D. D., Schwarz, S. P., Neff, D. F., & Gerardi, M. A. (1986). Psychological comparisons of irritable bowel syndrome to chronic tension and migraine headache and non-patient controls. *Biofeedback and Self-Regulation, 11,* 221–230.

Blanchard, E. B., Radnitz, C., Schwarz, S. P., Neff, D. F., & Gerardi, M. A. (1987). Psychological changes associated with self-regulatory treatments of irritable bowel syndrome. *Biofeedback and Self-Regulation, 12,* 31–38.

Blanchard, E. B., Scharff, L., Payne, A., Schwarz, S. P., Suls, J. M., & Malamood, H. (1992). Prediction of outcome from cognitive–behavioral treatment of irritable bowel syndrome. *Behaviour Research and Therapy, 30,* 647–650.

Blanchard, E. B., Scharff, L., Schwarz, S. P., Suls, J. M., & Barlow, D. H. (1990). The role of anxiety and depression in the irritable bowel syndrome. *Behaviour Research and Therapy, 28,* 401–405.

Blanchard, E. B., & Schwarz, S. P. (1987). Adaptation of a multicomponent treatment program for irritable bowel syndrome to a small group format. *Biofeedback and Self-Regulation, 12,* 63–69.

Blanchard, E. B., & Schwarz, S. P. (1988). Clinically significant changes in behavioral medicine. *Behavioral Assessment, 10,* 171–188.

Blanchard, E. B., Schwarz, S. P., & Neff, D. F. (1988). Two-year follow-up of behavioral treatment of irritable bowel syndrome. *Behavior Therapy, 19,* 67–73.

Blanchard, E. B., Schwarz, S. P., Suls, J. M., Gerardi, M. A., Scharff, L., Greene, B., Taylor, A. E., Berreman, C., & Malamood, H. S. (1992). Two controlled evaluations of multicomponent psychological treatment of irritable bowel syndrome. *Behaviour Research and Therapy, 30,* 175–189.

Borkovec, T. D., & Mathews, A. M. (1988). Treatment of nonphobic anxiety disorders: A comparison of nondirective, cognitive, and coping desensitization therapy. *Journal of Consulting and Clinical Psychology, 56,* 877–884.

Derogatis, L. I. (1983). *The SCL-90-R: Administration, scoring, and procedures manual II.* Towson, MD: Psychometric Research.

DiNardo, P. A., & Barlow, D. H. (1988). *Anxiety Disorders Interview Schedule–Revised (ADIS-R).* (Available from the Phobia and Anxiety Disorders Clinic, Center for Stress and Anxiety Disorders, State University of New York at Albany, Albany, NY 12222)

Drossman, D. A., McKee, D. C., Sandler, R. S., Mitchell, C. M., Cramer, E. M., Lowman, B. C., & Burger, A. L. (1988). Psychosocial factors in the irritable bowel syndrome: A multivariate study of patients and non-patients with irritable bowel syndrome. *Gastroenterology, 95,* 701–708.

Drossman, D. A., Sandler, R. S., McKee, D. C., & Lovitz, A. J. (1982). Bowel patterns among subjects not seeking health care: Use of a questionnaire to identify a population with bowel dysfunction. *Gastroenterology, 83,* 529–534.

Ellis, A. (1962). *Reason and emotion in psychotherapy.* New York: Lyle Stuart.

Ferguson, A., Sircus, W., & Eastwood, N. A. (1977). Frequency of "functional" gastrointestinal disorders. *Lancet, 2,* 613–614.

Greene, B., & Blanchard, E. B. (in press). Cognitive therapy for irritable bowel syndrome. *Journal of Consulting and Clinical Psychology.*

Guthrie, E., Creed, F., Dawson, D., & Tomenson, B. (1991). A controlled trial of psychological treatment for the irritable bowel syndrome. *Gastroenterology, 100,* 450–457.

Harvey, R. F., Hinton, R. A., Gunary, R. N., & Barry, R. E. (1989). Individual and group hypnotherapy in treatment of refractory irritable bowel syndrome. *Lancet,* 424–425.

Holroyd, K. A., & Andrasik, F. (1982). A cognitive–behavioral approach to recurrent tension and migraine headache. In P. E. Kendall (Ed.), *Advances in cognitive–behavioral research and therapy* (Vol. 1, pp. 275–320). San Diego, CA: Academic Press.

Holroyd, K. A., Andrasik, F., & Noble, J. (1980). Comparison of EMG biofeedback and a credible pseudotherapy in treating tension headache. *Journal of Behavioral Medicine, 3,* 29–39.

Jacobson, E. (1976). *You must relax* (5th ed.). New York: McGraw-Hill.

Latimer, P. R. (1983). *Functional gastrointestinal disorders: A behavioral medicine approach.* New York: Springer.

Liss, J. L., Alpers, D. H., & Woodruff, R. A. (1973). The irritable colon syndrome and psychiatric illness. *Diseases of the Nervous System, 34,* 151–157.

Lynch, P. N., & Zamble, E. (1989). A controlled behavioral treatment of irritable bowel syndrome. *Behavior Therapy, 20,* 509–523.

Meichenbaum, D. (1977). *Cognitive behavior modification: An integrative approach.* New York: Plenum.

Neff, D. F., & Blanchard, E. B. (1987). A multicomponent treatment for irritable bowel syndrome. *Behavior Therapy, 18,* 70–83.

Plotkin, W. B., & Rice, K. M. (1981). Biofeedback as a placebo: Anxiety reduction facilitated by training in either suppression or enhancement of alpha brain waves. *Journal of Consulting and Clinical Psychology, 49,* 590–596.

Schwarz, S. P., Blanchard, E. B., Berreman, C. F., Scharff, L., Taylor, A. E., Greene, B. R., Suls, J. M., & Malamood, H. S. (1993). Psychological aspects of irritable bowel syndrome: Comparisons with inflammatory bowel disease and nonpatient controls. *Behaviour Research and Therapy, 31,* 297–304.

Schwarz, S. P., Taylor, A. E., Scharff, L., & Blanchard, E. B. (1990). A four-year follow-up of behaviorally treated irritable bowel syndrome patients. *Behaviour Research and Therapy, 28,* 331–335.

Spielberger, C. D., Gorsuch, R. L., & Lushene, R. E. (1970). *STAI manual for the state–trait anxiety inventory.* Palo Alto, CA: Consulting Psychologists Press.

Svedlund, J., Sjodin, I., Ottosson, J.-O., & Dotevall, G. (1983). Controlled study of psychotherapy in irritable bowel syndrome. *Lancet,* 589–592.

Switz, D. N. (1976). What the gastroenterologist does all day. *Gastroenterology, 70,* 1048–1050.

Talley, N. J., Phillips, S. F., Melton, L. J., Mulvihill, C., Wiltgen, C., & Zinsmeister, A. R. (1990). Diagnostic value of the Manning criteria in irritable bowel syndrome. *Gut, 31,* 77–81.

Talley, N. J., Phillips, S. F., Melton, L. J., Wiltgen, C., & Zinsmeister, A. R. (1989). A patient questionnaire to identify bowel disease. *Annals of Internal Medicine, 111,* 671–674.

Talley, N. J., Zinsmeister, A. R., VanDyke, C., & Melton, L. J. (1991). Epidemiology of colonic symptoms and the irritable bowel syndrome. *Gastroenterology, 101,* 927–934.

Thompson, W. G. (1984). Gastrointestinal symptoms in the irritable bowel compared with peptic ulcer and inflammatory bowel disease. *Gut, 25,* 1089–1092.

Thompson, W. G., Creed, F., Drossman, D. A., Heaton, K. W., & Mazacca, G. (1992). Functional bowel disease and functional abdominal pain. *Gastroenterology International, 5,* 75–91.

Walker, E. A., Roy-Byrne, P. P., & Katon, W. J. (1990). Irritable bowel syndrome and psychiatric illness. *American Journal of Psychiatry, 147,* 565–572.

Whitehead, W. E., Bosmajian, L., Zonderman, A. B., Costa, P. T., & Schuster, M. M. (1988). Symptoms of psychologic distress associated with irritable bowel syndrome: Comparison of community and medical clinic samples. *Gastroenterology, 95,* 709–714.

Whitehead, W. E., Winget, C., Fedoravicius, A. S., Wooley, S., & Blackwell, B. (1982). Learned illness behavior in patients with irritable bowel syndrome and peptic ulcer. *Digestive Diseases and Sciences, 27,* 202–208.

Whorwell, P. J., Prior, A., & Colgan, S. M. (1987). Hypnotherapy in severe irritable bowel syndrome: Further experience. *Gut, 28,* 423–425.

Whorwell, P. J., Prior, A., & Faragher, E. B. (1984). Controlled trial of hypnotherapy in the treatment of severe refractory irritable bowel syndrome. *Lancet,* 1232–1234.

Young, S. J., Alpers, D. H., Norland, C. C., & Woodruff, R. A. (1976). Psychiatric illness and the irritable bowel syndrome: Practical implications for the primary physician. *Gastroenterology, 20,* 162–166.

Chapter 3

Nonpharmacological Treatment of Essential Hypertension: Research and Clinical Applications

Raymond C. Rosen, Elizabeth Brondolo, and
John B. Kostis

Hypertension is a significant risk factor for stroke, myocardial infarction, and congestive heart failure, which together account for more than 50% of deaths in the United States (Wollam & Hall, 1988). Despite significant advances in treatment and prevention, it is estimated that about 50 million Americans have elevated blood pressure (BP), which is defined as systolic blood pressure (SBP) 140 mmHg or greater or diastolic blood pressure (DBP) 90 mmHg or greater (Joint National Committee on Detection, Evaluation, and Treatment of High Blood Pressure [JNC-V], 1993). The prevalence of hypertension in-

The preparation of this chapter was supported by National Institutes of Health grants HL33960-04 and HL48642-02 to John B. Kostis and Raymond C. Rosen. We gratefully acknowledge the assistance of our graduate students, Chris Kotsen and Jennifer Follitico-Taylor.

creases steadily with age, is about twice as common among Blacks than among Whites, and is negatively related to socioeconomic status (Rowland & Roberts, 1982). In women, the prevalence increases markedly following menopause (Stamler, Stamler, Riedlinger, Algera, & Roberts, 1976). According to recent data from the 1991 National Health and Nutrition Examination Survey (NHANES III; in JNC-V, 1993), approximately 85% of hypertensive individuals are aware of their condition, and 55% have their blood pressure controlled by drugs.

Methodological changes in the approach to detection and management of hypertension have recently been published by the JNC-V (1993). First, a new four-stage classification system is recommended for classifying the severity of hypertension (see Table 1). This system is based on elevations in either SBP or DBP, with the higher category determining the individual's BP status. The revised classification draws attention to the risks associated with increased SBP as well as DBP and attempts to replace the possible "reverse-stigma" effect of

Table 1

High Blood Pressure (BP) Classification System

Diastolic BP (mmHg)	Systolic BP (mmHg)				
	<140	140–159	160–179	180–209	>210
<90		1	2	3	4
90–99	1	1	2	3	4
100–109	2	2	2	3	4
110–119	3	3	3	3	4
>120	4	4	4	4	4

Note. This classification system replaces the previous categories of *mild, moderate,* and *severe* hypertension. From "Fifth Report" by Joint National Committee on Detection, Evaluation, and Treatment of High Blood Pressure, 1993, *Archives of Internal Medicine, 153,* p. 161. Copyright 1993 by the American Medical Association. Adapted by permission.

the labels *mild* and *moderate* hypertension. Long-term therapy continues to be advised for all four levels of hypertension. Finally, the report highlights the special place of nonpharmacological therapy, to which it refers as "lifestyle modification." Several areas of specific behavior change are proposed, each of which is evaluated in detail later.

In this chapter, we critically review studies of nonpharmacological treatment of hypertension, as well as outline our clinical approach to patient management. Several arguments favor the use of nonpharmacological therapy, including recent evidence of the role of life-style factors, such as diet, exercise, and stress in the etiology of hypertension (National High Blood Pressure Education Program, 1992). Epidemiological studies have strongly implicated such factors as obesity, alcohol and salt consumption, and lack of exercise in the development and maintenance of high BP (Blair, Goodyear, Gibbons, & Cooper, 1984; Stamler, Stamler, Riedlinger, Algera, & Roberts, 1978). Other arguments in favor of nondrug therapy are the high cost and potential side effects associated with long-term pharmacotherapy. For example, commonly used antihypertensive drugs such as thiazide diuretics and beta blockers may adversely affect carbohydrate and lipid metabolism (Medical Research Council Working Party, 1985; Pollare, Lithell, Selinus, & Berne, 1989). Mood state, cognitive functioning, and sexual performance are also adversely affected by drug therapy (Croog et al., 1986; Kostis et al., 1990). In contrast, life-style modification has been associated with reduced overall cardiovascular risk and improved quality of life (Kostis et al., 1992; Rosen, Kostis, & Brondolo, 1989). According to the Joint National Committee Report, life-style modification can provide "multiple benefits at little cost and minimal risk" (JNC-V, 1993) and may be used as either a "first-step therapy" for individuals with high normal or Stage 1 hypertension or as a means for reducing the number and doses of antihypertensive medications required (Little, Girling, Hasler, & Trafford, 1991).

In general, the issue of wide-scale treatment of hypertension is increasingly seen as a major public health concern in the United States. Considering the large number of individuals who must be maintained on lifelong therapy, the costs and benefits associated with treatment must be carefully evaluated. As noted by Kaplan (1985, p. 359), "The steadily rising pressure to treat all such patients is bringing millions of asymptomatic people into lifetime drug therapy." The value of life-style modification in this context may ultimately lie in its cost saving, possible health benefits for the individual, and suggestion of enhanced "self-efficacy" following treatment. On the other hand, not all studies have shown positive effects for nondrug therapy, as is discussed later.

Dietary Interventions

Dietary changes are among the oldest and most widely used forms of life-style modification for hypertension (Blanchard, Martin, & Dubbert, 1988; Blaufox & Langford, 1987). Although many aspects of diet may influence BP in specific individuals, three dietary interventions are generally recommended: weight reduction for overweight individuals, sodium restriction, and moderation of alcohol intake. Additional recommendations generally include reduction of saturated fat intake and maintenance of adequate dietary levels of potassium, calcium, and magnesium, although these last interventions are not reliably associated with BP reduction (JNC-V, 1993).

Weight Reduction

Studies of weight loss and hypertension date back to the early 1920s, when it was shown that modest weight loss can lead to significant BP reduction in obese, hypertensive individuals (Rose, 1922; Terry, 1923). Further evidence of the relationship between obesity and hypertension has come from population studies showing that hypertension is two to three times more prevalent in overweight individuals than in nonoverweight individuals (Kannel, Brand, Skinner, Dawber, & McNamara, 1967; Stamler et al., 1978). Conversely, it has been shown that as many as 60% of hypertensive individuals are above 120% of ideal body weight (Velasquez & Hoffman, 1985). Overweight individuals are also more likely to suffer from cardiovascular complications, such as hyperlipidemia and coronary artery disease (Wollam & Hall, 1988). Several mechanisms, such as increased adrenergic tone, endocrine factors (i.e., hyperinsulinemia and increased plasma renin levels), and increased salt intake, have been proposed to account for the relationship between obesity and hypertension (Maxwell & Waks, 1987). In severely obese individuals (i.e., those above 150% of ideal body weight), hypertension is related to an increased cardiac output in relation to peripheral vascular resistance (Messerli et al., 1983).

The effects of weight loss on hypertension have been studied extensively in the past 2 decades (see Table 2). Using a variety of research designs and subject groups, investigators at numerous sites have documented a strong relationship between weight loss and a reduction in hypertension. As noted by Hall (1988), however, the interpretation of findings from these studies is not always clear cut, given the potential confounding effects of decreased sodium intake, increased physical activity, and concomitant use of various antihypertensive drugs. Most studies have also lacked attention-placebo controls or adequate follow-up assessment. Despite these limitations, there is increasing evidence of a direct therapeutic effect of weight loss in overweight hypertensive individuals, independent of other changes in life-style (Goldstein, 1992; Singh, Rastogi, Singh, & Mehta, 1990). Table 2 summarizes the major controlled trials of weight loss as therapy for hypertension.

Among the early studies, an Australian group (MacMahon, MacDonald, Bernstein, Andrews, & Blacket, 1985) compared the effects of weight reduction, beta blocker therapy, and double-blind placebos for a 5-month treatment period. Significant weight loss (M = 7.5 kg) was associated with a marked drop in both SBP and DBP ($-13.3/-9.8$), and a greater reduction in BP was noted in the weight loss compared with the drug condition. Furthermore, patients in the weight reduction condition showed a significant decrease in both total and high-density lipoprotein (HDL) cholesterol. Thus, this well-controlled, randomized study demonstrated that weight reduction was associated not only with effective treatment of mild hypertension but also with positive changes in the plasma lipid profiles of the patients. Similar results were obtained in our own recent trial with multifaceted nondrug therapy (Kostis et al., 1992).

Not all studies of dietary weight loss effects showed satisfactory reductions in BP, however. For example, one study of weight loss in obese, hypertensive patients found little difference in BPs at 6 months ($-0.2/-0.1$), compared with a no-treatment control (Haynes et al., 1984). Average weight loss in the treatment group was only 4.1 kg, compared with 0.8 kg in the control group. In accounting for the different outcomes of these two studies, we can hypothesize that a minimum level of weight loss may be needed to achieve significant BP changes. Subjects in the last study had considerably lower levels of weight loss compared with the levels achieved in early studies by

Table 2

Weight Reduction for Treatment of Hypertension (Controlled Trials)

Study	Subjects	Study design	Duration	Weight loss (kg)	Blood pressure (BP) change (mmHg), SBP/DBP
Heyden et al. (1973)	127 overweight hypertensive men and women	Random assignment to either weight loss diet or usual care	1 year	−7.8	−18/−13
Reisen et al. (1978)	24 overweight hypertensive men and women	Comparison to several parallel drug conditions	4 months	−8.8	−26/−20
Tuck et al. (1981)	25 obese hypertensive men and women	Random assignment to weight loss with or without Na restriction	3 months	−20.2	−15 (arterial pressure)
Fagerberg et al. (1984)	30 middle-aged, obese hypertensive men	Random assignment to weight loss with or without Na and energy restriction	13 weeks	−8.7	−12/−9
Maxwell et al. (1984)	30 obese hypertensive men and women	Random assignment to weight loss with or without Na restriction	12 weeks	−21.6	−16/−12

continued

Study	Sample	Design	Duration		
Haynes et al. (1984)	60 mildly hypertensive men and women	Random assignment to weight loss or no-treatment control	6 months	−4.1	−0.2/−0.1
Wing et al. (1984)	52 mildly hypertensive men and women	Random assignment to weight loss or Na restriction diet	8 weeks	−4.4	−13.9/−7.7
MacMahon et al. (1985)	56 mildly hypertensive overweight men and women	Random assignment to weight loss, metoprolol, or placebo	21 weeks	−7.4	−13/−10
Rissanen et al. (1985)	24 moderately obese hypertensive men and women	Sequential assignment to weight loss and control groups	1 year	−6.9	−11.5/−7.1
Rocchini et al. (1988)	72 obese male and female adolescents	Random assignment to weight loss with or without exercise	20 weeks	−2.5	−10/−12
Cohen et al. (1991)	30 moderately obese men and women patients	Effects of weight loss or concomitant drug therapy	1 year	−0.88	Reduction in BP medications
Wassertheil-Smoller et al. (1992)	878 overweight hypertensive men and women	TAIM trial of drug versus nondrug treatments for hypertension	6 months	−4.35	−11.9/−9.5

Note. TAIM = Trial of Antihypertensive Interventions and Management study; SBP = systolic blood pressure; DBP = diastolic blood pressure; Na = sodium.

McMahon et al. (1985), as well as other studies by Reisen et al. (1978) and Tuck, Sowers, Dornfeld, Kledzik, and Maxwell (1981).

Some investigators have attempted to separate the effects of weight loss from sodium restriction and other dietary factors. Results of these studies have generally been inconclusive, to date. Whereas some investigators have found significant changes in BP from weight loss alone (Maxwell, Kushiro, & Dornfeld, 1984; Tuck et al., 1981), others have noted a strong interaction with sodium restriction effects (Fagerberg, Anderson, Isaksson, & Bjorntrop, 1984). Again, the discrepancy in the amount of weight loss between the different studies and the importance of controls for exercise training or other nonspecific effects of treatment need to be underscored.

In the recent multicenter Trial of Antihypertensive Interventions and Management study, a large, prospective trial of various dietary and drug interventions for mild hypertension was conducted (Wassertheil-Smoller, Oberman, Blaufox, Davis, & Langford, 1992). During the treatment phase, 787 patients were randomly assigned to one of three drug conditions (atenolol, chlorthalidone, or placebo), combined with one of three dietary conditions (weight reduction, sodium restriction and potassium increase, or usual diet). After 6 months of treatment, DBP was found to be significantly reduced in all nine diet and drug combinations, including the placebo–usual diet condition. However, both drugs produced significantly greater BP decreases than placebo, and weight reduction was more effective than either sodium restriction or the usual diet condition. The addition of weight loss to either drug condition resulted in a greater BP reduction overall. In contrast, the addition of sodium restriction to either drug did not result in a lowering of BP beyond that achieved by either drug alone.

An additional noteworthy finding in this trial was the significant improvement in quality-of-life measures associated with weight reduction. Total physical complaints and sexual disturbances were significantly reduced among patients in the weight loss groups, compared with those in the other dietary conditions. Sexual problems were most common in patients who received chlorthalidone, although this effect was ameliorated somewhat by the effects of concomitant weight loss. Quality-of-life differences were reported for both men and women participants. Surprisingly, sodium restriction was associated with markedly adverse effects on quality of life, including increased sleep disturbances when combined with atenolol and greater fatigue when combined with placebo. Wassertheil-Smoller et al. (1992,

p. 42) noted that, "among those receiving a placebo drug, fatigue was made significantly worse by sodium restriction, with 32.7% reporting worsening compared to 13.6% under usual diet/placebo ($p = .02$) and compared to 14.1% under weight reduction/placebo ($p = .02$)." The mechanism for this effect is uncertain, and the results warrant further replication.

Weight loss has also been found to be superior to sodium restriction and stress management in the recent Trials of Hypertension Prevention (TOHP) for persons with high normal DBP (TOHP Collaborative Research Group, 1992). In this large-scale, multicenter trial, 2164 patients with DBP of 80–89 mmHg were randomly assigned to one of several nondrug conditions (weight loss, sodium reduction, stress management, or usual care) or to a crossover evaluation of various dietary supplements (calcium, magnesium, potassium, and "fish oil"). Results at 6 months indicated a small but significant advantage of weight loss compared with sodium restriction and no change in the stress reduction and other dietary supplement groups. The mean net weight loss of 5.7 kg reported at 6 months was the maximum weight loss achieved in the study and was associated with a BP-lowering effect of 3.8/2.5 mmHg. This result was considerably diminished, although still significant, at 18-month follow-up.

Finally, weight loss can be an effective means of maintaining treatment effects after withdrawal of medication. This was demonstrated in the multicenter Dietary Intervention Study in Hypertension (DISH; Langford et al., 1985), in which a large cohort ($N = 496$) of men and women hypertensive patients were followed for 1 year after withdrawal of drug therapy. Patients were randomly assigned to either weight reduction, sodium restriction, or a no-medication control group. Average weight loss for overweight patients in the weight reduction group was 4.5 kg, which resulted in a 60% success rate in maintaining normal BP without drug therapy after 1 year. By comparison, 45% of overweight patients in the sodium restriction and 35% of overweight patients in the no-medication control group maintained normal BP without drug therapy. The effectiveness of weight loss was markedly greater in patients with lower initial BP values, as well as in those who experienced greater weight loss during the course of the intervention.

Taken together, these studies provide convincing evidence of the role of dietary weight loss in the treatment of essential hypertension. Further research into the role of patient selection factors in determining the effectiveness of weight loss therapy is needed. For example, it is unclear whether this approach to treatment is likely to be equally effective for mildly overweight patients compared with those with moderate or severe obesity. Conversely, it has not been established whether a minimum level of weight loss is necessary to achieve significant BP control in specific patient groups (Haynes et al., 1984). The mechanism by which weight loss lowers BP is not well understood either. In markedly obese patients who lose a substantial amount of body weight, there is a corresponding decrease in total blood volume, cardiopulmonary blood volume, and cardiac output (Reisen et al., 1983). Other factors, such as a reduction in plasma norepinephrine levels, a decrease in plasma renin activity and plasma aldosterone, and a decrease in fasting levels of serum insulin, have also been implicated, however (Wollam & Hall, 1988). Another issue is the relative value of weight loss for older hypertensive patients, which is currently being addressed in the multicenter Trial of Non-Pharmacological Therapy in the Elderly. Finally, the question of long-term maintenance of treatment gains has not been sufficiently considered in the research to date.

Despite these limitations, an active weight loss program is strongly recommended for all hypertensive patients at or above 115% of ideal body weight. The expected average reduction in BP is approximately 1/1 mmHg for every 2–3 lb of weight loss (Wollam & Hall, 1988). In hypertensive patients receiving drug therapy, weight loss should also be recommended as a means of reducing the number or dosage of medications required (Langford et al., 1985). Aside from improvements in BP, weight reduction is usually associated with a decrease in cholesterol, low-density lipoprotein (LDL) cholesterol, and triglycerides, as well as improvement of cardiac function and reduction of left ventricular hypertrophy in some patients (MacMahon, Wilcken, & MacDonald, 1986).

Sodium Restriction

Low-salt diets for hypertension were first popularized in the 1940s, when the "rice–fruit diet" (Kempner, 1948) was prescribed for individuals with moderate or severe hypertension. This unpalatable diet was difficult to maintain, however, and was largely abandoned with the advent of modern pharmacotherapeutic approaches in the 1950s and 1960s (Wollam & Hall, 1988). In the early 1970s, a resurgence of interest in the topic was sparked by Dahl's (1972) proposal that hypertension in westernized cultures is primarily due to excessive dietary salt intake. Subsequent epidemiological studies have provided increasing support for this hypothesis (e.g., Intersalt Cooperative Research Group, 1988; Law, Frost, & Wald, 1991). Furthermore, a substantial number of intervention trials have been conducted in the past 2 decades, the results of which are briefly reviewed as follows (see Table 3).

Several early studies demonstrated positive effects of sodium restriction on BP changes in hypertensive patients (MacGregor et al., 1982; Morgan et al., 1978; Watt et al., 1983). However, other investigators reported that weight loss effects accounted for much of the variance in BP changes observed (Wing et al., 1984), as was discussed earlier. The issue of salt sensitivity is also important because certain individuals are likely to be more sensitive than others to sodium restriction (Hall, 1988). There may also be interactions with sympathetic nervous system activity and the adrenergic tone of the individual that need to be taken into account.

Modest effects of dietary sodium restriction were obtained in the recent multicenter Australian trial (Australian National Health and Medical Research Council Dietary Salt Study Management Committee, 1989). In this study, 111 mildly hypertensive patients were randomly assigned to either a low-sodium diet plus placebo or the same low-salt diet plus tablets containing slow-release sodium chloride. After 8 weeks of treatment, patients in the low-sodium group showed a small but significant decrease in both SBP and DBP (6.1/3.7 mmHg), compared with patients in the normal sodium group (0.6/0.9 mmHg). In the low-sodium group, older subjects and those with the highest initial SBP levels showed the greatest treatment effects. Weight loss was significantly correlated with changes in SBP, but not DBP, in both treatment groups. These findings suggest that a low-salt diet may have a mildly positive effect on BP control, independent of the associated effects of weight loss.

Two additional studies have provided evidence of the independent role of sodium restriction in the treatment of hypertension. MacGregor, Markandu, Sagnella, Singer, and Cappuccio (1989) evaluated the effects of three different levels of sodium reduction (50, 100, 200 mmol/day) in a double-blind crossover design with 20 mildly hyper-

Table 3

Salt Restriction for Hypertension (Randomized Controlled Studies)

Study	Subjects	Study design	Duration	Urinary Na change (meq/day)	Blood pressure change (SBP/DBP)
Morgan et al. (1978)	62 mildly hypertensive men	Random assignment to low salt or control group	24 months	−27	−1.5/−6.9
MacGregor et al. (1982)	19 mildly hypertensive men and women	Crossover study with low salt or salt additive	8 weeks	−76	−10/−5.0
Watt et al. (1983)	18 mildly hypertensive men and women	Crossover design study with low salt or salt additive	8 weeks	−56	−0.5/−0.3
Richards et al. (1984)	12 mildly hypertensive men and women	Crossover study with low Na and high K	12 weeks	−105	−5.2/−1.8
Fagerberg et al. (1984)	30 obese hypertensive men	Random assignment to low salt or control group	10 weeks	−89	−13.3/−6.7

continued

Study	Sample	Design	Duration	Na	SBP/DBP
Wing et al. (1984)	52 mildly hypertensive men and women	Random assignment to weight loss or low salt	8 weeks	−61	−6.2/−4.1
Grobbee et al. (1987)	40 mildly hypertensive men and women	Random assignment to low salt or placebo control	6 weeks	−72	−0.8/−0.8
Dodson et al. (1989)	34 Type II diabetics with mild hypertension	Random assignment to low salt or control group	12 weeks	−59	−13.0/−1.8
MacGregor et al. (1989)	20 mildly hypertensive men and women	Crossover design study with 3 levels of Na intake	12 weeks	−82	−8.0/−5.0
Australian National Health Study Management Committee (1989)	103 mildly hypertensive men and women	Random assignment to low salt or salt additive	8 weeks	−71	−5.5/−2.8
Benetos et al. (1992)	20 mildly hypertensive men and women	Crossover study with low salt or salt additive	9 weeks	−88	−11.4/−6.6

Note.   SBP = systolic blood pressure; DBP = diastolic blood pressure; Na = sodium; K = potassium.

tensive patients. Significant reductions in both SBP and DBP were obtained in the low- and medium-salt restriction conditions, as the low-sodium group was associated with a change of 16/9 mmHg, compared with 8/5 mmHg in the medium-sodium condition. The BP differences between the low- and medium-sodium conditions were also significant. No significant differences in weight were observed. This study included a 12-month follow-up assessment, which showed that 16 of 20 patients were adequately controlled on the basis of low-salt diet alone after 1 year of treatment. Similar effects were obtained by Richards et al. (1984) in a study with mildly hypertensive men and women.

Several studies have examined the effects of sodium restriction as adjunctive therapy for patients on antihypertensive medications. For example, Beard, Cooke, Gray, and Barge (1982) randomly assigned 90 medicated hypertensive patients to either a low-salt diet or a waiting-list control condition. After 12 weeks of treatment, patients in the low-salt condition showed a significant reduction in medication use compared to the controls, with 33% off medication altogether and 80% having significantly reduced the dosage. However, significant weight loss was again associated with sodium restriction in this trial. More recently, Weinberger et al. (1988) investigated the effects of a 30-week low-salt dietary intervention as adjunctive therapy for mild hypertension. Ninety-eight of 114 patients completed the dietary program, and a significant reduction in medication use was observed in patients with lower urinary sodium levels. Although significant weight loss was again associated with treatment, post-hoc analyses indicated that sodium restriction had resulted in BP changes independent of weight loss in these patients. As mentioned earlier, sodium restriction also played a beneficial role in maintaining BP levels in patients after withdrawal of medication in the multicenter DISH trial (Langford et al., 1985).

Despite the overall advantages of salt restriction as adjunctive therapy, recent studies have suggested that BP responses vary greatly, depending on the characteristics of patients and class of drugs involved (Muntzel & Drueke, 1992). Although low-sodium diets generally act to potentiate treatment with diuretics, at least one early study showed no benefit of salt restriction for patients receiving diuretic therapy (Parijs, Joossens, Van der Linden, Verstreken, & Amery, 1973). Other investigators have reported that a low-salt diet can potentiate adverse effects such as dizziness, weakness, and orthostatic hypotension in patients receiving thiazide diuretics (Van Brummelen, Schalekamp, & de Graeff, 1978). Dietary salt restriction may not be as effective in patients receiving beta blocker therapy (Kimura et al., 1988) and may actually inhibit the effects of treatment with calcium channel blockers (Morgan et al., 1986).

Several explanations of the mechanism of action of sodium restriction therapy have been offered (Hall, 1988; Muntzel & Drueke, 1992). As noted earlier, significant weight reduction is frequently seen in patients on a low-salt diet and may account for some of the variances in BP change. Sodium restriction has also been associated with reductions in plasma volume and extracellular fluid volume (Fagerberg, Isaksson, & Herlitz, 1986; Warren & O'Conner, 1981), which have been associated, in turn, with lower sympathetic tone (Ambrosioni et al., 1982). It has also been shown that sodium restriction is associated with decreased plasma renin levels and reduced cardiac output in some hypertensive patients (Omvik & Lund-Johansen, 1986). The salt-sensitivity hypothesis postulates that patients with enhanced responsiveness to dietary sodium may show a larger initial therapeutic response to sodium restriction (Muntzel & Drueke, 1992). Finally, a recent study by Benetos, Yang-Yan, Cuche, Hannaert, and Safar (1992) found that salt restriction was associated with specific decreases in resistance and increased diameter in the brachial artery. They suggested a difference in salt dependence among different arterial beds (Benetos et al., 1992).

Current guidelines suggest lowering dietary sodium to a level of less than 100 mmol/day (less than 6 g sodium chloride or less than 2.3 g sodium per day) in high normal or Stage 1 hypertensive individuals (JNC-V, 1993).

Moderation of Alcohol Intake

According to epidemiological data, the prevalence of hypertension is approximately 50% greater in individuals who consume three to five drinks per day and 100% greater in those consuming more than six drinks daily (Gordon & Kannel, 1983; Klatsky, Friedman, Siegelaub, & Gerard, 1977). The association between heavy drinking and hypertension has been demonstrated independent of the effects of weight gain in these patients (Friedman, Klatsky, & Siegelaub, 1982).

In contrast, the effects of moderate alcohol consumption (two drinks or fewer per day) on BP are uncertain, as some studies have suggested a U-shaped curve, with light drinkers having lower SBP and DBP than either abstainers or heavy drinkers (Harburg, Ozgoren, Hawthorne, & Schork, 1980; Jackson, Stewart, Beaglehole, & Scragg, 1985). Elevated plasma renin and catecholamine levels have been proposed as a possible mechanism for alcohol-induced hypertension (Kaysen & Noth, 1984). In a recent study of the acute pressor effects of ethanol, it was shown that at intake levels greater than 40.0 g/day the BP of patients was increased by 5–10 mmHg systolic, and 6–9 mmHg diastolic (Maheswaran, Gill, Davies, & Beevers, 1991).

Relatively few studies have directly assessed the effects of alcohol restriction intervention in hypertensive patients. One early study (Potter & Beevers, 1984) evaluated the effects of alcohol withdrawal in hypertensive men with a recent history of heavy drinking. Patients were admitted to an inpatient setting, where acute alcohol withdrawal occurred over a 3–6-day period. Results confirmed the acute pressor effects of alcohol on both SBP and DBP, independent of changes in plasma renin or cortisol levels. Similarly, Puddey, Beilin, Vandongen, and Rouse (1985) reported a significant decrease in both SBP and DBP when subjects substituted low-alcohol-content beer for normal alcohol consumption. Regression analysis of the data suggested that SBP decreased by 1 mmHg for each 100 ml/week change in alcohol consumption (Puddey et al., 1985).

In a recent controlled study of relaxation therapy for hypertension (Irvine & Logan, 1991), 110 hypertensive men and women were randomly assigned to either 12 weeks of relaxation therapy or a supportive therapy control condition. Blood pressure was significantly reduced in both conditions (relaxation group, −5.6/−5.1; support therapy, −5.8/−4.2), although the principal determinant of blood pressure change was the reduction of alcohol consumption. Both groups showed decreased alcohol intake levels, which were strongly correlated with BP changes over the course of treatment.

In addition to the direct BP-lowering effects of reduced alcohol intake, MacMahon and Norton (1986) suggested that restricting alcohol consumption in hypertensives may improve responsiveness to antihypertensive medications and increase adherence to either drug or nondrug interventions. Reduction in alcohol intake is also typically associated with weight loss and other positive effects on overall health

(Hall, 1988). According to present guidelines (JNC-V, 1993), hypertensive patients who drink alcohol-containing beverages should limit their daily intake to 1 oz or equivalent of ethanol per day (i.e., 2 oz of 100-proof whiskey, 8 oz of wine, or 24 oz of beer).

Other Dietary Interventions

Epidemiological studies have suggested an inverse relationship between dietary levels of potassium chloride and the prevalence of hypertension (Intersalt Cooperative Research Group, 1988; Khaw & Barret-Connor, 1984). Conversely, animal research has shown a beneficial effect of high potassium intake on the control of BP (Meneely & Battarbee, 1976). On the basis of these findings, several clinical trials have investigated the effects of supplemental potassium administration in hypertensive patients. Despite initial positive results, more recent studies have failed to document a consistent effect of potassium supplementation on BP control (Patki et al., 1990; Svetky, Yarger, Feussner, DeLong, & Klotman, 1987). In the recent multicenter TOHP trial (TOHP Collaborative Research Group, 1992), 178 subjects with high normal BP were randomly assigned to receive 4.5 g of supplemental potassium chloride per day for 6 months. Despite a marked increase in urinary potassium levels with treatment, no significant changes in SBP or DBP were observed.

Calcium and magnesium supplements have also been recommended for dietary control of hypertension (JNC-V, 1993). Calcium deficiency in the diet has been associated with an increased occurrence of hypertension in some studies (e.g., McCarron, Morris, Henry, & Stanton, 1984). In addition, recent evidence suggests that low calcium intake may amplify the effects of high sodium intake on BP (Hamet et al., 1991). The role of calcium may be particularly important for postmenopausal hypertensive women, who are also at risk for osteoporosis and other calcium-deficiency disorders. There is less evidence of the role of magnesium supplements, although it has been reported that hypertensive patients have reduced levels of intracellular magnesium (Resnick, Gupta, & Laragh, 1984). In the TOHP trial, subjects with high normal BP who received either calcium or magnesium supplements showed no significant changes in BP following 6 months of treatment (TOHP Collaborative Research Group, 1992). Similarly, no consistent findings have been reported for dietary supplementation with omega-3 polyunsaturated fatty acids (fish oil) or high-fiber foods (National High Blood Pressure Education Program, 1992).

Finally, dietary therapy for hypertension typically includes recommendations for reducing intake of dietary fats and cholesterol, as well as quitting smoking (Hall, 1988). Although these last interventions are not directly associated with lowering BP, the overall benefits in improved cardiovascular health are well established (JNC-V, 1993).

Exercise Training

Interest in the effects of exercise on the control of BP dates back to the 1930s, when Steinhaus (1933) observed that athletes and sports participants had lower resting BPs than their more sedentary counterparts. Since then, several large-scale epidemiological studies have confirmed that sedentary individuals, with low levels of physical activity, have a higher risk of becoming hypertensive (Blair et al., 1984; Paffenberger, Wing, Hyde, & Jung, 1983). Various exercise training regimens have recently been incorporated into nondrug treatment programs for hypertension (Blanchard, Martin, & Dubbert, 1988; Martin & Dubbert, 1985). In particular, it has been suggested that isotonic, or aerobic, forms of exercise, such as walking, jogging, or swimming, have positive effects on hypertension, as opposed to isometric, or static, types of exercise, such as weight lifting or body stretching. In the past 2 decades, several controlled studies of exercise training have been performed, as illustrated in Table 4.

Experimental studies in this area have shown generally positive effects, with a few notable exceptions. Until recently, most studies were performed on relatively small sample sizes, suitable controls were frequently lacking, and BP changes were often relatively small. Few earlier studies also attempted to control for the effects of concomitant weight loss or sodium restriction (Martin & Dubbert, 1985). However, several studies in the mid-1980s, performed at different sites in the U.S., Japan, and Australia have shown positive, and clinically meaningful, BP changes associated with aerobic exercise training (Duncan et al., 1985; Martin, Dubbert, Lake, & Burkett, 1982; Nelson, Jennings, Essler, & Korner, 1986).

Perhaps the strongest experimental data were obtained in a series of studies by Japanese investigators (Kinoshita et al., 1988; Urata et al., 1987). In their first study, 20 middle-aged men and women hypertensives were randomly assigned to either an exercise training (stationary bicycle three times weekly for 10 weeks) or a no-treatment control group. Exercise training was associated with not only significant BP changes, but also a significant decrease in plasma noradrenaline levels. This effect was independent of associated changes in body weight or sodium levels. Significant changes in plasma noradrenaline levels were found, which correlated with treatment outcome (Kinoshita et al., 1988).

Several studies of aerobic exercise training and hypertension have been conducted by investigators at the Jackson Veterans Affairs Medical Center (Dubbert et al., 1984; Martin, Dubbert, & Cushman, 1990; Martin et al., 1982). In the first two studies, middle-aged hypertensive men underwent a 10-week program of mixed aerobic exercises, including swimming, walking or jogging, or bicycling. Significant changes in both SBP and DBP, independent of weight loss or sodium excretion levels, were observed (Martin et al., 1982). Similar effects were observed in a second single-subject design study with two hypertensive male subjects (Dubbert et al., 1984). Neither of these studies, however, controlled for the possible nonspecific or attentional effects of the exercise training programs. Accordingly, a third study was conducted in which these factors were specifically controlled (Martin et al., 1990). Twenty-seven middle-aged men with mild hypertension were randomly assigned to either an aerobic exercise condition ($n = 13$) or an exercise control condition ($n = 14$). Subjects in the active exercise condition were required to perform aerobic activities such as jogging, walking, or riding a stationary bicycle, and controls received instruction in slow calisthenic and stretching exercises for a comparable period of time. Positive change expectations were provided for both groups. Results indicated a significant decrease in DBP of 9.6 mmHg for the aerobic exercise group, compared with an increase of 0.8 mmHg in the control group. A similar trend was observed in the SBP changes. Despite the addition of an active control group, this study suffered from the limitations of a small sample size and lack of follow-up assessment.

More recently, negative effects for the role of exercise in the treatment of hypertension have been reported by investigators at Duke University Medical Center (Blumenthal, Siegal, & Appelbaum, 1991). Ninety-nine men and women hypertensives were randomly assigned

Table 4

Exercise Training for Hypertension (Controlled Studies)

Study	Subjects	Exercise protocol	Duration	Study design	Outcome
Bonanno & Lies (1974)	27 hypertensive men, mean age = 41.3 years	Walking/jogging 40–55 min/3×/week	12 weeks	Matched control group with no change in diet	↓ DBP in both treatment and control
DePlaen & Detry (1980)	6 hypertensive men and women	Mixed exercise program 60 min/3×/week	12 weeks	Pre- and post treatment evaluation, no control group	↓ HR, but no change in DBP
Hagberg et al. (1983)	25 hypertensive adolescents, 19 men and 6 women	Walking/jogging 30–40 min/5×/week	6 months	Matched control group with no exercise training	↓ SBP and DBP in exercise group
Nomura et al. (1984)	21 hypertensive men and women mean age = 40.6 years	Bicycle ergometer 30 min/day/7×/week	3 weeks	Comparison of exercise with and without salt restriction	↓ SBP and DBP in both groups
Dubbert et al. (1984)	2 hypertensive men	Mixed aerobic exercises 30–40 min/5×/week	3–10 weeks	Single-subject, ABAB design	↓ DBP associated with exercise training

continued

Study	Subjects	Exercise	Duration	Design	Results
Duncan et al. (1985)	56 hypertensive men, mean age = 30.4 years	Walking/jogging 60 min/3×/week	16 weeks	Matched control group with no exercise training	↓ SBP and DBP in exercise group
Nelson et al. (1986)	13 hypertensive men and women, mean age = 44 years	Bicycle ergometer 45 min/3–7×/week	12 weeks	Within-subjects design with 3 levels of exercise	↓ SBP and DBP associated with increased exercise
Urata et al. (1987)	20 hypertensive men and women, mean age = 51.2 years	Bicycle ergometer 60 min/3×/week	10 weeks	Randomized control group with no exercise training	↓ SBP in exercise group compared with controls
Martin et al. (1990)	19 hypertensive men, mean age = 43.7 years	Mixed aerobic exercises 30 min/4×/week	10 weeks	Randomized control group with placebo exercise	↓ DBP in exercise group compared with controls
Blumenthal et al. (1991)	99 hypertensive men and women, mean age = 45.2 years	Walking/jogging 35 min/3×/week	16 weeks	Randomized prospective design with 2 control groups	↓ SBP and DBP in both treatment and control groups

Note. SBP = systolic blood pressure; DBP = diastolic blood pressure; HR = heart rate.

to 16 weeks of aerobic exercise, strength and flexibility training, or a waiting-list control group. Subjects for the study were relatively young (mean age = 45.2 years) and weighed less than 120% of ideal body weight. Aerobic exercise sessions were conducted three times weekly and consisted of 45-min sessions of walking or jogging, at an intensity of at least 70% of subjects' initial maximum volume of oxygen consumption (VO_2 max). Surprisingly, all three groups showed comparable decreases in both SBP and DBP following treatment. Changes in SBP and DBP were $-8/-6$ in the aerobic exercise group, $-7/-6$ in the strength and flexibility group, and $-9/-5$ in the waiting-list control. Although the investigators failed to account for the BP decline observed in the two control groups, it is possible that changes in exercise or dietary habits of control subjects confounded the effects of treatment. In addition, the intensity of exercise training appears to have been lower than in previous studies. Finally, the lack of a run-in period before onset of the study may have resulted in a significant regression effect in all three groups.

In summary, the effectiveness of aerobic exercise as a sole intervention for hypertension remains uncertain. Most studies to date have consisted of relatively small samples, without sufficient treatment controls, and have lacked adequate follow-up assessment. Arroll and Beaglehole (1992) concluded that most studies had critical design flaws, and that the better designed studies have reported smaller reductions in BP, overall, relative to studies with poorer designs. However, they also noted that studies that included daily exercise training produced noticeably greater effects than studies limited to two or three weekly sessions. The mechanism of action is also unclear and may involve either a decrease in noradrenaline or adrenaline secretion or changes in cardiac output and peripheral vascular resistance. A critical issue is the likely maintenance of treatment gains, and the possibility of discontinuation of regular exercise following termination of the experimental training period. The need for long-term follow-up in future studies of this type cannot be overemphasized.

Relaxation and Stress Management

Perhaps the most controversial aspect of life-style modification for hypertension is the use of relaxation or stress management techniques. A variety of approaches, including progressive muscle relaxation, yoga relaxation, transcendental meditation, autogenic training, thermal biofeedback, and cognitive relaxation techniques have all been investigated in recent years (Lehrer & Woolfolk, 1993). Unfortunately, there is little consensus at present regarding the effectiveness of these procedures, either alone or in combination with medication or other interventions. Although clinically impressive results have been obtained by several investigators (e.g., Agras, Southam, & Taylor, 1983; Aivazyan, Zaitsev, & Yurenev, 1988; Blanchard et al., 1986; Patel, Marmot, & Terry, 1981), others have failed to show a significant or lasting effect of relaxation training (see Table 5). Several factors, including differences in patient selection factors, research designs used, and specific types of relaxation or stress reduction procedures used, may account for this inconsistency. In general, relaxation training appears to be more successful in patients with higher baseline BP values (Kaufmann et al., 1988), although the only large-scale clinical trial to date of relaxation training was conducted on subjects with high normal BP readings (TOHP).

The first controlled studies of relaxation therapy for hypertension were reported by a group of British investigators (Patel, Marmot, & Terry, 1981; Patel & North, 1975). In these studies, a combination of yoga relaxation training and biofeedback (including both galvanic skin response and electromyographic biofeedback) was associated with significant reductions in both SBP and DBP in mildly hypertensive patients. Subsequent studies at Stanford University (Agras, Taylor, Kraemer, Allen, & Schneider, 1980; Brauer, Horlick, Nelson, Farquhar, & Agras, 1979; Taylor, Farquhar, Nelson, & Agras, 1977) demonstrated significant treatment effects with an abbreviated program of progressive muscle relaxation (PMR) training, compared with supportive therapy or no-treatment controls. Persistence of relaxation training was shown during 24-hr BP monitoring in an inpatient setting (Agras et al., 1980) and with ambulatory monitoring procedures in the workplace (Southam, Agras, Taylor, & Kraemer, 1982). In the latter study, 42 mildly hypertensive patients were randomly assigned to 8 weeks of relaxation training or a no-treatment control condition. Significant SBP and DBP changes were observed in both the clinic ($-11.7/-12.6$) and workplace ($-7.8/-4.6$) settings. These changes were maintained at a 15-month follow-up assessment (Agras, Southam, & Taylor, 1983).

Table 5

Relaxation and Stress Management Training for Hypertension (Controlled Studies)

Study	Subjects	Relaxation procedures	Duration	Study design	Blood pressure change (SBP, DBP)
Patel & North (1975)	34 mildly hypertensive men and women	Yoga relaxation and biofeedback vs. nonspecific relaxation	6 weeks	Random assignment to treatment and control	−26.1/−15.2 −8.9/−4.2
Taylor et al. (1977)	31 medicated patients (men and women)	PMR vs. nonspecific, supportive therapy	8 weeks	Random assignment to study groups	−13.6/−4.9 −2.8/−1.8
Brauer et al. (1979)	29 mildly hypertensive men and women	Therapist conducted vs. tape-recorded PMR training	10 weeks	Random assignment to study groups, psychotherapy control	−11.0/−6.1 −5.3/−1.0
Agras et al. (1980)	5 untreated hypertensive men and women	PMR training at 3×/day in inpatient setting	3 days	Within-subjects ABA design	−12.0/−9.0
Patel et al. (1981)	204 mildly hypertensive industry workers	Combined PMR and GSR biofeedback and stress management training	8 weeks	Random assignment to relaxation or control group	−13.8/−7.2 −4.0/−1.4
Southam et al. (1982)	42 mildly hypertensive men and women	PMR training vs. no-treatment control	8 weeks	Between-groups comparison and ambulatory monitoring	−7.8/−4.6 −0.1/+1.7
Glasgow et al. (1982)	90 high normal men and women	PMR and BP biofeedback training vs. no-treatment control	12 weeks	Random assignment to treatment or control group	−5.6/−4.4
Goldstein et al. (1982)	36 mildly hypertensive men and women	Relaxation vs. BP biofeedback vs. self-monitoring vs. drugs	8 weeks	Random assignment to study groups	+2.5/+3.5 −4.1/−4.4 +3.5/+2.6

continued

Study	Sample	Intervention	Duration	Design	Results
Jacob et al. (1986)	30 mildly hypertensive men and women	PMR and autogenic training vs. drug treatment	6 weeks	Crossover design with both drug and relaxation	-3.4/-1.5
Blanchard et al. (1986)	87 medicated hypertensive patients	PMR vs. thermal biofeedback training	8 weeks	Crossover design with decrease in BP drugs	Decreased drugs in both groups
Irvine et al. (1986)	32 mildly hypertensive men and women	Relaxation and stress management vs. mild physical exercise	10 weeks	Random assignment to study groups	-6.6/-5.2 +1.3/+4.5
Chesney et al. (1987)	158 mildly hypertensive industry workers	Thermal biofeedback and relaxation vs. PMR and cognitive relaxation	18 weeks	Stratified block design	-7.4/-4.5 -9.0/-5.9
Blanchard, Khramelashvili, et al. (1988)	59 mildly hypertensive patients in U.S. and USSR	Thermal biofeedback vs. autogenic training vs. self-relaxation	10 weeks	Random assignment to study groups	-6.7/-8.9 -8.4/-8.2 -4.1/-3.9
Aivazyan et al. (1988)	117 hypertensive men in the USSR	Autogenic training vs. thermal biofeedback vs. PMR and breathing	6 months	Random assignment to study groups	-10.3/-8.0
Lee et al. (1988)	92 hypertensive men	PMR and self-relaxation training vs. diet and exercise training	8 weeks	Random assignment to study groups	-6.0/-7.0 +1.0/-4.0
Davison et al. (1991)	58 high normal men	PMR and imagery relaxation vs. hygiene information	7 weeks	Random assignment to study groups	-6.1 (SBP) +1.2 (SBP)
Jacob et al. (1992)	19 mildly hypertensive men and women	PMR and thermal biofeedback vs. stress education control	12 weeks	Random assignment to study groups	-14.6/-5.8 -0.4/-1.0

Note. SBP = systolic blood pressure; DBP = diastolic blood pressure; PMR = progressive muscle relaxation; GSR = galvanic skin response.

Positive effects of relaxation training have also been found by Blanchard and associates at the State University of New York at Albany. Blanchard et al. (1986) randomly assigned 87 medicated hypertensive patients to either a PMR or a thermal biofeedback group for 8 weeks of training. Although clinical improvements were noted with both relaxation conditions, thermal biofeedback resulted in a significantly greater reduction in the use of BP medications. Changes in BP in the biofeedback condition were found to be related to positive treatment expectancies and degree of skill in controlling peripheral vasomotor activity, whereas self-perception of depth of relaxation was related to outcome in the PMR group (Wittrock, Blanchard, & McCoy, 1988). In addition, it was found that plasma norepinephrine levels were reduced in the thermal biofeedback condition but not in the PMR condition (McCoy et al., 1988).

Blanchard, Khramelashvili, et al. (1988) compared thermal biofeedback with autogenic training and self-relaxation (control) in two groups ($N = 59$) of unmedicated hypertensive patients in the Soviet Union and U.S. After 10 weeks of training, patients in each of the active treatment groups at both sites showed significant decreases in DBP (-8.5 mmHg). Changes in SBP were observed only in the Soviet patients, however. In a separate Soviet study of 117 hypertensive male patients randomly assigned to one of several relaxation groups or a no-treatment control (Aivazyan, Zaitsev, Salenko, Yurenev, & Patrusheva, 1988), thermal biofeedback and a deep-muscle relaxation training procedure were both associated with significant decreases in SBP and DBP ($-10.3/-8.0$). Significant treatment gains were maintained at 1-year follow-up in both relaxation groups. Aivazyan, Zaitsev, and Yurenev (1988) also reported 5-year follow-up results of a group of hypertensive patients receiving autogenic training.

Less positive results have been reported by other investigators. Goldstein, Shapiro, Thananopavarn, and Sambhi (1982) compared relaxation training, direct BP biofeedback, and self-monitoring with drug treatment in 36 mildly hypertensive patients. After 8 weeks of training, no changes in SBP or DBP were found in either of the relaxation or self-monitoring groups. Some improvement in DBP, but not SBP, was noted in the BP biofeedback group. None of the behavioral interventions achieved BP control comparable to that of antihypertensive medications. Similarly, Jacob et al. (1986) compared the effects of relaxation therapy with and without drug or placebo therapy in 30 mildly hypertensive patients. Results indicated a modest effect of relaxation therapy on clinic BP measures ($-3.4/-2.1$) but no significant changes in 24-hr ambulatory BP recordings. Antihypertensive drugs (atenolol and chlorthalidone) were again significantly more effective than relaxation therapy in controlling BP. In a subsequent study, Jacob et al. (1992) showed that relaxation effects show minimal generalization beyond the clinical situation. Finally, a combination of relaxation training, biofeedback, and cognitive restructuring was found to be no more effective than BP monitoring alone in an industry-based study of hypertension control (Chesney, Black, Swan, & Ward, 1987).

Few studies have compared relaxation training with other nondrug interventions. Irvine, Johnston, Jenner, and Marie (1986), for example, compared a combined program of relaxation and stress management with 10 weeks of physical exercise training in 32 mildly hypertensive patients. Half of the subjects in each condition received antihypertensive medications during the study period. Results indicated a significant improvement in both SBP and DBP ($-6.6/-5.2$) in the relaxation group compared with the exercise control condition ($+1.3/+4.5$). These differences were maintained at 3-month followup. Similarly, Lee et al. (1988) compared the effects of a combined hygienic informational and deep-muscle relaxation program with hygienic information alone in mildly hypertensive male patients. After 8 weeks of training, the relaxation training condition had achieved significantly greater reductions in both SBP and DBP compared with the hygienic informational condition. This study included measures of plasma norepinephrine, which were not significantly affected by either of the nondrug treatment interventions. However, Davison, Williams, Nezami, Bice, and DeQuattro (1991) subsequently demonstrated that the relaxation training procedure that they used caused a significant reduction in a cognitive measure of hostility, the Articulated Thoughts in Simulated Situations.

Overall, relaxation and stress management approaches have produced inconsistent results in the studies to date. On the basis of a meta-analysis of studies prior to 1987, Kaufmann et al. (1988) noted evidence of a "modest benefit of behavioral interventions with respect to DBP, and no benefit with respect to SBP" (p. 222). They also found that patients with higher baseline values were more likely to benefit from relaxation training, independent of possible regression effects.

Methodological problems, such as small sample sizes and lack of experimenter-blind assessment, have limited the generalizability of results from most studies. To date, only one large-scale clinical trial (TOHP) has included a randomized comparison of relaxation training with other nonpharmacological interventions (TOHP Collaborative Research Group, 1992). Although relaxation training in this trial was not associated with significant treatment effects, the trial was limited to subjects with high normal BPs. In addition, the relaxation training was of limited intensity and duration compared with other studies. Finally, it should be noted that, although most patients assigned to the weight loss condition were at least mildly overweight prior to treatment, there is no evidence that patients assigned to relaxation training had increased stress levels before treatment.

Combined Nondrug Therapy

Surprisingly, relatively few studies have evaluated the effects of combined or multifaceted nondrug therapy, despite the potential advantages of this approach for clinical practice (JNC-V, 1993). For example, a combined program of weight loss, sodium restriction, and alcohol moderation was evaluated in the Hypertension Control Program trial (Stamler et al., 1987). In this large-scale clinical trial, 189 previously well-controlled, middle-aged hypertensives were randomly assigned to combined nondrug therapy or a no-treatment control. After 4 years, 39% of the active treatment group ($n = 97$), compared to only 5% of the controls ($n = 44$) had maintained normotensive status without the need for antihypertensive medications (Stamler et al., 1987).

Jacob, Fortmann, Kraemer, Farquhar, and Agras (1985) evaluated a combined program of weight loss, sodium restriction, and relaxation training in subjects with high normal BP. Fifty men and women were randomly assigned to receive either 6 months of combined nondrug therapy or to a no-treatment control group. Results indicated a significant decline in SBP in both groups (-5.7 and -6.1 mmHg), although no significant change in DBP was observed. A small weight loss (1.2 kg) was observed in the nondrug intervention group, but not in the no-treatment control. The lack of effectiveness of combined nonpharmacological therapy in this study is likely due to several factors, including selection of borderline hypertensive patients, lack of significant weight loss, and evidence of significant behavioral changes in the control group (Jacob et al., 1985).

More recently, Applegate et al. (1992) reported positive effects of a 6-month, combined program of weight reduction, sodium restriction, and physical activity in elderly hypertensive patients. Patients in the combined nondrug therapy showed significant reductions in both SBP (−8.7 mmHg) and DBP (−6.8 mmHg) compared with a no-treatment control condition (−1.9/−4.5). Mean weight change in the intervention group was −2.1 kg, compared with 0.3 kg in the control group. Urinary sodium excretion was not different between the two groups.

Research in our own laboratory has evaluated the effects of a multifaceted nondrug intervention (The Heartsavers Lifestyle Program) that consists of dietary change, exercise training, and stress reduction, compared with both medication and placebo controls. We have evaluated the effects of this approach in both middle-aged (Kostis et al., 1992) and elderly hypertensives (Rosen et al., 1989). In the first study, 79 mildly hypertensive male patients were randomly assigned to receive either a 12-week, multifaceted nondrug treatment program or double-blind treatment with propranolol (80–160 mg/day) or placebo. The nondrug treatment program consisted of dietary weight loss and sodium restriction, graduated exercise training for 3–5 days/week up to 70% of maximum heart rate, and individualized relaxation training. All patients received a comprehensive physiological and psychological evaluation before and after treatment, which included exercise stress testing, serum lipid measures, and quality-of-life assessment.

As shown in Figure 1, both nondrug therapy and propranolol were associated with significant reductions in DBP and a trend toward decreased SBP. Sixty-eight percent of patients were classified as responding to nondrug therapy, with DBP reduced to 90 mmHg or less following treatment. Principal predictors of efficacy with nondrug therapy were baseline BP, weight reduction, and exercise tolerance changes (Kostis et al., 1992). In contrast to both propranolol and placebo, nondrug therapy was associated with significant weight loss, cholesterol reduction, and improved exercise tolerance and maximum oxygen consumption. A trend toward lower plasma insulin levels was also observed. Quality of life was significantly improved in the nondrug condition, as patients reported increased energy levels and improved sexual performance, compared with both drug and placebo.

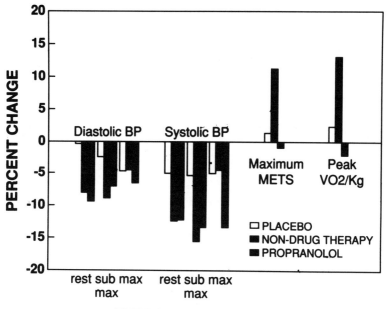

Figure 1. Effects of propranolol, combined nondrug therapy, and placebo on exercise tolerance and blood pressure (BP) after a 12-week intervention program. Measures represent diastolic and systolic BP at rest, submaximum and maximum exercise levels, exercise intensity (metabolic equivalents [METS] × 4), and oxygen consumption (VO$_2$/kg × 2). From "Superiority of Nonpharmacological Therapy Compared to Propranolol and Placebo in Men With Mild Hypertension: A Randomized, Prospective Trial" by Kostis et al., 1992, *American Heart Journal, 123,* p. 469. Copyright 1992 by Mosby-Yearbook. Reprinted by permission.

Similar results were obtained in a separate analysis of treatment effects with elderly male patients (Rosen et al., 1989).

Taken together, these findings suggest that a multifaceted or combined nondrug therapy approach may be the optimal strategy for treating Stage 1 or 2 hypertension (JNC-V, 1993). The fact that nondrug therapy can be implemented without special facilities, the potential "spill-over" benefits from weight loss, improved exercise tolerance, and lower serum lipid levels, as well as the potential quality-of-life improvements, are all advantages of this approach. Limitations are the potential lack of efficacy in some instances and the need for long-term maintenance and follow-up treatment for most patients (Rosen et al., 1989). It should be noted, however, that these concerns are not unique to life-style management approaches, as efficacy or maintenance problems may occur with pharmacotherapy as well. The percentage of hypertensive patients adequately controlled with one drug alone is less than 50% on average, compared with about 70% of patients on two medications and 90% of patients taking three drugs concurrently (Wollam, Hall, & Lowdon, 1988).

The Heartsavers Lifestyle Program: A Model Nonpharmacological Treatment Program for Hypertension

The Heartsavers Lifestyle Program was developed for either primary or adjunctive therapy for hypertension. It is based on a biopsychosocial model of hypertension (Obrist, 1981) and includes detailed assessment of biological, psychological, and social factors, followed by a 12-week multifaceted nondrug treatment intervention. All patients are carefully screened for a history of cardiovascular disease or other contraindications for regular exercise or dietary change. Patients with a recent history of alcohol or drug abuse, serious psychiatric illness, or symptoms of dementia are excluded from the program. A number of social and psychological variables are evaluated at baseline, including social support, access to medical care, treatment expectations, current life stresses, mood state, and anger management style (see Table 6).

Assessment

Blood pressure assessment should be based on standardized measures of SBP and DBP, obtained either in the clinic or home setting (American Society of Hypertension, 1992). In our program, a random-zero sphygmomanometer is used for three separate clinic readings, and 2 min apart, with the patient seated comfortably. As recommended by Blanchard, Martin, and Dubbert (1988), the same chair or couch is used at each visit because BP is highly susceptible to postural variations. Furthermore, BP readings are normally taken after the

Table 6

Clinical Assessment of Essential Hypertension

Medical assessment
    Physical examination and medical history
    Weight, height, and clinic blood pressure (SBP/DBP)
    24-hr ambulatory blood pressure, when indicated
    Exercise stress testing (HR, BP, VO_2)
    Blood chemistry and urinalysis (cholesterol, triglycerides)
    Urinary sodium level
Psychological variables
    Treatment expectations and experience
        Weight loss and dieting history
        Exercise training experience
        Relaxation and stress management skills
        Expectations for treatment adherence and outcome
    Mood state
        Presence of anxiety or depression
        Relation of mood state to blood pressure
    Anger management style
        Level of anger, hostility, and suspiciousness
        Characteristic coping responses, efficacy
        Situational triggers for anger or hostility
    Current life stresses
        Recent stressful events
        Degree of stability or instability in life situation
        Coping responses and resources
Professional and personal resources
    Access to physicians and other health professionals
    Adequate health insurance
    Access to health club or exercise facilities
    Access to "heart healthy" restaurants and supermarkets
    Social supports
        Family and friends
        Workplace programs
        Self-help and support groups (Overeaters Anonymous, Alcoholics
        Anonymous, Weight Watchers)

Note. BP = blood pressure; SBP = systolic blood pressure; DBP = diastolic blood pressure; HR = heart rate; VO_2 = volume of oxygen consumption.

patient has been comfortably seated and resting for at least 5–10 min. Measurements should be made at the same time of day because diurnal variations in pressure have also been documented (Kaplan, 1986). Patients should be encouraged to void prior to BP assessment and asked to refrain from smoking or caffeine intake for at least 30 min prior to the reading (Blanchard, Martin, & Dubbert, 1988).

Ambulatory BP studies are indicated for patients with a history of "white-coat hypertension" (Pickering & Devereux, 1987). Patients with episodic or seasonal fluctuations in BP may also benefit from ambulatory BP studies (JNC-V, 1993). The procedure may be valuable in assessing specific links between external stresses or mood states and daily BP fluctuations. However, given the expense and potential intrusiveness of the procedure, we have typically reserved ambulatory monitoring studies for selected cases only.

Exercise stress testing is recommended for all patients who are referred to an exercise training program. Measurements of BP, heart rate, and oxygen consumption are obtained under different levels of exercise intensity. On the basis of the results of this evaluation, a physician or exercise physiologist is able to screen out individuals at risk for cardiovascular complications. Specific recommendations are made regarding the optimal level and intensity of exercise for each patient. Stress testing also serves a valuable psychological function by reducing exercise-related anxiety and reassuring the patient of the relative safety of a structured exercise program.

In addition, blood chemistry and urinalysis are performed on all patients at baseline. Serum cholesterol (LDL, HDL, and total cholesterol) and triglyceride levels are routinely evaluated to determine the patient's overall risk for cardiovascular disease (Stamler et al., 1976). Patients with elevated cholesterol or triglyceride levels may require additional dietary interventions or adjunctive therapy with cholesterol-lowering agents. Similarly, blood sugar levels may be indicative of adult-onset diabetes, which may require additional dietary interventions.

A detailed behavioral history, including information about past dieting and exercise, is obtained. Past exercise behavior is the most reliable predictor of future exercise compliance (McAuley, 1992). Patients without past involvement in a regular exercise program may require additional support or encouragement to become fully engaged. Physical limitations to exercise such as orthopedic problems and chronic pain conditions, as well as the feasibility of engaging in regular exercise, should be carefully evaluated.

Other key areas of psychological assessment are mood state, anger and hostility, and current life stresses. Assessment is conducted by means of interview or paper-and-pencil approaches. Information obtained is used to tailor the stress management interventions to the needs of the patient (Rosen et al., 1989). For example, patients with high levels of hostility are provided with specific cognitive–behavioral interventions for anger management. It is also important to assess the patient's habitual style of coping with stress or anger situations and to enquire about perceived efficacy in managing conflict. One recent study demonstrated that when patients used a self-selected anger coping style, blood pressure responses to an experimental task were maximally attenuated (Engebretson, Matthews, & Scheier, 1989).

Finally, patient expectations for treatment efficacy and adherence may play a role in determining treatment outcome (Kirsch, 1985; McAuley, 1992). Specific areas to address by means of questionnaire or interview are (a) previous experience with nondrug therapy approaches, including past successes or failures; (b) current expectations regarding outcome of nondrug therapy; (c) expectations regarding likely effectiveness of nondrug therapy in lowering BP; (d) expectations for compliance and likely compliance difficulties; and (e) overall self-efficacy for behavior change.

Treatment Interventions

In accordance with the biopsychosocial model, a multidisciplinary approach is generally recommended for nondrug treatment of hypertension (Dubbert, 1992). Health professionals from several disciplines, including a nutritionist, exercise physiologist, cardiologist or internist, and health psychologist, should be involved in each case. In our program, psychologists have functioned both as treatment providers and as case managers and health care coordinators. In the latter role, the health psychologist identifies key patient needs, establishes appropriate referral sources, and facilitates compliance with recommended treatment. Further details of our program are as follows.

After assessment, all patients receive a comprehensive training manual and cassette tapes for home practice of relaxation. Included in the treatment manual are "heart healthy" recipes, calorie counting and food substitution tables, stress management guidelines, and exercise training schedules. Patients are carefully instructed in the use of self-monitoring assessment forms, which are completed on a weekly basis throughout the treatment period.

All participants are required to attend weekly group meetings, which are supplemented with individual or couples counseling sessions as needed. The initial 6 weeks of the program focus primarily on dietary changes; the second 6 weeks target stress management interventions. Exercise training is conducted on an individual basis throughout the 12-week period. Group meetings are used for several purposes, including patient education, training in specific intervention skills (such as calorie counting, food preparation, and meal planning), developing strategies for long-term behavior change, and soliciting support for adherence from significant others. The program emphasizes family involvement and social support for all aspects of behavior change.

Each group consists of up to six participants and their spouses or significant others. Group meetings last approximately 2 hr and include a combination of didactic instruction, behavioral modeling, weight and blood pressure assessment, and discussion of weekly self-monitoring data. Target goals for caloric intake are initially set at 1,500 kcal/day for men and 1,200 kcal/day for women. Average weight loss in our program is 6–8 kg (13–18 lb) over a 3-month period, and about two thirds of the patients achieve their weight loss goals by the end of treatment (Kostis et al., 1992). Sodium consumption is targeted for 1,500 mg/day for men and women. The recommended sodium intake is subsequently modified according to individual weight and BP responses. Dubbert (1992) advises frequent urinary sodium testing to monitor treatment efficacy, although we have not used this approach to date. A "balanced budget" approach to dietary substitution (Blanchard, Martin, & Dubbert, 1988) is generally used for salt and fat reduction. In addition, subjects are taught skills for coping with specific problem situations, such as eating in restaurants or at social engagements.

For the exercise training component, all subjects are encouraged to exercise for at least 20 min/day on a minimum of 3 days/week. Training levels are established at approximately 50% to 70% of maximum heart rate, determined during the initial exercise stress testing. Exercise self-monitoring includes the number of days per week that subjects exercise, duration of exercise, adverse symptoms, and pulse rates at 10-min intervals. With the assistance of an exercise physiologist, participants are encouraged to develop an individual exercise plan to practice at home or work. Most patients make extensive use of stationary bicycle exercises, jogging, or structured walking programs. Posttreatment evaluation indicated a significant improvement in aerobic fitness as a result of our exercise training program. Specifically, the maximum exercise level (maximum metabolic equivalents) was increased by approximately 15%, as were our measures of oxygen consumption (peak VO_2/kg) and average heart rate during exercise (Kostis et al., 1992).

The 6-week stress management component is divided into two phases: group instruction and individual application. In the group format, subjects are given instruction in the relationship between stress and hypertension, followed by a demonstration and guided practice of specific relaxation techniques. Participants are given brief training in yogic abdominal breathing, a modified progressive muscle relaxation program, and mantra meditation. As just noted, all subjects are also provided with two 30-min relaxation tapes, with detailed instructions for home practice. Taped instructions are supplemented with "in vivo" training in the first three sessions of relaxation. According to self-ratings of tension relaxation, subjects achieved an overall reduction of about 50% in their levels of subjective tension following treatment (Rosen et al., 1989).

During the second phase of training, subjects and their spouses receive individually tailored stress reduction strategies and thermal biofeedback training, as indicated. Anger management techniques are also emphasized during this phase of training. The final group session focused on relapse prevention and behavioral maintenance techniques (Blanchard, Martin, & Dubbert, 1988).

Adherence with nondrug therapy is assessed via attendance at intervention meetings, patient recording of home assessment data, and frequent monitoring by program staff of BP, weight, lipid levels, food records, and stress management practice. Currently, we are using 24-hr ambulatory BP monitoring to assess generalization of treatment efficacy. Patients who are able to achieve goal BP levels with life-style modification alone are provided with a long-term maintenance program and bimonthly follow-up assessments for at least 6 months following initial treatment. Patients who are unable to maintain goal

BP levels by nondrug means alone are referred for pharmacotherapy follow-up. These patients may be encouraged to use diet, exercise, or stress management techniques as adjunctive therapy and as a means of reducing the number or dosages of medications required (Hall, 1988).

We recently conducted a 9-month follow-up of all patients in the nondrug therapy condition (Kostis et al., 1992). Thirty-one subjects (94%) returned for this follow-up evaluation and were not receiving drug therapy at the time. Mean DBP continued to be significantly reduced compared with pretreatment levels, as was the average body mass index. Compared with DBP levels immediately after treatment, however, an average increase of 3.9 mmHg was noted at follow-up. Body mass index was essentially unchanged compared with the post-treatment levels, indicating that weight loss had been maintained.

The overall effectiveness of life-style modification for treatment of hypertension is related to the initial health of the patient, motivation for change, and involvement of spouses or significant others in the treatment process. According to Dubbert (1992), several additional factors need to be considered. First, support from collaborating clinics and medical center management is necessary to ensure adequate patient referrals, medical backup for patient safety and monitoring, and reimbursement for services provided. Special contingency plans are needed for patients who exercise regularly in the program facilities. Second, the use of accurate and reliable measures of BP is critical. Given the variability and potential for error in BP measurement, repeated measures should be taken under standardized conditions (JNC-V, 1993). Objective measures of weight loss, exercise tolerance, and urinary sodium levels should also be obtained whenever possible. Finally, patient selection criteria should be used to exclude individuals who are unlikely to benefit from nondrug therapy for medical or psychological reasons. Inclusion of such individuals may jeopardize the safety or efficacy of nondrug therapy.

Summary and Conclusion

Hypertension affects 20% or more of the adult population in Western societies and is a well-recognized risk factor for stroke, myocardial infarction, and congestive heart failure. Although antihypertensive drug therapy has been found to reduce morbidity and mortality significantly, the need to provide lifelong pharmacological therapy to vast numbers of people is highly controversial. In this context, nondrug treatment approaches are increasingly recommended for Stages 1 and 2 hypertension, either before or as an adjunct to, pharmacological therapy (JNC-V, 1993).

Among the various nondrug therapy approaches, we have reviewed in detail the use of dietary interventions, such as weight loss, sodium restriction, alcohol moderation, and dietary supplementation with potassium, calcium, and magnesium. Although there is strong support for the use of weight loss and sodium restriction, other dietary interventions have not been adequately evaluated to date. Aerobic exercise training has been found to have beneficial effects in selected studies, although results have not been wholly consistent. The use of relaxation or stress management approaches remains highly controversial because several controlled studies have failed to show significant effects of relaxation training. Surprisingly, relatively few studies have evaluated the effects of combined or multifaceted nondrug therapy, despite the potential clinical advantages of this approach (Applegate et al., 1992; Rosen et al., 1989). The Heartsavers Lifestyle Program, which we reviewed, is an example of one such successful program.

Key issues for future research are (a) the relative efficacy of combined versus individual nondrug interventions, (b) biological versus psychosocial determinants of outcome in nondrug therapy, (c) effectiveness of nondrug therapy in elderly hypertensives, and (d) long-term maintenance of behavior change. Treatment adherence is an important concern in nondrug therapy for hypertension, and controlled studies of long-term adherence with both drug and nondrug therapies are needed. These issues are currently under investigation in our laboratory.

REFERENCES

Agras, W. S., Southam, M. A., & Taylor, C. B. (1983). Long-term persistence of relaxation-induced blood pressure lowering during the working day. *Journal of Consulting and Clinical Psychology, 51*, 792–794.

Agras, W. S., Taylor, C. B., Kraemer, C., Allen, R. A., & Schneider, J. A. (1980). Relaxation training: Twenty-four-hour blood pressure reductions. *Archives of General Psychiatry, 37,* 859–863.

Aivazyan, T. A., Zaitsev, V. P., Salenko, B. B., Yurenev, A. P., & Patrusheva, I. F. (1988). Efficacy of relaxation techniques in hypertensive patients. *Health Psychology, 7,* 193–200.

Aivazyan, T. A., Zaitsev, V. P., & Yurenev, A. P. (1988). Autogenic training in the treatment and secondary prevention of essential hypertension: Five-year follow-up. *Health Psychology, 7*(Suppl.), 201–208.

Ambrosioni, E., Costa, F. V., Borghi, C., Montebugnoli, L., Giordani, M. F., & Magnani, B. (1982). Effects of moderate salt restriction on intralymphocytic sodium and pressor response to stress in borderline hypertension. *Hypertension, 4,* 789–794.

American Society of Hypertension. (1992). Recommendations for routine blood pressure measurement by indirect cuff sphygmomanometry. *American Journal of Hypertension, 5,* 207–209.

Applegate, W. B., Miller, S. T., Elam, J. T., Cushman, W. C., El Derwi, D., Brewer, A., & Graney, M. J. (1992). Nonpharmacologic intervention to reduce blood pressure in older patients with mild hypertension. *Archives of Internal Medicine, 152,* 1162–1166.

Arroll, B., & Beaglehole, R. (1992). Does physical activity lower blood pressure: A critical review of the clinical trials. *Journal of Clinical Epidemiology, 45,* 439–447.

Australian National Health and Medical Research Council Dietary Salt Study Management Committee. (1989). Fall in blood pressure with modest reduction in dietary salt intake in mild hypertension. *Lancet, i,* 399–402.

Beard, T. C., Cooke, H. M., Gray, W. R., & Barge, R. (1982). Randomised controlled trial of a no-added-sodium diet for mild hypertension. *Lancet, i,* 455–458.

Benetos, A., Yang-Yan, X., Cuche, J., Hannaert, P., & Safar, M. (1992). Arterial effects of salt restriction in hypertensive patients: A 9-week, randomized, double-blind, crossover study. *Journal of Hypertension, 10,* 355–360.

Blair, S. N., Goodyear, N. N., Gibbons, L. W., & Cooper, K. H. (1984). Physical fitness and incidence of hypertension in healthy normotensive men and women. *Journal of the American Medical Association, 252,* 487–490.

Blanchard, E. B., Khramelashvili, V. V., McCoy, G. C., Aivazyan, T. A., McCaffrey, R. J., Salenko, B. B., Musso, A., Wittrock, D. A., Berger, M., Gerardi, M. A., & Pangburn, L. (1988). The USA–USSR collaborative cross-cultural comparison of autogenic training and thermal biofeedback in the treatment of mild hypertension. *Health Psychology, 7,* 175–192.

Blanchard, E. B., Martin, J. E., & Dubbert, P. M. (1988). *Non-drug treatments for essential hypertension.* Elmsford, NY: Pergamon Press.

Blanchard, E. B., McCoy, G. C., Musso, A., Gerardi, M. A., Pallmeyer, T. P., Gerardi, R. J., Cotch, P. A., Siracusa, K., & Andrasik, F. (1986). A controlled comparison of thermal biofeedback and relaxation training in the treatment of essential hypertension: I. Short-term and long-term outcome. *Behavior Therapy, 17,* 563–579.

Blaufox, M. D., & Langford, H. G. (1987). *Non-pharmacologic therapy of hypertension.* Basel, Switzerland: Karger.

Blumenthal, J. A., Siegal, W. C., & Appelbaum, M. (1991). Failure of exercise to reduce blood pressure in patients with mild hypertension: Results of a randomized controlled trial. *Journal of the American Medical Association, 266,* 2098–2104.

Bonanno, J. A., & Lies, J. E. (1974). Effects of physical training on coronary risk factors. *American Journal of Cardiology, 33,* 760–764.

Brauer, A. P., Horlick, L., Nelson, E., Farquhar, J. W., & Agras, W. S. (1979). Relaxation therapy for essential hypertension: A Veterans Administration outpatient study. *Journal of Behavioral Medicine, 2,* 21–29.

Chesney, M. A., Black, G. W., Swan, G. E., & Ward, M. M. (1987). Relaxation training for essential hypertension at the worksite: I. The untreated mild hypertensive. *Psychosomatic Medicine, 49,* 250–263.

Cohen, M. D., D'Amico, F. J., & Merenstein, J. H. (1991). Weight reduction in obese hypertensive patients. *Family Medicine, 23,* 25–28.

Croog, S. H., Levine, S., Testa, M. A., Brown, B., Bulpitt, C. J., Jenkins, C. D., Klerman, G. L., & Williams, G. H. (1986). The effects of antihypertensive therapy on the quality of life. *New England Journal of Medicine, 314,* 1657–1664.

Dahl, L. K. (1972). Salt and hypertension. *American Journal of Clinical Nutrition, 25,* 231–244.

Davison, G. C., Williams, M. E., Nezami, E., Bice, T. L., & DeQuattro, V. L. (1991). Relaxation, reduction in angry articulated thoughts, and improvements in borderline hypertension and heart rate. *Journal of Behavioral Medicine, 14,* 453–468.

DePlaen, J. F., & Detry, J. M. (1980). Hemodynamic effects of physical training in established arterial hypertension. *Acta Cardiologica, 35,* 179–188.

Dodson, P. M., Beevers, M., Hallworth, R., Webberley, M. J., Fletcher, R. F., & Taylor, K. G. (1989). Sodium restriction and blood pressure in hypertensive Type II diabetics: Randomized blind controlled and cross-over studies of moderate sodium restriction and sodium supplementation. *British Medical Journal, 298,* 227–230.

Dubbert, P. M. (1992). Implementing behavioral treatment for hypertension: Considerations for health psychologists. *Behavior Therapist, 15,* 182–185.

Dubbert, P. M., Martin, J. E., Zimering, R. T., Burkett, P. A., Lake, M., & Cushman, W. C. (1984). Behavioral control of mild hypertension with aerobic exercise: Two case studies. *Behavior Therapy, 15,* 373–380.

Duncan, J. J., Farr, J. E., Upton, J., Hagan, R. D., Oglesby, M. E., & Blair, S. N. (1985). The effects of aerobic exercise in plasma catecholamines and blood pressure in patients with mild essential hypertension. *Journal of the American Medical Association, 254,* 2609–2613.

Engebretson, T., Matthews, K., & Scheier, M. (1989). Relations between anger expression and cardiovascular activity: Reconciling inconsistent findings

through a matching hypothesis. *Journal of Personality and Social Psychology,*
57, 513–521.

Fagerberg, B., Anderson, O. K., Isaksson, B., & Bjorntrop, P. (1984). Blood
pressure control during weight reduction in obese hypertensive men:
Separate effects of sodium and energy restriction. *British Medical Journal,*
288, 11–14.

Fagerberg, B., Isaksson, B., & Herlitz, H. (1986). Body composition, intra-
erythrocyte sodium content, volume regulation and blood pressure during moderate sodium restriction in hypertensive men. *Acta Medica Scan-*
dinavica, 219, 371–379.

Friedman, G. D., Klatsky, A. L., & Siegelaub, A. B. (1982). Alcohol, tobacco,
and hypertension. *Hypertension,* 4(Suppl. III), 143–150.

Glasgow, M. S., Gaarder, K. R., & Engel, B. T. (1982). Behavioral treatment
of high blood pressure: II. Acute and sustained effects of relaxation and
systolic blood pressure biofeedback. *Psychosomatic Medicine, 44,* 155–170.

Goldstein, D. J. (1992). Beneficial health effects of modest weight loss. *Inter-*
national Journal of Obesity, 16, 397–415.

Goldstein, I. B., Shapiro, D., Thananopavarn, C., & Sambhi, M. P. (1982).
Comparison of drug and behavioral treatments of essential hypertension. *Health Psychology, 1,* 7–26.

Gordon, T., & Kannel, W. B. (1983). Drinking and its relation to smoking,
BP, blood lipids, and uric acid: The Framingham study. *Archives of Internal*
Medicine, 143, 1366–1374.

Grobbee, D. E., Hofman, A., Roelandt, J. T., Boomsma, F., Schalekamp, M.
A., & Valkenburg, H. A. (1987). Sodium restriction and potassium supplementation in young people with mildly elevated blood pressure. *Jo-*
urnal of Hypertension, 5, 115–119.

Hagberg, J. M., Goldring, D., Ehsani, A. A., Heath, G. W., Hernandez, A.,
Schechtman, K., & Holloszy, J. O. (1983). Effect of exercise training on
the blood pressure and hemodynamic features of hypertensive adolescents. *American Journal of Cardiology, 52,* 763–768.

Hall, W. D. (1988). Nonpharmacologic treatment of hypertension. In G. L.
Wollam & W. D. Hall (Eds.), *Hypertension management: Clinical practice*
and therapeutic dilemmas (pp. 67–102). Chicago: Yearbook Publishers.

Hamet, P., Mongeau, E., Lambert, J., Bellavance, F., Gelinas, M. D., Ledoux,
M., & Cambiotti, L. W. (1991). Interactions among calcium, sodium, and
alcohol intake as determinants of blood pressure. *Hypertension,* 17(Suppl.
I), 150–154.

Harburg, E., Ozgoren, F., Hawthorne, V. M., & Schork, M. S. (1980). Community norms of alcohol usage and blood pressure: Tecumseh, Michigan. *American Journal of Public Health, 70,* 813–820.

Haynes, R. B., Harper, A. C., Costley, S. R., Johnston, M., Logan, A. G.,
Flanagan, P. T., & Sackett, D. L. (1984). Failure of weight reduction to
reduce mildly elevated blood pressure: A randomized trial. *Journal of*
Hypertension, 2, 535–539.

Heyden, S., Tyroler, H. A., Hames, C. G., Bartel, A., Thompson, J. W., Krishan, I., & Rosenthal, T. (1973). Diet treatment of obese hypertensives. *Clinical Science, 45*(Suppl.), 209s–212s.

Intersalt Cooperative Research Group. (1988). Intersalt: An international study of electrolyte excretion and blood pressure. Results for 24 hour urinary sodium and potassium excretion. *British Medical Journal, 297*, 319–328.

Irvine, M. J., Johnston, D. W., Jenner, D. A., & Marie, G. V. (1986). Relaxation and stress management in the treatment of essential hypertension. *Journal of Psychosomatic Research, 30*, 437–450.

Irvine, M. J., & Logan, A. G. (1991). Relaxation behavior therapy as sole treatment for mild hypertension. *Psychosomatic Medicine, 53*, 587–597.

Jackson, R., Stewart, A., Beaglehole, R., & Scragg, R. (1985). Alcohol consumption and blood pressure. *American Journal of Epidemiology, 122*, 1037–1044.

Jacob, R. G., Fortmann, S. P., Kraemer, H. C., Farquhar, J. W., & Agras, W. S. (1985). Combining behavioral treatments to reduce blood pressure. *Behavior Modification, 9*, 32–54.

Jacob, R. G., Shapiro, A. P., O'Hara, P., Portser, S., Kruger, A., Gatsonis, C., & Ding, Y. (1992). Relaxation therapy for hypertension: Setting-specific effects. *Psychosomatic Medicine, 54*, 87–101.

Jacob, R. G., Shapiro, A. P., Reeves, R. A., Johnsen, A. M., McDonald, R. H., & Coburn, C. (1986). Relaxation therapy for hypertension: Comparison of effects with concomitant placebo, diuretic, and beta-blocker. *Archives of Internal Medicine, 146*, 2335–2340.

Joint National Committee on Detection, Evaluation, and Treatment of High Blood Pressure (JNC-V). (1993). Fifth report. *Archives of Internal Medicine, 153*, 154–183.

Kannel, W. B., Brand, N., Skinner, J. J., Dawber, T. R., & McNamara, P. M. (1967). The relation of adiposity to blood pressure and development of hypertension: The Framingham study. *Annals of Internal Medicine, 67*, 48–59.

Kaplan, N. M. (1985). Non-drug treatment of hypertension. *Annals of Internal Medicine, 102*, 359–373.

Kaplan, N. M. (1986). *Clinical hypertension.* Baltimore: Williams & Wilkins.

Kaufmann, P. G., Jacob, R. G., Ewart, C. K., Chesney, M. A., Muenz, L. R., Doub, N., & Mercer, W. (1988). Hypertension intervention pooling project. *Health Psychology, 7*(Suppl.), 209–224.

Kaysen, G., & Noth, R. H. (1984). The effects of alcohol on blood pressure and electrolytes. *Medical Clinics of North America, 68*, 221–246.

Kempner, W. (1948). Treatment of hypertensive vascular disease with rice diets. *American Journal of Medicine, 4*, 545–577.

Khaw, K. T., & Barrett-Connor, E. (1984). Dietary potassium and blood pressure in a population. *American Journal of Clinical Nutrition, 39*, 963–968.

Kimura, G., Deguchi, F., Kojima, S., Ashida, T., Yoshimi, H., Abe, H., Kawano, Y., Yoshida, K., Imanishi, M., Kawamura, M., et al. (1988).

Antihypertensive drugs and sodium restriction. *American Journal of Hypertension, 1*, 372–379.

Kinoshita, A., Urata, H., Tanabe, Y., Ikeda, M., Tanaka, H., Shindo, M., & Arakawa, K. (1988). What types of hypertensives respond better to mild exercise therapy? *Journal of Hypertension, 6*(Suppl. 4), S631–S633.

Kirsch, I. (1985). Response expectancy as a determinant of experience and behavior. *American Psychologist, 40*, 1189–1202.

Klatsky, A. L., Friedman, G. D., Siegelaub, A. B., & Gerard, M. J. (1977). Alcohol consumption and blood pressure: Kaiser-Permanente multiphasic health examination data. *New England Journal of Medicine, 296*, 1194–1200.

Kostis, J. B., Rosen, R. C., Brondolo, E., Taska, L., Smith, D. E., & Wilson, A. C. (1992). Superiority of nonpharmacological therapy compared to propranolol and placebo in men with mild hypertension: A randomized, prospective trial. *American Heart Journal, 123*, 466–474.

Kostis, J. B., Rosen, R. C., Holzer, B. C., Randolph, C., Taska, L., & Miller, M. H. (1990). CNS side effects of centrally-active antihypertensive agents: A prospective, placebo-controlled study of sleep, mood state and cognitive and sexual function in hypertensive males. *Psychopharmacology, 102*, 163–170.

Langford, H. G., Blaufox, D., Oberman, A., Hawkins, C. M., Curb, D. J., Cutter, G. R., Wassertheil-Smoller, S., Pressel, S., Babcock, C., Abernethy, J. D., Hotchkiss, J., & Tyler, M. (1985). Dietary therapy slows the return of hypertension after stopping prolonged medication. *Journal of the American Medical Association, 253*, 657–664.

Law, M. R., Frost, C. D., & Wald, N. J. (1991). By how much does dietary salt reduction lower blood pressure? Analysis of data from trials of salt reduction. *British Medical Journal, 302*, 819–824.

Lee, D. D., DeQuattro, V. L., Allen, J., Kimura, S., Aleman, E., Konugres, G., & Davison, G. (1988). Behavioral vs β-blocker therapy in patients with primary hypertension: Effects on blood pressure, left ventricular function and mass, and the pressor surge of social stress anger. *American Heart Journal, 116*, 637–649.

Lehrer, P. M., & Woolfolk, R. (1993). *Principles and practice of stress management* (2nd ed., pp. 571–606). New York: Guilford Press.

Little, P., Girling, G., Hasler, A., & Trafford, A. (1991). A controlled trial of low sodium, low fat, high fiber diet in treated hypertensive patients: Effect on antihypertensive drug requirement in clinical practice. *Journal of Human Hypertension, 5*, 175–181.

MacGregor, G. A., Markandu, N. D., Best, F. E., Elder, D. M., Cam, J. M., Sagnella, G. A., & Squires, M. (1982). Double-blind randomised crossover trial of moderate sodium restriction in essential hypertension. *Lancet, i*, 351–355.

MacGregor, G. A., Markandu, N. D., Sagnella, G. A., Singer, D. R. J., & Cappuccio, F. P. (1989). Double-blind study of three sodium intakes and long-term effects of sodium restriction in essential hypertension. *Lancet, ii,* 1244–1247.

MacMahon, S. W., MacDonald, G. J., Bernstein, L., Andrews, G., & Blacket, R. B. (1985). Comparison of weight reduction with metoprolol in treatment of hypertension in young overweight patients. *Lancet, i,* 1233–1236.

MacMahon, S. W., & Norton, R. N. (1986). Alcohol and hypertension: Implications for prevention and treatment. *Annals of Internal Medicine, 105,* 124–125.

MacMahon, S. W., Wilcken, D. E., & MacDonald, G. J. (1986). The effect of weight reduction on left ventricular mass: A randomized controlled trial in young, overweight hypertensive patients. *New England Journal of Medicine, 314,* 334–339.

Maheswaran, R., Gill, J. S., Davies, P., & Beevers, D. G. (1991). High blood pressure due to alcohol: A rapidly reversible effect. *Hypertension, 17,* 787–792.

Martin, J. E., & Dubbert, P. M. (1985). Exercise in hypertension. *Annals of Behavioral Medicine, 7,* 13–18.

Martin, J. E., Dubbert, P. M., & Cushman, W. C. (1990). Controlled trial of aerobic exercise in hypertension. *Circulation, 81,* 1560–1567.

Martin, J. E., Dubbert, P. M., Lake, M., & Burkett, P. A. (1982, November). *The effects of exercise in mild hypertension.* Paper presented at the meeting of the Association for Advancement of Behavior Therapy, Los Angeles, CA.

Maxwell, M. H., Kushiro, T., & Dornfeld, L. P. (1984). Blood pressure changes in obese hypertensive subjects during rapid weight loss. *Archives of Internal Medicine, 144,* 1581–1584.

Maxwell, M. H., & Waks, A. U. (1987). Obesity and hypertension. In M. D. Blaufox & H. G. Langford (Eds.). *Non-pharmacologic therapy of hypertension* (pp. 29–39). Basel, Switzerland: Karger.

McAuley, E. (1992). The role of efficacy cognitions in the prediction of exercise behavior in middle-aged adults. *Journal of Behavioral Medicine, 15,* 65–88.

McCarron, D. A., Morris, C. D., Henry, H. J., & Stanton, J. L. (1984). Blood pressure and nutrient intake in the United States. *Science, 224,* 1392–1398.

McCoy, G. C., Blanchard, E. B., Wittrock, D. A., Morrison, S., Pangburn, L., Siracusa, K., & Pallmeyer, T. P. (1988). Biochemical changes associated with thermal biofeedback treatment of hypertension. *Biofeedback and Self-Regulation, 13,* 139–150.

Medical Research Council Working Party. (1985). MRC trial of treatment of mild hypertension: Principal results. *British Medical Journal, 291,* 97–104.

Meneely, G. R., & Battarbee, H. D. (1976). High sodium-low potassium environment and hypertension. *American Journal of Cardiology, 38,* 768–785.

Messerli, F. H., Sundgaard-Riise, K., Reisen, E., Dreslinski, G., Dunn, F. G., & Frohlich, E. (1983). Disparate cardiovascular effects of obesity and arterial hypertension. *American Journal of Medicine, 74,* 808–812.

Morgan, T., Adam, W., Gillies, A., Wilson, M., Morgan, G., & Carney, S. (1978). Hypertension treated by salt restriction. *Lancet, i*, 227–230.

Morgan, T., Anderson, A., Wilson, D., Myers, J., Murphy, J., & Nowson, C. (1986). Paradoxical effect of sodium restriction on blood pressure in people on slow-channel calcium drugs. *Lancet, 1*(8484), 793.

Muntzel, M., & Drueke, T. (1992). A comprehensive review of the salt and blood pressure relationship. *American Journal of Hypertension, 5*, 1S–42S.

National High Blood Pressure Education Program. (1992). *Working group report on primary prevention of hypertension.* Bethesda, MD: National Institutes of Health.

Nelson, L., Jennings, G. L., Essler, M. D., & Korner, P. I. (1986). Effect of changing levels of physical activity on blood-pressure and hemodynamics in essential hypertension. *Lancet, 2*, 473–476.

Nomura, G., Kumagai, E., Midorikawa, K., Kitano, T., Tashiro, H., & Toshima, H. (1984). Physical training in essential hypertension: Alone and in combination with dietary salt restriction. *Journal of Cardiac Rehabilitation, 4*, 469–475.

Obrist, P. A. (1981). *Cardiovascular psychophysiology: A perspective.* New York: Plenum.

Omvik, P., & Lund-Johansen, P. (1986). Is sodium restriction effective treatment of borderline and mild essential hypertension? A long-term hemodynamic study at rest and during exercise. *Journal of Hypertension, 4*, 535–541.

Paffenberger, R. S., Wing, A. L., Hyde, R. T., & Jung, D. L. (1983). Physical activity as an index of hypertension in college alumni. *American Journal of Epidemiology, 117*, 245–257.

Parijs, J., Joossens, J. V., Van der Linden, L., Verstreken, G., & Amery, A. K. P. C. (1973). Moderate sodium restriction and diuretics in the treatment of hypertension. *American Heart Journal, 85*, 22–34.

Patel, C., Marmot, M. G., & Terry, D. J. (1981). Controlled trial of biofeedback-aided behavioural methods in reducing mild hypertension. *British Medical Journal, 282*, 2005–2008.

Patel, C., & North, W. R. S. (1975). Randomised controlled trial of yoga and bio-feedback in management of hypertension. *Lancet, ii*, 93–95.

Patki, P. S., Singh, J., Gokhale, S. V., Bulakh, P. M., Shrotri, D. S., & Patwardhan, B. (1990). Efficacy of potassium and magnesium in essential hypertension: A double-blind, placebo-controlled, crossover study. *British Medical Journal, 301*, 521–523.

Pickering, T. G., & Devereux, R. B. (1987). Ambulatory monitoring of blood pressure as a predictor of cardiovascular risk. *American Heart Journal, 114*, 925–928.

Pollare, J., Lithell, H., Selinus, I., & Berne, C. (1989). A comparison of the effects of hydrochlorthiazide and captopril on glucose and lipid metabolism in patients with hypertension. *New England Journal of Medicine, 321*, 868–873.

Potter, J. F., & Beevers, D. G. (1984). Pressor effect of alcohol in hypertension. *Lancet, i*, 119–122.

Puddey, I. B., Beilin, L. J., Vandongen, R., & Rouse, I. L. (1985). A randomized controlled trial of the effect of alcohol consumption on blood pressure. *Clinical and Experimental Pharmacology and Physiology, 12*, 257–261.

Reisen, E., Abel, R., Modan, M., Silverberg, D. S., Eliahou, H. E., & Modan, B. (1978). Effect of weight loss without salt restriction on the reduction of blood pressure in overweight hypertensive patients. *New England Journal of Medicine, 298*, 1–6.

Reisin, E., Frohlich, E. D., Messerli, F. H., Dreslinski, G. R., Dunn, F. G., Jones, M. M., & Batson, H. M. (1983). Cardiovascular changes after weight reduction in obesity hypertension. *Annals of Internal Medicine, 98*, 315–319.

Resnick, L. M., Gupta, R. K., & Laragh, J. H. (1984). Intracellular free magnesium in erythrocytes of essential hypertension: Relation to blood pressure and serum divalent cations. *Proceedings of the National Academy of Science (USA), 81*, 6511–6515.

Richards, A. M., Nicholls, M. G., Espiner, E. A., Ikram, H., Maslowski, A. H., Hamilton, E. J., & Wells, J. E. (1984). Blood pressure response to moderate sodium restriction and to potassium supplementation in mild essential hypertension. *Lancet, i*, 351–355.

Rissanen, A., Pietinen, P., Siljamaki-Ojansuu, U., Piirainen, H., & Reissel, P. (1985). Treatment of hypertension in obese patients: Efficacy and feasibility of weight and salt reduction programs. *Acta Medica Scandinavica, 218*, 149–156.

Rocchini, A. P., Katch, V., Anderson, J., Hinderliter, J., Becque, D., Martin, M., & Marks, C. (1988). Blood pressure in obese adolescents: Effect of weight loss. *Pediatrics, 82*, 16–23.

Rose, R. H. (1922). Weight reduction and its remarkable effect on high blood pressure. *New York Medical Journal Medical Record, 115*, 752–759.

Rosen, R. C., Kostis, J. B., & Brondolo, E. (1989). Nondrug treatment approaches for hypertension. *Clinics in Geriatric Medicine, 5*, 791–802.

Rowland, M., & Roberts, J. (1982). Blood pressure levels and hypertension in persons ages 6–74 years: United States, 1976–1980. In National Center for Health Statistics, *Vital and Health Statistics* (84th ed., pp. 1–11). Washington, DC: U.S. Government Printing Office.

Singh, R. B., Rastogi, S. S., Singh, D. S., & Mehta, P. J. (1990). Effect of obesity and weight reduction in hypertension. *Acta Cardiologica, 45*, 45–56.

Southam, M. A., Agras, W. S., Taylor, C. B., & Kraemer, H. C. (1982). Relaxation training: Blood pressure lowering during the working day. *Archives of General Psychiatry, 39*, 715–717.

Stamler, J., Stamler, R., Reidlinger, W. F., Algera, G., & Roberts, R. H. (1976). Hypertension screening of one million Americans: Community hypertension evaluation clinic program, 1973 through 1975. *Journal of the American Medical Association, 235*, 2299–2306.

Stamler, R., Stamler, J., Grimm, R., Gosch, F. C., Elmer, P., Dyer, A., Berman, R., Fishman, J., Van Heel, N., Civinelli, J., & MacDonald, A. (1987). Nutritional therapy for high blood pressure: Final report of a four-year randomized controlled trial—The hypertension control program. *Journal of the American Medical Association, 257,* 1484–1491.

Stamler, R., Stamler, J., Reidlinger, W. F., Algera, G., & Roberts, R. H. (1978). Weight and blood pressure: Findings in hypertension screening of 1 million Americans. *Journal of the American Medical Association, 240,* 1607–1610.

Steinhaus, A. H. (1933). Chronic effects of exercise. *Physiological Review, 12,* 103–147.

Svetkey, L. P., Yarger, W. E., Feussner, J. R., DeLong, E., & Klotman, P. E. (1987). Double-blind, placebo-controlled trial of potassium chloride in the treatment of mild hypertension. *Hypertension, 9,* 444–450.

Taylor, C. B., Farquhar, J. W., Nelson, E., & Agras, W. S. (1977). Relaxation therapy and high blood pressure. *Archives of General Psychiatry, 34,* 339–342.

Terry, A. H. (1923). Obesity and hypertension. *Journal of the American Medical Association, 81,* 1283–1292.

The Trials of Hypertension Prevention Collaborative Research Group. (1992). The effects of nonpharmacologic interventions on blood pressure of persons with high normal levels. *Journal of the American Medical Association, 267,* 1213–1220.

Tuck, M. L., Sowers, J., Dornfeld, L., Kledzik, G., & Maxwell, M. (1981). The effect of weight reduction on blood pressure, plasma renin activity and plasma aldosterone levels in obese patients. *New England Journal of Medicine, 304,* 930–933.

Urata, H., Tanabe, Y., Kiyonaga, A., Ikeda, M., Tanaka, H., Shindo, M., & Arakawa, K. (1987). Antihypertensive and volume-depleting effects of mild exercise on essential hypertension. *Hypertension, 9,* 245–252.

Van Brummelen, P., Schalekamp, M., & de Graeff, J. (1978). Influence of sodium intake on hydrochlorthiazide-induced changes in blood pressure and serum electrolytes. *Acta Medica Scandinavica, 204,* 151–157.

Velasquez, M. T., & Hoffman, R. G. (1985). Overweight and obesity in hypertension. *Quarterly Journal of Medicine, 54,* 205–212.

Warren, S. E., & O'Conner, D. T. (1981). The antihypertensive mechanism of sodium reduction. *Journal of Cardiovascular Pharmacology, 3,* 781–790.

Wassertheil-Smoller, S., Oberman, A., Blaufox, M. D., Davis, B., & Langford, H. (1992). The Trial of Antihypertensive Interventions and Management (TAIM) study: Final results with regard to blood pressure, cardiovascular risk, and quality of life. *American Journal of Hypertension, 5,* 37–44.

Watt, G. C., Edwards, C., Hart, J. T., Hart, M., Walton, P., & Foy, C. J. (1983). Dietary sodium restriction for mild hypertension in general practice. *British Medical Journal, 286,* 432–435.

Weinberger, M. H., Cohen, S. J., Miller, J. Z., Luft, F. C., Grim, C. E., & Fineberg, N. S. (1988). Dietary sodium restriction as adjunctive treatment of hypertension. *Journal of the American Medical Association, 259,* 2561–2565.

Wing, R. R., Caggiula, A. W., Nowalk, M. P., Koeske, R., Lee, S., & Langford, H. (1984). Dietary approaches to the reduction of blood pressure: The independence of weight and sodium/potassium interventions. *Preventive Medicine, 13,* 233–244.

Wittrock, D. A., Blanchard, E. B., & McCoy, G. C. (1988). Three studies on the relation of process to outcome in the treatment of essential hypertension with relaxation and thermal biofeedback. *Behaviour Research and Therapy, 26,* 53–66.

Wollam, G. L., & Hall, W. D. (Eds.). (1988). *Hypertension management: Clinical practice and therapeutic dilemmas.* Chicago: Yearbook Publishers.

Wollam, G. L., Hall, W. D., & Lowdon, J. D. (1988). Approach to pharmacologic therapy for mild, moderate, severe and resistant hypertension. In G. L. Wollam & W. D. Hall (Eds.), *Hypertension management: Clinical practice and therapeutic dilemmas* (pp. 365–383). Chicago: Yearbook Publishers.

Chapter 4

Headache

John P. Hatch

Headache is prevalent in all civilized societies, yet it remains one of the most perplexing of problems for patients and therapists alike. Over 90% of people report having at least one headache per year (Linet, Stewart, Celentano, Ziegler, & Sprecher, 1989). For most of these people, headaches are mild and infrequent and are relieved by over-the-counter analgesics or a period of quiet rest, but headache occasionally is a symptom of catastrophic illness. Few people ever consult a physician about their headaches, but, at the same time, headache is one of the most common causes of physician visits. Headaches can be severe or frequent enough to cause social, recreational,

I sincerely appreciate the helpful comments of Lawrence S. Schoenfeld, Elizabeth Brummage, and Robert B. Nett on early drafts of this chapter.

or occupational disability. Over 11 million people in the United States suffer mild to severe disability because of headaches (Stewart, Lipton, Celentano, & Reed, 1992). For a few people, headaches become totally disabling.

The pathophysiological mechanisms responsible for the pain of headache are unknown. Therefore, the symptom of pain often is treated as if it were the disease, and pain relief becomes the primary therapeutic objective. Understanding of the pain phenomenon is also limited, but it must be viewed as a subjective psychological experience. For this reason, the psychologist has much to offer the headache patient. The psychologist's theoretical training in such fields as perception, motivation, learning, emotion, and personality can be called on in formulating an understanding of the factors initiating and maintaining the headache experience and associated behaviors. Moreover, the psychologist's technical skills in measuring cognitive, physical, and physiological behavior are put to good use in assessing headache. In this chapter, I show how the psychologist's knowledge and skills can be used in the evaluation and treatment of the headache patient. I also define the context in which these abilities are best used by describing the diagnosis, epidemiology, and medical treatment of headache.

Diagnosis

In 1988, the Headache Classification Committee of the International Headache Society published operational diagnostic criteria for the headache disorders (International Headache Society, 1988). Over 100 different types of headache were described, so a detailed discussion of diagnosis is beyond the scope of this chapter. Most headaches are the benign, idiopathic varieties such as migraine and tension-type, and these are the ones that I consider in detail. I do not list all the specific diagnostic criteria here, but list only the general description of each type of headache. Much of the literature reviewed in this chapter was published before the operational criteria were available. However, I use the terms *migraine* and *tension-type* consistently to refer to these common forms of headache, even though diagnostic criteria are not entirely constant across studies. It should also be recognized that headache is a symptom of some life-threatening conditions, so even though diagnosis is not emphasized in this chapter, it should be remembered that not all headaches are benign. Surveys show that between 1.2% and 16% of patients who seek emergency treatment for headache have a serious neurological condition (Silberstein, 1992). Because headache is so prevalent in the general population, it is common for a serious neurological disorder to develop in a benign headache sufferer.

The diagnosis of primary headache disorders is controversial. A growing number of researchers view vascular and tension-type headaches on a quantitative intensity continuum rather than as qualitatively distinct illnesses (Smith & Jensen, 1988). Furthermore, recent theories propose that most headaches originate in the central nervous system, with both vascular and muscular mechanisms being either epiphenomena or sufficient, but not necessary, causes of pain (Raskin, 1988). The mixed results obtained from studies of the pathophysiological mechanisms (vasomotor dysregulation and muscular hypertonicity) that are presumed to underlie vascular and tension-type headaches are at the heart of the controversy. Nonetheless, operational diagnostic criteria are now available, and it is usually possible to classify patients accordingly.

Migraine Headache

Two broad categories of migraine headache are recognized: *migraine with aura* and *migraine without aura*. Migraine with aura replaces the former diagnosis of classic migraine, and migraine without aura replaces the former diagnosis of common migraine. The general description of migraine without aura (International Headache Society, 1988) is as follows:

> Idiopathic, recurring headache disorder manifesting in attacks lasting 4–72 hours. Typical characteristics of headaches are unilateral location, pulsating quality, moderate or severe intensity, aggravation by routine physical activity, and association with nausea, photo- and phonophobia. (p. 19)

Migraine with aura (International Headache Society, 1988) is described as follows:

> Idiopathic recurring disorder manifesting with attacks of neurological symptoms unequivocally localizable to cerebral cortex or brain stem, usually gradually developed over 5–20 minutes and usually lasting less than 60 minutes. Headache, nausea, and/or photophobia usually follow neurological aura symptoms directly or after a

free interval of less than an hour. The headache usually lasts 4–72 hours, but may be completely absent. (pp. 20–21)

Tension-Type Headache

The term *tension-type headache* replaces the former diagnosis of muscle contraction headache. Tension-type headache is described as chronic if the patient reports that headache is present for an average of 15 or more days per month and episodic if headache is present for fewer than 15 days per month. Some studies suggest that tension-type headache may be related to hypertonicity in the skeletal muscles of the head and neck, but this is controversial. Therefore, tension-type headache may be further subclassified according to whether the diagnostician finds evidence of pericranial muscle hyperactivity. If palpation of muscles reveals increased tenderness or if electromyography reveals increased electrical activity, then the diagnosis of tension-type headache associated with disorder of pericranial muscles is given. Otherwise, the diagnosis of tension-type headache unassociated with disorder of pericranial muscles is given.

The general description of tension-type headache according to the International Headache Society (1988) criteria is as follows:

> Recurrent episodes of headache lasting minutes to days. The pain is typically pressing/tightening in quality, of mild or moderate intensity, bilateral in location and does not worsen with routine physical activity. Nausea is absent, but photophobia, or phonophobia may be present. (p. 29)

The occasional tension-type headaches that are experienced by most people are of little concern. These headaches usually are relieved by over-the-counter analgesics or a brief period of rest and relaxation, and few sufferers ever seek professional therapy. However, the headaches sometimes increase in severity and occur on a daily or almost daily basis. Such chronic tension-type headaches can be among the most difficult and frustrating headache disorders to treat, particularly if the patient has become dependent on analgesics or other medications.

Cluster Headache

This chapter addresses primarily migraine and tension-type headaches. However, the characteristics of another type of benign headache that is occasionally encountered should also be recognized. This is the *cluster headache* (Diamond & Dalessio, 1992a). The International Headache Society (1988) description of cluster headache is as follows:

> Attacks of severe strictly unilateral pain orbitally, supraorbitally and/or temporally, lasting 15–180 minutes and occurring from once every other day to 8 times a day. Are associated with one or more of the following: conjunctival injection, lacrimation, nasal congestion, rhinorrhea, forehead and facial sweating, miosis, ptosis, and eyelid edema. Attacks occur in series lasting for weeks or months (so-called cluster periods) separated by remission periods usually lasting months or years. About 10 per cent of the patients have chronic symptoms. (p. 35)

Little research has addressed the behavioral treatment of cluster headache, although it often is assumed that behavioral treatment is ineffective. Blanchard, Andrasik, Jurish, and Teders (1982) provided some information on treating cluster headache patients using progressive relaxation training and thermal biofeedback. Blanchard and Andrasik (1985) also discussed the behavioral treatment of cluster headache.

Epidemiology

Epidemiological research on headache has focused primarily on prevalence, a measure of the number of cases in existence at a particular time. Information on headache incidence, which is the rate at which new cases occur in the population, has become available only recently. Measures of prevalence reflect both the incidence of new cases and the persistence of headache disorders in the population. One recent population-based telephone survey showed that 90% of male and 95% of female adolescents and young adults reported one or more headaches during the previous 12 months (Linet et al., 1989). This study also showed that 57.1% of males and 76.5% of females experienced a headache during the 4 weeks immediately prior to the interview, and 7.9% of males and 13.9% of females missed time from school or work because of their most recent headache. On the basis of questionnaire data and physical examinations performed by a neurologist, Rasmussen, Jensen, Schroll, and Olesen (1991) reported that 93% of men and 99% of women in a random sample of the general population of Denmark experienced headache. Rasmussen et al. also studied the point prevalence of headache by asking the question, "Do you have a headache today?" Eleven percent of male and 22% of female subjects responded in the affirmative. On the basis of this prevalence data alone, headache must be considered a major health problem.

Migraine Headache

Migraine prevalence has been estimated to range from 5% to 19% for men and from 11% to 28% for women; however, population-based studies involving large samples have been published only recently. Two studies conducted in Europe used the International Headache Society diagnostic criteria. Rasmussen and Olesen (1992) found a lifetime prevalence of 5% for migraine with aura and 8% for migraine without aura in a random sample of the Danish population. The male-to-female ratios were 1:2 for migraine with aura and 1:7 for migraine without aura. In a nationwide survey of France (Henry et al., 1992), the lifetime prevalence of migraine was 6.1% for males and 17.6% for females. Another recent study (Stewart et al., 1992) showed that 5.7% of males and 17.6% of females have one or more migraine headaches per year.

Prevalence of migraine is highest between the ages of 35 and 45 years for both sexes (Stewart et al., 1992). Migraine prevalence increases with age in people 12–35 years old and declines with advancing age in people older than 45 years (Stewart et al., 1992). The initial onset of migraine comes at a later age for girls than for boys (Stewart, Linet, Celentano, Van Natta, & Ziegler, 1991). For girls, the incidence of migraine peaks between 12 and 17 years of age, whereas the peak for boys occurs between 5 and 11 years. New onset of migraine during the late 20s is rare in men but relatively common in women (Stewart et al., 1991). Among young adults 21–30 years old, 7% of men and 16.3% of women have experienced migraine at some point in their lives (Breslau, Davis, & Andreski, 1991). Among older adults, 65–69 years old, 10% of men and 14% of women had a migraine headache in the past year (Cook et al., 1989). After the age of 90 years, migraine prevalence dropped to less than 1% of men and 6% of women (Cook et al., 1989).

The prevalence of migraine appears to be increasing in the United States. Between 1980 and 1989, the prevalence of migraine rose from 25.8 per 1,000 persons to 41.0 per 1,000 persons, nearly a 60% increase (National Health Interview Survey, 1991). People younger than 45 years of age accounted for 71% of the increase.

Stewart et al. (1992) projected that approximately 2.6 million U.S. men and 8.7 million U.S. women suffer moderate to severe disability from migraine headache. During the 3-year period from 1986 to 1988 more than 70% of male and 80% of female chronic migraine sufferers made one or more physician visits per year for treatment of headache, and 7% of men and 8% of women patients were hospitalized at least once for headache (National Health Interview Survey, 1991).

In the U.S., migraine headache is most prevalent in the western and mountain states and least prevalent in the northeastern states (Stewart et al., 1992; National Health Interview Survey, 1991). It is also more prevalent at high altitudes. In Peru, 12.4% of persons living 14,200 feet above sea level were found to have migraine headaches compared with only 3.6% of persons living 330 feet above sea level (Arregui et al., 1991). In contrast, tension-type headache was found in 9.6% and 9.5% of the high- and low-altitude samples, respectively. Chronic hypoxia, altered neurotransmitters, increased blood viscosity, cold temperatures, living conditions, and diet were mentioned as possible explanations for the differences observed (Arregui et al., 1991).

Migraine headache is also associated with anxiety and depression (Breslau et al., 1991; Merikangas, Angst, & Isler, 1990; Nappi, Bono, Sandrini, Martignoni, & Micieli, 1991). Also, migraine is associated with low income (Stewart et al., 1992), fewer years of education, and lower socioeconomic level (Cook et al., 1989). These relationships may reflect differences in life stress, diet, and access to health care in high and low socioeconomic groups. On the other hand, migraine may help determine income, educational level, and socioeconomic level by interfering with school and work performance (Stewart et al., 1992).

Tension-Type Headache

The lifetime prevalence of tension-type headache was found to be 78% in the Danish population study that used International Headache Society diagnostic criteria (Rasmussen et al., 1991). The prevalence in men was 69%, and in women it was 88%. The male-to-female ratio was 4:5. Approximately 36% of the population experienced tension-type headache several times per month, and 44% reported headaches from 1 to 14 days per year. Three percent of the population experienced headache for 180 days or more per year, thereby meeting the diagnostic criteria for chronic tension-type headache. Typical headache pain intensity was rated as severe by 1% of respondents, moderate by 58%, and mild by 41%.

Pathophysiology

Migraine Headache

The migraine attack can be divided into the prodrome or aura, the headache, and the postheadache phases. Before the onset of pain, some patients experience sensory, motor, or psychological changes, which constitute the aura. The aura is believed to be caused by vasoconstriction in various parts of the brain. The headache phase may be caused by dilation of large extracranial arteries and a lowering of the pain threshold. Pain during the headache and postheadache phases may also depend on edema of blood vessels and a sterile inflammatory response.

On the basis of their recent studies of regional cerebral blood flow in migraine patients undergoing angiography, Oleson et al. (1990) raised questions about changes in blood flow as the primary cause of pain. The first observed event was a focal reduction of blood flow in the posterior portion of one cerebral hemisphere. This was followed by the migraine aura. Regional cerebral blood flow remained low as the aura abated and the headache began. During the headache, regional cerebral blood flow changed from abnormally low to abnormally high, without change in the character of pain. In some patients, headache ended while cerebral blood flow remained elevated. Olesen et al. (1990) concluded that migraine pain is unrelated to increased cerebral blood flow, but this conclusion has not been accepted by all authorities (e.g., see Diamond, 1991). Olesen (1991) hypothesized that a pathophysiological disturbance in one cerebral hemisphere causes the aura and headache. Pain was hypothesized to be caused by pain-producing substances liberated from the cerebral cortex and stimulating pial arterial nociceptors. A myogenic nociceptive mechanism also has been implicated in the pathogenesis of migraine (Olesen, 1991). The relative importance of vascular, muscular, and central mechanisms in migraine headache is not known. A more detailed discussion of migraine pathophysiology can be found in Dalessio (1990).

Tension-Type Headache

The pathophysiology of tension-type headache is also unknown. It once was believed that involuntary tonic muscular contraction caused muscle ischemia, which was responsible for pain. Although muscle contraction may be present, this has by no means been universally demonstrated to be the primary cause of pain. It also has been demonstrated (Langemark, Jensen, & Olesen, 1990) that temporal muscle blood flow is normal in tension-type headache patients, which suggests that muscle ischemia probably is not a primary source of pain. However, abnormal blood flow patterns were noted in the cerebral vessels of tension-type headache patients, which suggests the involvement of an intracranial vascular mechanism (Wallasch, 1992). It is likely that similarly experienced headaches are sometimes associated with muscle spasm and sometimes not. When muscle spasm is present, it is seldom possible to determine whether it is the primary cause of pain or only a consequence of pain caused by a central mechanism.

Several investigators have compared electromyographic activity in the pericranial muscles of tension-type headache sufferers with that in various types of controls (for reviews see Flor & Turk, 1989; Hatch, Moore, Borcherding, et al., 1992; Pikoff, 1984). Most studies failed to reveal evidence of muscular hyperactivity during headaches or during headache-free periods. Also, there is little evidence to suggest that tension-type headache patients show extraordinary electromyographic activity during psychological or physical stress or that they are unable to relax normally following exposure to stress. Recent studies using ambulatory recording techniques to monitor electromyographic activity, psychological stress, and headache pain in the patient's natural environment (Hatch et al., 1991; Rugh et al., 1990) also failed to show a relation between muscle activity and pain.

Patients diagnosed with tension-type headache show increased tenderness to manual palpation of the pericranial muscles compared with normal controls (Hatch, Moore, Cyr-Provost, et al., 1992; Langemark, Jensen, Jensen, & Olesen, 1989; Lous & Olesen, 1982), which suggests a muscular source of pain. However, both muscle tenderness and elevated electromyographic activity may be found in groups of tension-type headache patients, whereas measures of muscle tenderness and hyperactivity are only weakly associated (Hatch, Moore, Cyr-Provost, et al., 1992). This suggests that muscle tenderness and elevated electromyographic activity may be associated with different aspects of muscle dysfunction. One study found pericranial muscle tenderness to be as common among migraine patients as among tension-type headache patients (Lous & Olesen, 1982). Schoenen, Bottin, Hardy, and Gerard (1991) recently demonstrated elevated pressure pain sensitivity not only in the pericranial muscles of chronic tension-type headache patients but also in their Achilles' tendons. Following muscular biofeedback therapy, pressure pain thresholds were increased, which suggests the action of a central mechanism (Schoenen et al., 1991).

The Relation of Personality to Headache

Migraine headache patients are often described as rigid, obsessional, hostile, ambitious, perfectionistic, compulsive, and full of repressed anger (Adler, Adler, & Packard, 1987; Anderson, 1980; Packard, 1987). Tension-type headache patients are described as angry, anxious, depressed, and dependent, with unresolved dependency needs and psychosexual conflicts (Adler et al., 1987; Packard, 1987). However, recent studies using standardized psychological tests to measure these traits have generated little evidence of a typical headache personality (Kohler & Kosanic, 1992; Pfaffenrath, Hummelsberger, Pollmann, Kaube, & Rath, 1991). Although it is clear that certain psychological traits, such as depressed mood and anxiety, are slightly elevated in headache patients in relation to normal controls, the concept of a headache-prone personality type has been overemphasized as a cause of headache.

Evaluation

Headache, like any other painful condition, should be viewed as a multidimensional phenomenon, and the clinician who is treating the headache patient should seek to understand the problem on behavioral, emotional, social, motivational, cognitive, and physiological bases. The psychologist must combine knowledge about mental health with knowledge about chronic pain disorders in general and headache in particular during evaluation. Throughout evaluation, emphasis should be placed on understanding the interrelationships among the different dimensions of the disorder. In most cases, it is impossible to learn the specific causes of headache, and patients should not be led to expect simple explanations. Also, it is usually difficult to unravel the complex relationship between cause and effect when considering the various dimensions of the pain experience. Interventions at each level are effective with some patients and ineffective with others, so good clinical judgment is needed in designing an integrated treatment plan.

Headache History

The importance of taking a thorough headache history cannot be overemphasized. The use of a structured interview is recommended for this purpose. An outline of such an interview that has much to recommend it is published in Blanchard and Andrasik's (1985) useful primer on the psychological management of headache. The interview should at a minimum cover a careful description of the headaches; their history, duration, frequency, and severity; precipitating factors; previous treatments; and current health status. Detailed information on taking a headache history can also be found in Diamond and Dalessio's (1992c) recent chapter on the subject.

Evaluation usually includes an attempt to identify the type of headache the patient has. Many patients know the diagnosis given by their physician and are knowledgeable about their disorder, but a surprising number know little. The psychologist should be able to elicit enough information to determine whether the patient presents symptoms that are typical of migraine or tension-type headache or that are atypical. Given the current uncertainty over the diagnosis and pathophysiology of migraine and tension-type headaches, the value of a correct diagnosis for behaviorally oriented treatment is debatable. Many of the treatment goals are the same for either type of headache. There are, however, some behavioral techniques that are designed specifically for one type of headache. For example, electromyographic biofeedback is usually selected for treating tension-type headache, whereas hand temperature biofeedback is usually selected for migraine. There is insufficient research on how effective each of these two treatments is in treating the other type of headache.

All headache patients must be evaluated by a physician before behavioral therapy begins, and the psychologist should request a copy of the patient's medical record from the treating physician. The medical record should state that the evaluation included a neurological examination and should clearly state the diagnosis. If the symptoms described by the patient are not typical of one of the benign headache disorders or if the patient reports a recent change in the headaches, then referral to a neurologist is recommended. Silberstein (1992) listed the following as causes for concern in diagnosing the headache patient:

> The first or worst headache of the patient's life, (particularly if it is of acute onset or has associated neurological symptoms).
> A headache that is subacute in onset and gets progressively worse over days or weeks.
> A headache associated with fever, nausea, and vomiting that cannot be explained by a systemic illness.
> A headache associated with focal neurological findings, papilledema, changes in consciousness or cognition (such as difficulty in reading, writing, or thinking), or a stiff neck.
> No obvious identifiable headache etiology. (p. 399)

Because some of these features may occur in a benign headache, either as part of the headache itself (e.g., stiff neck or vomiting) or as part of an associated aura (e.g., focal neurological symptoms), the importance of a good medical diagnosis is apparent.

Also, if after taking the headache history and reviewing the medical record, the psychologist is not certain that the patient has received a thorough medical workup, then the patient should be referred to a neurologist. If the headache history and medical record prove that a thorough medical evaluation has recently been performed and if the headaches have not changed recently, then patients usually can be spared the expense of yet another medical examination. Also, if the patient has not received recent medical care, then the psychologist should advise the patient that medical treatment may be highly effective and offer to cooperate with the patient's physician.

Psychological Evaluation

As already noted, the evidence supporting a particular headache-prone personality type is not strong. Certain personality characteristics are more common in headache patients than in the general population, and symptoms of minor psychological distress (e.g., depression or anxiety) are rather common. However, frank psychopathology is not common among headache patients, and psychological disturbance can seldom be identified as the primary cause of pain. Still, it is important to carefully assess the headache patient's psychological status before beginning treatment. Individual differences in personality color the perception of pain, the patient's response to pain, and the behavior of others toward the patient. The evaluation should include a psychodiagnostic interview and the administration of selected standardized tests. Some patients resist answering psychologically oriented questions or completing psychological inventories because of fear that the clinician may think the disorder is purely psychological in nature. For this reason it often is advisable to introduce psychological questions by explaining that all aspects of the problem need to be explored and that the validity of their pain is not being questioned. Taking a careful headache history before addressing psychological issues can also help convince patients that their pain will be taken seriously.

Depression is probably the most common psychological disturbance encountered in the headache patient population (Adler et al., 1987; Breslau et al., 1991; Nappi et al., 1991). Also, about 52% of psychiatric patients being treated for depression also suffer from headaches (Marchesi et al., 1989). It has been suggested that headache and depression are linked independently of their clinical expression (Marchesi et al., 1989). Some depression in headache patients is to be expected as a result of living with pain. Chronic pain can cause sleep disturbances, disruption of occupational and psychosocial activities, overuse of medications, financial difficulties, and severe strain on social support mechanisms. These factors may further contribute to a depressed mood. The relationship between depression and pain is further complicated by the fact that depression can alter the patient's perception of pain. Depression may be associated with a lowering of pain threshold and pain tolerance level (Rome, Harness, & Kaplan, 1990) or may cause the patient to experience headaches as more distressful.

Because headache and depression are so commonly associated, the psychological evaluation should include a careful inquiry into depressive symptoms. If clinical depression is found, then it may require conventional psychological treatment. The potential for suicide should also be considered. The odds ratio for a suicide attempt was found to be 3.0 among patients suffering from migraine with aura, compared with 1.6 for patients with migraine without aura and 5.5

for patients with major depression (Breslau et al., 1991). There is approximately a three-fold increase in risk of a suicide attempt in patients with migraine with aura in relation to people without migraine, independent of major depression, sex, or other psychiatric comorbidity. It also is important to realize that antidepressant medications are effective in treating migraine and tension-type headache regardless of whether the patient is experiencing depression. Therefore, the patient who reports taking antidepressant medication is not necessarily under treatment for depression by a physician.

In addition to the clinical interview, the psychologist will probably wish to include standardized psychological tests as a part of the patient evaluation. The Minnesota Multiphasic Personality Inventory (MMPI) is the most widely used standardized test for measuring the psychological functioning of pain patients, and norms for headache patients have been published (Blanchard & Andrasik, 1985). Blanchard and Andrasik (1985) found that cluster headache patients generally do not differ from normal controls in psychological functioning, and migraine patients show mean t scores greater than 60 only on MMPI Scale 3 (Hysteria). Patients with mixed migraine and tension-type headaches show the next highest level of psychological disturbance. Tension-type headache patients show the greatest psychological disturbance, with elevated t scores on Scales 1 (Hypochondriasis), 2 (Depression), 3 (Hysteria), 7 (Psychasthenia), and 8 (Schizophrenia). A similar ranking of patients who were diagnosed with different types of headaches was obtained for scores on the Beck Depression Inventory, the State–Trait Anxiety Inventory, and the Psychosomatic Symptom Checklist (Cox, Freundlich, & Meyer, 1975). This pattern of results led Blanchard and Andrasik (1985) to conclude that the degree of psychological disturbance is related to the number of days of headache suffering experienced per week, which they called "headache density."

In 1989, the MMPI was revised, which resulted in publication of the MMPI-2 (Butcher, Dahlstrom, Graham, Tellegen, & Kaemmer, 1989). Changes made to the MMPI included rewording of items, a new normative population, a new method of computing t scores, and a new set of content scales. Keller and Butcher (1991) published a monograph on their use of the MMPI and MMPI-2 with a group of 502 chronic pain patients. They concluded that the two instruments produced similarly shaped profiles, although the MMPI-2 produced *t* scores that were approximately 5 points lower. There is little information available now on how headache patients perform on this test.

The Beck Depression Inventory also has been found to be useful for evaluating depression in the headache patient, and Blanchard and Andrasik (1985) provided norms for small samples of migraine and tension-type headache patients. Because it can be quickly administered and scored, the Beck Depression Inventory is useful for monitoring change in a patient who is depressed. For evaluating anxiety, which frequently accompanies headache, the State–Trait Anxiety Inventory has been recommended by Blanchard and Andrasik (1985), who published some normative data for this test on headache patients.

Evaluation of Pain

Psychological tests have been developed specifically for measuring the pain experience. The most widely known of these tests is the McGill Pain Questionnaire (Holroyd et al., 1992; Melzack, 1975). The unique feature of the McGill Pain Questionnaire is that it requires patients to rate their pain using adjectives designed to describe the sensory (e.g., aching, crushing, or throbbing), affective (e.g., cruel, killing, or sickening), and evaluative (e.g., mild, strong, or excruciating) dimensions of the pain experience. Unfortunately, few studies using this test with headache patients have been published. The McGill Pain Questionnaire is sensitive to change in some types of clinical pain, and it may prove useful in monitoring change in headaches along the three dimensions that are purportedly measured.

For evaluating the intensity dimension of pain, a simple visual analogue scale has many advantages (Huskisson, 1983). The visual analogue scale usually consists of a 100-mm-long line with endpoints labeled *no pain* and *pain as severe as possible*. The patient is asked to make a mark at the point along the line that best denotes the intensity of his or her current pain. The test is scored as the distance in millimeters from the left (*no pain*) point to the patient's mark. Because many headache patients do not have constant pain, it also is recommended that patients rate their worst pain during a headache and their typical or average pain during a headache. Some clinicians also ask patients to rate their degree of improvement since starting therapy on a visual analogue scale.

Headache Diary

Another important component of evaluation is the headache diary, in which the patient periodically records information about headaches. It can be helpful, although not always clinically practical, to have patients keep a headache diary for a few weeks before treatment begins. The information provided via the diary is useful in establishing a baseline of headache activity and for monitoring improvement. Regular discussion of the diary data during therapy also serves as a basis for patient education, identifying problem areas, identifying headache triggers, and setting therapeutic goals.

It is useful to have the patient provide brief information four times per day (at each meal and at bedtime). A simple 6-point rating scale, such as that recommended by Blanchard and Andrasik (1985), works well. A visual analogue scale can also be used. Because some patients have nearly continuous headaches, it can be difficult for them to determine exactly when one headache ends and another begins. Therefore, some investigators use the number of days on which the patient reports no headache activity (headache-free days) as the unit of headache frequency. Patients should also provide information about their degree of disability because of headaches and the amount and type of medication taken for headaches. The headache diary can also be tailored to meet individual therapeutic objectives or to identify factors that precipitate headaches. For example, it may be useful to have certain patients provide information about their mood, diet, life stress, menstrual cycle, weather changes, physical activities, or work habits during the preheadache period.

Headaches can change in different ways, and various aspects of headache activity can change at different rates. A decrease in headache frequency, lower pain intensity, less reliance on medication, and fewer lost workdays may all be signs of therapeutic progress. Different indices of headache activity are not independent of one another and should be interpreted within the context of the overall treatment strategy. The patient who shows a decrease in headache frequency or severity but an increase in medication use may be headed for additional problems.

Behavioral Evaluation

The overt behaviors exhibited by the patient during a headache can be an important source of clinical information. Because most headaches are episodic, patients usually do not experience headaches during the evaluation session. If the patient does have a headache, then the psychologist should carefully observe any outward signs of pain and note how frequent and expressive these behaviors are. Pain patients often show guarding, bracing, rubbing, grimacing, and sighing behaviors (Keefe & Block, 1982). Patients who engage in such behaviors to an extreme are sending a message that they are in pain, and they may be attempting to elicit attention, sympathy, or solicitous behavior from others (Keefe, 1988).

Regardless of whether the patient can be directly observed while in pain, it is important to inquire of the patient and significant others exactly what the patient does when he or she has a headache and what other people do in response to the pain behaviors. It is well known (Sternbach, 1980) that pain behaviors can be learned through operant conditioning. These behaviors become more frequent when they are rewarded and eventually can interfere with effective functioning or an active life-style. Also, healthy, nonpain behaviors sometimes are punished or selectively not rewarded. Therefore, it is important for the psychologist to identify what pain behaviors the patient typically exhibits and what the potentially rewarding or punishing consequences might be. Possible reinforcers include such things as avoidance of work, opportunities to rest in bed, attention or preferential treatment by others, continued access to addictive drugs, and avoidance of performance demands and other stressors.

Because some types of headache are familial, it is not unusual for a parent or other member of the patient's family to have suffered from headaches. If this is so, then it is important to determine how that person typically behaved and was treated by others while in pain. Pain behaviors may be learned through modeling, and knowledge about how family members respond to their own pain and that of others may give insight into the patient's pain behaviors.

Psychophysiological Profiling

Many research studies of headache have included various psychophysiological measurements in evaluating patients. For example, Philips (1977) treated tension-type headache patients with biofeedback aimed at whatever muscle was found to be most tense during a psychophysiological evaluation session. This type of screening of patients for muscle hyperactivity has recently been advocated under the term *muscle scanning.* The rationale for such screening is that if isolated areas of muscle hyperactivity can be identified, then therapy can be optimized by training patients to reduce muscle tension in the problem areas. More elaborate psychophysiological evaluations, sometimes called *stress profiling,* usually involve measuring electromyographic or autonomic nervous system activity to identify some relation between exposure to standardized laboratory stressors and a physiological response pattern that could be implicated in headache. It is often assumed that the response of headache patients to stress is unusually large or long lasting after stress exposure. Although some research supports this hypothesis, the techniques of muscle scanning and stress profiling have not been validated to the point where they can be recommended for evaluating individual patients (Flor & Turk, 1989; Hatch, Moore, Borcherding, et al., 1992; Hatch, Prihoda, & Moore, 1992). In spite of our limited ability to evaluate it, the physiological component of pain remains an important part of theories that direct behavioral treatment.

Medical Treatment

Migraine Headache

Abortive treatment.   For many patients, the abortion of migraine attacks is readily achieved with ergotamine tartrate (e.g., Cafergot, Wigraine, Bellergal-S) or other vasoconstrictors (e.g., Midrin). When taken at the first sign of aura or at the earliest stages of pain, ergotamine preparations can be highly effective in aborting migrainous attacks (Raskin, 1988; Saper, 1990; Ziegler, 1987). Ergotamine tartrate is administered in oral, rectal, and sublingual forms. Ergotamine causes constriction of arterial smooth muscle, and it is presumed that this action is responsible for the symptomatic relief of migraine. However, ergotamine also affects turnover of brain serotonin and can suppress the firing rate of serotonergic neurons in the brain (Raskin, 1988). These central effects may be responsible for the clinical response to ergotamine. The hydrogenated form of ergotamine, dihydroergotamine (D.H.E. 45), is available in parenteral form for abortive migraine therapy and currently is being tested in oral and nasal forms.

Sumatriptan, a drug that acts as an agonist at the vasoconstrictor 5-HT1 receptor, was recently studied for its efficacy in abortive migraine therapy. A multicenter study conducted in Europe (Subcutaneous Sumatriptan International Study Group, 1991; Visser et al., 1992) showed that a subcutaneous injection of sumatriptan was associated with headache relief in over 70% of patients, compared with 25% of placebo-treated patients. Similar results have been reported by a group working in the U.S. (Cady et al., 1991).

Prophylactic treatment. When headaches are so frequent and severe that abortive therapy is not practical, various medications are used prophylactically to interrupt the cycle of attacks. The most widely used medications for this purpose are β-adrenergic blocking agents. The first beta blocker that was used in treating migraine, and one that remains in use, is propranolol (Inderal). Propranolol is a nonselective β-adrenergic blocker. This means that it blocks the effects of norepinephrine at both β1-adrenergic receptors, which are found primarily in the heart and cause myocardial excitation, and β2-adrenergic receptors, which are found primarily in the smooth muscle of blood vessels and lungs and cause vasodilation and bronchodilation when stimulated. The clinical response to propranolol may be related to its ability to prevent vasodilation; however, this has been called into question (Saper, 1990). Nadolol (Corgard) and timolol (Blocadren) are other nonselective beta blockers that are used for migraine prophylaxis. Selective β1-adrenergic blockers such as metoprolol (Lopressor) and atenolol (Tenormin) also are effective in the prevention of migraine headaches.

Calcium channel blockers such as verapamil (Isoptin, Calan) are another class of drugs that have recently been used for migraine prophylaxis. Contraction of vascular smooth muscle depends on the influx of calcium ions into the cell through specialized channels. By blocking the flow of calcium ions through such channels, these drugs may prevent migraine headaches by preventing sustained vasoconstriction (Ziegler, 1987). Other medicines that are used in migraine prophylaxis include the tricyclic antidepressants, Bellergal-S, Depakote, and Sansert.

Tension-Type Headache

Abortive treatment. Mild episodic tension-type headaches are often relieved by self-medication with over-the-counter analgesics.

With chronic or near daily headache, dependence on analgesics or other medications can become a serious problem, so most authorities recommend cautious use of analgesics for patients who suffer frequent headaches. Raskin (1988) felt that incapacitating attacks of tension-type headache are just as effectively aborted by intravenous dihydroergotamine as are attacks of migraine. Nonsteroidal anti-inflammatory agents such as naproxen (Naprosyn) and various analgesic–sedative combinations (e.g., Fioricet or Fiorinal) are also effective (Kunkel, 1989) in treating episodic attacks. Because they contain a barbiturate, the analgesic–sedative combinations are believed to have a high potential for abuse.

Prophylactic treatment. For the prophylaxis of chronic tension-type headache the tricyclic antidepressants such as amitriptyline (Elavil) and doxepin (Sinequan) are the first-line therapy, but the monoamine oxidase inhibitors are also effective (Kunkel, 1989). Although depression is often comorbid with headache, it is unlikely that these drugs reduce headache activity through their antidepressive action. Nonsteroidal anti-inflammatory agents, Depakote, and Sansert are also used in the prophylaxis of tension-type headache.

Drug-Induced Headache

Many medications have the undesirable effect of causing headaches (Mathew, 1990). Unfortunately, even medications frequently prescribed for headache may actually cause headaches to become worse. For example, ergotamine tartrate, if overused, can lead to a serious problem known as ergotamine-rebound headache. If ergotamine is taken frequently, it leads to a form of recurring headache, which is relieved only by ergotamine (Kunkel, 1990; Raskin, 1988). These headaches may increase in frequency until they occur on a daily or near daily basis. At this point, patients may begin using ergotamine even before headache onset in an effort to prevent the expected attack. The physiological mechanism responsible for rebound headaches is unknown but may be a drug-induced sensitization of the vasomotor reflex. When patients are found to be using ergotamine more than two times per week to abort migraine attacks, the possibility of rebound headaches should be considered (Raskin, 1988). When rebound headaches occur, it is necessary to remove patients from ergotamine before any other therapy can be expected to succeed. The withdrawal from ergotamine is often a difficult and painful process, which may require hospitalization.

Rebound headaches also occur in response to the overuse of prescription analgesics and over-the-counter preparations such as aspirin and acetaminophen. Patients who use analgesics at a high rate experience more headaches (Isler, 1982) and are less responsive to prophylactic therapy (Kudrow, 1982) compared with patients who use analgesics less often. Simply eliminating all symptomatic medications for headache results in significant improvement and enhances the effects of prophylactic medications in these patients (Mathew, Kurman, & Perez, 1990). Up to 12 weeks may be required for the maximum benefit to be obtained following elimination of analgesics (Rapoport, Weeks, Sheftell, Baskin, & Verdi, 1986). Isler (1982) found a strong tendency for detoxified migraine patients to relapse and return to high analgesic consumption if analgesics were later prescribed for pain other than headache. Such relapses were always associated with an increase in headaches. On the contrary, patients from a rheumatology clinic who were taking high doses of analgesics did not suffer from more headaches than did controls who were not taking analgesics (Lance, Parkes, & Wilkinson, 1988). This apparent difference in sensitivity to analgesics between headache and nonheadache pain patients has led to speculation that headache patients may have an inherent abnormality that predisposes them to drug-induced headache (Mathew et al., 1990).

Behavioral Treatment

The behavioral treatment of headache uses patient education, modification of illness behaviors, and techniques aimed at effective stress management. At the outset of therapy, it is important to ascertain how the patient perceives his or her headaches, correct any misconceptions, and clarify treatment expectations. Patients should understand that headaches do not result from a constitutional weakness, either psychological or physiological, but rather are the product of environmental, social, psychological, and physiological variables over which he or she can exercise considerable control. Patients should also understand that there are a number of times in their lives when interventions could be effective and that their headaches could improve in several ways. Many chronic pain patients feel helpless, hopeless, and demoralized; and they may engage in catastrophic thoughts. These patients in particular need to be encouraged to develop positive expectations and adopt a sense of self-control. Patients should also be led to expect that they will be active participants in therapy. Finally, patients should understand that they will learn new skills in therapy. These skills must be mastered, practiced until proficiency is achieved, and then incorporated into daily life.

Headache Triggers

There are several environmental factors that can precipitate or trigger a headache in certain individuals (Diamond, 1991; Diamond & Dalessio, 1992b; Gallagher, 1990). The most common triggering agents are stress, alcohol, certain foods, sleep dysregulation, and menstruation. Many patients are unable to identify any precipitating factors and describe their headaches as purely random events. Others know of specific events that cause headaches, or they have a hunch about possible precipitating events. The most common precipitating factors should be discussed with patients to identify provocative events or alert patients to possible critical events. If patients can avoid precipitating factors or be taught to cope more effectively with them, then significant headache improvement can result.

Psychological stress. The triggering factor most commonly mentioned by migraine and tension-type headache patients is psychological stress. In one prospective study, Kohler and Haimerl (1990) showed that migraine headache is associated with psychological stress on the day of the attack or on the day before. Of course, stress is a difficult term to define clinically, but most patients have a good general idea of what they perceive to be stressful. This should be elicited and discussed with the patient. The report of stress-triggered headaches should be carefully investigated. In Western society, headaches and stress are so strongly linked that patients may report a relationship almost automatically. The therapist should try to identify specific examples of stressors that are reliably linked to headaches and then explore how the patient appraises the stressful events and what his or her resources are for coping with them. If specific stressors are identified, it might be useful to have the patient record data about them in the headache diary. Such information can be used to document the relationship between events and headaches.

Headache patients often are presumed to be unusually reactive to stress, but there is little evidence that headache sufferers endure greater life stress, except the stress caused by chronic pain itself, than any other group. It is more likely that headache patients appraise stressful life events, particularly minor hassles, more negatively and cope with them less effectively than do pain-free people (De Benedittis & Lorenzetti, 1992; Holm, Holroyd, Hursey, & Penzien, 1986). Patients should be helped to realize that chronic pain is itself a type of stress that can be expected to affect other areas of their lives. The therapist should explore the pain behaviors in which the patient engages during a headache and how significant other people behave in response to the patient's pain behaviors.

One other rather curious feature of the stress–headache relationship deserves brief attention. It is frequently noted that headaches may not occur during a period of stress but rather after the crisis has ended. At other times a seemingly trivial frustration may trigger a headache.

Dietary factors.   Dietary factors constitute another common class of headache precipitant. Migraine patients in particular report that their headaches follow the ingestion of certain foods or drinks. Many patients report that they have headaches as a result of an allergy to certain foods. Although the possibility of allergic headache has been debated for years, headaches probably are not the result of a true antigen–antibody reaction but rather are a response to vasoactive substances found in foods (Diamond & Dalessio, 1992b). Therefore, the term *dietary migraine* is preferred. Some of the chemicals found naturally in foods, or added during food processing, that may trigger headaches in susceptible individuals include tyramine, sodium nitrite, caffeine, alcohol, monosodium glutamate, aspartame, and phenylethylamine. These dietary ingredients are listed in Table 1 along with some examples of foods in which they are commonly found.

Caffeine and nicotine, both of which are vasoconstrictors, are believed to cause rebound vasodilation and headache if taken in large amounts (Diamond, 1991). Few double-blind studies of these triggering agents have been conducted, and the available information comes from a few surveys and from clinical reports. Patients who are sufficiently motivated to try can be assisted in eliminating potentially

Table 1

Common Types of Foods That May Precipitate Headache

Food ingredient	Common sources
Tyramine	Avocados, broad beans, aged cheese, yogurt, sour cream, chicken liver, bananas, pickled foods, fresh-baked yeast breads
Sodium nitrate, sodium nitrite	Cured and aged meats including ham, bacon, salami, hot dogs, cured fish
Monosodium glutamate	Chinese foods, many processed foods and frozen foods, seasonings
Phenylethylamine	Chocolate, cheeses, red wines
Alcohol	Beer, wine, liquor (especially red wine, brandy, and gin)
Caffeine	Coffee, tea, soft drinks, chocolate, over-the-counter analgesics (e.g., Excedrin, Vanquish, Midol)

Note. From *Migraine Headache Prevention and Management* (p. 33) edited by S. Diamond, 1990, New York: Marcel Dekker; copyright 1990 by Marcel Dekker; adapted by permission; and *The Practicing Physician's Approach to Headache* (p. 56–57) edited by S. Diamond and D. J. Dalessio, 1992, Baltimore: Williams & Wilkins; copyright 1992 by Williams & Wilkins; adapted by permission.

provocative elements from their diet. In a recent study, Radnitz and Blanchard (1991) evaluated dietary restriction therapy in a small group of vascular headache patients who had failed to achieve clinically meaningful benefit from prior stress management therapy. Six of 10 patients reduced their headaches by 50% or more.

Diamond and Dalessio (1992b) published an extensive list of foods allowed and foods to avoid on a migraine diet. Eliminating all the foods on such a list would be a challenge for any patient. A practical alternative approach is to allow patients to examine the list and identify foods that they suspect may be a cause of headaches. It may be helpful to have them identify foods that they eat frequently. The identified foods can then be eliminated from the patient's diet a few at a time and the effect on headaches noted. The relation between dietary factors and headache seems to be highly individualistic, so flexibility in working with patients is recommended.

Fasting or skipping meals can reportedly trigger a headache. Presumably the resulting fall in blood sugar, which causes vasodilation, is responsible for the headache. Patients who experience this type of headache should eat meals at regular intervals and eat balanced meals containing adequate amounts of protein, which is digested more slowly than carbohydrates (Gallagher, 1990). Patients who frequently awaken with a headache may benefit from eating something before retiring.

Hormones.   Much attention has been given to the role of the female reproductive hormones in headache disorders. Headaches are known to be significantly affected by menarche, menses, pregnancy, menopause, and the use of oral contraceptives. Menstruation is a very common precipitant of headache among female patients. Between 60% and 70% of female migraine sufferers report that some of their headaches are temporally linked to their menses. The physiological mechanism that triggers these attacks may be the premenstrual withdrawal of estradiol (Somerville, 1972). Little is known about the effectiveness of behavioral treatment for menstrual migraine, but preliminary evidence suggests that behavioral therapy may be effective (Blanchard, 1992).

Sleep patterns.   Another factor associated with headache is dysregulation of sleep. Patients often report headaches on awakening, particularly following an unusually long or deep sleep. Other patients report headaches in association with loss of sleep, and some find that a period of sleep may abort a headache. Little is known about how sleep affects headache, but headache patients are often advised to maintain a regular sleep schedule.

Other headache triggers.   Other possible headache triggers include physical exertion, sexual activity, changes in the weather, exposure to glare or bright sunlight, odors, and high altitude.

A curious fact about precipitating factors is that they rarely trigger a headache on every exposure. For example, alcohol is a common precipitant of migraine headache, but most patients are able to drink alcohol on some occasions without developing a headache. It may be that a cascade phenomenon occurs whereby a patient's vulnerability to a headache increases as multiple precipitating factors occur in close temporal proximity. For example, a glass of wine that normally would not precipitate a headache may do so if the patient also oversleeps, has a stressful day, skips lunch, or is beginning her menstrual period.

Stress Management

Another important component in the behavioral treatment of headache is stress management. Progressive muscle relaxation (PMR) training, biofeedback, and cognitive behavioral therapy have all been used successfully as stress management techniques in treating headache patients.

Mechanisms of action. It is often presumed that relaxation training and electromyographic biofeedback work with tension-type headache by making patients aware of muscle tension and fostering relaxation of painful skeletal muscles. As noted earlier, however, the role of muscle hyperactivity in tension-type headache is controversial, and there are no published studies on the relative effectiveness of electromyographic biofeedback in tension-type headache patients with and without pericranial muscle involvement. Holroyd et al. (1984) conducted a clever experiment that raises further questions about the importance of muscle relaxation in behavioral therapy. In this experiment, students with tension-type headache were treated with electromyographic biofeedback and led to believe that they were learning muscle relaxation. In reality, only half received biofeedback contingent on reduced muscle activity, and the other half received biofeedback contingent on increased muscle activity. Also, at the end of each session half of the subjects in each feedback condition viewed bogus computer information that depicted great success on the task whereas the other half viewed information that depicted only moderate success. Neither the type of biofeedback given nor the actual level of muscle activity achieved had a significant effect on headaches. Only the bogus computer feedback given at the end of the session affected headaches, with subjects given high success feedback experiencing significantly greater headache reduction than subjects receiving moderate success feedback. On the basis of this and other experiments, Holroyd challenged the physiological model of biofeedback and proposed a cognitive–attributional mechanism of action.

Thermal biofeedback aimed at teaching patients to warm their fingers through digital vasodilation is used primarily to treat migraine headache. It is not known how thermal biofeedback works. Because migraine sufferers have been described as showing instability or imbalance of the autonomic nervous system, it has been speculated that thermal biofeedback might promote autonomic quieting or reduced sympathetic tone. This theory seems doubtful in light of evidence that voluntary finger warming in normal subjects probably is not mediated by the withdrawal of sympathetic vasoconstrictor tone (Freedman et al., 1988) but rather by a nonneural β-adrenergic mechanism acting on arteriovenous shunts.

Effectiveness.   Blanchard (1992) extensively reviewed the research findings on the behavioral treatment of headache, and his article should be consulted for additional detail. Almost all published studies that compared subjects in any form of active behavioral therapy with an untreated control group have shown behavioral treatment to be more effective than no treatment (see Blanchard, 1992). Also, biofeedback and relaxation training were more effective in treating tension-type headache than a medication placebo, which patients were told was a muscle relaxant (Cox et al., 1975). When behavioral therapy is compared with a credible behavioral placebo, however, the picture is less clear. Electromyographic biofeedback is more effective than a credible meditation placebo treatment with tension-type headache (Holroyd, Andrasik, & Noble, 1980). When headache diary data are used as the outcome measure, active behavioral therapy (relaxation or relaxation combined with cognitive stress management) is significantly more effective than "pseudomeditation" in treating tension-type headache (Blanchard, Appelbaum, Radnitz, Michultka, et al., 1990). However, active treatment (thermal biofeedback plus relaxation or thermal biofeedback plus cognitive stress management) is not significantly more effective than pseudomeditation in treating vascular headache (Blanchard, Appelbaum, Radnitz, Morrill, et al., 1990). When the proportion of patients in each group achieving a clinically significant (more than 50%) reduction in headaches is used as the outcome measure, active treatment produces slightly superior results compared with the credible placebo. Blanchard, Appelbaum, Radnitz, Michultka, et al. (1990) argued post hoc that the pseudomeditation condition contained elements similar to relaxation and actually promoted relaxation. In summary, behavioral treatment has been shown to be more effective than a medication placebo and a credible behavioral placebo in treating tension-type headache but not migraine.

Treatment combinations.   When comparing various combinations of behavioral therapy, the literature is complex. In general, the addition of cognitive stress coping therapy to relaxation therapy yields an increase in treatment effectiveness with tension-type headache, but there is no advantage to adding cognitive therapy to thermal biofeedback for migraine (Blanchard, 1992). With minimal therapist contact, in largely home-based therapy, there is little advantage in adding cognitive therapy in treating migraine or tension-type headache. Holroyd and Andrasik (1978) compared tension-type headache patients receiving cognitive stress management training alone or cognitive therapy plus relaxation training with a control group that merely discussed the history of headache symptoms but was given no strategies for coping with stress. All three treated groups improved more than did an untreated control group, but there were no significant differences among the three treated groups. Neither the addition of relaxation training nor the elimination of cognitive stress management therapy modified the benefits obtained by the headache discussion group. In a mixed group of tension-type and migraine headache patients, the addition of electromyographic biofeedback to autogenic relaxation training resulted in additional headache improvement, but the addition of thermal biofeedback did not (Cott, Parkinson, Fabich, Bedard, & Marlin, 1992).

Comparison of Behavioral and Pharmacological Treatments

Behavioral and pharmacological treatments for headache have also been compared. Holroyd and Penzien (1990) performed a meta-analysis of 25 trials of propranolol and 35 trials of relaxation therapy combined with thermal biofeedback in the treatment of migraine headache. Using headache diary data as the outcome measure, both treatments produced a 43% average reduction in headache activity. Placebo medication produced an average improvement of 14%, and untreated controls did not improve. Therefore, the meta-analysis showed both behavioral and pharmacological therapy to be more effective than a medication placebo, and the two therapies were equally effective.

Behavioral and pharmacological therapies have also been directly compared in a single study, and behavioral therapy compares favorably. In one early study (Sovak, Kunzel, Sternbach, & Dalessio, 1981), 54% of migraine patients treated with autogenic relaxation and thermal biofeedback showed clinically significant improvement, compared with 45% treated with propranolol. In a large study, Mathew

(1981) reported that 35% of migraine patients treated with autogenic relaxation and thermal biofeedback were clinically improved, compared with 42% of those treated with amitriptyline alone and 62% of those treated with propranolol alone. When behavioral therapy was combined with propranolol, the percentage of patients who were clinically improved increased to 74%. Holroyd and co-workers (Holroyd et al., 1988) treated one group of migraine patients with a home-based program of relaxation training and thermal biofeedback and another group with ergotamine tartrate as an abortive medication. Headache diary data indicated a 52% reduction in headache activity for the behaviorally treated patients, compared with a 41% reduction for those taking medication. The difference was not statistically significant, but there were other differences noted. Drug treatment worked faster than did behavioral treatment. Also, behavioral treatment was associated with reduced analgesic use, but drug treatment was not. Three years after treatment (Holroyd et al., 1989), patients in both groups continued to show lower headache activity compared with the pretreatment period. Patients treated with ergotamine were less likely to still rely on the therapy they were given, were more likely to have received additional treatment for headaches, and were more likely to be using prophylactic or narcotic medications.

Behavioral and pharmacological treatments for tension-type headache have also been directly compared. In an early study (Paiva et al., 1982), the muscle relaxant diazepam was compared with frontal electromyographic biofeedback in tension-type headache patients. The drug seemed to work faster than the biofeedback, which did not produce significant improvement during the treatment period. However, during the follow-up period, only the behaviorally treated patients showed clinical improvement. In a recent study, Holroyd and co-workers (Holroyd, Nash, Pingel, Cordingley, & Jerome, 1991) compared the antidepressant amitriptyline with a minimal therapist contact program consisting of relaxation training combined with cognitive stress coping training. The behaviorally treated patients showed a tripling of headache-free days and a 56% reduction in headache activity as revealed by headache diary data. The patients treated with the antidepressant showed a doubling of headache-free days and a 27% reduction in headache activity. The difference was statistically significant. If neurologist ratings were taken as the outcome measure, then both groups showed even greater improvements.

A potential advantage of behavioral treatments over pharmacological treatments lies in the fact that no significant side effects or adverse reactions associated with behavioral treatment of headache have been reported. The same cannot be said of pharmacological treatment. In fact, some side effects of behavioral treatment have been reported to be beneficial. Patients treated with relaxation or biofeedback show lowered scores on the Beck Depression Inventory and the State–Trait Anxiety Inventory, regardless of headache type or treatment outcome (Blanchard et al., 1986). Therefore, behavioral treatment may improve psychological function in treated patients even if headaches do not improve.

Long-Term Maintenance of Treatment Effects

The maintenance of behavioral treatment effects for 1–3 years posttreatment is well documented (Blanchard, 1992). Several additional studies have documented good maintenance of treatment effects following biofeedback and relaxation training for 5–7 years posttreatment (Blanchard, Andrasik, Guarnieri, Neff, & Rodichok, 1987; Blanchard, Appelbaum, Guarnieri, Morrill, & Dentinger, 1987; Gauthier & Carrier, 1991; Lisspers & Ost, 1990). In one study (Blanchard, Andrasik, et al., 1987), vascular headache patients showed progressive but nonsignificant deterioration during the 4-year follow-up period, but other studies have shown solid long-term maintenance (Gauthier & Carrier, 1991) or even enhancement of treatment effects during long-term follow-up. The fact that one study (Gauthier & Carrier, 1991) showed that 51% of the originally treated sample had received additional treatment for headaches during the follow-up period, however, suggests that these results should be cautiously interpreted.

Booster Treatments

The value of booster treatments after the completion of an original course of behavioral therapy to increase the maintenance of treatment effects has also been studied. The administration of booster treatments once per month for 6 months after initial therapy produced no added benefit beyond that obtained through brief monthly contacts without additional therapy (Andrasik, Blanchard, Neff, & Rodichok, 1984; Blanchard, Andrasik, et al., 1987).

Home Practice

The effect of requiring patients to practice at home the skills they are taught in therapy has also received some attention. One study showed that in the treatment of migraine with thermal biofeedback there is no advantage to giving patients home practice assignments (Blanchard, Nicholson, Radnitz, et al., 1991). Another study suggested a possible advantage of home practice when relaxation therapy is used to treat tension-type headache (Blanchard, Nicholson, Taylor, et al., 1991). Although the limited research available at this time does not strongly support the value of home practice, most clinicians will probably continue to recommend home practice for their clients because they believe it facilitates the generalization of skills learned in the clinic to real life.

Behavioral Treatment of Cluster Headache

As already noted, little research has addressed the behavioral treatment of cluster headache, and behavioral treatment is often presumed to be ineffective in treating this type of headache. Blanchard and colleagues provided information on their treatment of 11 cluster headache patients with abbreviated progressive relaxation training and thermal biofeedback (Blanchard et al., 1982). Of the seven patients who completed treatment, three reported some degree of improvement.

Behavioral Treatment of High-Medication-Consumption Headache

As noted earlier, the consumption of high doses of ergotamine tartrate or analgesics can result in increased headache frequency. Blanchard and co-workers (Blanchard, Taylor, & Dentinger, 1992; Michultka, Blanchard, Appelbaum, Jaccard, & Dentinger, 1989) provided preliminary information on the behavioral treatment of what they termed "high-medication-consumption headache." Although patients who are consuming large amounts of medication appear to be more difficult to treat than patients who are not overusing medication (Michultka et al., 1989), a treatment program that combines behavioral treatment with the gradual withdrawal of medications is associated with reduced medication use and headache frequency in some patients (Blanchard et al., 1992).

Summary

By virtue of their theoretical and technical training, psychologists have much to offer in the behavioral management of migraine and tension-type headache. In addition, psychological research has made significant contributions to the understanding of these disorders. Because the pathophysiology of headache is not well understood, symptomatic pain reduction often is the primary objective of treatment. Although the vast majority of headaches are benign, this cannot be assumed without a medical evaluation. Therefore, the evaluation must include an assessment of what medical diagnostic procedures have been performed and the diagnosis given. If there is any question about the diagnosis, then the patient must be referred for a neurological examination before behavioral therapy is begun.

In both evaluating and treating headache patients, it is important to keep in mind that pain is a subjective and personal experience that can be measured only indirectly. Pain is also a multidimensional experience, and there is much interaction among the various dimensions. The relationships between causes of pain and effects of pain tend to be blurred. Therefore, the psychologist must combine knowledge about mental health, pain, and headache in particular with sound clinical judgment in formulating and executing a behavioral treatment plan. Available research suggests that behavioral interventions can produce clinically meaningful change in headaches, and the efficacy of behavioral interventions compares favorably with the efficacy of several currently used pharmacological interventions.

REFERENCES

Adler, C. S., Alder, S. M., & Packard, R. C. (1987). *Psychiatric aspects of headache*. Baltimore: Williams & Wilkins.

Anderson, R. W. (1980). The relation of life situations, personality features, and reactions to the migraine syndrome. In D. J. Dalessio (Ed.), *Wolf's headache and other head pain* (4th ed., pp. 403–417). New York: Oxford University Press.

Andrasik, F., Blanchard, E. B., Neff, D. F., & Rodichok, L. D. (1984). Biofeedback and relaxation training for chronic headache: A controlled comparison of booster treatments and regular contacts for long-term maintenance. *Journal of Consulting and Clinical Psychology, 52*, 609–615.

Arregui, A., Cabrera, J., Leon-Velarde, F., Paredes, S., Viscarra, D., & Arbaiza, D. (1991). High prevalence of migraine in a high-altitude population. *Neurology, 41*, 1668–1669.

Blanchard, E. B. (1992). Psychological treatment of benign headache disorders. *Journal of Consulting and Clinical Psychology, 60*, 537–551.

Blanchard, E. B., & Andrasik, F. (1985). *Management of chronic headaches: A psychological approach.* Elmsford, NY: Pergamon Press.

Blanchard, E. B., Andrasik, F., Appelbaum, K. A., Evans, D. D., Myers, P., & Barron, K. D. (1986). Three studies of the psychologic changes in chronic headache patients associated with biofeedback and relaxation therapies. *Psychosomatic Medicine, 48*, 73–83.

Blanchard, E. B., Andrasik, F., Guarnieri, P., Neff, D. F., & Rodichok, L. D. (1987). Two, three, and four-year follow-up on the self-regulatory treatment of chronic headache. *Journal of Consulting and Clinical Psychology, 55*, 257–259.

Blanchard, E. B., Andrasik, F., Jurish, S. E., & Teders, S. J. (1982). The treatment of cluster headache with relaxation and thermal biofeedback. *Biofeedback and Self-Regulation, 7*, 185–191.

Blanchard, E. B., Appelbaum, K. A., Guarnieri, P., Morrill, B., & Dentinger, M. P. (1987). Five-year prospective follow-up on the treatment of chronic headache with biofeedback and/or relaxation. *Headache, 27*, 580–583.

Blanchard, E. B., Appelbaum, K. A., Radnitz, C. L., Michultka, D. M., Morrill, B., Kirsch, C., Hillhouse, J., Evans, D. D., Guarnieri, P., Attanasio, V., Andrasik, F., Jaccard, J., & Dentinger, M. P. (1990). A placebo-controlled evaluation of abbreviated progressive muscle relaxation and relaxation combined with cognitive therapy in the treatment of tension headache. *Journal of Consulting and Clinical Psychology, 58*, 210–215.

Blanchard, E. B., Appelbaum, K. A., Radnitz, C. L., Morrill, B., Michultka, D., Kirsch, C., Guarnieri, P., Hillhouse, J., Evans, D. D., Jaccard, J., & Barron, K. D. (1990). A controlled evaluation of thermal biofeedback and thermal biofeedback combined with cognitive therapy in the treatment of vascular headache. *Journal of Consulting and Clinical Psychology, 58*, 216–224.

Blanchard, E. B., Nicholson, N. L., Radnitz, C. L., Steffek, B. D., Appelbaum, K. A., & Dentinger, M. P. (1991). The role of home-practice in thermal biofeedback. *Journal of Consulting and Clinical Psychology, 59*, 507–512.

Blanchard, E. B., Nicholson, N. L., Taylor, A. E., Steffek, B. D., Radnitz, C. L., & Appelbaum, K. A. (1991). The role of regular home-practice in the relaxation treatment of tension headache. *Journal of Consulting and Clinical Psychology, 59*, 467–470.

Blanchard, E. B., Taylor, A. E., & Dentinger, M. P. (1992). Preliminary results from the self-regulatory treatment of high-medication-consumption headache. *Biofeedback and Self-Regulation, 17*, 179–202.

Breslau, N., Davis, G. C., & Andreski, P. (1991). Migraine, psychiatric disorders, and suicide attempts: An epidemiologic study of young adults. *Psychiatry Research, 37,* 11–23.

Butcher, J. N., Dahlstrom, W. G., Graham, J. R., Tellegen, A., & Kaemmer, B. (1989). *Manual for administration and scoring: MMPI-2.* Minneapolis, MN: University of Minnesota Press.

Cady, R. K., Wendt, J. K., Kirchner, J. R., Sargent, J. D., Rothrock, J. F., & Skaggs, Jr., H. (1991). Treatment of acute migraine with subcutaneous sumatriptan. *Journal of the American Medical Association, 265,* 2831–2835.

Cook, N. R., Evans, D. A., Funkenstein, H. H., Scherr, P. A., Ostfeld, A. M., Taylor, J. O., & Hennekens, C. H. (1989). Correlates of headache in a population-based cohort of elderly. *Archives of Neurology, 46,* 1338–1344.

Cott, A., Parkinson, W., Fabich, M., Bedard, M., & Marlin, R. (1992). Long-term efficacy of combined relaxation:biofeedback treatments for chronic headache. *Pain, 51,* 49–56.

Cox, D. J., Freundlich, A., & Meyer, R. G. (1975). Differential effectiveness of electromyographic feedback, verbal relaxation, and medication placebo with tension headaches. *Journal of Consulting and Clinical Psychology, 43,* 892–898.

Dalessio, D. J. (1990). The pathology of migraine. *Clinical Journal of Pain, 5,* 235–239.

De Benedittis, G., & Lorenzetti, A. (1992). The role of stressful life events in the persistence of primary headache: Major events vs. daily hassles. *Pain, 51,* 35–42.

Diamond, S. (1991). Migraine headaches. *Medical Clinics of North America, 75,* 545–566.

Diamond, S., & Dalessio, D. J. (1992a). Cluster headache. In S. Diamond & D. J. Dalessio (Eds.), *The practicing physician's approach to headache* (pp. 80–92). Baltimore: Williams & Wilkins.

Diamond, S., & Dalessio, D. J. (1992b). Migraine headache. In S. Diamond & D. J. Dalessio (Eds.), *The practicing physicians's approach to headache* (pp. 51–79). Baltimore: Williams & Wilkins.

Diamond, S., & Dalessio, D. J. (1992c). Taking a headache history. In S. Diamond & D. J. Dalessio (Eds.), *The practicing physician's approach to headache* (pp. 11–24). Baltimore: Williams & Wilkins.

Flor, H., & Turk, D. C. (1989). Psychophysiology of chronic pain: Do chronic pain patients exhibit symptom-specific psychophysiological responses? *Psychological Bulletin, 105,* 215–259.

Freedman, R. R., Sabharwal, S. C., Ianni, P., Desai, N., Wenig, P., & Mayes, M. (1988). Nonneural beta-adrenergic vasodilating mechanism in temperature biofeedback. *Psychosomatic Medicine, 50,* 394–401.

Gallagher, R. M. (1990). Precipitating causes of migraine. In S. Diamond (Ed.), *Migraine headache prevention and management* (pp. 31–44). New York: Marcel Dekker.

Gauthier, J. G., & Carrier, S. (1991). Long-term effects of biofeedback on migraine headache: A prospective follow-up study. *Headache, 31,* 605–612.

Hatch, J. P., Moore, P. J., Borcherding, S., Cyr-Provost, M., Boutros, N. N., & Seleshi, E. (1992). Electromyographic and affective responses of episodic tension-type headache patients and headache-free controls during stressful task performance. *Journal of Behavioral Medicine, 15,* 89–112.

Hatch, J. P., Moore, P. J., Cyr-Provost, M., Boutros, N. N., Seleshi, E., & Borcherding, S. (1992). The use of electromyography and muscle palpation in the diagnosis of tension-type headache with and without pericranial muscle involvement. *Pain, 49,* 175–178.

Hatch, J. P., Prihoda, T. J., & Moore, P. J. (1992). The application of generalizability theory to surface electromyographic measurements during psychophysiological stress testing: How many measurements are needed? *Biofeedback and Self-Regulation, 17,* 17–39.

Hatch, J. P., Prihoda, T. J., Moore, P. J., Cyr-Provost, M., Borcherding, S., Boutros, N. N., & Seleshi, E. (1991). A naturalistic study of the relationships among electromyographic activity, psychological stress, and pain in ambulatory tension-type headache patients and headache-free controls. *Psychosomatic Medicine, 53,* 576–584.

Henry, P., Michel, P., Brochet, B., Dartigues, J. F., Tison, S., Salamon, R., & Groupe de Recherche Interdisciplinaire sur la Migraine. (1992). A nationwide survey of migraine in France: Prevalence and clinical features in adults. *Cephalalgia, 12,* 229–237.

Holm, J. E., Holroyd, K. A., Hursey, K. G., & Penzien, D. B. (1986). The role of stress in recurrent tension headache. *Headache, 26,* 160–167.

Holroyd, K. A., & Andrasik, F. (1978). Coping and the self-control of chronic tension headache. *Journal of Consulting and Clinical Psychology, 46,* 1036–1045.

Holroyd, K. A., Andrasik, F., & Noble, J. (1980). Comparison of EMG biofeedback and credible pseudotherapy in treating tension headache. *Journal of Behavioral Medicine, 3,* 29–39.

Holroyd, K. A., Holm, J. E., Hursey, K. G., Penzien, D. B., Cordingley, G. E., Theofanous, A. G., Richardson, S. C., & Tobin, D. L. (1988). Recurrent vascular headache: Home-based behavioral treatment versus abortive pharmacological treatment. *Journal of Consulting and Clinical Psychology, 56,* 218–223.

Holroyd, K. A., Holm, J. E., Keefe, F. J., Turner, J. A., Bradley, L. A., Murphy, W. D., Johnson, P., Anderson, K., Hinkle, A. L., & O'Malley, W. B. (1992). A multicenter evaluation of the McGill Pain Questionnaire: Results from more than 1700 chronic pain patients. *Pain, 48,* 301–311.

Holroyd, K. A., Holm, J. E., Penzien, D. B., Cordingley, G. E., Hursey, K. G., Martin, N. J., & Theofanous, A. (1989). Long-term maintenance of improvements achieved with (abortive) pharmacological and nonpharmacological treatments for migraine: Preliminary findings. *Biofeedback and Self-Regulation, 14,* 301–308.

Holroyd, K. A., Nash, J. M., Pingel, J. D., Cordingley, G. E., & Jerome, A. (1991). A comparison of pharmacological (amitriptyline HCL) and non-pharmacological (cognitive–behavioral) therapies for chronic tension headaches. *Journal of Consulting and Clinical Psychology, 59,* 387–393.

Holroyd, K. A., & Penzien, D. B. (1990). Pharmacological versus nonpharmacological prophylaxis of recurrent migraine headache: A meta-analytic review of clinical trials. *Pain, 42,* 1–13.

Holroyd, K. A., Penzien, D. B., Hursey, K. G., Tobin, D. L., Rogers, L., Holm, J. E., Marcille, P. J., Hall, J. R., & Chila, A. G. (1984). Change mechanisms in EMG biofeedback training: Cognitive changes underlying improvements in tension headache. *Journal of Consulting and Clinical Psychology, 52,* 1039–1053.

Huskisson, E. C. (1983). Visual analogue scales. In R. Melzack (Ed.), *Pain measurement and assessment* (pp. 33–37). New York: Raven Press.

International Headache Society. (1988). Classification and diagnostic criteria for headache disorders, cranial neuralgias and facial pain. *Cephalalgia, 8*(Suppl. 7), 1–96.

Isler, H. (1982). Migraine treatment as a cause of chronic migraine. In F. C. Rose (Ed.), *Advances in migraine research and therapy* (pp. 159–164). New York: Raven Press.

Keefe, F. J. (1988). Behavioral assessment methods for chronic pain. In R. D. France & K. Ranga Rama Krishnan (Eds.), *Chronic pain* (pp. 298–320). Washington DC: American Psychiatric Press.

Keefe, F. J., & Block, A. R. (1982). Development of an observation method for assessing pain behavior in chronic low back pain. *Behavior Therapy, 13,* 363–375.

Keller, L. S., & Butcher, J. N. (1991). *Assessment of chronic pain patients with the MMPI-2.* Minneapolis, MN: University of Minnesota Press.

Kohler, T., & Haimerl, C. (1990). Daily stress as a trigger of migraine attacks: Results of thirteen single-subject studies. *Journal of Consulting and Clinical Psychology, 58,* 870–872.

Kohler, T., & Kosanic, S. (1992). Are persons with migraine characterized by a high degree of ambition, orderliness, and rigidity? *Pain, 48,* 321–323.

Kudrow, L. (1982). Paradoxical effects of frequent analgesic use. *Advances in Neurology, 33,* 335–341.

Kunkel, R. S. (1989). Muscle contraction (tension) headache. *Clinical Journal of Pain, 5,* 39–44.

Kunkel, R. S. (1990). Abortive treatment of migraine. In S. Diamond (Ed.), *Migraine headache prevention and management* (pp. 45–55). New York: Marcel Dekker.

Lance, F., Parkes, C., & Wilkinson, M. (1988). Does analgesic abuse cause headaches de novo? *Headache, 28,* 61–62.

Langemark, M., Jensen, K., Jensen, T. S., & Olesen, J. (1989). Pressure pain thresholds and thermal nociceptive thresholds in chronic tension-type headache. *Pain, 38,* 203–210.

Langemark, M., Jensen, K., & Olesen, J. (1990). Temporal muscle blood flow in chronic tension-type headache. *Archives of Neurology, 47,* 654–658.

Linet, M. G., Stewart, W. F., Celentano, D. D., Ziegler, D., & Sprecher, M. (1989). An epidemiologic study of headache among adolescents and young adults. *Journal of the American Medical Association, 261,* 2211–2216.

Lisspers, J., & Ost, L. G. (1990). Long-term follow-up with migraine treatment: Do the effects remain up to 6 years? *Behaviour Research and Therapy, 28,* 313–322.

Lous, I., & Olesen, J. (1982). Evaluation of pericranial tenderness and oral function in patients with common migraine, muscle contraction headache and 'combination headache. *Pain, 12,* 385–393.

Marchesi, C., DeFerri Ferri, A., Petrolini, N., Govi, A., Manzoni, G. C., Coiro, V., & DeFerri Risio, C. (1989). Prevalence of migraine and muscle tension headache in depressive disorders. *Journal of Affective Disorders, 16,* 33–36.

Mathew, N. T. (1981). Prophylaxis of migraine and mixed headache: A randomized controlled study. *Headache, 21,* 105–109.

Mathew, N. T. (1990). Drug-induced headache. *Neurologic Clinics, 8,* 903–912.

Mathew, N. T., Kurman, R., & Perez, F. (1990). Drug induced refractory headache—Clinical features and management. *Headache, 30,* 634–638.

Melzack, R. (1975). The McGill Pain Questionnaire: Major properties and scoring methods. *Pain, 1,* 277–299.

Merikangas, K. R., Angst, J., & Isler, H. (1990). Migraine and psychopathology: Results of the Zurich cohort study of young adults. *Archives of General Psychiatry, 47,* 849–853.

Michultka, D. M., Blanchard, E. B., Appelbaum, K. A., Jaccard, J., & Dentinger, M. P. (1989). The refractory headache patient: II. High medication consumption (analgesic rebound) headache. *Behavior Research and Therapy, 27,* 411–420.

Nappi, G., Bono, G., Sandrini, G., Martignoni, E., & Micieli, G. (Eds.). (1991). *Headache and depression: Serotonin pathways as a common clue.* New York: Raven Press.

National Health Interview Survey. (1991). Prevalence of chronic migraine headaches in the United States, 1980–1989. *Morbidity and Mortality Weekly Report, 40,* 331, 337–338.

Olesen, J. (1991). Clinical and pathophysiological observations in migraine and tension-type headache explained by integration of vascular, supraspinal and myofascial inputs. *Pain, 46,* 125–132.

Olesen, J., Friberg, L., Olsen, T. S., Iverson, H. K., Lassen, N. A., Anderson, A. R., & Karle, A. (1990). Timing and topography of cerebral blood flow, aura, and headache during migraine attacks. *Annals of Neurology, 28,* 791–798.

Packard, R. C. (1987). Life stress, personality factors, and reactions to headache. In D. J. Dalessio (Ed.), *Wolf's headache and other head pain* (5th ed., pp. 370–387). New York: Oxford University Press.

Paiva, T., Nunes, J. S., Moreira, A., Santos, J., Teixeira, J., & Barbosa, A. (1982). Effects of frontalis EMG biofeedback and diazepam in the treatment of tension headache. *Headache, 22,* 216–220.

Pfaffenrath, V., Hummelsberger, J., Pollmann, W., Kaube, H., & Rath, M. (1991). MMPI personality profiles in patients with primary headache syndromes. *Cephalalgia, 11,* 263–268.

Philips, C. (1977). The modification of tension headache pain using EMG biofeedback. *Behaviour Research and Therapy, 15,* 119–129.

Pikoff, H. (1984). Is the muscular model of headache still viable? A review of conflicting data. *Headache, 24,* 186–198.

Radnitz, C. L., & Blanchard, E. B. (1991). Assessment and treatment of dietary factors in refractory vascular headache. *Headache Quarterly, 2,* 214–220.

Rapoport, A. M., Weeks, R. E., Sheftell, F. D., Baskin, S. M., & Verdi, J. (1986). The "analgesic washout period": A critical variable in the evaluation of headache treatment efficacy. *Neurology, 36*(Suppl. 1), 100–101. (Abstract)

Raskin, N. H. (1988). *Headache* (2nd ed.). New York: Churchill Livingstone.

Rasmussen, B. K., Jensen, R., Schroll, M., & Olesen, J. (1991). Epidemiology of headache in a general population—A prevalence study. *Journal of Clinical Epidemiology, 44,* 1147–1157.

Rasmussen, B. K., & Olesen, J. (1992). Migraine with aura and migraine without aura: An epidemiological study. *Cephalalgia, 12,* 221–228.

Rome, H. P., Jr., Harness, D. M., & Kaplan, H. J. (1990). Psychologic and behavioral aspects of chronic facial pain. In A. L. Jacobson & W. C. Donlon (Eds.), *Headache and facial pain* (pp. 25–52). New York: Raven Press.

Rugh, J. D., Hatch, J. P., Moore, P. J., Cyr-Provost, M., Boutros, N., & Pellegrino, C. S. (1990). The effects of psychological stress on electromyographic activity and negative affect in ambulatory tension-type headache patients. *Headache, 30,* 216–219.

Saper, J. R. (1990). Migraine, migraine variants, and related vascular headaches. In A. L. Jacobson & W. C. Donolon (Eds.), *Headache and facial pain* (pp. 81–107). New York: Raven Press.

Schoenen, J., Bottin, D., Hardy, F., & Gerard, P. (1991). Cephalic and extracephalic pressure pain thresholds in chronic tension-type headache. *Pain, 40,* 65–75.

Silberstein, S. D. (1992). Evaluation and emergency treatment of headache. *Headache, 32,* 396–407.

Smith, M. J., & Jensen, N. M. (1988). The severity model of chronic headache. *Journal of General Internal Medicine, 3,* 396–409.

Somerville, B. (1972). The role of estradiol withdrawal in the etiology of menstrual migraine headache. *Neurology, 22,* 355–365.

Sovak, M., Kunzel, M., Sternbach, R. A., & Dalessio, D. J. (1981). Mechanism of the biofeedback therapy of migraine: Volitional manipulation of the psychophysiological background. *Headache, 21,* 89–92.

Sternbach, R. A. (1980). Behavioral therapies and headache. In D. J. Dalessio (Ed.), *Wolf's headache and other head pain* (4th ed., pp. 440–449). New York: Oxford University Press.

Stewart, W. F., Linet, M. S., Celentano, D. D., Van Natta, M., & Ziegler, D. (1991). Age- and sex-specific incidence rates of migraine with and without visual aura. *American Journal of Epidemiology, 134,* 1111–1120.

Stewart, W. F., Lipton, R. B., Celentano, D. D., & Reed, M. L. (1992). Prevalence of migraine headache in the United States. Relation to age, income, race, and other sociodemographic factors. *Journal of the American Medical Association, 267,* 84–89.

Subcutaneous Sumatriptan International Study Group. (1991). Treatment of migraine attacks with sumatriptan. *New England Journal of Medicine, 325,* 316–321.

Visser, W. H., Ferrari, M. D., Bayliss, E. M., Ludlow, S., & Pilgrim, A. J., for the Subcutaneous Sumatriptan International Study Group. (1992). Treatment of migraine attacks with subcutaneous sumatriptan: First placebo-controlled study. *Cephalalgia, 12,* 308–313.

Wallasch, T. M. (1992). Transcranial Doppler ultrasonic features in episodic tension-type headache. *Cephalalgia, 12,* 293–296.

Ziegler, D. K. (1987). The treatment of migraine. In D. J. Dalessio (Ed.), *Wolf's headache and other head pain* (5th ed., pp. 87–111). New York: Oxford University Press.

Chapter 5

Asthma

Thomas L. Creer and Bruce G. Bender

Considerable progress in treating asthma has been made during the past 25 years. All veteran practitioners or investigators would agree with this statement. However, if the same professionals were asked to describe where science stands with respect to the control of asthma, they would be less than sanguine. Terms such as "perplexing," "paradoxical," and "complex" would be liberally sprinkled throughout their discussion as they summarized their views regarding asthma. The reason for these words is, perhaps, best illustrated by describing epidemiological data, definitions of asthma, characteristics of the disorder, and the pathophysiology of asthma.

Epidemiology

Prevalence

In the past 2 decades, the prevalence, morbidity, and mortality of asthma in the United States and other Western countries have increased. Approximately 80 million Americans—one third of the U.S. population—suffer from a chronic respiratory disease, a category that includes asthma. This translates to a conservative estimate of 10–15 million individuals in the U.S. with asthma. On the basis of National Health Interview Survey data from 1980 through 1990 (reported in Asthma, 1992), the age-adjusted prevalence rate of self-reported asthma increased by 38%; this included a 50% increase for females and a 27% increase for males. From 1981 through 1988, the annual prevalence rate for Black females increased by 45%; the annual prevalence rate for White females increased by 63% (Asthma, 1992). Also on the basis of the National Health Interview Survey, Taylor and Newacheck (1992) reported a statistically significant increase from 3.2% in 1981 to 4.3% in 1988 in the prevalence of asthma in children younger than 18 years of age. It is known that racial or ethnic minorities who are poor and who reside in urban environments are at high risk for asthma (Weiss, Gergen, & Crain, 1992). Weiss, Gergen, and Crain (1992) noted that less is known about those who live in rural areas, in part because these populations are rarely studied. However, a report prepared for U.S. Congress (U.S. Congress, Office of Technical Assistance, 1990) indicated that chronic illness and disability affect a greater proportion of the rural than the urban population (14% vs. 12%, respectively). These data, found in several surveys by the National Center for Health Statistics, suggest the prevalence of asthma may be higher in rural than in urban areas; there simply have not been the necessary epidemiological studies to demonstrate this.

Morbidity

Morbidity data reflect the quantitative and qualitative conditions or states influenced by asthma. A number of types of data were described in a report from the Centers for Disease Control (Asthma, 1992). Results from the National Ambulatory Medical Care Survey indicated that physician visits for asthma as a first-listed diagnosis increased from 6.5 million in 1985 to 7.1 million in 1990. The age-adjusted rate of physician visits increased 35% for Blacks, but decreased 8% for Whites. For Blacks, the rate of visits decreased 46% for males, but increased 98% for females. For Whites, the rate decreased 23% for males, but increased 8% for females. From 1980 through 1990, the age-adjusted hospital discharge rate for asthma as the first-listed diagnosis varied slightly (from 180 to 188 per 100,000). Females had higher hospital discharge rates than males each year; Blacks were more than twice as likely as Whites to be hospitalized. Taylor and Newacheck (1992) reported that, compared with children without asthma, youngsters with asthma missed 10.1 million more days of school, had 12.9 million more contacts with physicians, and experienced 200,000 more hospitalizations in 1988. Almost 30% of children with asthma in the U.S. had some limitation in activity, as compared with only 5% of children without asthma.

Weiss, Gergen, and Hodgson (1992) evaluated the economic impact of asthma in the U.S. They estimated the cost of asthma at $6.206 billion in 1990. Direct costs included expenditures for hospitalizations; these costs approached $1.6 billion. Hospitalization represented the largest single direct medical expenditure for the condition, and reflected an increase of $500,000 over comparable costs reported in 1985. Costs for outpatient hospital care were estimated at $190.3 million; expenditures for care provided in hospital emergency rooms were approximately $295 million. Asthma is generally treated in outpatient settings (Sheffer, 1991). Costs for inpatient services were estimated to be $146 million; costs for outpatient services were approximately $347 million. It is paradoxical that the total estimated costs for hospital services for the treatment of asthma ($2.045 billion) far exceeded the total costs of the services received by the majority of patients with asthma ($493 million). Medications contributed approximately $1.010 billion in direct expenditures; total direct costs estimated for asthma were $3.638 billion. Indirect expenditures included reduced productivity because of loss of school days; this represented the largest single indirect cost ($899.7 million). Other indirect costs included loss of work ($849.3 million) and income lost to premature death ($819.3 million). All indirect costs for asthma were estimated at $2.568 billion. Weiss, Gergen, and Hodgson (1992) concluded that although asthma is often a mild chronic illness that can be treated with ambulatory care, 43% of its economic impact was associated with emergency room use, hospitalization, and death.

Mortality

Murray and Enarson (1992) reported that 1.5 billion people in the world are infected with the tubercle bacillus. There are 20 million active cases of the disease; moreover, 8 million new cases of tuber-culosis and 3 million deaths from the disease are reported each year. Although mortality attributed to asthma pales compared with the findings on tuberculosis, the increase in deaths from asthma is alarm-ing for two reasons. First is the magnitude of change in recent years. As noted by the Centers for Disease Control, the age-adjusted death rate for asthma as the underlying cause of death increased 45%, from 1.3 per 100,000 to 1.9 per 100,000 from 1980 through 1989 (Asthma, 1992). During this period, the death rate increased 54% for females and 23% for males. The annual death rate from asthma was consist-ently higher for Blacks than for Whites; for Blacks, the rate increased 52%, compared with a 45% increase for Whites. The increase in death rate for Black and White females was similar (63% and 64%, respec-tively). However, the increase in the death rate for Black males was more than twice that for White males (Asthma, 1992).

The second reason reflects the perplexing and paradoxical nature of asthma. New and better treatments are available for what is usually a reversible condition. There is national (Sheffer, 1991) and interna-tional (National Heart, Lung and Blood Institute, 1992) agreement on the use of these medications. Instead of an increase in death rates, the data should show a decrease in mortality from asthma; as noted, however, the opposite trend has been found. This finding is alarming to experts, who have futilely sought to determine the reason (Sheffer & Buist, 1987). The paradox of increased deaths when better treat-ments are available is enhanced by the knowledge that, as aptly pointed out by Ellis (1988), any mortality is unacceptable with a po-tentially reversible disorder such as asthma.

Definition of Asthma

Over the past few decades, a number of attempts to define asthma have been made. Committees of experts in the field have attempted to develop consensual definitions of the condition. Past efforts have failed. Reasons for the failure were summarized by Busse and Reed (1988). They noted that a clinician treating patients requires a different definition than an immunologist investigating the pathogenesis of the disorder or an epidemiologist tracking populations of patients with asthma. The frames of reference are so diverse and the types of in-formation required so different, suggested Busse and Reed, that it is not surprising that agreement on a definition of asthma is impossible to attain. In addition, the difficulty of defining asthma is increased "by the complexity and heterogeneity of the genetic, environmental, psychosocial, physiologic, and molecular biologic factors in its pathogenesis, course, and manifestations" (Busse & Reed, 1988, p. 969). Various attempts to define the disorder in terms of its cause have also failed because the cause of asthma is unknown.

A number of operational definitions have been proposed for asthma. It was assumed that the definition proposed by U.S. experts, assembled by the National Heart, Lung and Blood Institute, would provide an operational definition that would be used by all scientists who work with asthma. This definition states that:

> Asthma is a lung disease with the following characteristics: (1) airway obstruction (or airway narrowing) that is reversible (but not completely so in some patients) either spontaneously or with treatment; (2) airway inflammation; and (3) airway hyperresponsiveness to a variety of stimuli. (Sheffer, 1991, p. 57)

This description creates an operational definition of value to many scientists, particularly physicians. However, a panel of international experts on asthma, also assembled by the National Heart, Lung and Blood Institute, prepared a more comprehensive operational definition of asthma:

> Asthma is a chronic inflammatory disorder of the airways in which many cells play a role, including mast cells and eosinophils. In susceptible individuals, this inflammation causes symptoms which are usually associated with widespread but variable airflow obstruction that is often reversible, either spontaneously or with treatment, and causes an associated increase in airway responsiveness to a variety of stimuli. (National Heart, Lung and Blood Institute, 1992, p. 1)

Differences in the two definitions, both prepared by expert panels, illustrate the complexity of asthma. Confusion with respect to asthma, however, is highlighted by the knowledge that these definitions reflect only operational definitions of asthma per se. Developing an operational definition of what is referred to as an asthma attack, flare, or episode is a totally separate process that entails obtaining agreement among medical personnel, behavioral scientists, and patients (Creer, 1992).

Characteristics of Asthma

The perplexing nature of asthma is also evident in descriptions of the characteristics of the disorder. These characteristics include the intermittent, variable, and reversible nature of the disorder.

Intermittency

The number of attacks experienced varies from patient to patient and, for a given individual, from time to time. A patient may suffer a burst of attacks over a span of a few days and then go several months or even years between episodes. A second patient may have perennial asthma and have attacks on most days throughout the year. The frequency of attacks experienced by patients is a function of a number of variables, including the number and diversity of stimuli that trigger their episodes, the degree of hyperreactivity of their airways, the degree of control established over their disorder, health care variables such as access to asthma specialists, and patient variables such as medication compliance. Any of these variables may produce dramatic changes in a given individual's asthma.

The intermittent nature of asthma presents three problems to scientists (Renne & Creer, 1985). First, the intermittency of attacks makes it difficult, if not impossible, to recruit a homogeneous population of asthmatic subjects. Recruiting only patients with perennial asthma does not control the problem because these patients may be differentially affected by factors unrelated to a study, such as an outbreak of flu or changes in medical treatment, that independently alter their rates of attacks. Second, the intermittent nature of asthma makes it difficult to gather long-term data on it. This can be a problem for scientists who seek to determine if various interventions, including behavioral approaches, have long-term benefits. Changes may occur because of the treatment; however, particularly with children, these changes may be inextricably woven into maturational transitions. Finally, the intermittency of attacks generates different expectations in patients. Those with perennial asthma anticipate they will experience asthma throughout the year; consequently, they are usually prepared to manage episodes. Patients with more intermittent asthma, however, acquire different expectations. They often are not only unprepared to manage occasional episodes, but also fail to anticipate what may be a severe attack of asthma.

Variability

Variability is a term used to refer both to the severity of a patient's asthma and to the intensity of discrete attacks. Use of the term is confusing in that it is not always clear whether *severity* is being used to refer to the general condition of patients or to the specific attacks they experience. Two additional issues are raised by the ambiguity of the term *severity*. First, until recently, there has been no consensual agreement as to how to classify either a given attack or the asthma per se of a patient as mild, moderate, or severe. Although the terms were used throughout the asthma literature, there were, paradoxically, no established criteria for their use. This situation may be changing as the "Guidelines for the Diagnosis and Management of Asthma" (Sheffer, 1991) and the *International Consensus Report* (National Heart, Lung and Blood Institute, 1992) both offered a general classification of asthma severity and a guide for treatment of patients who experience mild, moderate, or severe asthma attacks. Second, Renne and Creer (1985) cautioned that patients acquire different expectations as a function of the severity of their attacks. If their episodes are mild, they tend to anticipate that all future attacks will be mild and are unprepared to cope with more severe attacks if they occur. A single severe attack not only can lead to psychological and behavioral reactions that can exacerbate a given attack, but it also may alter, sometimes unrealistically, the patient's anticipation of future attacks. Creer (1979), for example, noted that patients who panic during asthmatic episodes usually acquired the behavior because of a single incident when they or those around them became overly frightened. Expectations that they will experience only mild attacks of asthma can lead patients to delay seeking medical attention for severe episodes when they occur. Failure to seek prompt and aggressive medical action for attacks that increasingly intensify in severity is an oft-cited factor contributing to deaths from asthma (e.g., Sheffer & Buist, 1987).

Reversibility

McFadden (1980) noted that reversibility was the sine qua non of asthma; it distinguished the condition from other respiratory disorders, particularly emphysema, which is not reversible. As with other characteristics of asthma, however, the characteristic is perplexing. First, reversibility may be relative. Although most patients show complete reversibility of airway obstruction with appropriate treatment, others do not totally reverse their asthma with intensive therapy (Loren et al., 1978). Because total reversibility of asthma does not occur in all patients, the reports of experts in both the U.S. (Sheffer, 1991) and internationally (National Heart, Lung and Blood Institute, 1992) note this fact in their definitions of asthma. Second, the spontaneous remission of some attacks makes it impossible to prove a cause–effect relationship between changes in a patient's asthma and an intervention for the disorder (Creer, 1982). Although outcome data may support a particular intervention, a remission of symptoms can occur spontaneously and coincidentally to the intervention.

Pathophysiology of Asthma

The perplexing and paradoxical nature of asthma has been described. The complexity of asthma, however, is best revealed in discussing current knowledge and thought regarding the pathogenesis of the disorder. It is imperative that behavioral scientists understand current findings on the pathogenesis of asthma if they are to collaborate with medical and biological scientists. A model of the pathogenesis of asthma, expanded from a version by Creer and Bender (in press), is presented in Figure 1.

Stimuli

Stimuli implicated in the pathogenesis of asthma include irritants, exercise and cold air, respiratory infections, allergens, aspirin and related substances, and emotional situations and responses (Reed & Townley, 1983). Irritants, exercise and cold air, and respiratory infections influence anyone with asthma; allergens, aspirin and related substances, and emotional situations and responses affect only some patients. The specific stimuli that provoke given attacks vary both across patients and within a given individual. It is impossible to say with certainty what stimulus or set of stimuli caused a given attack; all that can be identified are the stimuli correlated with a specific episode (Creer & Kotses, 1990). A stimulus may interact with other stimuli, often in an additive manner, to induce an attack, which thereby increases the difficulty of identifying what stimulus or set of stimuli produced a particular episode. For this reason, Reed and Townley (1983) pointed out that "some episodes of asthma do not have a recognizable stimulus" (p. 813).

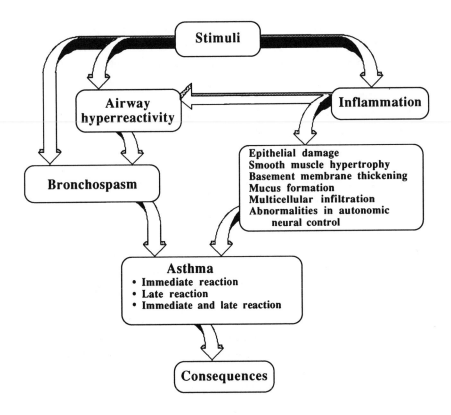

Figure 1.   Model of asthma.

Linking Stimuli to Physiological Responses

A number of factors have been proposed as linking stimuli to the respiratory responses that constitute asthma. As depicted in Figure 1, two are prominent: airway hyperreactivity and inflammation. Asthma is characterized by airway hyperreactivity or hyperresponsiveness, a condition characterized by an exaggerated bronchoconstrictor response both to physical changes and to chemical and pharmacological agents. In addition, the level of airway reactivity to different stimuli is usually correlated with the severity of asthma (Sheffer, 1991). Airway hyperresponsiveness is ubiquitous in patients with asthma; Ellis (1988) referred to hyperreactivity as "a fundamental and intrinsic characteristic of all individuals with asthma, both children and adults" (p. 1039). A number of mechanisms of airway hyperreactivity in asthma, including "airway inflammation, abnormalities in bronchial epithelial integrity, alterations in autonomic neural control of airways, changes in intrinsic bronchial smooth muscle function, and baseline airflow obstruction" (Sheffer, 1991, p. 58), have been proposed.

In recent years, evidence has indicated that airway inflammation plays a significant role in asthma. As Madison (1991) explained, "Inflammation of the airways, whether it be stimulated by immunological or nonimmunological mechanisms, may be the critical event that promotes the development of asthma in general" (p. 175). Mechanisms contributing to airway inflammation in asthma are multiple and involve a number of different inflammatory cells. It is unlikely that asthma is caused by either a single cell or a single inflammatory mediator. Rather, "asthma results from complex interactions among inflammatory cells, mediators, and the cells and tissues resident in the airways" (Sheffer, 1991, p. 58). Results may involve changes noted in Figure 1; these include epithelial damage, smooth muscle hypertrophy, basement membrane thickening, mucus formation, multicellular infiltration, and abnormalities in autonomic neural control (Busse, 1992; Sheffer, 1991). Proposed pathways in the pathogenesis of airway hyperreactivity and inflammation in asthma were outlined by the panel of experts on asthma (Sheffer, 1991).

Asthma

Characteristics of asthma have been described. However, Figure 1 shows that, with exposure to a precipitating stimulus or set of stimuli, a patient may experience an immediate (within minutes of exposure) reaction, a late (hours after exposure) response, or both an immediate and a delayed reaction (Busse, 1992; Larson, 1992). These reactions not only further obscure the question of causality between stimuli and asthma but make it difficult for patients to correlate specific stimuli to given asthmatic episodes. Different reactions to precipitating stimuli pose further difficulties to scientists who work with asthma.

Behavioral scientists have primarily investigated stimuli correlated with asthma and psychological or behavioral responses to the disorder. The focus in the past was often on delineating the role of specific stimuli correlated with asthma, such as suggestion and emotions. Suggestion and asthma were reviewed by Kotses, Hindi-Alexander, and Creer (1989); the evidence suggests that psychologically induced airway changes may be a function of variation in general activation level and not changes in asthma severity. The relationship of emotions, personality, and asthma was thoroughly reviewed by Lehrer, Isenberg, and Hochron (1993); they successfully conveyed the complexity of delineating these variables and how they relate to one another. Although additional research must be conducted on the nature of the relationship of various psychological or behavioral stimuli to asthma, such as occurs with risk factor analyses, recent investigation has veered more toward the investigation of responses to asthma. Psychologists have cooperated with other asthma experts in the treatment of asthma. Working with physicians, nurses, educators, and allied health personnel, health psychologists have contributed their unique expertise to achieving the goals both of controlling asthma and of permitting patients to experience life to the same degree as individuals without asthma. Although a myriad of topics can be covered in describing the contributions of psychology, this chapter reviews assessment of responses and behavioral interventions to change asthma and reactions to the disorder.

Assessment

A number of topics have generated research. Included are the assessment of asthma knowledge and management, attitudes toward asthma and asthma management, quality of life, compliance, and neuropsychological changes.

Asthma Knowledge and Management

Evaluations of asthma knowledge and management have included a number of approaches and a wide diversity of content. Four of the nine questionnaires listed in Table 1 were designed to assess the knowledge of children (or children with their parents), and the remaining four were designed to evaluate the knowledge base in asthmatic adults. One questionnaire contained over 100 items (Quirk & Jones, 1990; Tehan, Sloane, Walsh-Robart, & Chamberlain, 1989), and another contained only 12 items (Bauman et al., 1989). Although some instruments were aimed at college-educated asthmatic patients

Table 1

Asthma Knowledge and Management

Study	Test name	Number of items	Content areas	Target group	Method of administration
Donnelly, Spykerboer, & Thong (1985); Spykerboer, Donnelly, & Thong (1986); Donnelly, Donnelly, & Thong (1987)	Unnamed	77	Parent knowledge and misconceptions about etiology, pathophysiology, symptomatology, triggers, outcome, and environmental factors (outdoor play, urban vs. rural living, effect of diet)	Parents of asthmatic children	Interviewer-administered questionnaire
Eiser, Town, & Tripp (1988)	Unnamed	30	General knowledge about the body; knowledge and attitudes about asthma (including attacks, attack avoidance, allergens, exercise, food, and emotions)	7–16-year-old asthmatic children	Interviewer-administered questionnaire with discussion probe
Tehan, Sloane, Walsh-Robart, & Chamberlain (1989)	Asthma Knowledge Test	29	Knowledge about asthma, anatomy and physiology of the lungs, asthma triggers, early warning signs, self-management, decision making, problem solving, and medications	Asthmatic college students	Self-administered questionnaire

continued

Quirk & Jones (1990)	Unnamed	76	29 items pertain to severity and frequency of symptoms; 47 pertain to the effects of asthma on daily living	Asthmatic adults	Interviewer-administered questionnaire
Taggart et al. (1991)	Unnamed	16	Child's asthma management knowledge in 3 areas: response to identified triggers	9–12-year-old inner-city, hospitalized asthmatic children	Self-administered questionnaire (parents were allowed to read items to child)
Taylor et al. (1991)	Test of Management Competency	3	Family asthma management knowledge and behavior was scored following presentation of 3 types of asthma episodes	5–11-year-old asthmatic children	Interviewer-presented; responses were videotaped
Jenkinson, Davison, Jones, & Hawtin (1988)	Unnamed	Unknown	Instrument assesses patients' knowledge of the use of bronchodilators and prophylactic drugs, if applicable; perceived disability from asthma is also measured	Asthmatic children	Self-administered, or with younger child, parent-administered
Bauman et al. (1989)	Unnamed	12	Knowledge of pathophysiology of attacks; perceptions of preventive behavior; attitudes toward self and others; and perception of personal control	Asthmatic adults	Self-administered questionnaire

Table 1 (*continued*)

Study	Test name	Number of items	Content areas	Target group	Method of administration
Parcel, Nader, Tiernan (1980)	Parcel Knowledge of Asthma Questionnaire	27	Knowledge of childhood asthma	Children with asthma and their parents	Self-administered questionnaire
Mesters, Pieterse, & Meertens (1991)	Unnamed	43 (knowledge and attitudes only)	Three-part questionnaire that includes demographic items: 10 items on medication instruction, 17 items on knowledge of asthma symptoms, 12 items on knowledge about actions during an asthma attack; and 4 items regarding parental perceived satisfaction with provided care from general practitioner	Asthmatic children	Completed by child's parents

continued

Ringsberg, Wiklund, & Wilhelmsen (1990)	Unnamed	Not cited	Three-part questionnaire concerned with treatment of asthma and information given to patient, as well as work and leisure activities; questions from the Nottingham Health Profile, the Mood Adjective Checklist, and the Quality of Life in Severe Heart Failure; and knowledge about asthma.	Asthmatic adults	Self-administered questionnaire
McNabb, Wilson-Pessano, & Jacobs (1986)	Critical Incident Study		Competency was assessed in four areas: prevention, intervention, compensatory behaviors, and external controlling factors.	Asthmatic children (and their parents, physicians, teachers)	Informants were asked to think of a time when the child effectively or ineffectively managed asthma symptoms

(Tehan et al., 1989), at least one measure was constructed to evaluate knowledge in low-income, inner-city children with asthma (Taggart et al., 1991).

Asthma knowledge and management questionnaires target several objectives. In several cases, questionnaires were introduced to evaluate changes in asthma and asthma management knowledge that occurred as a result of a specific intervention program. For example, Taggart and colleagues (1991) used their brief questionnaire in a pre- and posttest design to evaluate, in part, the effectiveness of a 3-month educational program that included a variety of written materials, videotape presentations, and discussions with a nurse aimed at improving asthma knowledge and self-management in 6- to 16-year-old low-income children. Parcel, Nader, and Tiernan (1980) provided a school-based educational program to 53 children whose parents identified them as having asthma, using child and parent questionnaires developed specifically to detect pre- and posttest changes in asthma knowledge.

A second objective of asthma knowledge and management questionnaires has been to reveal misconceptions regarding asthma that might cause underutilization of medical care and noncompliance. For example, Spykerboer, Donnelly, and Thong (1986) included items in their questionnaire designed to measure not only knowledge but also blatant misperceptions about asthma (e.g., that asthma can be caused by swallowing a hard object). A third objective has been to identify within a single questionnaire the relationship between the degree of asthma knowledge and the behaviors and psychological constructs related to asthma care. Bauman et al. (1989) attempted to profile asthma knowledge, perceptions of preventive behavior, attitudes toward self and others, and perceptions of personal control, all within an instrument that included only 12 items. At least two asthma knowledge and management questionnaires added items that assess quality of life, that is, the impact of asthma on work and leisure activities (Quirk & Jones, 1990; Ringsberg, Wiklund, & Wilhelmsen, 1990).

Excluding assessment of attitudes, perceptions, and quality of life, the evaluations of knowledge and management are diverse and can be broadly grouped into three categories: (a) evaluation of knowledge of the body, including pathophysiology, asthma symptoms, and early warning signs; (b) evaluation of knowledge of what triggers or exacerbates asthma, including allergens, smoke, emotions, exercise, food, and viral infections; and (c) evaluation of specific management behaviors, including behaviors aimed at preventing asthma attacks, as well as behaviors exhibited during an asthma attack that might result in symptom improvement or exacerbation.

The assessment format varies across instruments. Most instruments consist of questionnaires. In the case of child-completed questionnaires, some reports indicated that parents were allowed to read items to the child if the child's reading level was not adequate for the level of the items (Taggart et al., 1991); other instruments sought to evaluate parental knowledge and therefore required only the parent to complete the questionnaire (Mesters, Pieterse, & Meertens, 1991). Three questionnaires were administered by a trained interviewer (Donnelly, Spykerboer, & Thong, 1985; Quirk & Jones, 1990; Taylor et al., 1991), thus allowing additional probes in order to reveal more about the subjects' understanding of asthma. At least two sets of investigators altered the questionnaire approach to use innovative procedures to evaluate capacity for asthma management. Taylor et al. (1991) presented families of asthmatic children with descriptions of three asthma episode scenarios; the families' responses were videotaped and scored according to their demonstrated capacity to intervene. McNabb, Wilson-Pessano, and Jacobs (1986) used the critical incident technique, which consisted of asking the child, the parents, or both to describe a recent incident that demonstrated effective or ineffective handling of the child's asthma symptoms; the various adaptive behaviors reported by many different patients were documented, although no approach to quantifying management competency for each individual was clearly described.

In summary, the objectives, content, format, and target populations of asthma knowledge and management assessment tools are heterogeneous, making comparisons difficult and sometimes meaningless. Nonetheless, several criticisms can be proffered. Instruments that attempt to accomplish numerous goals, such as measuring knowledge, management competency, attitudes, belief systems, and quality of life, seldom accomplish all their objectives; they frequently yield a complex and confusing series of scores whose meaning is difficult to interpret, particularly in the absence of reliability or validity data. Those questionnaires that appear to have the clearest meaning and greatest utility attempt to attain a specific goal, such as assessing knowledge of a specific body of information. Jenkinson, Davison,

Jones, and Hawtin (1988), for example, included a series of questions about the use of bronchodilators and prophylactic drugs. However, rapidly changing approaches to asthma treatment greatly limit the ongoing use of any single questionnaire. Therefore, selection of assessment instruments for research or clinical purposes may depend on the use of instruments that are clear and specific in their goals and that are repeatedly updated as knowledge about asthma and its treatment increases.

Attitudes Toward Asthma and Asthma Management

Attempts to evaluate attitudes toward asthma have been even more problematic than attempts to evaluate asthma knowledge and management. The use of the term *attitudes* suggests the sharing of a singular concept across studies that, on close inspection, reveal an enormous range of objectives, some of which have little to do with attitudes. The collection of asthma attitude questionnaires in Table 2 includes attempts to measure a variety of psychological constructs, sometimes poorly defined, which include ego strength, vulnerability, panic–fear, belief in treatment efficacy, self-efficacy, and locus of control. Although some of these instruments are theory based, it is frequently difficult to determine whether the labeled theoretical construct is in fact being measured. Although evaluation of a child's perception of "self-efficacy to prevent illness" is laudable (Clark et al., 1988), it is difficult to determine whether scores produced by a self-efficacy questionnaire clearly reflect the child's belief that he or she can alter the course of his or her own illness, particularly when information about reliability and validity is unavailable. Although asthma attitude questionnaires are of interest in their attempt to build a theoretical foundation regarding perceptions and beliefs about asthma, none can be adopted as a dependent measure in a study of asthmatic children unless a primary objective is to evaluate further the characteristics of the instrument.

In many cases, asthma attitude questionnaires appear to evaluate constructs not labeled as such in the questionnaires. Specifically, many instruments contain questions whose answers may in fact reflect feelings of hopelessness and depression. In the questionnaire used by Bauman et al. (1989), for example, subject questions appeared to be loaded for depressive symptomatology (e.g., "I often feel angry about my asthma," or "asthma affects my moods and feelings"). At a minimum, the correlation between scores from these instruments and instruments that more directly evaluate children's depression, such as the Beck Depression Inventory and the Children's Depression Inventory, must be examined before further conclusions about what they measure can be drawn. Some asthma attitude questionnaires, such as the Asthma Self-Efficacy Scale (Tobin, Wigal, Winder, Holroyd, & Creer, 1987), may have a significant association with compliance. Mothers who express the belief that their behavior can significantly affect their child's illness (i.e., belief in self-efficacy) were found in one study to be more adherent to prescribed medical procedures (Radius et al., 1978). Other "attitudes" may demonstrate a similar relationship to compliance and provide important information about subject variables to mediate compliance. Again, the utility of these measures will be realized only when it is clear what they are measuring.

Quality of Life

Attempts to measure quality of life result from a desire to evaluate the broad impact of specific diseases or disabilities and to compare the effects of different treatments in controlled outcome studies. Life-quality measures were preceded by traditional approaches to health measurement that include the assessment of mortality and morbidity. As noted earlier, the concept of morbidity has sometimes been expanded to include work or school days missed because of illness or disability. Life-quality assessment assumes a broader look at the impact of illness on the individual's well-being and may include the assessment of work, income, physical activity, social life, sexual activity, and mood states.

The measurement of life quality is not new. The Karnofsky Performance Status scale was one of the earliest measures of life quality and is based on physician or observer appraisals of physical functioning (Karnofsky, Abelman, Carver, & Burchenal, 1948). The assessment of life quality in adults with chronic obstructive pulmonary disease (COPD) includes a brief instrument, adopted by the American Lung Association (1975), that assigns patients to one of five functional levels reflecting global assessment of work ability, physical activity, and self-care. As with the Karnofsky scale, this instrument had the

Table 2
Asthma Attitudes

Study	Test name	Number of items	Content areas	Target group	Method of administration
Deynes (1980); Gochman & Saucier (1982); Gaut & Kieckhefer (1988)	Deynes	77	42 items: 6 factors of health care agency; ego strength and decision-making capabilities; relative valuing of health; knowledge and decision-making experiences; physical energy; feelings; attitudes toward health 22 items: self-care practices 13 items: health status	Chronically ill adolescents	Self-administered questionnaire
Richards et al. (1989)	Asthma Opinion Survey	33	Attitudes regarding asthma, falling into 11 clusters: general vulnerability, specific vulnerability, attitudes toward patient knowledge, recognition of airway obstruction, accessibility of health care, panic–fear, belief in treatment efficacy, staff–patient relationships, sense of control, personal impact, social impact	Asthmatic adults	Self-administered questionnaire
Sibbald (1989); Sibbald, Collier, & D'Souza (1986)	Unnamed	31	Statements regarding attitudes and beliefs that determine illness behavior in asthma; patients indi-	Adults	Self-administered questionnaire

continued

Source	Name	No.	Description	Population	Administration
Clark et al. (1988)	Unnamed	7	cate their view on each item on a 4-point scale anchored by *strongly agree* at one end and *strongly disagree* at the other. Three models used: Model 1 assesses beliefs, including child's perception of self-efficacy to prevent illness, and behaviors; Model 2 is composed of three nonbehavioral variables influential in self-management, e.g., child's age, history of hospitalization, and whether child has participated in health education and self-management program; Model 3 is a combination of Models 1 and 2	Asthmatic children between 7 and 17 years	Interviewer-administered questionnaire
Tobin, Wigal, Winder, Holroyd, & Creer (1987)	Asthma Self-Efficacy Scale	80	Assesses the self-efficacy of patients in managing their asthma	Asthmatic adults	Self-administered questionnaire
Parcel & Meyer (1978)	Children's Health Locus of Control Scale	20	Instrument assesses children's locus of control with respect to the management of asthma	Asthmatic children	Self-administered
Tehan, Sloane, Walsh-Robart, & Chamberlain (1989)	Asthma Attitudes Test	20	Attitudes about asthma: self-confidence, satisfaction with activity level, understanding and control of asthma, and perception of personal health	Asthmatic college students	Self-administered questionnaire

advantage of allowing the clinician to assess quickly the patient's functional level on a single continuum of adaptation, thus providing a straightforward, global picture of the quality of the patient's daily life. Although such instruments have provided a picture of the physical incapacity rendered by a particular disease, they are narrow in their definition of life quality. Subsequently developed life-quality instruments have attempted to include numerous areas of behavior and subjective states, including leisure activity, sports, eating, home management, body care, communication skills, interactions with family members, psychological outlook, feelings of hopelessness, and general emotional adjustment.

Table 3 contains a selected number of life-quality instruments, including three developed specifically for use with adult asthmatic patients and five scales that have been widely used with a variety of chronically ill patient groups. The number of items is variable; the Sickness Impact Profile, one of the longest, includes 136 items. Because they are specific to asthmatic populations, the Living With Asthma Questionnaire and the Asthma Quality-of-Life Questionnaire have several advantages for this population: they include questions about asthma symptoms and the use of asthma medication and are not focused on the more severely disabling conditions that some life-quality instruments attempt to assess.

The diversity of instruments described in Table 3 reflects both the strengths and weaknesses of this area of assessment. Clearly, the meaning of life quality is broad, and there is no standard operational definition that has been widely accepted. The clinician or investigator who wishes to include life-quality assessment in clinical outcome trials may choose from a variety of instruments, depending on what content appears relevant to a particular investigation. It is apparent that outcomes may vary considerably, depending on the instrument chosen; at the same time, comparison of life-quality outcomes across investigations using different instruments may have no validity. An interesting alternative to most of the other life-quality instruments is the use of "well-years" or "quality-adjusted life-years" (Kaplan, 1985). The primary goal of quality-adjusted survival analysis is to estimate a level of wellness between optimal functioning and death. The quality-adjusted life-years analysis attempts to take into consideration the quality-of-life consequences of specific illnesses. Using a formula that assigns a numerical value to the reduction in life quality imposed by the disease, the system simultaneously and quantitatively attempts to consider mortality, morbidity, and preference weights for behavioral states of function on a 0–1.0 wellness scale. This well-quantified system provides a single number, which simplifies between-group comparisons within studies as well as comparisons across separate outcome trials. However, the conceptual utility of this approach is questionable. The primary motivation for using life-quality measures is to better understand the real-world impact of a disease on patients' day-to-day living. The quality-adjusted survival analysis approach, although it provides a well-defined numerical measurement system, provides little insight into the personal world of chronically ill patients.

The impact of chronic asthma on the individual's life can be significant, and the success of asthma intervention must continue to be measured not only by the presence of illness symptoms but also by changes in the individual's capacity to lead a fulfilling life. At present, no available life-quality measure is sufficient to stand alone in a clinical outcome study. The "battery approach" remains the best alternative for providing adequate assessment of life-quality changes. The battery approach involves the selection of a set of behavioral instruments, each of which measures a different area of functioning and behavioral adaptation. This approach has several advantages. First, it allows for the selection of tests and questionnaires that have been well investigated and are known to provide valid assessment of a particular area of functioning. For example, there are several well-standardized instruments that can provide a clearer understanding of the impact of a specific illness on mood than can a subset of questions about hopelessness and future outlook in a life-quality questionnaire whose validity with respect to changes in mood state has not been adequately researched. The second advantage of the battery approach is that it allows investigators to select functional areas of relevance to individual studies. If the physical adaptation, social adaptation, and cognitive alertness of a patient population are of particular interest, specific instruments that address each area in question can be selected. Third, the inclusion of life-quality instruments with other standardized behavioral measures allows the life-quality instrument to be validated against and compared with other specific measures.

Life-quality instruments are best viewed as one component of the battery approach and not as instruments that can by themselves eval-

Table 3
Quality of Life

Study	Test name	Number of items	Content areas	Target group	Method of administration
American Lung Association (1975)	Unnamed	5	Clinician assigns patient to 1 of 5 functional levels reflecting global assessment of work ability, physical activity, and self-care	Adult COPD patients	Clinician-assigned rating
Hyland, Finnis, & Irvine (1991)	Living With Asthma Questionnaire	68	Social/leisure, sport, sleep, holidays, work and other activities, colds, mobility, effects on others, medication usage, doctors, and dysphoric states and attitudes	Adult asthma patients	Self-administered questionnaire
Juniper et al. (1992)	Asthma Quality of Life Questionnaire	32	Asthma symptoms, responses to environmental stimuli, avoidance of these stimuli, activity limitation, dysfunction	Adult asthma patients	Self-administered questionnaire
Spitzer et al. (1981)	Quality of Life Index	15	Activity of daily living, health, social support, feelings of healthiness, and psychological outlook	Adults with cancer	Self- or interviewer-administered

continued

Bergner, Bobbitt, Carter, & Gilson (1981)	Sickness Impact Profile	136	Sleep and rest, eating, work, home management, recreation, ambulation, mobility, body care, social interaction alertness, emotional behavior, and communication	Adults with varying chronic illness	Self-administered
Bush (1983)	Quality of Well-Being Scale		"Functional levels" are established for each of 3 function scales: mobility, physical activity, and social activity	Adult patients with various diseases and disabilities	Self-report and structured interview
Katz, Ford, Moskowitz, Jackson, & Jaffee (1963)	Index of Activities of Daily Living	6	The patient is placed on 1 of 7 levels of self-care in bathing, dressing, toileting, transfer, continence, and feeding	Elderly and chronically ill adult patients	Clinician-assigned rating
Chambers, MacDonald, Tugwell, Buchanan, & Kraag (1982)	McMaster Health Index Questionnaire	74	Physical adjustment (mobility, self-care, communication), social adjustment (general well-being, work/social role performance, family and friend support/participation), and emotional adjustment (self-esteem, personal relationships, thoughts about the future, and critical life events)	Adult patients with various illnesses and disabilities	Self-administered questionnaire

Note. COPD = chronic obstructive pulmonary disease.

uate the physical, social, and psychological ramifications of chronic illness. Two investigations demonstrated the use of life-quality instruments in a larger behavioral test battery (McSweeny, Grant, Heaton, Adams, & Timms, 1982; Prigatano, Wright, & Levin, 1984). In both studies, COPD patients completed a test battery that included the Sickness Impact Profile, the Profile of Mood States, the Minnesota Multiphasic Personality Inventory, and the Katz Adjustment Scale. The battery allowed multiple comparisons of results from psychological tests and medical evaluations to provide a comprehensive picture of the impact of COPD on the lives of patients. A similar strategy is recommended for the assessment of life-quality in patients with asthma.

Compliance

The measurement of compliance in the use of asthma medications has received considerable attention because noncompliance has generally been found to fall between 25% and 50% among asthmatic patients (Eraker, Kirscht, & Becker, 1984). In a study conducted by the Upjohn Company, 14% of patients receiving a prescription did not fill their prescription (Market Facts, Inc., 1985). Noncompliance is not unique to asthma; it is common for situations in which long-term medications are required to control chronic illness. For example, patients requiring medication to control hypertension are frequently noncompliant, a finding linked to the fact that, as with some asthma medications, the benefits of taking antihypertensive medications are not immediately apparent to patients (Krall, 1991).

A number of factors complicate attempts to measure and understand noncompliance. The initial question of noncompliance is, "Is the patient taking his medication?" However, observations of medication-taking behavior indicate that patterns of noncompliance may be complex. Lasagna and Hutt (1991) suggested that noncompliance can take four forms: (a) taking more medication than prescribed; (b) taking less medication than prescribed; (c) taking the medicine at different times or different intervals than instructed; and (d) taking medication under contraindicated conditions (e.g., at mealtime, before bedtime, etc.). Noncompliant medication-taking behavior may also be distinguished as "active," versus "passive." Passive noncompliance occurs when patients forget to take their medication; active noncompliance involves patient behaviors deliberately designed to misrepresent their compliance. In a study of 115 asthmatic adults, Rand et al. (1992) found that 14% "dumped" the contents of their aerosolized medication canisters within 3 hours of a scheduled visit in an apparent attempt to appear compliant to study personnel who weighed canister contents at each visit. Active noncompliance is troubling both because it contradicts the notion that noncompliance occurs because patients are naive and forgetful and because it indicates that patients may manipulate information available to physicians and study personnel. In terms of individual patient care, such action may cause the physician to prescribe a different medication or a stronger dosage of a medication in a well-meaning but ill-informed attempt to foster better control of asthma symptoms. When noncompliance occurs in clinical drug studies, several undesirable outcomes can occur: (a) Noncompliance may reduce the likelihood that an effective medicine will in fact be shown to be effective, (b) investigators may compensate for the absence of drug efficacy by increasing the dose to alter undercompliance, and (c) higher doses may result in increased incidence of more severe adverse reactions (Lasagna & Hutt, 1991).

Most physicians are not adept at judging noncompliance in their patients, even when they believe they have an accurate perception of their patients' medication-taking behavior (Spector & Mawhinney, 1991). Two techniques commonly used in clinical trials to evaluate patient compliance, pill counts and medication diaries, are often inaccurate. In a study of antacid consumption in ulcer patients, a 36% discrepancy was identified between pill counts and physiological measures (Roth, Carson, & Hsi, 1970); in numerous instances, the physiological measures showed lower compliance than indicated by the volume of returned pills. A technique similar to pill counting involves the weighing of canisters of aerosolized medication to determine the amount of medication used. As just described, patients may discharge their aerosol canisters before scheduled visits; the result is that canister weights suggest a level of compliance that is inaccurate (Rand et al., 1992). Medication diaries, completed by patients at home, may also overstate compliance. A recent study of asthmatic adults revealed that, although 87% of adult asthmatic patients reported on their diary cards that they used their inhaler at least twice daily, electronic recordings of inhaler use indicated only 52% of the patients used the inhaler with that frequency (Tashkin et al., 1991).

Because neither physicians nor patients can be relied on to provide accurate assessments of compliance, more objective assessment procedures must be used. Two such procedures are blood screening and electronic monitoring. Measuring the presence of a specific drug in the blood stream can be achieved with some drugs, such as theophylline, directly through blood serum analysis (Ellis, 1988). Unfortunately, many medications cannot be directly detected in blood or urine analysis. In some cases, a riboflavin tracer can be added to a medication to assess compliance (Cluss, Epstein, Galvis, Fireman, & Friday, 1984). Although this approach is objective and quantifiable, measurement of theophylline or riboflavin in the blood can be complicated by variations in rates of absorption, metabolism, and elimination. In addition, as is the case with pill counts, patients may increase their intake of the medication shortly before a scheduled appointment to artificially create an image of compliance. Microprocessor-chip recording of medication use provides the most reliable evidence of patient compliance because it records the exact date and time an aerosol medication is discharged or a pill is removed from a container. Several studies of compliance in asthmatic adults have used a nebulizer chronolog, a portable device that houses a standard nebulizer canister capable of recording the date and time of each use of aerosolized medication (Mawhinney et al., 1991; Rand et al., 1992; Spector et al., 1986; Tashkin et al., 1991). Two methods for recording the date and time of medication removal from pill containers have been used in clinical trials (Cramer, Mattson, Prevey, Scheyer, & Oulette, 1989; Eisen, Miller, Woodward, Spitnagel, & Przybeck, 1990). The first method, labeled the Medication Event Monitoring System, consists of a bottle cap equipped with a microprocessor chip that registers each time the cap is removed from the bottle (Cramer et al., 1989; Oliverieri, Matsui, Hermann, & Koren, 1991); the second records individual pill removal from a blister sheet wired with loops carrying low-voltage current and including an electronic memory that records pill removal (Eisen et al., 1990). The use of microprocessors to record medication usage in each of these approaches advances compliance methodology significantly by providing the capacity to determine not only how much medication has been consumed, but also patterns of medication usage. Such patterns may reveal whether patients skip medication dosages at regular or random intervals, whether they consume a double dose of a particular medication when they omit a previous dose, whether compliance is higher immediately before and after scheduled visits, and whether compliance is greater during periods when the patient's asthma symptoms are worse. Given the complexity of measuring patient compliance and the potential gravity of misrepresenting medication-taking behaviors, it has been strongly recommended that two or more measures of compliance be used in any single investigation (Rapoff & Barnard, 1991).

For the practicing clinician, medication monitoring may be useful with individual patients, particularly for situations in which noncompliance is suspected or in which adequate control of asthma symptoms has been elusive. One of the simplest ways to assess compliance in a clinical setting is to check pharmacy records to determine whether the number of medication refills matches the amount of medication prescribed. When the clinician has evidence that a patient has been significantly noncompliant, confronting the individual with this information may defeat attempts to alter the behavior. Instead, further education about the role of medications in controlling asthma and more frequent monitoring by clinical personnel may help ensure that the patient will appropriately use medications.

Neuropsychological Changes

A number of investigations have been conducted to determine (a) whether patients with asthma have an increased incidence of neuropsychological dysfunction, (b) whether there are common neuropsychological problems in this population, and (c) whether the specific source of these deficits can be identified. Neuropsychological impairment, most frequently in the form of deficits in abstract reasoning, memory, and speed of performance, has been reported in adult patients with COPD (Grant, Heaton, McSweeney, Adams, & Timms, 1980; Krop, Block, & Cohen, 1973). Prigatano, Parsons, Wright, Levin, and Hawryluk (1983) also identified mild neuropsychological impairments in 100 COPD patients, compared with 25 healthy controls, and found a correlation between these findings and resting partial oxygen pressure. They concluded the neuropsychological deterioration in a COPD population was likely the result of oxygen deprivation to the brain. In another study, a single measure of visuoconstructive ability, the Bender Gestalt Test, was administered to 95 adult asthmatic patients but to no controls (Schraa, Dirks, Jones,

& Kinsman, 1981). Schraa and co-workers found memory and motor impairment sufficient to conclude that 65% of the patients were experiencing cerebral dysfunction.

Focusing on asthmatic children, Dunleavy and colleagues (Dunleavy, 1981; Dunleavy & Baade, 1980; Dunleavy, Hansen, & Baade, 1981) argued that hypoxia produced neuropsychological damage in a significant proportion of severely asthmatic children. Using the Halstead Neuropsychological Test Battery for Children, these investigators found perceptual and motor impairments; they concluded that 7 of 20 (35%) of the asthmatic children showed brain damage traceable to histories of hypoxia. Although a relationship between asthma, anoxia, and brain damage in children was suggested both in these studies and by others (Bierman, Pierson, Shapiro, & Simmons, 1975; Nellhaus, Newman, Ellis, & Pirnat, 1975), there is little evidence that its prevalence approaches that suggested by Dunleavy (1981). In a study of psychomotor adaptation in sixty-seven 9–14-year-old hospitalized children, Bender, Beleau, Fukuhara, Mrazek, and Strunk (1987) found significantly reduced neuromotor scores in one of five patients. The neuromotor scores were not accompanied by reduced cognitive abilities but were significantly correlated with measures of child and family psychosocial adjustment. This led Bender and colleagues to conclude that impaired motor skills in some asthmatic children (a) were the result of psychological withdrawal and physical activity, (b) were not the result of hypoxia, and (c) did not reflect an increase in brain damage. That deficient motor skills are secondary to passivity and reversible with intensive physical therapy has been demonstrated in a study of cardiopulmonary exercise with 65 severely asthmatic children (Ludwick, Jones, Jones, Fukuhara, & Strunk, 1986).

Suess and Chai (1981) contested the conclusion of Dunleavy and Baade (1980) that neuropsychological deficit in asthmatic children is hypoxia-induced by arguing that subtle cognitive impairment in this population may be the product of asthma medications, particularly corticosteroids. Suess and Chai described preliminary results of a 3-year study that revealed visual memory deficits as a function of steroid use. Results published 5 years later (Suess, Stump, Chai, & Kalisker, 1986) detailed a comprehensive study that included 39 asthmatic children treated with theophylline, 51 asthmatic children treated with theophylline and systemic steroids, and 30 nonasthmatic control children. Several tests of visual retention and paired associate learning were administered to every child twice, once each at the same time on 2 consecutive days. For the asthmatic children who received steroids twice a day, the design provided test results 8 and 24 (or 48) hours after steroid ingestion. Test results indicated reduced visual and memory scores in the steroid-treated group on the day of steroid treatment but not 24 or 48 hours later; no such pattern emerged in either of the remaining groups. The investigators concluded that corticosteroids impair memory in asthmatic children, but that acute neuropsychological effects are present only in the immediate aftermath of steroid ingestion. Findings from the study thus demonstrated that a relationship exists between memory and steroids in asthmatic children. Although irreversible brain damage is an unlikely outcome, steroids can measurably alter brain function.

The measurement of medication-related neuropsychological changes in asthmatic patients turned to a second medication commonly used to treat childhood asthma, theophylline. The stimulant effects of theophylline on the central nervous system have led parents of many asthmatic children to complain that the medication causes their children to become restless and hyperactive (Research and Forecasts, Inc., 1989). Investigators have reported a variety of neuropsychological side effects of theophylline, mostly in open-label studies, that include decreased memory (Rachelefsky et al., 1986; Springer, Goldenberg, Ben Dov, & Godfrey, 1985; Williams-McCargo, 1984), attention (Furukawa et al., 1988; Springer et al., 1985), and motor skills (Springer et al., 1985; Williams-McCargo, 1984). Evidence from blinded studies, in contrast, indicates that theophylline side effects are relatively infrequent and appear to be similar to the effects of a closely related xanthine compound, caffeine. These subtle effects include anxiety (Bender & Milgrom, 1992), increased hand tremor (Bender & Milgrom, 1992; Joad, Ahrens, Lindgren, & Weinberger, 1986; Springer et al., 1985), and improved attention or memory (Bender & Milgrom, 1992; Joad et al., 1986; Rappaport et al., 1989). Stein and Lerner (1993) documented decreased parental complaints about behavioral problems in the second week of theophylline treatment and concluded that theophylline-induced behavior change decreases with initial habituation to the drug. Thus, the double-blind, randomized, crossover trials of placebo versus theophylline indicate a few subtle neuropsychological changes in asthmatic children treated with theophylline that include increased anxiety, attention, and tremor.

In conclusion, investigations intent on identifying the presence of brain damage in asthmatic populations by using standardized neuropsychological test batteries have not been fruitful. Mild neuropsychological deficits have been identified in both adult and pediatric patients with pulmonary disease; these changes are best understood as an indication of alteration of brain function, but not irreversible, localized brain damage. Future investigations in these populations will yield more helpful information if, rather than screening for damage using large, traditional neuropsychological batteries, they focus on specific neuropsychological functions and allow for exploration of potential causal factors. Assessment of alteration in neuropsychological functions after steroid or theophylline ingestion is an example of the kind of event-specific investigation that has increased the understanding of the effects of these medications and dispelled misunderstandings about the extent of these effects. Creer and Bender (in press) recommended that future studies of medication side effects include several important components, including parent and teacher observations by way of standardized questionnaires. Tests should be used that (a) measure each function believed affected by the medications, (b) can be administered on repeated occasions without large practice effects; and (c) are time efficient and do not place excessive demands on patients who must take them on repeated occasions.

Psychological or Behavioral Intervention

In the past 2 decades, a number of approaches to applying psychological and behavioral techniques to help control asthma have been taken. Several methods, including stress management, biofeedback, and family therapy, were succinctly summarized by Lehrer, Sargunaraj, and Hochron (1992). The principal focus of psychological and behavioral research in the past 2 decades, as also noted by Lehrer et al. (1992), has been on the development and evaluation of educational and self-management programs for patients with asthma.

Self-Management of Asthma

The goal of self-management programs is to teach patients to perform self-initiated skills and competencies so they can become partners with medical and behavioral scientists in managing their asthma. There are three phases to achieving the goal: First, patients must integrate medical and behavioral knowledge and expertise with such personal factors as individual abilities, experience, and expectations regarding the control of asthma. Second, patients must select the skills they should perform to control their asthma. Each patient should balance what he or she has learned with flexible and dynamic problem solving to resolve issues generated by asthma. Finally, patients must perform skills required to establish and maintain control over the particular intricacies of their asthma. Wigal, Creer, Kotses, and Lewis (1990) summarized evidence from 19 educational and self-management programs that showed self-management techniques have a primary role in the overall treatment of asthma. Although there were methodological shortcomings in many of these first-generation programs, the results demonstrated that self-management skills and techniques permit patients to become partners with health care personnel in the control of asthma (Creer, Wigal, Kotses, & Lewis, 1990).

The need to educate patients to manage their asthma was stressed by both U.S. and international panels of experts on asthma (National Heart, Lung and Blood Institute, 1992; Sheffer, 1991). Attaining effective self-management requires more effective and refined techniques than incorporated into first-generation asthma self-management programs. A second-generation model for the self-management of asthma, depicted in Figure 2, was proposed by Creer, Kotses, and Wigal (1992). The model was suggested for four reasons. First, it permits the synthesis of significant components of first-generation asthma self-management with recent trends in self-management. The result should be programs that establish more effective and efficient control of asthma. Second, the model permits medical and behavioral scientists to tailor strategies to meet the needs of individual patients. Previous research was conducted to develop and evaluate educational and self-management programs that could be generally applied with patients or members of their families. However, none of the programs provided guidance toward fitting a specific treatment protocol to the idiopathic nature of a given patient's asthma. Third, the model reflects considerable multidirectional interaction among components. Although the result makes for more difficult science, it more closely approximates the experience of patients with asthma and those who

CONTEXT

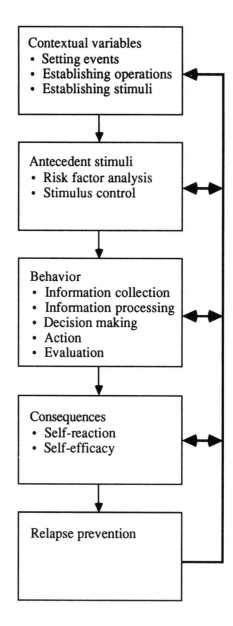

Figure 2. Second-generation model of asthma self-management.

treat them (Thoresen & Kirmil-Gray, 1983). Finally, the second-generation model suggests future directions that can be taken to reduce the impact of asthma. In this respect, it raises more questions than answers (Creer & Bender, in press). The relevance of each component or element of the model is as follows.

Context.   Context refers to the setting where a particular event or set of events occurs. There is multidirectional interaction between the context and elements of a self-management model; that is, they influence one another. The importance of context in asthma has long been recognized (Creer & Christian, 1976); indeed, many behavioral scientists propose that context be considered in designing and conducting any behavioral study (e.g., Sulzer-Azaroff & Mayer, 1991). The model of asthma self-management depicted in Figure 2 is embedded within the context. The result is a complex matrix that accounts for events, including patients preventing attacks by taking prescribed medications, avoiding or escaping from known triggers of asthma, reacting appropriately to abort episodes, and developing self-efficacy to perform the skills required to help control their asthma. Four events involved in the context constitute a four-term contingency that characterizes the relationship among contextual variables, antecedent stimuli, behavior, and consequences (Sulzer-Azaroff & Mayer, 1991).

Contextual variables.   Three types of contextual variables have been identified as relevant to the management of asthma: setting events, establishing operations, and establishing stimuli (Creer & Bender, in press; Creer et al., 1992).

Setting events.   These refer to complex antecedent stimuli, events, and stimulus–response interactions (Sulzer-Azaroff & Mayer, 1991). Maintenance medications are increasingly prescribed for patients to prevent asthma attacks (e.g., Sheffer, 1991). Although adherence to their physicians' instructions would likely reduce the frequency and severity of their attacks, evidence indicates that patients' rate of compliance to instructions for prescribed prophylactic medications varies between 2% and 100% in children (Creer, 1993). As adherence to medication regimens may be a setting event for a patient's attacks, there is a need for systematic investigation of the behaviors that constitute medication compliance.

Establishing operations.   These are the stimuli or events that alter the rates of responses associated with a reinforcer or change the effectiveness of the reinforcer (Sulzer-Azaroff & Mayer, 1991). Creer and Bender (in press) provide an example of establishing operations: If patients perceive that medications prevent, halt, or lessen the severity of attacks, the drugs become reinforcers for compliant behavior. If patients believe medications do not manage their asthma or they are concerned about adverse side effects of the drugs, the medications fail to reinforce and patients are likely not to adhere. Arkes (1991) described another type of establishing operation: sunk cost effects. This is illustrated by patients who continue to use a medication even when they perceive that it is not achieving its desired effect. The result may be overuse of the drug, a behavior that can have fatal consequences (Spitzer et al., 1992).

Establishing stimuli.   These stimuli are paired with an establishing operation. The response or change they evoke becomes a conditioned stimulus for that operation. An establishing stimulus cues or prompts the occurrence of the establishing operation (Sulzer-Azaroff & Mayer, 1991). The use of medications to control attacks provides an illustration of an establishing operation. When patients begin to have an attack, they seek their medication, usually inhaled through a nebulizer, because the drug has been established as a conditioned stimulus for relieving episodes. When the nebulizer is not immediately present, however, patients may desperately seek it because they recognize they cannot halt the attack without the drug contained in the inhaler. This situation is an establishing stimulus. Complicating the situation is that, as noted earlier, many patients fail to fill their prescriptions or to store medications where they can be readily located. If the needed medication is not available and used quickly, two consequences may occur. First, the patient may seek attention at a hospital emergency room, a practice noted by Weiss, Gergen, and Hodgson (1992) as increasing the cost of asthma care. Second, the patient may acquire inappropriate behavioral patterns, such as panic, that exacerbate ongoing attacks and interfere with the management of future episodes.

Antecedent stimuli.   Contingencies are specified dependencies between patients' asthma or behavior and their antecedents and consequences. The focus of research on asthma contingencies has been on analyzing risk factors for asthma and their relationship to attacks. Such analyses permit patients to establish control over some stimuli and, in turn, to reduce the number of attacks they experience.

Risk factor analysis.   Risk factor analysis involves a probability analysis of discrete events related to asthma. Characteristics of asthma, including the intermittency of attacks, severity of episodes, and the degree of reversibility, are probabilistic variables. Combinations and permutations of these variables constitute the topography of each asthma attack; they also are the conditions that must be considered in establishing control over asthma and asthmatic episodes. Risk factors associated with the pathogenesis of asthma include heredity, atopy, exercise and cold air, infections, indoor and outdoor pollutants and irritants, aspirin and related substances, diet, and emotional reactions (Reed & Townley, 1983). Not all of these factors lend themselves to risk factor analysis. Research to determine the probability that information concerning known precipitants of asthma or respiratory responses will predict patients' attacks is summarized in Table 4. Initial studies in risk prediction were based on respiratory responses, namely patients' peak flow values (PEFs). PEFs are obtained with a peak flow meter; the values indicate the fastest air flow rate sustained by a patient for at least 10 ms during a forced exhalation (Wright & McKerrow, 1959). Taplin and Creer (1978) demonstrated the use of PEFs to predict asthma. Flow values obtained from 2 children were entered into a conditional probability equation to predict the occurrence of asthma. The base rate or prior probability of the occurrence of an attack and a critical PEF that most enhanced the predictability of asthma were determined for each youngster. Two conditional probabilities were calculated for each child: (a) the probability of asthma occurring in a 12-hour period following a flow rate less than or equal to the critical value, and (b) the probability of asthma occurring in a 12-hour period following a flow rate greater than the critical value. Taplin and Creer (1978) reported an approximately 300% increase over the base rate in predicting asthma using this procedure. Harm, Kotses, and Creer (1985) extended this basic procedure with 25 asthmatic children and found an average improvement of approximately 500% in predicting the probability of asthma.

Research in risk factor analysis has been extended in other directions. Pinzone, Carlson, Kotses, and Creer (1991) examined medication compliance and exercise data in an attempt to predict asthmatic episodes in 10 patients. Exercise predicted the probability of attacks in 2 of 5 subjects with exercise-induced asthma; no results were obtained with medication compliance, although Creer (1979) reported that a missed medication dose predicted 100% of the attacks experienced by a child in an earlier study. Pinzone and her co-workers (1991) found that PEF predicted attacks in 9 of 10 subjects; in addition,

Table 4
Risk Factor Analysis of Precipitating Stimuli for Asthma

Stimuli	Probability equation	Reference
PEFR	$P_t(A) = F(P_{t-k}, B_{t-k})$	Harm, Kotses, & Creer (1985) Kotses, Stout, Wigal, Carlson, Creer, & Lewis (1991) Pinzone, Carlson, Kotses, & Creer (1991) Taplin & Creer (1978)
Medication compliance	$P_t(A) = F(B_{t-k})$	Creer (1979) Kotses et al. (1991) Kotses, Winder, Stout, McConnaughy, & Creer (1993) Pinzone et al. (1991)
Environmental factors Mold Ragweed	$P_t(A) = F(E_{t-k})$	Kotses et al. (1991) Kotses et al. (1993) Stout, Kotses, Carlson, & Creer (1991)

continued

Temperature change		
Dust		
Pollen		
Humidity		
Cigarette smoke		
Heat		
Odors		
Wind		
Animal dander		
Air pollution		
Emotional factors	$P_t(A) = F(Em_{t-k})$	Kotses et al. (1991)
Anxiety		Kotses et al. (1993)
Physiological	$P_t(A) = F(P_{t-k}, B_{t-k})$	Kotses et al. (1991)
Exercise		Kotses et al. (1993)
Alcohol consumption		Pinzone et al. (1991)
Fatigue		

Note. PEFR = peak expiratory flow rate; $P_t(A)$ = probability of asthma at a given moment; F = function; P = physiological; B = behavior; E = environment; Em = emotion; t − k = past history.

the prediction of attacks was enhanced by using a combination of factors including PEF, exercise, and time of day. Stout, Kotses, Carlson, and Creer (1991) investigated the degree to which asthmatic episodes were associated with seven environmental variables determined for each of 17 adults with asthma. Using stepwise regression procedures, cladosporium mold, ragweed pollen, and temperature change were found to be significant predictors of attacks. Stout et al. (1991) concluded that knowledge of the probability of the occurrence of known risk factors, unique to each individual, predicted the likelihood patients would experience asthma within a predetermined time frame.

Research on risk prediction has three implications (Creer & Bender, in press; Creer et al., 1992). First, information on risk factors can be used by physicians not only to refine their predictions of future attacks of individual patients but also to tailor preventive strategies for the patients. Second, with the experimental foundation of attack prediction established, simple tactics have been developed to permit patients to predict, on the basis of changes detected through self-monitoring of specific stimuli or responses, the probability that they will experience an asthma attack within a set period of time. Finally, use of risk factor data can serve as the foundation for individualized self-management programs for patients with asthma. Kotses et al., (1991) determined which stimuli were correlated with the attacks experienced by 8 patients. The data were entered into an equation to determine the probability that specific stimuli would induce asthma in individual patients within a predetermined period of time. Subjects were then randomly assigned to an experimental or control group; experimental patients received a brief individualized self-management program aimed at teaching them risk prediction to prevent attacks, and patients in the control group received their usual medical care. Results indicated a 22% decrease in the number of attacks in the experimental group. In a larger study using risk prediction, Kotses, Winder, Stout, McConnaughy, and Creer (1993) randomly assigned a group of 36 patients to one of three conditions: (a) individualized self-management, (b) group asthma self-management, and (c) control. Results showed that the PEF improved in both intervention conditions. However, there was a 38% drop in the number of attacks experienced by patients assigned to the control group. This indicated that the patients were able to predict many attacks and prevent them from occurring.

Stimulus control. This refers to changing antecedent events to alter the occurrence of a response. Narrowing and reducing the impact that antecedent stimuli have in triggering asthma, as in risk factor analysis, is one tactic. Stimulus control can also be established through two other approaches. First, patients can escape from or control known precipitants, narrow stimulus control, or promote self-generated stimulus or response change. This might be achieved, for example, by escaping from a smoke-filled room when smoke triggers attacks or by limiting jogging to prevent exercise-induced asthma. Second, patients can avoid, escape, or control their asthma by arranging antecedents. Specific strategies that can be used include environmental programming, initiating positive self-instruction, generating patient commitment to help control the asthma, and establishing response generalization. An example of environmental programming is to remove potential triggers of asthma from the home. Common examples include house dust and dust mites, feather pillows, and pets. Establishing response generalization can be illustrated by the case of patients with asthma who like to jog each morning. Provided that the patient does not overexercise, this is a healthy activity most of the year. However, the degree of airway obstruction that may develop is a function of the temperature and humidity of inhaled air; for example, the colder and drier the air, the greater the likelihood of bronchoconstriction. To promote the exercise across all seasons, psychologists who hear patients complain that jogging promotes asthma may recommend to them that they explore with their physicians the desirability of using a pre-exercise bronchodilator or cromolyn sodium to prevent exercise-induced asthma on cold and dry days.

Behavior.   Self-management involves both the acquisition of self-management skills and their subsequent performance. Teaching patients about asthma and its management was the basis for the 19 programs developed for childhood asthma (Wigal et al., 1990). Asthma knowledge was commonly assessed across all programs. Information on the skills performed by patients in the self-management of asthma was far more ambiguous. Nevertheless, most of the programs emphasized the skills of information collection, information processing, decision-making, action, and evaluation.

Information collection.   In most instances, this involved self-monitoring, or the self-collection and self-recording of data. In the case of younger children, however, data were gathered by parents. Because patients can provide both the best and the worst data about their asthma (Creer & Winder, 1986), it is important that they (a) observe only phenomena operationally defined and agreed on by them and their physicians; (b) attend only to specific changes in their respiration and behavior; and (c) add an objective measure, such as readings from a peak flow meter, to the more subjective information often collected with respect to asthma. Documenting information, usually by means of self-recording, requires patients to (a) record data on a daily basis when possible and (b) observe and record data only during particular windows of time (e.g., seasons when they are most apt to experience asthma). As much as possible, children should be taught to self-monitor their own responses and to allow their parents to serve as a reliability check.

Information processing. This usually involved teaching patients to process the information they gathered about themselves and their asthma (Creer, 1991). Three basic steps in information processing are as follows. First, patients must evaluate both the symptoms they experienced (private events) and signs of respiratory distress as observed by others (public events). As much as possible, they have to reconcile recognition of their symptoms with the signs seen by others. Second, they have to analyze "the ABCs" of their attacks by (a) looking at the antecedent conditions correlated with changes in their respiration, (b) performing the behaviors needed to correct any breathing difficulty, and (c) attending to the consequences of their action. Finally, patients must make judgments as to the meaning of the data they collect. This often means that they compare the data they collect against personal standards, such as their personal best PEF, or referential standards, such as their predicted PEF. Making such comparisons using the peak flow meter was recommended by both the U.S. and international panels of experts on asthma (National Heart, Lung and Blood Institute, 1992; Sheffer, 1991).

Decision-making. This is a critical function in self-management in that patients are asked to make pertinent judgments and decisions about their asthma based on the information they collect. Decision-making strategies common to Gold Standard Physicians and Gold Standard Patients have been described (Creer, 1990). Gold Standard Physicians were the physicians considered most capable of managing asthma, as determined both by their peers and by their responses to how they would treat hypothetical cases of asthma. Gold Standard

Patients were children and their parents who, on the basis of their responses to a standardized questionnaire administered after each of their attacks, were regarded as the most competent in managing asthmatic episodes. Research is needed on two topics: (a) how to teach every patient with asthma to make decisions similar to those made by the two Gold Standard groups, and (b) how to refine the strategies and heuristics of decision-making for asthma.

Action. Action is the performance of self-management skills developed to help control asthma. It is a function of the self-instruction patients provide to themselves. Self-instruction includes the prompting, directing, and maintaining of the performance of self-management skills. Self-instruction is significant in two respects (Creer & Bender, in press). First, establishing control over attacks requires that patients perform, in a stepwise manner, strategies recommended by their physicians for the management of asthma. The stepwise management of asthma by both physicians and patients was a strong recommendation of both the U.S. and international panels of experts on asthma (National Heart, Lung and Blood Institute, 1992; Sheffer, 1991). Second, instruction can promote coping strategies. These could include those developed not only for asthma, such as self-generated stimulus and response change, but those used in the self-regulation of other physical problems (Creer et al., 1992). Coping tactics include relaxation, with or without biofeedback; biofeedback; systematic desensitization, including self-desensitization; skill rehearsal and modeling, sometimes with guided participation; linking or unlinking behavioral chains; and self-reinforcement, particularly when used with self-instruction.

Evaluation. In some patients, asthma has been characterized as reflecting steady-state variability (Creer, 1979). Because changes in their asthma may constantly occur, there is a need for patients to evaluate their respiration continually and reverse breathing difficulties as they occur. Assessing the effectiveness of self-management skills in achieving this aim is also a component of the self-evaluation of asthma.

Consequences. The consequences of performing self-management skills to help control asthma require more investigation. Two components that merit research are self-reaction and self-efficacy.

Self-reaction. Self-reaction refers to the attention patients direct toward evaluating their performance (Bandura, 1986). On the basis of their evaluation, patients can establish realistic expectations about their performance, as well as evaluate whether they need more training and expertise. Patients should also develop realistic expectations about the limits of self-management in controlling asthma. They should recognize that they are unlikely to control all their attacks through self-management. Asthma is complex, and no patient is capable of performing all actions necessary to manage all episodes. When attacks rapidly intensify in severity, the patients need to add to the ABCs of asthma: what Winder (1984) referred to as (d)—call their doctor—and (e)—go to a hospital emergency room.

Self-efficacy. Self-efficacy is the belief of patients that they can adequately perform specific skills in a given situation (Bandura, 1977). As noted earlier, reliable and valid methods for assessing self-efficacy have been developed for patients with asthma.

Relapse prevention. Marlatt (1982) proposed a relapse prevention model as a paradigm for understanding patient relapse. Relapse refers to a violation of self-imposed rules or sets of rules patients have been taught to use in managing their asthma. Specific steps that might be incorporated into an asthma intervention program, particularly one that incorporates self-management procedures, would include (a) taking prescribed prophylactic medications; (b) avoiding high-risk situations; (c) escaping from high-risk situations; (d) mastering the performance of self-management skills; (e) rehearsing asthma self-management competencies between attacks; (f) reducing the impact of factors that weaken self-management performance, such as reliance on memory; (g) taking remedial steps when necessary; and (h) developing new coping strategies when appropriate. Relapse prevention should become a component of any future asthma self-management program (Creer & Bender, in press; Creer et al., 1992).

Conclusion

The complex and perplexing nature of asthma has been described. The unfolding intricacies and nuances of the disorder lead to the conclusion that current knowledge of the disorder is but a faint outline consisting of fragments of scientific data. Asthma is ripe for experimentation, including research by behavioral scientists. A potpourri of topics, particularly the stimuli and responses correlated with asthma, can be investigated. In this chapter, we elected to focus on the assessment of such asthma-related topics as knowledge of asthma and asthma management, attitudes toward the disorder, quality of life, compliance, neuropsychological changes, and medication side effects as illustrations of the wealth of research subjects. We could have just as easily discussed other variables, including the relationship of familial or environmental factors to asthma. Both U.S. (Sheffer, 1991) and international (National Heart, Lung and Blood Institute, 1992) panels of experts recommended that self-management be the cornerstone for establishing control over asthma. Achieving this goal will require a more thorough integration of the knowledge and competencies of medical, biological, and behavioral scientists with the skills of patients, families, and other segments of the community. Because self-management is a set of behavioral techniques, there are endless possibilities for psychologists and other behavioral scientists who strive to control what, for the foreseeable future, is an incurable condition.

REFERENCES

American Lung Association. (1975). *Report of the task force on comprehensive and continuing care for patients with chronic obstructive pulmonary disease.* New York: Author.

Arkes, H. (1991). Costs and benefits of judgment errors: Implications for debiasing. *Psychological Bulletin, 110,* 486–498.

Asthma—United States, 1980–1990. (1992). *Morbidity and Mortality Weekly Report, 41,* 733–735.

Bandura, A. (1977). *Social learning theory.* Englewood Cliffs, NJ: Prentice-Hall.

Bandura, A. (1986). *Social foundations of thought and action: A social cognitive theory.* Englewood Cliffs, NJ: Prentice-Hall.

Bauman, A. E., Craig, A. R., Dunsmore, J., Browne, G., Allen, D. H., & Vandenberg, R. (1989). Removing barriers to effective self-management of asthma. *Patient Education and Counseling, 14,* 217–226.

Bender, B. G., Beleau, L., Fukuhara, J. T., Mrazek, D. A., & Strunk, R. C. (1987). Psychomotor adaptation in children with severe chronic asthma. *Pediatrics, 79,* 723–727.

Bender, B., & Milgrom, H. (1992). Theophylline-induced behavior change in children: An objective evaluation of parents' perceptions. *Journal of the American Medical Association, 267,* 2621–2624.

Bergner, M., Bobbitt, R. A., Carter, W. B., & Gilson, G. S. (1981). The Sickness Impact Profile: Development and final revision of a health status measure. *Medical Care, 19,* 787–805.

Bierman, C., Pierson, W., Shapiro, G., & Simmons, E. (1975). Brain damage from asthma in children. *Journal of Allergy and Clinical Immunology, 55,* 126.

Busse, W. (1992). Mechanisms of inflammation and their therapeutic implications in the asthmatic patient. *Annals of Allergy, 69,* 261–266.

Busse, W. W., & Reed, C. E. (1988). Asthma: Definitions and pathogenesis. In E. Middleton, Jr., C. E. Reed, E. F. Ellis, N. F. Adkinson, Jr., & J. W. Yunginer (Eds.), *Allergy: Principles and practice* (pp. 969–998). St. Louis, MO: Mosby.

Bush, J. W. (1983). *Quality of Well-Being Scale: Function Status Profile and Symptom/Problem Complex Questionnaire.* San Diego, CA: Health Policy Project, University of California at San Diego.

Chambers, L. W., MacDonald, L. A., Tugwell, P., Buchanan, W. W., & Kraag, G. (1982). The McMasters Health Index Questionnaire as a measure of the quality of life for patients with rheumatoid disease. *Journal of Rheumatology, 9,* 780–784.

Clark, N. M., Rosenstock, I. M., Hassan, H., Evans, D., Wasilewski, Y., Feldman, C., & Mellins, R. B. (1988). The effect of health beliefs and feelings of self-efficacy on self-management behavior of children with a chronic disorder. *Patient Education and Counseling, 11,* 131–139.

Cluss, P. A., Epstein, L. H., Galvis, S. A., Fireman, P., & Friday, G. (1984). Effects of compliance for chronic asthmatic children. *Journal of Consulting and Clinical Psychology, 52,* 909–910.

Cramer, J. A., Mattson, R. H., Prevey, M. L., Scheyer, R. D., & Oulette, V. L. (1989). How often is medication taken as prescribed? *Journal of the American Medical Association, 261,* 3273–3277.

Creer, T. L. (1979). *Asthma therapy: A behavioral health-care system for respiratory disorders.* New York: Springer.

Creer, T. L. (1982). Asthma. *Journal of Consulting and Clinical Psychology, 50,* 912–921.

Creer, T. L. (1990). Strategies for judgment and decision-making in the management of childhood asthma. *Pediatric Asthma, Allergy, and Immunology, 4,* 253–264.

Creer, T. L. (1991). The application of behavioral procedures to childhood asthma: Current and future perspectives. *Patient Education and Counseling, 17,* 9–22.

Creer, T. L. (1992). Psychological and behavioral assessment of childhood asthma: Part II. Behavioral approaches. *Pediatric Asthma, Allergy, and Immunology, 6,* 21–34.

Creer, T. L. (1993). Medication compliance and childhood asthma. In N. A. Krasnegor, L. Epstein, S. B. Johnson, & S. J. Yaffe (Eds.), *Developmental aspects of health compliance behavior* (pp. 303–333). Hillsdale, NJ: Erlbaum.

Creer, T. L., & Bender, B. G. (in press). Recent trends in asthma research. In A. J. Goreczny (Ed.), *Handbook of health and rehabilitation psychology.* New York: Plenum.

Creer, T. L., & Christian, W. P. (1976). *Chronically-ill and handicapped children: Their management and rehabilitation.* Champaign, IL: Research Press.

Creer, T. L., & Kotses, H. (1990). An extension of the Reed and Townley conception of the pathogenesis of asthma: The role of behavioral and psychological stimuli and responses. *Pediatric Asthma, Allergy, and Immunology, 2,* 169–184.

Creer, T. L., Kotses, H., & Wigal, J. K. (1992). A second-generation model of asthma self-management. *Pediatric Asthma, Allergy, and Immunology, 6,* 143–165.

Creer, T. L., Wigal, J. K., Kotses, H., & Lewis, P. D. (1990). A critique of 19 self-management programs for childhood asthma: Part II. Comments regarding the scientific merit of the programs. *Pediatric Asthma, Allergy, and Immunology, 4,* 41–55.

Creer, T. L., & Winder, J. A. (1986). Asthma. In K. A. Holroyd & T. L. Creer (Eds.), *Self-management of chronic disease: Handbook of clinical interventions and research medicine* (pp. 29–55). San Diego, CA: Academic Press.

Denyes, M. J. (1980). Development of an instrument to measure self-care agency in adolescents (Doctoral dissertation, University of Michigan, 1980). *Dissertation Abstracts International, 41,* 1716.

Donnelly, J. E., Donnelly, W. J., & Thong, Y. H. (1987). Parental perceptions and attitudes toward asthma and its treatment: A controlled study. *Social Sciences in Medicine, 24,* 431–437.

Donnelly, J. E., Spykerboer, J. E., & Thong, Y. H. (1985). Are patients who use alternative medicine dissatisfied with orthodox medicine? *Medical Journal of Australia, 142,* 539–541.

Dunleavy, R. A. (1981). Neuropsychological correlates of asthma: Effect of hypoxia or drugs? *Journal of Consulting and Clinical Psychology, 49,* 137.

Dunleavy, R. A., & Baade, L. E. (1980). Neuropsychological correlates of severe asthma in children 9–14 years old. *Journal of Consulting and Clinical Psychology, 48,* 214–219.

Dunleavy, R. A., Hansen, J., & Baade, L. E. (1981). Discriminating powers of Halstead battery tests in assessment of 9- to 14-year old severe asthmatic children. *Clinical Neuropsychologist, 3,* 9–12.

Eisen, S. A., Miller, D. K., Woodward, R. S., Spitnagel, E., & Przybeck, T. R. (1990). The effect of prescribed daily dose frequency on patient medication compliance. *Archives of Internal Medicine, 150,* 1881–1884.

Eiser, C., Town, C., & Tripp, J. H. (1988). Illness experience and related knowledge amongst children with asthma. *Child Care Health Development, 14,* 11–24.

Ellis, E. F. (1988). Asthma in infancy and childhood. In J. E. Middleton, Jr., C. E. Reed, E. F. Ellis, J. N. F. Adkinson, & J. W. Yunginer (Eds.), *Allergy: Principles and practice* (pp. 969–998). St. Louis, MO: Mosby.

Eraker, S. A., Kirscht, J. P., & Becker, M. H. (1984). Understanding and improving patient compliance. *Annals of Internal Medicine, 100,* 258–268.

Furukawa, C. T., DuHamel, T. R., Weimer, L., Shapiro, G. G., Pierson, W. E., & Bierman, C. W. (1988). Cognitive and behavioral findings in children taking theophylline. *Journal of Allergy and Clinical Immunology, 81,* 83–88.

Gaut, D. A., & Kieckhefer, G. M. (1988). Assessment of self-care agency in chronically ill adolescents. *Journal of Adolescent Health Care, 9,* 55–60.

Gochman, D., & Saucier, J. F. (1982). Perceived vulnerability in children and adolescents. *Health Education Quarterly, 9,* 46–59.

Grant, I., Heaton, R. K., McSweeney, A. J., Adams, K. M., & Timms, R. M. (1980). Brain dysfunction in COPD. *Chest, 77,* 308–309.

Harm, D. L., Kotses, H., & Creer, T. L. (1985). Improving the ability of peak expiratory flow rates to predict asthma. *Journal of Allergy and Clinical Immunology, 76,* 688–694.

Hyland, M. E., Finnis, S., & Irvine, S. H. (1991). A scale for assessing quality of life in adult asthma sufferers. *Journal of Psychosomatic Research, 35,* 99–110.

Jenkinson, D., Davison, J., Jones, S., & Hawtin, P. (1988). Comparison of effects of a self-management booklet and audiocassette for patients with asthma. *British Medical Journal, 297,* 267–270.

Joad, J., Ahrens, R. C., Lindgren, S. D., & Weinberger, M. M. (1986). Extrapulmonary effects of maintenance therapy with theophylline and inhaled albuterol in patients with chronic asthma. *Journal of Allergy and Clinical Immunology, 78,* 1147–1153.

Juniper, E. G., Guyatt, G. H., Epstein, R. S., Ferrie, P. J., Jaeschke, R., & Hiller, T. K. (1992). Evaluation of impairment of health related quality of life in asthma: Development of a questionnaire for use in clinical trials. *Thorax, 47,* 76–83.

Kaplan, R. M. (1985). Quality-of-life measurement. In P. Karoly (Ed.), *Measurement strategies in health psychology* (pp. 115–146). New York: Wiley.

Karnofsky, D. A., Abelman, W. H., Carver, L. F., & Burchenal, J. H. (1948). The use of nitrogen mustards in the palliative treatment of carcinoma. *Cancer, 1,* 634–656.

Katz, S. T., Ford, A. B., Moskowitz, R. W., Jackson, B. A., & Jaffee, M. W. (1963). Studies of illness in the aged: The index of ADL. *Journal of the American Medical Association, 185,* 914–919.

Kotses, H., Hindi-Alexander, M., & Creer, T. L. (1989). A reinterpretation of psychologically-induced airway changes: From asthma to activation. *Journal of Asthma, 26,* 53–63.

Kotses, H., Stout, C., Wigal, J. K., Carlson, B., Creer, T. L., & Lewis, P. (1991). Individualized asthma self-management: A beginning. *Journal of Asthma, 28,* 287–289.

Kotses, H., Winder, J. A., Stout, C., McConnaughy, K., & Creer, T. L. (1993). *A comparison of individual and group formats for asthma self-management.* Manuscript submitted for publication.

Krall, R. L. (1991). Interaction of compliance and patient safety. In J. A. Cramer & B. Spilker (Eds.), *Patient compliance in medical practice and clinical trials* (pp. 19–26). New York: Raven Press.

Krop, H. D., Block, A. J., & Cohen, E. (1973). Neuropsychological effects of continuous oxygen therapy in chronic obstructive pulmonary disease. *Chest, 64,* 317–322.

Larson, G. L. (1992). Asthma in children. *New England Journal of Medicine, 326,* 1540–1545.

Lasagna, L., & Hutt, P. B. (1991). Health care, research, and regulatory impact of noncompliance. In J. A. Cramer & B. Spilker (Eds.), *Patient compliance in medical practice and clinical trials* (pp. 393–403). New York: Raven Press.

Lehrer, P. M., Isenberg, S., & Hochron, S. M. (1993). Asthma, emotion, and personality style: A review. *Journal of Asthma, 30,* 5–21.

Lehrer, P. M., Sargunaraj, D., & Hochron, S. (1992). Psychological approaches to the treatment of asthma. *Journal of Consulting and Clinical Psychology, 60,* 639–643.

Loren, M. L., Leung, P. K., Cooley, R. L., Chai, H., Bell, T. D., & Buck, V. M. (1978). Irreversibility of obstructive changes in severe asthma in children. *Chest, 74,* 126–129.

Ludwick, S. K., Jones, J. W., Jones, T. K., Fukuhara, J. T., & Strunk, R. C. (1986). Normalization of cardiopulmonary endurance in severely asthmatic children after bicycle ergometry therapy. *Journal of Pediatrics, 109,* 446–451.

Madison, J. M. (1991). Chronic asthma in the adult: Pathogenesis and pharmacotherapy. *Seminars in Respiratory Medicine, 12,* 175–184.

Market Facts, Inc. (1985). *National prescription buyers' survey.* Kalamazoo, MI: Author.

Marlatt, G. A. (1982). Relapse prevention: A self-control program for the treatment of addictive behaviors. In R. B. Stuart (Ed.), *Adherence, compliance and generalization in behavioral medicine* (pp. 117–153). New York: Brunner/Mazel.

Mawhinney, H., Spector, S. L., Kinsman, R. A., Siegel, S. C., Rachelefsky, G. S., Katz, R. M., & Rohr, A. S. (1991). Compliance in clinical trials of two nonbronchodilator, antiasthma medications. *Annals of Allergy, 66,* 294–299.

McFadden, Jr., E. R. (1980). Asthma: Airway reactivity and pathogenesis. *Seminars in Respiratory Medicine, 1,* 287–296.

McNabb, W. L., Wilson-Pessano, S. R., & Jacobs, A. M. (1986). Critical self-management competencies for children with asthma. *Journal of Pediatric Psychology, 11,* 103–117.

McSweeny, A. J., Grant, I., Heaton, R. K., Adams, K. M., & Timms, R. M. (1982). Life quality of patients with chronic obstructive pulmonary disease. *Archives of Internal Medicine, 142,* 473–478.

Mesters, I., Pieterse, M., & Meertens, R. (1991). Pediatric asthma, a qualitative and quantitative approach to needs assessment. *Patient Education and Counseling, 17,* 23–34.

Murray, J. F., & Enarson, D. A. (1992). World lung health: A concept that should become a reality. *American Review of Respiratory Disease, 146,* 818–822.

National Heart, Lung and Blood Institute. (1992). *International consensus report on diagnosis and treatment of asthma* (Publication No. 92-3091). Washington, DC: U.S. Department of Health and Human Services.

Nellhaus, G., Newman, I., Ellis, E., & Pirnat, M. (1975). Asthma and seizures in children. *Pediatric Clinics of North America, 22,* 89–100.

Oliverieri, N. F., Matsui, D., Hermann, C., & Koren, G. (1991). Compliance assessed by the Medication Event Monitoring System. *Archives of Disease in Childhood, 66,* 1399–1402.

Parcel, G. S., & Meyer, M. P. (1978). Development of an instrument to measure children's health locus of control. *Health Education Monographs, 6,* 149–159.

Parcel, G. S., Nader, P. R., & Tiernan, K. (1980). A health education program for children with asthma. *Journal of Developmental and Behavioral Pediatrics, 1,* 128–132.

Pinzone, H. A., Carlson, B. W., Kotses, H., & Creer, T. L. (1991). Prediction of asthma episodes in children using peak expiratory flow rates, medication compliance, and exercise data. *Annals of Allergy, 67,* 461–467.

Prigatano, G. P., Parsons, O., Wright, E., Levin, D. C., & Hawryluk, G. (1983). Neuropsychological test performance in mildly hypoxemic patients with chronic obstructive pulmonary disease. *Journal of Consulting and Clinical Psychology, 51,* 108–116.

Prigatano, G. P., Wright, E. C., & Levin, D. (1984). Quality of life and its predictors in patients with mild hypoxemia and chronic obstructive pulmonary disease. *Archives of Internal Medicine, 144,* 1613–1619.

Quirk, F. H., & Jones, P. W. (1990). Patients' perception of distress due to symptoms and effects of asthma on daily living and an investigation of possible influential factors. *Clinical Science, 79,* 17–21.

Rachelefsky, G., Wo, J., Adelson, J., Spector, S., Katz, R., Siegel, S., & Rohr, A. (1986). Behavior abnormalities and poor school performance due to oral theophylline usage. *Journal of Allergy and Clinical Immunology, 77,* 145.

Radius, R. M., Becker, M. H., Rosenstock, I. M., Drachman, R. H., Schuberth, K. C., & Teets, K. C. (1978). Factors influencing mothers' compliance with a medication regimen for asthmatic children. *Journal of Asthma Research, 15,* 133–149.

Rand, C. S., Wise, R. A., Nides, M., Simmons, M. S., Bleecker, E. R., Kusek, J. W., Li, V. C., & Tashkin, D. P. (1992). Metered-dose inhaler adherence in a clinical trial. *American Review of Respiratory Diseases, 146,* 1559–1564.

Rapoff, M. A., & Barnard, M. U. (1991). Compliance with pediatric medical regimens. In J. A. Cramer & B. Spilker (Eds.), *Patient compliance in medical practice and clinical trials* (pp. 73–98). New York: Raven Press.

Rappaport, L., Coffman, H., Guare, R., Fenton, T. DeBraw, C., & Twarog, F. (1989). Effects of theophylline on behavior and learning in children with asthma. *American Journal of Diseases of Children, 143,* 368–372.

Reed, C. E., & Townley, R. G. (1983). Asthma: Classification and pathogenesis. In E. Middleton, Jr., C. E. Reed, & E. F. Ellis (Eds.), *Allergy: Principles and practice* (pp. 811–831). St. Louis, MO: Mosby.

Renne, C. M., & Creer, T. L. (1985). Asthmatic children and their families. In M. L. Walraich & D. K. Routh (Eds.), *Advances in developmental and behavioral pediatrics* (pp. 41–81). Greenwich, CT: Jai Press.

Research and Forecasts, Inc. (1989). *American asthma report.* New York: Author.

Richards, J. M., Jr., Dolce, J. J., Windsor, R. A., Bailey, W. C., Brooks, C. M., & Soong, S.-J. (1989). Patient characteristics relevant to effective self-management: Scales for assessing attitudes of adults toward asthma. *Journal of Asthma, 26,* 99–108.

Ringsberg, K. C., Wiklund, I., & Wilhelmsen, L. (1990). Education of adult patients at an "asthma school": Effects on quality of life, knowledge and need for nursing. *European Respiratory Journal, 3,* 33–37.

Roth, H. P., Carson, H. S., & Hsi, B. P. (1970). Measuring intake of prescribed medication: A bottle count and tracer technique compared. *Clinical Pharmacological Therapy, 11,* 228–237.

Schraa, J. C., Dirks, J. F., Jones, N. F., & Kinsman, R. A. (1981). Bender-Gestalt performance and recall in an asthmatic sample. *Journal of Asthma, 18,* 7–9.

Sheffer, A. L. (1991). Guidelines for the diagnosis and management of asthma. *Pediatric Asthma, Allergy, and Immunology, 5,* 57–188.

Sheffer, A. L., & Buist, A. S. (1987). Proceedings of the asthma mortality task force. *Journal of Allergy and Clinical Immunology, 80,* 361–514.

Sibbald, B. (1989). Patient self-care in acute asthma. *Thorax, 44,* 97–101.

Sibbald, G., Collier, J., & D'Souza, M. (1986). Questionnaire assessment of patients attitudes and beliefs about asthma. *Family Practice, 3,* 37–41.

Spector, S. L., Kinsman, R., Mawhinney, H., Siegel, S. C., Rachelefsky, G. S., Katz, R. M., & Rohr, A. S. (1986). Compliance of patients with asthma with an experimental aerosolized medication: Implications for control clinical trials. *Journal of Allergy and Clinical Immunology, 77,* 65–70.

Spector, S. L., & Mawhinney, H. (1991). Aerosol inhaler monitoring of asthmatic medication. In J. A. Cramer & B. Spilker (Eds.), *Patient compliance in medical practice and clinical trials* (pp. 149–162). New York: Raven Press.

Spitzer, W. O., Dobson, A. J., Hall, J., Chesterman, E., Levi, J., Shepherd, R., Battista, R. N., & Catchlove, B. R. (1981). Measuring the quality of life of cancer patients: A concise QL-index for use by physicians. *Journal of Chronic Diseases, 34,* 585–597.

Spitzer, W. O., Suissa, S., Ernst, P., Horwitz, R. I., Habbick, B., Cockcroft, D., Boivan, J. F., McNutt, M., Buist, A. S., & Rebuck, A. S. (1992). The use of β-agonists and the risk of death and near death from asthma. *New England Journal of Medicine, 326,* 501–506.

Springer, C., Goldenberg, B., Ben Dov, I., & Godfrey, S. (1985). Clinical, physiologic, and psychologic comparison of treatment by cromolyn or theophylline in childhood asthma. *Journal of Allergy and Clinical Immunology, 76,* 64–69.

Spykerboer, J. E., Donnelly, W. J., & Thong, Y. H. (1986). Parental knowledge and misconceptions about asthma: A controlled study. *Social Science Medicine, 22,* 553–558.

Stein, M. A., & Lerner, C. A. (1993). Behavioral and cognitive effect of theophylline. *Annals of Allergy, 70,* 135–140.

Stout, C., Kotses, H., Carlson, B. W., & Creer, T. L. (1991). Predicting asthma in individual patients. *Journal of Asthma, 28,* 41–47.

Suess, W. M., & Chai, H. (1981). Neuropsychological correlates of asthma: Brain damage or drug effects? *Journal of Consulting and Clinical Psychology, 49,* 135–136.

Suess, W., Stump, N., Chai, H., & Kalisker, A. (1986). Mnemonic effects of asthma medication in children. *Journal of Asthma, 23,* 291–296.

Sulzer-Azaroff, B., & Mayer, G. R. (1991). *Behavior analysis for lasting change.* New York: Holt, Rinehart & Winston.

Taggart, V. S., Zuckerman, A. E., Sly, R. M., Steinmueller, C., Newman, G., O'Brien, R. W., Schneider, S., & Bellanti, J. A. (1991). You can control asthma: Evaluation of an asthma education program for hospitalized inner-city children. *Patient Education and Counseling, 17,* 35–47.

Taplin, P. S., & Creer, T. L. (1978). A procedure for using peak expiratory flow-rate data to increase the predictability of asthma episodes. *Journal of Asthma Research, 16,* 15–19.

Tashkin, D., Rand, C., Nides, M., Simmons, M., Wise, R., Coulson, A. H., Li, V., & Gong, H. (1991). A nebulizer chronolog to monitor compliance with inhaler use. *American Journal of Medicine, 91,* 33–36.

Taylor, G. H., Rea, H. H., McNaughton, S., Smith, L., Mulder, J., Asher, M. I., Mitchell, A., Seelve, E., & Stewart, A. W. (1991). A tool for measuring the asthma self-management competency of families. *Journal of Psychosomatic Research, 35,* 483–491.

Taylor, W. R., & Newacheck, P. W. (1992). Impact of childhood asthma on health. *Pediatrics, 90,* 657–662.

Tehan, N., Sloane, B. C., Walsh-Robart, N., & Chamberlain, M. D. (1989). Impact of asthma self-management education on the health behavior of young adults. *Journal of Adolescent Health Care, 10,* 513–519.

Thoresen, C. E., & Kirmil-Gray, K. (1983). Self-management psychology and the treatment of childhood asthma. *Journal of Allergy and Clinical Immunology, 72,* 596–606.

Tobin, D. L., Wigal, J. K., Winder, J. A., Holroyd, K. A., & Creer, T. L. (1987). A self-efficacy scale for asthma. *Annals of Allergy, 59,* 273–277.

U.S. Congress, Office of Technical Assistance. (1990). *Health care in rural America* (OTA-H-434). Washington, DC: U.S. Government Printing Office.

Weiss, K. B., Gergen, P. J., & Crain, E. F. (1992). Inner-city asthma: The epidemiology of an emerging U.S. public health concern. *Chest, 101,* 362S–367S.

Weiss, K. B., Gergen, P. J., & Hodgson, T. A. (1992). An economic evaluation of asthma in the United States. *New England Journal of Medicine, 326,* 862–866.

Wigal, J. K., Creer, T. L., Kotses, H., & Lewis, P. D. (1990). A critique of 19 self-management programs for childhood asthma: Part I. The development and evaluation of the programs. *Pediatric Asthma, Allergy, and Immunology, 4,* 17–39.

Williams-McCargo, C. (1984). The effect of theophylline on the attention span, behavior, and short-term memory of asthmatic children (Doctoral dissertation, Kent State University, 1984). *Dissertation Abstracts International, 45,* 1315B.

Winder, J. A. (1984). Keep asthma patients in your practice and out of the ER. *Practice, 1,* 19–25.

Wright, B. M., & McKerrow, C. B. (1959). Maximum forced expiratory flow rate as a measure of ventilatory capacity: With a description of a new portable instrument for measuring it. *British Medical Journal, 2,* 1041–1047.

Chapter 6

Dermatological Disorders

Steven Friedman, Marjorie Hatch, and Cheryl Paradis

The contribution of psychological factors to dermatological disorders was first discussed by Wilson in his book *Diseases of the Skin*, published in 1842 (Gil et al., 1988). Modern psychosomatic research in dermatology began in the 1930s, when a number of physicians wrote about the relationship between specific skin diseases and unconscious conflictual and personality constellations (Koblenzer, 1983). Despite the flurry of interest earlier in this century and the work of current dermatologist-psychiatrists such as Koblenzer, material on the

The research described in this chapter was supported, in part, by National Institute of Mental Health grant 42545 and by funds from the Department of Psychiatry's Practice Plan (State University of New York at Brooklyn).

psychological aspects of skin disease appears infrequently. For example, a well-known 2,400-page textbook of dermatology (Rook, Wilkinson, & Ebling, 1979) devotes only 1 page to psychological factors. This situation is changing, however, with the publication of specialty journals such as *Psyche and Cutis,* among other factors. Still, what has been published consists primarily of clinical case examples and theoretical speculation on the subject rather than systematic empirical and experimental observation.

Some of the sparseness of clinical research in this area may be due to the fact that dermatological patients are extremely reluctant to take a referral to a mental health professional because there is still a severe stigma associated with mental illness and because such patients, by consulting a dermatologist, have defined themselves as having a medical rather than an emotional or psychological illness (Koblenzer, 1987).

The general importance of psychological factors in dermatological disorders has been illustrated in several studies. For example, Sanborn, Sanborn, Cimbolic, and Niswander (1972) found that 2.7% of admissions to a United States Veterans Affairs hospital were for skin disorders. Sanborn et al. also found that 6 of 64 patients (9.4%) who had completed suicides suffered from dermatological disease and associated anxious and depressive symptoms. This is a higher rate than would be expected for nonpsychiatric patients. All of the patients who committed suicide had seen a physician within 6 weeks of committing suicide, two thirds of them within 14 days. Sanborn et al. also reported that the occurrence of dermatological flare-ups seemed to be associated with emotional stress for these patients, and they concluded that "treatment of dermatological problems that appeared to be stress-related must include treatment of emotional reaction as well as for the dermatological reaction" (p. 393). This admonition is repeated over and over in the medical and specifically dermatological literature, but it appears that, despite these exhortations, little systematic or prospective research has been done.

Some research has been done on establishing dermatology–psychiatry liaison clinics, in which dermatological problems complicated by psychopathology are identified and treated on site. Gould and Gragg (1983) examined the incidence of psychiatric disorder in a series of 60 consecutive patients admitted to a dermatology–psychiatry liaison clinic and found that the three most common psychiatric diagnoses were depression, anxiety, and obsessive–compulsive disorder (OCD). However, these investigators did not appear to use any structured interviews, report reliability checks on their diagnosis (either psychiatric or dermatological), or report any results of standardized psychological testing. It is also unclear what percentage of patients who were referred by the dermatologists were eventually seen by the liaison service, which makes it impossible to judge the true prevalence of these disorders in dermatological settings.

In reviewing the psychosomatic dermatology research, it is clear that psychological symptoms and disorders are often confused. There are few studies that used predefined objective diagnostic criteria and standardized interviewing techniques. One exception is a recent study (Hatch, Paradis, Friedman, Popkin, & Shalita, 1992) that used structured psychiatric interviews of a random, consecutive sample of patients attending a dermatological clinic to show a relationship between certain dermatological conditions and revised third edition of the *Diagnostic and Statistical Manual of Mental Disorders (DSM-III-R)* anxiety disorders (American Psychiatric Association, 1987). A particularly interesting finding was the high prevalence of OCD in this population.

In this study, 34 dermatology patients were evaluated with a structured psychiatric interview, the *Anxiety Disorders Interview Schedule—Revised (ADIS-R;* DiNardo & Barlow, 1988). The patients were diagnosed with several nonspecific pruritic ("itchy") conditions: atypical dermatitis, eczema, psoriasis, prurigo nodularis, or pruritis. Twenty-six percent of the patients were found to suffer from one or more anxiety disorders. Of 5 patients (14%) diagnosed with OCD, 4 of them described contamination obsessions, with washing as their primary obsessive-compulsive problem. They described washing anywhere from 1 to 12 hours per day, often using abrasive cleansers that clearly affected their dermatological conditions. Of the 5 OCD patients, 1 patient was comorbid for both panic disorder and generalized anxiety disorder (GAD), and 1 was comorbid for GAD. Two of these patients had a primary diagnosis of panic disorder, 1 had GAD, and 1 had posttraumatic stress disorder. Axis II disorders (American Psychiatric Association, 1987) were not assessed in this study. The Epidemiologic Catchment Area Program (Robins et al., 1984) demonstrated that anxiety disorders are the most common psychiatric condition and that the lifetime prevalence rate for OCD may be as high as 1–3%. This study indicates, however, that many patients with anxiety disorders, and in particular OCD, are presenting to dermatologists.

It is clear from the just-described studies that psychological disturbance is prevalent in dermatology patients but is rarely diagnosed, treated, or referred for psychological treatment. At the same time, it is clear from reviewing the literature that approaches that have looked at dermatological disorders from either a strictly psychological or a physiological perspective have proven insufficient. The goal of this chapter is to familiarize the health psychologist with the range of disorders that present in dermatological settings and that are hypothesized to be affected by psychological factors. With this goal in mind, we briefly review the importance of skin as an organ and examine studies done in dermatological settings and clinics that have looked at the incidence and prevalence of psychological conditions. The format of our literature review is based on a model of "psychocutaneous disorders" presented by Koblenzer (1983). This model, in many ways a traditional psychosomatic perspective on dermatological disorders, is useful to familiarize the health psychologist with the many disorders that are of potential interest. Finally, illustrative clinical examples that are specific to the health or clinical psychologist and guidelines for clinical work and research that stress the need to move toward an integrated diathesis–stress model are presented.

The Importance of Skin as an Organ

The important role of the skin as a pathway between the inner self and the outer environment has too often been unrecognized. The skin is one of the infant's first means of contact with the outside world. Relationships with the mother and other caretakers are built on bodily sensations and skin contact. Stroking and close physical contact provide stimulation and are soothing for the developing infant. It has been hypothesized that these early relationships, which are mediated through skin contact, establish a way for the infant to develop an internalized psychological structure of body image and to learn to regulate self-esteem (Koblenzer, 1987).

Observational infant research, longitudinal studies, and animal studies have shown that a disruption of early physical contact can be an important factor in the emergence of serious physical and emotional disturbances, including colic, infantile eczema, and infantile depression. Spitz (1965), in his classic studies of institutionalized infants, found that impairment of the mother–child relationship had a detrimental impact on the young infant. Although these infants received physical and nutritional care, they were deprived of physical contact and emotional nurturing from caretakers. Fifteen percent of infants in these institutionalized settings developed infantile eczema. This reflects a significant increase from the 2–3% incidence reported in the general population. Spitz believed that two coexisting conditions, emotional deprivation and genetic predisposition, must be present to produce infantile eczema. The work by Spitz is an early example of a model postulating an interaction between biological vulnerability and environmental stressors in dermatological disorders.

Spitz's (1965) clinical observations are supported by clinical research that has demonstrated that psychological disturbances often occur after the onset of dermatological disease. Serious dermatological disease in infants, because of the disease's capacity to evoke disgust, avoidance, and other severe emotional reactions in parental figures, can easily result in a disruption of the tactile stimulation needed for proper development. In addition, many dermatological conditions, such as eczema or alopecia (loss of hair), cause the sufferer difficulties because of society's focus on the importance of physical appearance and beauty (Gupta, Gupta, Schork, Ellis, & Voorhees, 1990). An inability to achieve the ideal appearance can cause self-esteem and self-image problems in vulnerable individuals, such as adolescents who are afflicted with severe acne (Wu, Kinder, Trunnel, & Fulton, 1988).

Jowett and Ryan (1985) analyzed the effects of three skin disorders on patients' overall emotional, social, and functional relationships. Using a semistructured interview, they interviewed 100 patients over the age of 16 years with a dermatological illness for at least 12 months. Subjects included 30 patients with acne, 38 with psoriasis, and 32 with eczema. Eighty-two percent of the patients had noticeable skin lesions on their hands, face, and other visible areas. In terms of psychiatric dysfunction, 61% of the patients experienced anxiety, and 29% experienced depression. In addition, 64% of the patients reported that the skin conditions adversely affected their socioeconomic activity, and 40% said that their social life was adversely affected. Forty-seven percent of the patients with eczema, 3% with acne, and 26%

with psoriasis reported family friction. Jowett and Ryan found that 80% of these patients reported severe shame and embarrassment, but those patients who developed the condition either late in life or had it from the earliest days of infancy reported less shame and embarrassment. In summary, this survey clearly demonstrates that skin disease can be associated with severe emotional and functional handicaps.

Etiology and Course of Psychosomatic Dermatological Disorders

Various theories are influential in understanding the etiology or course of psychocutaneous diseases. Theories of primary importance include (a) the *psychoanalytic model*, (b) the *behavioral model*, and (c) the *diathesis–stress model*.

Freud and his followers in the psychoanalytic movement viewed psychosomatic conditions as the outward expression of inner unconscious conflict (Koblenzer, 1987). Conversion symptoms, in particular, were viewed as a representation of the patient's unconscious conflicts and the compromise made when unacceptable thoughts or wishes were repressed. The location of a dermatological lesion was hypothesized as having symbolic meaning for the patient; dermatitis on the hands, for example, reflected possible conflict over masturbation.

One clinician, writing about his research with dermatology patients, stated that symptom formation "occurs when an aggressive impulse is warded off and this energy is discharged into the pathway of organic functionings" (Musaph, 1969). He cited his belief that facticial dermatitis (self-inflicted skin lesions) is influenced in part by "sexualized aggressive feelings originally aimed at key figures from the first years of life." Spitz (1965) concluded that chronic eczema resulted from the "infant's libidinal and aggressive drives which normally would be discharged" in the course of the handling by the mother but were blocked from being discharged. To the best of our knowledge, although the psychoanalytic approach has been the dominant approach in the clinical dermatological literature, few if any empirical or experimental studies have tested these theories.

The second influential model of psychosomatic disease, the behavioral model, has focused more on the course of a dermatological condition than on etiology. In this model, psychosomatic dermatological conditions are thought to be influenced by reinforcement of maladaptive behaviors. Most of the research based on this theoretical approach has focused on the treatment of patients with compulsive scratching (Gil et al., 1988). Scratching episodes are viewed as being inadvertently reinforced by the outside world as well as by the temporary relief afforded by the scratching behavior itself. Behavioral or social learning factors are seen as one important factor in a complex disease process. In addition, in childhood dermatological conditions, a parent's attention to the child's scratching episodes may serve as an important maintaining variable for scratching (Gil et al., 1988).

As an example of this approach, Welkowitz, Held, and Held (1989) described a multicomponent behavioral program to lessen the frequency and duration of scratching in a patient with neurotic excoriation. The program included self-monitoring procedures, such as daily records of scratching episodes, which were designed to separate the seemingly automatic behavior, or scratching, from its controlling stimuli. Similar behavioral approaches have been described by others (Allen & Harris, 1966; Rosenbaum & Ayllon, 1981; Watson, Tharp, & Krisberg, 1972).

Aversive procedures based on behavioral principles have also been reported to be effective in the treatment of excessive scratching. In one study (Ratliff & Stein, 1968), when scratching episodes occurred during a therapy session patients were administered a shock and were encouraged to say aloud, "Don't scratch!" Progressive relaxation was successfully taught as a competing response. Limitations of the behavioral approaches include that, historically, they have consisted of clinical case studies with little or no follow-up. In addition, behavioral therapy has guided interventions, but has not offered a comprehensive approach to understanding the etiology of these disorders.

The third model of psychocutaneous disease is the diathesis–stress model. According to this model, genetically vulnerable individuals may develop dermatological diseases under conditions such as exposure to allergens and psychosocial stressors (Arnetz, Fjellner, Eneroth, & Kallner, 1991). Clinicians have hypothesized that stress can alter physiological processes and lead to disease. Stress can be defined as resulting from either major life events, such as marriage, divorce, or the death of a family member, or an excess of minor life events, such as numerous daily hassles.

Clinical researchers working with dermatological patients have not generally used a comprehensive diathesis–stress model. Rather, research to date has tended to focus on measuring stress levels and how various stressors may affect bodily processes and influence the onset and course of certain dermatological disorders.

Stress has been shown to affect bodily processes, causing increased sympathetic arousal, peripheral vascular changes, liberation of histamine in the skin, and a lowered itch threshold (Fjellner & Arnetz, 1985). In an example of this approach, Arnetz et al. (1991) conducted a study of the endocrine and dermatological concomitants of stress. They compared patients with psoriasis and atopic dermatitis with control subjects on tests of skin reactivity. They concluded that there were individual variations, rather than group differences, in dermatological reactivity within each group. For example, skin reactivity appeared to be associated more with differences in coping style and mood than with a specific dermatological disease condition. The only significant group difference was that both patient groups, in contrast to normals, showed lower growth hormone secretion during a stressful experimental condition. Although various bodily changes have been linked with stress, there appear to be no long-term prospective studies linking stress with specific dermatological disease.

Other clinicians have linked psychosocial stressors with the onset and course of psoriasis and atopic dermatitis. Faulstich, Williamson, Duchman, Conerly, and Brantley (1985) hypothesized that flares of atopic dermatitis resulted from stress. Graham and Wolff (1953) found that emotional stress caused blood vessel dilation, which they hypothesized could lead to an onset of eczema, hives, or pruritus. The mechanism by which stress affects skin and dermatological conditions is hypothesized to be a complex process involving changes in immune function, pain and itch perception, and inflammatory responses.

Another link between the psyche and the soma has been investigated through the study of hypnosis, which has been regarded as helpful in the treatment of viral warts, dermatitis, and hives (Surman, Gottlieb, Hackett, & Silverberg, 1973). Hypnotic inhibition of the flare reaction to a histamine prick test has been demonstrated (Zachariae, Bjerring, & Arendt-Nielsen, 1989). This suggests that if hypnosis can lead to changes in the inflammatory processes, then psychosocial stressors could also mediate the course of skin disorder in a similar fashion.

Recent research further supports the belief that pain perception and the inflammatory response are mediated by the central nervous system and may be modulated by psychological interventions. For example, in a study by Zachariae and Bjerring (1990), 10 normal college students who scored high on hypnotic susceptibility were screened for their cutaneous reactivity to a histamine prick test. Brain-related evoked potentials were measured on the basis of eight argon laser stimulations (a mildly painful stimulus). These measurements were repeated under hypnosis, in which one arm was given repeated suggestions of analgesia. Zachariae and Bjerring found a significant reduction in subjectively reported pain as well as in brain-related evoked potentials. In addition, a significant difference between prehypnotic and hypnotic analgesia condition was found in the histamine flare area. The study supports the hypothesis that higher cortical activity could be involved in the interaction of inflammatory and pain processes and bears replication in clinical samples.

In summary, stress may lead to changes in bodily processes, such as immune function and pain and itch perception, and may be hypothesized to be an important factor in the development and course of the dermatological disorder.

Psychocutaneous Disorders

In our review of psychological factors in dermatological disorders we present a system of classification of psychocutaneous diseases. We define each disorder, evaluate the literature on the psychological factors in the disorder, and describe psychological or psychiatric treatment that has been used. Although reviews of literature have traditionally focused on the empirically or experimentally collected evidence, our review is necessarily more broad because of the lack of research that meets even minimal standards for scientific rigor. Dermatological disorders have often been defined in idiosyncratic ways, standardized assessment tools have not been developed for either the medical/dermatological or psychological aspects of skin disorders, and the treatment literature consists almost entirely of unreplicated clinical single-case studies with little follow-up. In group treatment studies, there has been little attempt at random assignment, to use placebo or waiting list controls, to use independent blind assessors, or to follow up for any appreciable amount of time.

Any classification of dermatological disorders in which psychological factors are imputed will be somewhat arbitrary. We use a three-part classification system that was originally proposed by Koblenzer (1987; see Table 1). This system is one developed by, and well recognized by, clinical dermatologists. Clinical researchers generally have not relied on any single model of dermatological disorder. In the model by Koblenzer (1983), diseases are organized through a presumed common etiology. These include (a) conditions that are strictly psychological in origin, (b) dermatological conditions in which strong psychogenic factors are thought to be involved in the etiology

Table 1

Classification of Psychocutaneous Diseases

Conditions with clear psychological etiology
    Dermatitis artefacta
    Delusions as they relate to skin
        Parasitosis
    Obsessions/compulsions relating to skin
        Body dysmorphic disorder
        Trichotillomania
        Neurotic excoriations
    Psychogenic pain syndromes
        Glossodynia
        Glossopyrusis
Conditions in which psychogenic factors are reportedly involved in etiology and maintenance of the disorder
    Urticarias (hives)
    Alopecia (loss of hair)
    Hyperhydrosis (excessive sweating)
    Erythema (blushing)
Conditions dependent on both genetic or environmental and stress factors
    Atopic dermatitis (neurodermatitis, eczema)
    Psoriasis
    Acne

Note. From *Psychocutaneous Disease* (p. 32) by C. S. Koblenzer, 1987, New York: Grune & Stratton. Copyright 1987 by Grune & Stratton. Adapted by permission.

and maintenance of the disorder, and (c) conditions that appear to be related to the interplay between genetic and environmental factors and whose course appears to be affected by emotional distress.

Conditions With Psychological Etiology

Conditions that have clear psychological etiology include disorders such as dermatitis artefacta and neurotic excoriations, as well as parasitosis, body dysmorphophobia, trichotillomania, and psychogenic pain syndromes. These disorders are seen as "self-inflicted." Because the task of diagnosing and treating malingering patients often falls to the dermatologist, with the clinical health psychologist acting as a consultant or adjunct, such patients are not covered in this review. As in other areas of health psychology, developing a close working relationship with the physician is of critical importance. This is greatly aided if the psychologist recognizes and masters some of the basic medical terminology used in dermatological settings.

Neurotic excoriations and dermatitis artefacta. Neurotic excoriations are characterized by lesions on the skin that occur because of severe burning or itching sensations that result in patients scratching themselves repetitively. Patients often report that they "want to dig into the skin." Dermatitis artefacta consists of similar self-inflicted dermatological lesions, but which are distinguished from neurotic excoriations by the fact that in dermatitis artefacta the patient is consciously, or unconsciously, holding back information and will not admit self-mutilation to the health care provider (Doran, Roy, & Wolkowitz, 1985). The wide spectrum of presentations ranges from patients who unconsciously pick at small irregularities in the skin, often around the fingertips, to uncontrolled picking resulting in severe lesions. Self-inflicted excoriations may also be secondary to delusions of parasitosis, which will be reviewed later in this chapter.

The lesions of severe dermatitis artefacta are often seen as bizarre in configuration and are confined to areas that are easily accessible to the hands. Dermatologists, if they actively confront these patients with their self-inflicted wounds, are faced with strenuous denial. Clinically, it has been reported that many of these patients, if not actively psychotic, have borderline personality structures.

Sneddon and Sneddon (1975) reported a long-term follow-up study of 43 patients with dermatitis artefacta. They noted that their sample consisted primarily of young women in which the dermatological disorder was only one incident in a long history of psychogenic illness. Fully 30% of patients continued to self-inflict injury, or were disabled with other psychiatric disorders, over 12 years after the initial onset of the disorder. These investigators reported that recovery, when it did occur, was associated with changes of life circumstances rather than any specific medical or psychological treatment, or both.

Neurotic excoriations have also been reported to occur primarily in women in their 20s and 30s (Doran et al., 1985). As in dermatitis artefacta, the lesions characteristic of neurotic excoriations are frequently localized in the upper back, face, legs, and arms. Doran et al. concluded that these patients suffer from an "inhibited repressed and internally directed rage with an inability to overcome their difficult life situations" (p. 294). Clinicians have hypothesized that repressed rage and guilt feelings can trigger scratching and that the function of such scratching and physical damage is either self-punishment, a physiological release for psychological tension with rage repression, gratification of the need for love, or all three. However, a thorough search of the literature does not report any empirical investigations of these hypothesized etiological causes for such self-inflicted lesions. As just noted, there have been some case reports touting the efficacy of a behavioral approach (Welkowitz et al., 1989) to neurotic excoriations, and these reports are reviewed later in this chapter.

Delusions of parasitosis.   Another group of dermatological disorders with clear psychogenic etiology are delusions that relate to the skin. Primarily, these patients have delusions of parasitosis (also referred to as monosymptomatic hypochondriacal syndrome). A patient with delusions of parasitosis, typically a middle-aged woman, will report to the dermatologist that she is "infected with some parasite or vermin." Bishop (1983), in his review of the literature, found that over 400 cases have been reported, with the first being described by dermatologists in 1894 as a syndrome called "acarophobia," or fear of scabies. However, delusions of parasitosis are no longer considered an anxiety disorder but rather a psychotic syndrome characterized by the encapsulated belief of being infected by scabies, lice, fleas, microbes, worms, or other parasites.

The patients usually complain to the dermatologist about itching, tickling, or prickling sensations that they believe are caused by vermin infesting their body. No objective evidence of any infestation can be found, but frequently the dermatologist will notice excoriations and skin inflammations secondary to scratching. Patients have also been known to bathe in kerosene and other noxious liquids as a means of killing the supposed vermin.

Frequently, patients will come to the dermatologist with a little container holding a variety of different materials as "evidence" of the infestation. If told that their specimen has been examined under a microscope and does not contain any parasites, they will usually provide an elaborate rationalization of why the dermatologist could not find the infestation. These patients rarely accept referrals to mental health providers. It has been reported that one remarkable aspect of delusions of parasitosis is the frequency with which it has been reported to be shared or induced in others; classical folie à deux has been described in at least 22 different cases (Bishop, 1983).

Munro and Chmara (1982) in reviewing 50 cases of monosymptomatic hypochondriacal psychosis reported that this disorder is a subtype of paranoia, accompanied by illusional misperceptions or poorly defined hallucinations. The investigators' impressions were that their patients had a premorbid personality described as "schizoid type," in that they were angry and suspicious, and often experienced high levels of anxiety and shame. In addition, these patients tended to suffer from "secondary depression" and insomnia and had a history of alcohol abuse. Most of the patients had seen numerous physicians and had undergone repeated medical exams and procedures. One third of the patients remembered a significant incident such as an actual skin infection that appeared to trigger their psychological illness.

Paulson and Petrus (1969) reported on the psychological assessment of 5 patients with these encapsulated delusional systems. Results showed evidence of neurotic symptomatology with depression and somatization but no gross evidence of paranoid thinking. Paulson and Petrus concluded that these patients suffered from somatic delusions and that the "unconscious derivatives of this somatic delusion appeared related to strongly expressed conflicts over sexuality and aggression."

For patients suffering from monosymptomatic delusions of parasitosis the efficacy of pimozide (a high-potency neuroleptic) has been widely reported (Koblenzer, 1987). Again, as best as we are able to ascertain, the reports of the effectiveness of pimozide, or any other treatment, have been reported only in uncontrolled case studies. Patients on pimozide are reported to experience significant relief within 2 weeks. Even though 80% improve, most still believe in the physical nature of their disorder. This continued lack of insight requires that most patients remain on long-term psychopharmacological treatment.

There have also been occasional claims of successful treatment with tricyclic antidepressants, monoamine oxidase inhibitors, and other neuroleptic drugs (Koblenzer, 1987). Other treatments for these disorders have included supportive psychotherapy, with the therapist gradually encouraging a psychological rather than psychosomatic framework to express conflict. All investigators agree that engaging patients with these disorders in psychotherapy is a difficult, if not impossible, task. Psychotherapeutic treatment, if possible, involves gradually changing patients' conception that there is "something wrong with my body" to the idea that there is "something wrong with me." Successful treatment, in the opinion of Torch and Bishop (1981), comes from mental health professionals "accepting the patients' distress on a physical level." This concept of accepting a patient's distress essentially means never directly challenging a patient's belief in the organic cause of his or her dermatological condition. This observation is an important one, and in our experience is the key to engaging any dermatological patient in psychological treatment. What is usually necessary to engage a patient in a psychological or psychopharmacological intervention is to help the patient accept the idea that other factors, such as stress and anxiety, can contribute to the worsening or maintenance of symptoms. We address this point in more detail toward the end of this chapter.

There do not appear to be any descriptions of treatment for parasitosis from a cognitive or behavioral perspective. Eventually, most dermatologists find the clinical management of these patients frustrating and seeking to refer them away from their dermatology practice. In our experience, when a psychologist begins collaborating with a dermatologist, the first patient who is likely to be referred—although this disorder is exceedingly rare—is the patient with delusions of parasitosis.

Body dysmorphic disorder (dermatological hypochondriasis). Body dysmorphic disorder, or dermatological hypochondriasis, can also be included under dermatological disorders whose primary etiology is psychological in nature. A recent review article by Phillips (1991) reported that body dysmorphic disorder, which is defined as a preoccupation with an imagined defect in physical appearance (American Psychiatric Association, 1987), has long been recognized in European psychiatry but has largely been neglected in the United States. The term *dysmorphophobia* was coined by Morselle in 1891 and is generally defined as the "subjective feeling of ugliness or physical defect" that the patient thinks is noticeable to others despite normal appearance. The features of greatest concern tend to be the nose, teeth, skin, and hair. *Dermatological hypochondriasis* (Bishop, 1983) is another term generally used to describe a body dysmorphic disorder-like syndrome that has focused on defects in the skin and hair. To dermatologists, patients may present with a variety of different believed symptoms, such as skin distortion when actual examination may show mild, if any, postacne symptomatology, excessive hair loss that is not documented, or deformities in their scrotum, penis, or other areas around the perineum. A related syndrome is bromidrosiphobia, fear that the body may emit a bad odor, especially through sweating; however, we were unable to locate any studies of this disorder.

Cotterill (1981) has described a series of 28 patients (12 men and 16 women) diagnosed with "dermatological nondisease" or "psychocutaneous disease." Their complaints included burning and itching in their face, hair loss, and itching, discomfort, and burning around the perineum. Cotterill found that these patients were at increased risk for both attempted and successful suicide; over the course of the study three patients attempted suicide, one successfully. In addition, 57% of the patients met criteria for body dysmorphic disorder with depression. Again, no systematic diagnostic interview was used, leaving open the question of the reliability of the diagnosis.

Hardy and Cotterill (1982) compared 12 patients with body dysmorphobia who consulted a dermatologist with 12 patients with psoriasis and 12 normal controls (matched for age, sex, and educational status). They found that both the dysmorphophobic and psoriatic patients scored higher on obsessionality measures of the Leyton Obsessional Inventory but were not significantly different from each other. The score on the Beck Depression Inventory was mildly elevated for the dysmorphophobic group, whereas psoriatic patients and normals were not found to be depressed. Further clinical evaluation suggested that 5 of 12 body dysmorphophobia patients were moderately to severely depressed, which suggests that a subgroup of dermatological body dysmorphophobic patients were suffering from a mood disorder rather than OCD as initially thought.

A case description of a body dysmorphic disorder may be helpful. A 35-year-old single White man was referred for the evaluation and treatment of his "obsession" when he consulted a dermatologist regarding the "skin around my scrotum and penile area." The patient stated that at the age of 18 he developed "a spontaneous infection" in his penis. He also reported that he was "too embarrassed" to see a physician. He waited until the infection became more severe and he was in excruciating pain. At that point he confided in his mother and was encouraged to consult the family practitioner. The patient recalls that the practitioner examined his penis and said with shock, "What the hell happened here!" He was placed on a trial of antibiotics and was referred to a urologist, who followed the patient for several months for treatment with a series of broad-spectrum antibiotics.

The patient reported that, since that time, "my penis has not been the same. It doesn't feel the same and in many ways it doesn't look the same. I know what it looked like then and now it looks like an old man's penis." Since the initial episode 18 years before, the patient had consulted at least four different urologists, several family practitioners, several plastic surgeons, and five different dermatologists with requests that they examine his penis. Each of these physicians over the years reassured the patient that there was nothing wrong with his penis. For a number of years reassurance by a physician would calm him for a short period. At the time of the referral, the patient had seen a dermatologist and insisted that the skin around the penis and scrotal area was damaged. The dermatologist spent some time talking to him and the patient reported, "The doctor asked me what was *really* bothering me." After several short consultations with the dermatologist, the patient for the first time took a psychological referral.

There have been a number of case reports describing the successful resolution of body dysmorphic disorder with antidepressants, primarily serotoninergic agonists (Hollander, Liebowitz, Winchel, Klumker, & Klein, 1989). Theoretically, many clinicians have noted the similarity between body dysmorphic disorder and OCD. In one series of 3 patients with dermatological body dysmorphophobia, all of the patients appeared to meet *DSM-III-R* criteria for OCD and reportedly improved on fluoxetine (Prozac) or behavioral treatment, or both (Brady, Austin, & Lydiard, 1990).

Little is known about the course or outcome of this disorder in dermatological settings. Numerous investigators have reported that body dysmorphic disorder patients are usually symptomatic for years, if not decades (Phillips, 1991). Symptoms are unremitting, often worsening at times, and as noted earlier, these patients are often at risk for severe depression as well as suicide. Speculation on the etiology of this disorder has ranged from identifying defense mechanisms and displacement to neurotransmitter dysfunctions as the causes (Phillips, 1991). It appears most likely that the etiology of dysmorphic disorder is quite complex.

Dermatological conditions also may result from excessive washing or other rituals associated with OCD. One of the earliest reports of OCD in dermatology practice was by Rasmussen (1985). He reported that, in each of three cases, referral to a mental health professional by the dermatologist occurred only after several years of unsuccessful medical treatment. More systematic research has indicated that the incidence of OCD in a dermatological setting may be quite high. In one study of 34 dermatological patients examined in a structured interview, a 15% incidence of OCD was found (Friedman, Hatch, Paradis, Popkin, & Shalita, in press). As noted earlier, this incidence is much higher than the 1–3% rate of OCD cited in the ECA study (Robins et al., 1984).

Trichotillomania.   Among other disorders that appear to be entirely psychogenic are those characterized by primary obsessions or compulsions that relate to the skin or hair. The most common and well-recognized of these is trichotillomania, a disorder of chronic hair pulling, which some investigators (Koblenzer, 1987) have suggested is a variant of obsessive–compulsive disorder.

The term *trichotillomania* was coined by Hallopaeu in 1889 to describe a condition provoked by pulling one's own head hair, resulting in irregular loss. Cossidente and Sarti (1981) reported that this habit is seen most in children and adolescents and is often preceded by a compulsive tendency to touch the hair, smooth it, twist it around, or put it in the mouth with stereotypic movements. The behavior appears to be more frequent and intense when the patient is totally or partially distracted, such as when reading or watching TV. Cases of trichotillomania are most often initially seen by dermatologists, because hair pulling results in irritation of various hair sites, particularly the scalp, eyebrows, and eyelashes. Trichotillomania may occur in isolation but is often comorbid with other mood, anxiety, substance abuse, and eating disorders.

There have been several case reports, as well as open trials, demonstrating the successful use of fluoxetine in the treatment of trichotillomania (Primeau & Fontaine, 1987; Swedo et al., 1989). In addition, there has been at least one placebo-controlled double-blind study of fluoxetine (Christenson, Mackenzie, Mitchell, & Callies, 1991). In that study, 34 potential subjects were recruited by newspaper advertisements, and 14 agreed to participate. Seven additional subjects were recruited from a trichotillomania clinic. The total sample consisted of 21 subjects, who underwent 18 weeks of treatment at a maximum dose of 80 mg fluoxetine per day. The investigators used five measures of improvement. The subjects kept daily diaries and reported the number of hair pulling episodes per week, estimated the number of hairs pulled per week, and counted the number of hairs pulled per week (collected in an envelope). In addition, subjects reported the weekly subjective severity of the urge to pull out hair and subjective rating of the severity of hair pulling. Christenson et al. concluded that there was no short-term efficacy of fluoxetine.

A variety of clinical reports have suggested the utility of a behavioral approach. A comprehensive review of the behavioral modification literature was done by Friman, Finney, and Christopherson (1984). Typical of this approach is a case report by Bayer (1972) of a 22-year-old female with a 2-year history of hair pulling. Bayer described the patient as being shy and socially avoidant. Behavioral treatment consisted of a combination of self-monitoring and mild aversive treatment. After 5 days of simply monitoring the number of hairs that she pulled, the client decreased hair pulling from an average of 20 hairs per day to between 13 and 15. The second part of treatment consisted of asking the patient to give the hairs to the therapist. This was obviously embarrassing, and the patient reported that she then pulled an average of less than 1 hair per day. Unfortunately, there was no long-term follow-up of this patient.

Psychogenic pain syndromes.   The final set of dermatological disorders that are thought to be psychogenic in origin comprises the psychogenic pain syndromes, glossodynia (painful tongue), and glossopyrosis (burning tongue). Under these conditions, a painful or burning portion of the tongue is localized particularly above the tip on the lower half. Sometimes other sensations, such as itching or a sandy feeling and dryness, may be present, and the patient may often unconsciously or unwittingly aggravate these unpleasant sensations by rubbing or biting the tongue, occasionally even touching the tongue repetitively. Clinically, it has been hypothesized that patients with this disorder in fact suffer from a form of depression (Koblenzer, 1987) and may respond to treatment with antidepressants and low-dose neuroleptics. To the best of our knowledge, no empirical data describing either the phenomenology or treatment exist for these syndromes.

Conditions in Which Strong Psychogenic Factors Are Imputed

Dermatological conditions in this group include skin conditions that, although initially caused by biological or environmental factors, are believed to be perpetuated by psychological factors. This group includes urticarias (hives), alopecia areata (hair loss), hyperhydrosis (excessive sweating), and symptomatic erythema (blushing).

Urticaria (hives).   Chronic urticaria (hives) is a dermatological condition characterized by wheals, which are pustules that appear suddenly over portions of the body. Urticaria is often associated with allergic reactions. However, when symptoms occur on a daily basis and extend beyond a few weeks, the condition is often considered to be influenced by psychological factors. Most of the clinical data on urticaria have relied on clinical reports and case studies. These reports have significant limitations, including a failure to choose patients on a random basis, a lack of comparison or control groups, and evaluators who were not blind to the diagnosis and hypothesis being examined.

One exception is the research of Lyketsos, Stratigos, Tawil, Psaras, and Lyketsos (1985), who performed a well-controlled study of 28 patients diagnosed with urticaria. This study is especially important because of its relatively large sample size, its inclusion of appropriate control groups, and its use of reliable psychological measures. All consecutive admissions of patients diagnosed with urticaria not judged to be related to allergies or medical infection were included. This study also included 38 nonpsychosomatic dermatology patients, diagnosed with conditions such as herpes zoster, genital warts, chicken pox, and impetigo, as a control group. All patients were administered a battery of questionnaires. The results indicated that the urticaria patients, in comparison with controls, scored significantly lower on measures of dominance and higher on measures of extrapunitiveness, intrapunitiveness, anxiety, and depression.

Werth (1978) examined the relationship between emotional conflict and recurrent or persistent urticaria in her clinical report of 5 patients. She concluded that these patients' outbreaks of urticaria were related to their experiencing an insoluble dilemma or conflict. Little has been published on treatment approaches, although Tsushima (1988) reported that biofeedback was helpful for the treatment of hives.

Alopecia areata (hair loss).   Alopecia areata (hair loss) is a dermatological condition with great variability in etiology, response to treatment, and prognosis. Alopecia has been associated with endocrine disorders, oral–dental infections, metabolic disorders, congenital syphilis, and other skin diseases (Koblenzer, 1987). A subset of alopecia cases can be considered primarily psychosomatic. These patients' alopecia appears to be related to stressful life events and premorbid personality factors.

Research by Lyketsos and colleagues (1985), just described, also included 26 patients diagnosed with alopecia, unrelated to other medical disorders. The results indicated that patients with alopecia had significantly lower scores on psychological measures of dominance and higher scores on measures of extrapunitiveness, intrapunitiveness, anxiety, and depression when compared with controls.

Perini et al. (1984) compared the life circumstances of 48 patients with alopecia, 30 patients with common baldness, and 30 patients with fungal infections. Life events were measured by the Paykel Revised Interview for Recent Life Events (Paykel, Emms, Fletcher, & Rassaby, 1980). This scale was administered in a semistructured interview and covers 64 life events. Events were recorded only when they occurred 6 months before the onset of various dermatological diseases. The psychological impact of the event was rated on a 5-point scale. Patients with alopecia experienced significantly more life events (123 events) as compared with the patients with common baldness (22 events) and patients with fungal infections (15 events). These life events included, for example, losses, martial problems, car accidents, and financial difficulties. Perini et al. hypothesized that alopecia resulted from stress, which affected immune function.

Hyperhidrosis (sweating). Hyperhidrosis (excessive sweating) typically occurs on the palms, soles, and axillae (armpits). As in many dermatological conditions, it is associated with feelings of shame and anxiety. Most of the research on hyperhidrosis is limited to single-case treatment studies. Lerer and Jacobowitz (1981) describe the psychological treatment of a 19-year-old woman who had experienced hyperhidrosis since the age of 5. This case report is especially interesting in that it included pretreatment, posttreatment, and 2-year follow-up results on a battery of psychological tests. Test results indicated that prior to treatment she was experiencing high anxiety, fearfulness, and difficulty in interpersonal relationships and coping, in addition to deficits in ego functioning and a hysterical personality organization. After completion of a course of insight-oriented psychotherapy, testing indicated decreased anxiety and aggression and increased self-assertiveness and coping. Two-year follow-up measures revealed that she continued to show clinical improvement in both her hyperhidrosis and psychological symptoms.

Other clinicians working with patients with hyperhidrosis recommend assertiveness training and desensitization (Bar and Kuypers, 1973). Patients are encouraged to use graduated exposure to feared situations and thereby extinguish anxiety. Koblenzer (1987), based on her clinical experience, recommends the use of biofeedback techniques and psychotherapy in the treatment of hyperhydrosis.

Kuypers and Cotton (1972) demonstrated the effectiveness of instrumental conditioning in lowering the rate of sweating. They measured the thermal sweat responses of 8 normal male volunteers under three conditions: for 10 minutes before a sauna was turned on, for 10 minutes with the sauna on, and for 10 minutes after the sauna was turned off. Subjects were administered increasingly painful shocks as their sweat rate increased. Results indicated that, under these experimental conditions, subjects were able to markedly decrease their sweat rate. Limitations of this study, however, were that the subjects were taken from a normal population and that patients with hyperhidrosis were not specifically included. To the best of our knowledge, there have been no controlled studies documenting the effectiveness of any of the aforementioned behavioral techniques with a clinical sample. Patients who do not participate or benefit from these psychological techniques may decide to use medical interventions. These include the use of sedatives and surgical excision of the axillary vault (Koblenzer, 1987).

Erythema (blushing).   Another dermatological condition in which strong psychological factors are imputed is symptomatic erythema (blushing). Clinicians who work with patients with this condition describe them as having psychological problems similar to those of patients with hyperhydrosis. They are described as socially phobic, inhibited, and having difficulty expressing emotions (Bar & Kuypers, 1973; Gibbs, 1969). Case reports (Bar & Kupers, 1973) have shown the usefulness of a paradoxical approach to erythema. Patients are instructed to try to blush in as many situations as possible, and these reports suggest that patients are able to achieve voluntary control over involuntary blushing. Gibbs (1969), in a single-case report with 6-month follow-up, described the use of assertiveness training and interpersonal skills training.

Conditions Equally Dependent on Genetic or Environmental and Stress Factors

Most research examining the interaction between skin disease and psychological factors has focused on three diseases considered to reflect equal contributions of genetic or environmental factors and stress: atopic dermatitis, psoriasis, and acne. These three disorders, although having their own distinct symptoms and etiologies, share the common label *pruritic disorders,* meaning they are characterized by itching or picking. In addition, patients having these conditions have been studied in similar types of research, focusing on the effect of skin disorders on specific psychological states and social functioning, the relationship between psychopathology and skin disorders, and psychological factors that maintain and exacerbate skin problems.

Pruritus (itching) is often seen as part of many dermatological disorders (e.g., eczema, psoriasis, etc.) but can also occur in isolation. Beare (1976) reviewed 43 cases of generalized pruritus in patients without any other visible skin disorder. The majority of patients had suffered for approximately $10\frac{1}{2}$ months before symptoms spontaneously disappeared.

Atopic dermatitis (eczema).   *Dermatitis* is a highly generalized term that originally referred to an inflammation of the skin. The most common form, atopic dermatitis, is marked by erythema (redness), oozing and crusting, excoriation (removal of the skin by scratching), and lichenification (thickening of the skin) (Leider & Rosenblum,

1976). It has been estimated that atopic dermatitis affects 7–24 people per 1,000, and accounts for up to 20% of all patients treated by dermatology clinics (Faulstich & Williamson, 1985). Pruritus, or itchiness, is usually intense, and chronicity and recurrences are problematic. Other terms for this disease include *neurodermatitis, prurigo Besbier,* and *atopic eczema* (Miller & Keane, 1987).

In terms of psychological antecedents to atopic dermatitis, Brown (1967) found that his patients reported significantly more separation experiences in the year previous to the onset of their symptoms compared with a control sample of dental patients, and that 48% suffered from "severe shock, worry, or emotional upset" in the 6 months preceding the outbreak of their eczema. The atopic dermatitis group also reported significantly more frustration and anger under stress as compared with the control group. This suggests that a combination of both objective life situations and reaction to the stress generated by these situations may relate to dermatitis.

Similarly, an early study using a large sample of atopic dermatitis patients ($N = 100$) found that over 70% reported antecedent emotional stressors related to disease onset (Wittkower & Russell, 1953). Two more recent studies reported significantly higher state and trait anxiety ratings for atopic dermatitis patients compared with clinical and no-disease control groups (Faulstich, Williamson, Duchmann, Conerly, & Brantley, 1985; Garrie, Garrie, & Mote, 1974). However, a more appropriate comparison group for studies such as these would be patients with a dermatological disorder that is thought to be primarily of biological etiology (i.e., fungal infection).

It has been speculated that emotional reactions in dermatological conditions may lead to altered autonomic activity, resulting in peripheral vascular changes and a lowering of itch thresholds, leading to a vicious itch–scratch cycle (Beerman, 1962). Jordan and Whitlock (1974) tested this hypothesis with patients with atopic dermatitis ($N = 18$). Using a classical conditioning paradigm, an itch stimulus (electrical stimulation) was applied to each subject's hand, and the skin reaction (GSR) and scratching behavior were measured to determine itch threshold. Results indicated that the dermatological patients developed conditioned scratch responses much sooner than healthy controls, lending some support to the hypothesis that stress and anxiety may mediate atopic dermatitis. In summary, although there is a relatively large body of literature implicating stressful life situations in precipitating or exacerbating atopic dermatitis, the nature of this association remains unclear.

It has long been assumed in the clinical literature that environmental factors are an especially important variable in childhood dermatological disorders. Clearly, dermatological disorders with onset in childhood and adolescence have a great potential to inhibit normal developmental processes. A comprehensive review and assessment of research on childhood dermatological disorders is beyond the scope of this chapter, but it is worth noting some of the most relevant findings.

Among early researchers in this area, Beare (1976) concluded, in a subjective evaluation of 11 cases of children with generalized itching, that "itching is nearly always emotional in origin." Gil et al. (1987) examined this idea empirically, conducting a series of studies of atopic dermatitis in children and basing their research on a biopsychosocial model that highlights the role of environmental and social learning factors in the maintenance of scratching behavior.

Although other investigators have proposed that scratching behavior is under operant control, Gil et al. (1988) provided one of the only well-controlled studies examining this hypothesis. They examined the scratching behavior of 33 children with severe atopic dermatitis in the presence of one parent, using an observational system that recorded scratching requests, actual behavior on the part of both child and parent, and parental prevention of scratching. Results indicated that parent behaviors predicted a large and significant amount of the variance in scratching-related behaviors, even after controlling for demographic and medical status variables. Parental attention, typically given after the child scratched, appeared to reinforce scratching behavior. This was true even when the response was to stop the child from scratching. Noncontingent attention, on the other hand, was related to a lower incidence of scratching.

Gil and her colleagues (Gil et al., 1987; Gil & Sampson, 1989) also examined the relation of stress and family environment to symptom severity in children with atopic dermatitis. Chronic problems associated with atopic dermatitis, such as lifestyle adjustments (e.g., not being able to eat certain foods) and home treatments (e.g., taking frequent baths), were found to be strongly related to atopic dermatitis symptom severity. In terms of family environment factors, children from well-organized families that allowed their members relative autonomy had fewer and less severe dermatological symptoms than children in enmeshed and chaotic families. Gil et al. (1987) and Gil and Sampson (1989) speculated that some families' emphasis on self-reliance, planning, and regular routines may serve as a buffer against stress for children with atopic dermatitis. Compliance with treatment recommendations also seems to be greater in such families.

In terms of psychological treatment for atopic dermatitis, different modalities, including insight-oriented psychotherapy and behavioral therapies, have been researched. Brown and Bettley (1971), in a well-designed study of traditional psychotherapy for eczema patients, randomly assigned 72 patients to either a medication group or a medication group plus psychotherapy for 4 months. Some of the psychotherapy patients also received relaxation training and hypnosis. The psychotherapy consisted of a focused approach on awareness and verbalization of resentment and hostility, with an aim of changing life situations of conflict and frustration. Change in all groups was measured by the Cornell Medical Index (Brodman, Erdman, Lorge, Wolff, & Broadbent, 1949) and a symptom rating scale of the investigators' devising. Although the difference between the psychotherapy and medication groups was not statistically significant in general, a subset of the patients who received psychotherapy had significantly clearer skin than the patients who received medication alone. This subgroup included those in whom the onset of psychological symptoms occurred within 1 year of getting eczema (and thus were judged to have an emotional disturbance that was "highly relevant" to the eczema) and those with high motivation for psychological treatment. These patients' improvements in psychological symptoms were maintained over a 14-month period. This study thus provides evidence of the use of psychological treatment for skin disorders that are linked to emotional disturbance, particularly when the disturbance is temporally related to the dermatological conditions and when the patient is motivated for this form of treatment.

In addition, a number of single-case studies have demonstrated significant reductions in severe scratching behavior in both children and adults. Cataldo, Varni, Russo, and Estes (1980) successfully used a combination of techniques including verbal reminders from the therapist (e.g., "You're scratching"), the use of an incompatible response (having the patient fold hands), distraction (e.g., having the patient think of a favorite food), and differential social attention by the therapist to treat a patient with long-standing dermatitis. Allen and Harris (1966) trained a mother in reinforcement procedures to eliminate scratching in a 5-year-old girl. In this case, the mother was successfully trained to withhold all reinforcement contingent on the child's scratching herself but to reinforce desirable behavior by providing attention and verbal approval. By the end of 6 weeks, the child's body was clear of sores, and these gains were maintained at a 4-month follow-up. Manuso (1977) reported success in treating a 60-year-old woman with chronic atopic dermatitis on her hands by using biofeedback-assisted vasodilatation training. However, in these studies random assignments to well-defined treatment protocols, checking the reliability of ratings to control for potential investigator bias, and adequate follow-up were not done.

In one well-controlled group study (Haynes, Wilson, Jaffe, & Britton, 1979), 12 patients with atopic dermatitis were instructed in frontal electromyographic feedback and relaxation training. Participants were exposed to a fixed sequence of treatment phases: a no-treatment baseline phase, a phase incorporating nonspecific treatment factors (listening to a tone in the biofeedback room), and the aforementioned treatment. Photographic analyses of the skin, which consisted of both subjective severity ratings of pictures by two independent raters and an inch-by-inch determination of percentage of affected skin before and after treatment, revealed significant remission of dermatological problems across the entire program. Ratings of itching level decreased within but not across treatment sessions. Haynes et al. interpreted their findings as offering mixed support for the hypothesis that atopic dermatitis is amenable to psychobiological procedures. Their study is particularly important in that they carefully assessed actual skin changes in a reliable and objective manner, and it is unfortunate that subsequent studies have not used this advanced methodology. This is perhaps due to its time-consuming and costly nature, or because researchers are reluctant to assess skin severity in new and unfamiliar ways.

Psoriasis. Psoriasis is a common, recurrent condition marked by discrete, bright red spots or reddened patches of thick, leaflike scales, with a 1–2% prevalence in the general population (Miller & Keane, 1987). Psychosocial factors have been reported to be important in the onset and exacerbation of symptoms in 39–80% of psoriasis patients, compared to 10–50% of controls, both dermatological and asymptomatic (Fava, Perini, Santonastoso, & Farnaso, 1980; Seville, 1977). These striking results have not been replicated by others (Haynes et al., 1979; Payne, Rowland Payne, & Marks, 1985). However, the studies that failed to replicate these findings used small samples, and the research focused merely on counting the number of stressful events in the subjects' lives without regard for the personal relevance that the stressors had for subjects.

In a further examination of psychosocial factors in psoriasis, Gupta et al. (1988, 1989) looked at the psychocutaneous characteristics of patients who reported that stress exacerbated their psoriasis. Compared with a group of psoriasis patients who reported stress not to be a factor in their illness, the high stress reactors had a more clinically disfiguring disease and more frequent flare-ups. These patients were judged to rely more on the approval of others and experienced more stress related to having psoriasis.

Most attempts to delineate specific personality characteristics in patients with psoriasis have failed to yield significant results, although there have been isolated reports of high levels of outward aggression (Matussek, Agerer, & Seibt, 1985), high depression (Fava et al., 1980; Hughes, Barraclough, Hamblin, & White, 1983), high anxiety (Fava et al., 1980), and high obsessionality (Hardy & Cotterill, 1982) in this group. In addition, in one study psoriasis was reported to affect sexual functioning in 72% of the subjects (Weinstein, 1984). Clearly, the onset of psoriasis during developmentally critical periods such as adolescence may more severely affect the psychological growth of an individual (Dungey & Buselmeier, 1982). However, it is likely that some of the abnormal psychological characteristics reported in psoriatics are typical reactions to any chronic, cosmetically disfiguring disease.

A limited number of prospective studies have also been done. Gaston and colleagues (Gaston, Crombez, Lassonde, Bernier-Buzzanga, & Hodgins, 1991), for example, examined the role of psychological stress on psoriasis patients prospectively over a period of 20 weeks using standardized measures. A time-series analysis indicated a positive correlation between the severity of dermatological symptoms and psychological distress or adverse life events.

More recently, some clinical researchers have emphasized the need for more complex psychosocial models to elucidate the role of stress in skin diseases. Arnetz and colleagues' (1991) research led them to conclude that patients suffering from psoriasis and atopic dermatitis cannot be differentiated from healthy controls solely on the basis of dermal and neuroendocrine reactivity to psychosocial stressors. Rather, individual subjects' skin reactivity was to a large extent dependent on coping style, availability and use of social support, and mood. Although this is an interesting observation, no details of the research that led to this conclusion were provided.

Psychological treatment for psoriasis has focused, for the most part, on a multimodal approach incorporating both behavioral and traditional elements. Waxman (1973), using a single-subject design, examined a six-pronged treatment including hypnosis, relaxation, insight therapy, and behavioral techniques (counterconditioning and assertiveness training) for a 38-year-old woman with a 20-year history of psoriasis. Although he reported disappearance of the rash and attendant improvement in psychological symptoms, his research design provides no way to identify the "active ingredient" in his treatment, leaving questions about the efficiency of the individual components.

In an attempt to determine the components of effective treatment, Gaston et al. (1991) used a dismantled time-series research design to assign 18 subjects with psoriasis to one of four groups: meditation, meditation plus imagery, waiting list, and no-treatment control. Treatment lasted 12 weeks, with 4-week pre- and postbaseline periods. The severity of psoriasis was determined by a dermatologist on a four-point scale on three dimensions (thickness, erythema, and silvery plaques), as well as on the basis of the amount of the scalp covered with lesions. Analysis revealed a significant difference between the mean ratings of treatment and control groups after treatment. Interestingly, no additional impact was associated with the use of the imagery technique. Subjects' continuing use of dermatological medication while participating in the study was not found to be a significant factor in improvement. Despite the small sample size, this study used sound methodology and adequate controls and is a good model for future research.

As a means of providing more efficient psychological services for dermatology patients, group therapy has become increasingly popular. Unfortunately, little systematic evaluation of such groups has been done. One exception is the study by Bremer-Schulte, Cormane, Van Dijk, and Wuite (1985), who conducted research on the group therapy of patients with psoriasis using a trained patient and professional as group coleaders. They provided 10-week group treatment to 42 psoriasis patients. The treatment focused on the following aspects of psoriasis: (a) somatic (information about causes and medical treatments), (b) emotional (concomitants such as anxiety, depression, and shame), and (c) social (lack of understanding by others and isolation). The group treatment consisted of lectures, discussion, and the teaching of techniques such as relaxation and respiratory exercises. Compared with a group of waiting-list controls, the experimental group required significantly less medication, reported less shame and shyness, and rated their disease as less important in their daily lives. In addition, group participants were found to have developed an increase in interactional skills and problem-solving ability. Follow-up data 2 years later showed an overall continuation of these effects. On the basis of an informal review of the group treatment literature since 1968, Bremer-Schulte et al. concluded that, in general, the coleader format produces better outcomes than do traditional formats in which groups are run by professionals or peers alone.

Acne. Acne is another common pathological condition of the skin. The term *acne* is used in conjunction with a number of descriptive labels referring to the size, shape, color, and extent of papules (pimples). Severe acne is most commonly seen in teenagers, having an incidence of 0.5–5% in people ages 15–21, but it can also occur in adults (Miller & Keane, 1987). There is great individual variation in the effects of these dermatological conditions on psychological states, often mediated by the severity of the disease, coping ability, age, family and peer support systems, and patients' perception of their disease (Fried & Shalita, 1992).

Recent studies have nicely documented the fact that acne may significantly interfere with social interactions such as dating and sports participation and is implicated in poor academic functioning and unemployment (Jowett & Ryan, 1985; Motley & Finlay, 1989). Perhaps related to social impairments, a link has been found between the severity of acne and the extent of self-image impairment (Wu et al., 1988) and clinical depression (Cunliffe, Hull, & Hughes, 1989). In addition, several well-controlled studies have shown increased levels of anxiety and anger in acne patients when compared with patients with pityriasis rosea (periodically erupting patches of scaly red skin) and controls with no skin condition (Garrie & Garrie, 1978; Van der Meeren, Van der Schaar, & Van den Hurk, 1985).

A relevant case report usefully illustrates the range of possible reactions that patients may have to acne. A 49-year-old single White man referred himself for psychological treatment because he was "having difficulty in obtaining an erection." He reported in the initial session that he had never been involved in any long-term emotional relationship until 6 months prior to the interview, when he had become increasingly involved with a woman.

He reported having a "happy and comfortable childhood" until he suddenly developed severe and disfiguring acne at the age of 13 years. The patient reported, "I was a very happy-go-lucky child with a lot of friends and I actually started to date when I got this severe acne. It was so horrible that I withdrew from social situations, with my school work suffering. I remember spending hours of every day fantasizing over and over again that I hoped each day the lesions on my face would heal. I would be constantly watching them to see that they would. Of course, the problem was that when some would heal, new ones would constantly appear." The patient reported that he had consulted numerous dermatologists but had not had significant improvement in spite of aggressive medical treatment, which was prior to the availability of Accutane (isotretinoin).

The patient reported that for approximately 30 years, even 13 years after the acne disappeared on its own, he was a complete social recluse. He also reported that he had developed several habits, which he found "too humiliating to discuss." One of these habits was "always shaving in the dark because it was just too painful to look at my face in the mirror." Further evidence of shame and embarrassment was that the patient had no photographs of himself from the age of 13 until the age of 30 years, when his acne spontaneously remitted. The occasional picture taken by a family member would be destroyed.

Treatment followed a psychoeducational approach, which consisted of educating the client regarding the common pattern of social anxiety and isolation that affects many patients with acne. In combination with anxiety management training (Suinn, 1977), social skills training was highly effective in alleviating both his social isolation and sexual difficulties. In this particular case no specific sex therapy techniques were necessary, but the supportive environment in the psychotherapy process seemed to enable the man to face a lifetime of avoided social situations.

The little research that has been published on psychological treatment for severe acne has focused on stress reduction techniques.

Hughes, Brown, Lawlis, and Fulton (1983), for example, successfully used a combination of biofeedback, relaxation, and cognitive imagery to treat a case of severe acne. Using a multiple baseline design, they showed that patients experienced increased acne severity when the relaxation component was temporarily suspended.

In conclusion, research on pruritic conditions tends not to suffer from methodological inadequacies to the same degree as research on the dermatological conditions already discussed. This likely reflects the greater interest, and longer history of research, on these common disorders. Difficulty in developing reliable assessment instruments for use with skin disorders remains, however, and is exemplified by research by Berg (1991). He asked patients to describe the part of their body with the skin disorder, the objective skin problems (i.e., redness, pimples, etc.), and subjective symptoms (i.e., burning, pain, and itching) that they found disturbing. Results were compared with actual dermatological examination as well as a questionnaire retest 6 weeks later. Berg concluded that the questionnaire was a poor measure of mild skin disease, and 6-week test–retest reliability was low. However, questions that assessed skin status (redness, pimples, and skin dryness) did show adequate test–retest reliability and did correlate with actual physical exams. This indicates that one of the important tasks to be accomplished in this field is the development of reliable and valid assessment tools.

Up to now, medical interventions have been widely considered the treatment of choice for dermatological conditions. A growing body of research suggests, however, that the efficacy of current medical approaches is largely palliative and that a combination of medical and psychological modalities is the treatment of choice (Faulstich & Williamson, 1985). Further research of a well-designed and sophisticated nature is necessary, both to identify what kinds of psychological interventions are effective for treating dermatological conditions and to refine those already in use.

Practical Suggestions and Future Directions

Although psychological factors have long been implicated in the etiology and maintenance of certain dermatological conditions, the current empirical evidence of this is rather modest at best. Historically, approaches that have emphasized purely psychological (primarily psychodynamic or learning) or biological factors have failed to explain convincingly the onset, exacerbation, or alleviation of dermatological disorders and symptoms. The complexity of dermatological disorders calls for an integrated approach that considers biological vulnerability, personality and individual coping styles, and familial support systems.

Clinical Implications

Some of the most serious problems facing psychologists interested in this area are practical ones. Where is the patient seen—in a dermatology clinic or in a psychiatric or behavioral medicine clinic? What kind of treatment is given, for what type of dermatological disorder, and who pays?

Other problems relate to referral and collaboration issues. First, who makes the referral? It has long been documented in the clinical dermatological literature that patients are reluctant to accept a psychological referral, or even explanation, for their disorder (Koblenzer, 1983). A similar problem exists in working with most dermatologists. As is probably true of other physicians, dermatologists rarely recognize the importance of psychological stresses to their patients' symptoms because of inexperience and poor training in psychological issues; as a result they are less likely to consider nonmedical interventions. Dermatologists themselves often spend barely a few minutes with each patient. It has been our experience that both patients and physicians are more likely to consider behavioral and psychological interventions when the health care professional uses a stress model rather than a psychoanalytic model. The goal of treatment is best described as lowering, changing, or controlling stress. However, we have found that even under the best circumstances only a minority of patients take a psychological referral if it requires them to leave the dermatologist's office.

Providing treatment and conducting research is best done within the domain of the dermatologist's office or clinic. Unfortunately, aside from academic medical centers, where some internal support may exist for research and treatment, financial considerations remain a crucial issue in most settings. Health psychologists must provide evidence of the efficacy and cost efficiency of their interventions so that patients, and their insurers, will pay for psychological treatment. Yet at the same time the difficulty in engaging dermatological patients in psychological treatments impedes progress.

One concrete suggestion for mental health practitioners in collaborating with dermatologists is to provide practical and timely solutions. The likelihood of developing a lasting collaboration is greatly increased if the treating psychologist can be of use to both the patient and the physician. The psychologist must be familiar with the wide range of dermatological disorders in which psychosocial factors are reported to be involved. Then the ability to offer a precise treatment plan (e.g., exposure and response prevention) focused on a specific behavior (e.g., excessive washing) within a concrete diagnosis (e.g., OCD) is likely to be appreciated by both the patient and referring dermatologist.

Physicians throughout their medical school training and clinical careers are taught to focus on physical disorders (e.g., heart disease or diabetes). Medical school curricula have recently encouraged expanding the focus from the "disease state" to include a comprehensive biopsychosocial approach (Engel, 1980). It has been our experience that most dermatologists, like other physicians, lack training in this comprehensive approach. The psychologist can educate the dermatologist to the importance of a comprehensive biopsychosocial approach most effectively when it can make a concrete difference in the day-to-day management of the dermatological patient. For example, the ability to diagnose and treat OCD in a neurodermatitis patient with a lessening of compulsive ritualistic washing that ultimately leads to improvement in the skin condition is an intervention dermatologists themselves will greatly appreciate (Friedman et al., in press).

Research Implications

Clinical research needs to focus on numerous variables, including medical diagnosis, personality factors, life situation, and the patient's response to different treatment approaches. Research or treatment protocols provided to dermatology patients need to consider the many issues we have raised in this chapter; for example, how is the disorder defined? Are all patients with the same disorder (e.g., eczema) necessarily the same? As described earlier in this chapter, some researchers have identified homogeneous subgroups of patients (e.g., those eczema patients who identify stress as a major variable affecting their disorder). What is the reliability of the medical and the psychological diagnosis? What is the reliability of the assessment measures? Are assessment techniques standardized? How does one reliably assess change? Is the intervention well defined? What kind of comparison or control group is used? Is there random assignment, a waiting-list control, and adequate follow-up?

For research in the field of psychological factors and dermatology to progress, researchers need to go beyond the simple descriptive level of most of the research summarized in this chapter. To be truly comprehensive, researchers need to focus on one type of disorder (e.g., atopic dermatitis) while looking at one type of behavior (e.g., excessive scratching) and perhaps across a subset of individuals (e.g., anxious dermatitis patients). Unfortunately, the more focused the programmatic research becomes, the less likely it is that clinical dermatologists will see it as relevant to their day-to-day management of patients.

Dermatological disorders of all types can cause an untold amount of suffering for the afflicted. Psychological factors such as stress play an important role for a significant proportion of these patients. Previous research has been primarily descriptive. An important new direction is to view dermatological disorders in a truly comprehensive stress–diathesis model. Health psychologists are just beginning to answer some of the fundamental questions that have long existed in the dermatological literature. Psychologists can have a major impact in the lives of countless patients and at the same time contribute to understanding the relationship between psyche and soma.

REFERENCES

Allen, K. E., & Harris, F. R. (1966). Elimination of a child's excessive scratching by training the mother in reinforcement procedures. *Behavior Research and Therapy, 4*, 79–84.

American Psychiatric Association. (1987). *Diagnostic and statistical manual of mental disorders* (3rd ed., rev.). Washington, DC: Author.

Arnetz, B. B., Fjellner, B. O., Eneroth, P., & Kallner, A. (1991). Endocrine and dermatological concomitants of mental stress. *Acta Dermato-Venereologica, 156*, 9–12.

Bar, L. H. J., & Kuypers, B. R. M. (1973). Behavior therapy in dermatological practice. *British Journal of Dermatology, 88,* 591–598.

Bayer, C. A. (1972). Self-monitoring and mild aversion treatment of trichotillomania. *Journal of Behavior Therapy and Experimental Psychiatry, 3,* 139–141.

Beare, J. M. (1976). Generalized pruritus: A study of 43 cases. *Clinical and Experimental Dermatology, 1,* 343–352.

Beerman, H. (1962). Aetiology and mechanisms in development of neurodermatitis. In N. J. Mayer (Ed.), *Psychosomatic medicine.* London: Kimpton.

Berg, M. (1991). Evaluation of a questionnaire used in dermatological epidemiology: Discrepancy between self-reported symptoms and objective signs. *Acta Dermato-Venereologica, 156,* 13–17.

Bishop, E. R. (1983). Monosymptomatic hypochondriacal syndromes in dermatology. *Journal of the American Academy of Dermatology, 9,* 152–157.

Brady, K. T., Austin, L., & Lydiard, R. B. (1990). Body dysmorphic disorder: The relationship to obsessive–compulsive disorder. *Journal of Nervous and Mental Disease, 178,* 538–540.

Bremer-Shulte, M., Cormane, R. H., Van Dijk, E., & Wuite, J. (1985). Group therapy of psoriasis. *Journal of the American Academy of Dermatology, 12,* 61–66.

Brodman, K., Erdman, A. J., Lorge, I., Wolff, H. G., & Broadbent, T. H. (1949). The Cornell Medical Index: An adjunct to medical interviewing. *Journal of the American Medical Association, 140,* 530–534.

Brown, D. G. (1967). Emotional disturbance in eczema: A study of symptom reporting behavior. *Journal of Psychosomatic Research, 11,* 27–40.

Brown, D. G., & Bettley, F. R. (1971). Psychiatric treatment of eczema: A controlled trial. *British Medical Journal, 2,* 729–734.

Cataldo, M. F., Varni, J. W., Russo, R. C., & Estes, S. A. (1980). Behavior therapy techniques in treatment of exfoliative dermatitis. *Archives of Dermatology, 116,* 919–922.

Christenson, G. A., Mackenzie, T. B., Mitchell, J. E., & Callies, A. L. (1991). A placebo-controlled, double-blind crossover study of fluoxetine in trichotillomania. *American Journal of Psychiatry, 148,* 1566–1571.

Cossidente, A., & Sarti, M. G. (1981). Psychiatric syndromes with dermatologic expression. *Clinics in Dermatology, 4,* 201–220.

Cotterill, J. A. (1981). Dermatological non-disease: A common and potentially fatal disturbance of cutaneous body image. *British Journal of Dermatology, 104,* 611–619.

Cunliffe, W. J., Hull, S. M., & Hughes, B. R. (1989). *The benefit of isotretinoin for the severely depressed/dysmorphophobic patient.* Abstract presented at the Second International Congress on Psychiatry and Dermatology, University of Leeds, Leeds, UK.

DiNardo, P. A., & Barlow, D. H. (1988). *Anxiety Disorders Interview Schedule–Revised (ADIS-R).* (Available from the Phobia and Anxiety Disorders

Clinic, Center for Stress and Anxiety Disorders, State University of New York at Albany, Albany, NY 12222)

Doran, A. R., Roy, A., & Wolkowitz, O. M. (1985). Self-destructive dermatoses. *Psychiatric Clinics of North America, 8,* 291–298.

Dungey, R. K., & Buselmeier, T. J. (1982). Medical and psychosocial aspects of psoriasis. *Health and Social Work, 7,* 140–147.

Engel, G. L. (1980). The clinical application of the biopsychosocial model. *American Journal of Psychiatry, 137,* 535–544.

Faulstich, M. E., & Williamson, D. A. (1985). An overview of atopic dermatitis: Toward a bio-behavioral integration. *Journal of Psychosomatic Research, 29,* 647–654.

Faulstich, M. E., Williamson, D. A., Duchman, E. G., Conerly, S., & Brantley, P. (1985). Psychophysiological analysis of atopic dermatitis. *Journal of Psychosomatic Research, 29,* 415–417.

Fava, G. A., Perini, G. I., Santonastoso, P., & Farnaso, C. V. (1980). Life events and psychological stress in dermatologic disorders: Psoriasis, chronic urticaria, and fungal infections. *British Journal of Medical Psychology, 53,* 277–282.

Fjellner, B., & Arnetz, B. B. (1985). Psychological predictors of pruritus during mental stress. *Acta Dermato-Venereologica, 65,* 504–508.

Fried, R. G., & Shalita, A. R. (1992). The reciprocal interaction between acne and the psyche. *Focus on Cutis and Psyche, 2,* 28–33.

Friedman, S., Hatch, M. L., Paradis, C. M., Popkin, M., & Shalita, A. R. (in press). Obsessive compulsive disorder in two Black ethnic groups: Incidence in an urban dermatology clinic. *Journal of Anxiety Disorders.*

Friman, P. C., Finney, J. W., & Christopherson, E. R. (1984). Behavioral treatment of trichotillomania: An evaluative review. *Behavior Therapy, 15,* 249–264.

Garrie, E. V., Garrie, S. A., & Mote, T. (1974). Anxiety and atopic dermatitis. *Journal of Consulting and Clinical Psychology, 42,* 742.

Garrie, S. A., & Garrie, E. V. (1978). Anxiety and skin diseases. *Cutis, 23,* 205–208.

Gaston, L., Crombez, J., Lassonde, M., Bernier-Buzzanga, J., & Hodgins, S. (1991). Psychological stress and psoriasis: Experimental and prospective correlational studies. *Acta Dermato-Venereologica, 156,* 37–43.

Gibbs, D. (1969). Reciprocal inhibition therapy of a case of symptomatic erythema. *Behavior Research and Therapy, 3,* 261.

Gil, K. M., Keefe, F. J., Sampson, H. A., McCaskill, C. C., Rodin, J., & Crisson, J. E. (1987). The relationship of stress and family environment to atopic dermatitis symptoms in children. *Journal of Psychosomatic Research, 31,* 673–684.

Gil, K. M., Keefe, F. J., Sampson, H. A., McCaskill, C. C., Rodin, J., & Crisson, J. E. (1988). Direct observation of scratching behavior in children with atopic dermatitis. *Behavior Therapy, 19,* 213–227.

Gil, K. M., & Sampson, H. A. (1989). Psychological and social factors of atopic dermatitis. *Allergy, 44,* 84–98.

Gould, W. M., & Gragg, T. M. (1983). A dermatology–psychiatry liaison clinic. *Journal of the American Academy of Dermatology, 9,* 73–77.

Graham, D. T., & Wolff, S. (1953). The relation of eczema to attitude and to vascular reaction of the human skin. *Journal of Clinical Medicine, 42,* 238–254.

Gupta, M. A., Gupta, A. K., Kirkby, S., Schork, N. J., Gorr, S. K., Ellis, C. N., & Voorhees, J. J. (1989). A psychocutaneous profile of psoriasis patients who are stress reactors: A study of 127 patients. *General Hospital Psychiatry, 11,* 166–173.

Gupta, M. A., Gupta, A. K., Kirkby, S., Weiner, H. K., Mace, T. M., Schork, N. J., Johnson, E. A., Ellis, C. N., & Voorhees, J. J. (1988). Pruritus in psoriasis: A prospective study of some psychiatric and dermatologic correlates. *Archives of Dermatology, 124,* 1052–1057.

Gupta, M. A., Gupta, A. K., Schork, N. J., Ellis, C. N., & Voorhees, J. J. (1990). The aging face: A psychocutaneous perspective. *Journal of Dermatologic Surgery and Oncology, 16,* 902–904.

Hardy, G. E., & Cotterill, J. A. (1982). A study of depression and obsessionality in dysmorphophobic and psoriatic patients. *British Journal of Psychiatry, 140,* 19–22.

Hatch, M. L., Paradis, C., Friedman, S., Popkin, M., & Shalita, A. R. (1992). Obsessive compulsive disorder in patients with chronic pruritic conditions: Case studies and discussion. *Journal of the American Academy of Dermatology, 26,* 549–551.

Haynes, S. N., Wilson, C. C., Jaffe, P. G., & Britton, B. T. (1979). Biofeedback treatment of atopic dermatitis. *Biofeedback and Self-Regulation, 4,* 195–209.

Hollander, E., Liebowitz, M. R., Winchel, R., Klumker, A., & Klein, D. F. (1989). Treatment of body dysmorphic disorder with serotonin reuptake blockers. *American Journal of Psychiatry, 146,* 768–770.

Hughes, J. E., Barraclough, B. M., Hamblin, L. G., & White, J. E. (1983). Psychiatric symptoms in dermatology patients. *British Journal of Psychiatry, 143,* 51–54.

Hughes, H., Brown, B. W., Lawlis, G. F., & Fulton, J. E. (1983). Treatment of acne vulgaris by biofeedback relaxation and cognitive imagery. *Journal of Psychosomatic Research, 27,* 185–191.

Jordan, J. M., & Whitlock, F. A. (1974). Atopic dermatitis: Anxiety and conditioned scratch responses. *Journal of Psychosomatic Research, 18,* 297–299.

Jowett, S., & Ryan, T. (1985). Skin disease and handicap: An analysis of the impact of skin conditions. *Social Science Medicine, 20,* 425–429.

Koblenzer, C. S. (1983). Psychosomatic concepts in dermatology: A dermatologist–psychoanalyst's viewpoint. *Archives of Dermatology, 119,* 501–511.

Koblenzer, C. S. (1987). *Psychocutaneous disease.* New York: Grune & Stratton.

Kuypers, B. R. M., & Cotton, D. W. K. (1972). Conditioning of sweating: A preliminary report. *British Journal of Dermatology, 87,* 154–160.

Leider, M., & Rosenblum, M. (1976). *A dictionary of dermatological words, terms and phrases.* West Haven, CT: Dome Laboratories.

Lerer, B., & Jacobowitz, J. (1981). Treatment of essential hyperhidrosis by psychotherapy. *Psychosomatics, 22,* 536–538.

Lyketsos, G. C., Stratigos, J., Tawil, G., Psaras, M., & Lyketsos, C. G. (1985). Hostile personality characteristics, dysthymic states and neurotic symptoms in urticaria, psoriasis and alopecia. *Psychotherapy and Psychosomatics, 44,* 122–131.

Manuso, J. S. J. (1977). The use of biofeedback-assisted hand warming training in the treatment of chronic eczematous dermatitis of the hands: A case study. *Journal of Behavior Therapy and Experimental Psychiatry, 8,* 445–446.

Matussek, P., Agerer, D., & Seibt, G. (1985). Aggression in depressives and psoriatics. *Psychotherapy and Psychosomatics, 43,* 120–125.

Miller, B. F., & Keane, C. B. (1987). *Encyclopedia and dictionary of medicine, nursing, and allied health* (4th ed.). Philadelphia: Saunders.

Motley, R. J., & Finlay, A. Y. (1989). How much disability is caused by acne? *Clinical and Experimental Dermatology, 14,* 194–198.

Munro, A., & Chmara, J. (1982). Monosymptomatic hypochondriacal psychosis: A diagnostic check list based on 50 cases of the disorder. *Canadian Journal of Psychiatry, 27,* 374–376.

Musaph, H. (1969). Aggression and symptom formation in dermatology. *Journal of Psychosomatic Research, 13,* 257–264.

Paulson, M. J., & Petrus, E. P. (1969). Delusions of parasitosis: A psychological study. *Psychosomatics, 10,* 111–120.

Paykel, E. S., Emms, E. M., Fletcher, J., & Rassaby, E. S. (1980). Life events and social support in puerperal depression. *British Journal of Psychiatry, 136,* 339–346.

Payne, R. A., Rowland Payne, C. M. E., & Marks, R. (1985). Stress does not worsen psoriasis? A controlled study of 32 patients. *Clinical and Experimental Dermatology, 10,* 239–245.

Perini, G. I., Fornasa, C. V., Cipriani, R., Bettin, A., Zecchino, F., & Peserico, A. (1984). Life events and alopecia areata. *Psychotherapy Psychosomatic, 41,* 48–52.

Phillips, K. A. (1991). Body dysmorphic disorder: The distress of imagined ugliness. *American Journal of Psychiatry, 148,* 1138–1149.

Primeau, F., & Fontaine, R. (1987). Obsessive disorder with self-mutilation: A subgroup responsive to pharmacotherapy. *Canadian Journal of Psychiatry, 32,* 699–701.

Rasmussen, S. A. (1985). Obsessive–compulsive disorder in dermatology practice. *Journal of the American Academy of Dermatology, 6,* 965–967.

Ratliff, R. G., & Stein, N. H. (1968). Treatment of neurodermatitis by behavior therapy: A case study. *Behavior Research and Therapy, 6,* 397–399.

Robins, L. N., Hezler, J. E., Weissmann, M. M., Orvaschel, H., Gruenberg, E., Burke, J. D., & Regier, D. A. (1984). Lifetime prevalence of specific psychiatric disorders in three sites. *Archives of General Psychiatry, 41,* 949–958.

Rook, A., Wilkinson, D. S., & Ebling, F. J. G. (Eds.). (1979). *Textbook of dermatology* (3rd ed.). Oxford, UK: Blackwell Scientific.

Rosenbaum, M. S., & Ayllon, T. (1981). The behavioral treatment of neuro-dermatitis through habit reversal. *Behavioral Research and Therapy, 19,* 313–318.

Sanborn, P. E., Sanborn, C. J., Cimbolic, P., & Niswander, G. P. (1972). Suicide and stress-related dermatoses. *Diseases of the Nervous System, 33,* 391–394.

Seville, R. H. (1977). Psoriasis and stress. *British Journal of Dermatology, 97,* 297–302.

Sneddon, I., & Sneddon, J. (1975). Self-inflicted injury: A follow-up study of 43 patients. *British Medical Journal, 3,* 527–530.

Spitz, R. A. (1965). *The first year of life: A psychoanalytic study of normal and deviant development of object relations.* Madison, CT: International Universities Press.

Suinn, R. (1977). *Manual for anxiety management training (AMT).* Fort Collins, CO: Rocky Mountain Behavioral Sciences Institute.

Surman, O. S., Gottlieb, S. K., Hackett, T. P., & Silverberg, E. L. (1973). Hypnosis in the treatment of warts. *Archives of General Psychiatry, 28,* 439–441.

Swedo, S. E., Leonard, H. L., Rapoport, J. L., Lenane, M. C., Goldberger, E. L., & Cheslow, D. L. (1989). A double-blind comparison of clomipramine and desipramine in the treatment of trichotillomania (hair pulling). *New England Journal of Medicine, 321,* 497–501.

Torch, E. M., & Bishop, E. R. (1981). Delusions of parasitosis: Psychotherapeutic engagement. *American Journal of Psychotherapy, 35,* 101–106.

Tsushima, W. T. (1988). Current psychological treatments for stress-related skin disorders. *Cutis, 42,* 402–404.

Van der Meeren, H. L. M., Van der Schaar, W. W., & Van den Hurk, C. M. (1985). The psychological impact of severe acne. *Cutis, 7,* 84–86.

Watson, D. L., Tharp, R. G., & Krisberg, J. (1972). Case study in self-modification: Suppression of inflammatory scratching while awake and asleep. *Journal of Behavior Therapy and Experimental Psychiatry, 3,* 213–215.

Waxman, D. (1973). Behavior therapy of psoriasis: A hypnoanalytic and counter-conditioning technique. *Postgraduate Medical Journal, 49,* 591–595.

Weinstein, M. Z. (1984). Psychosocial perspectives on psoriasis. *Dermatology Clinics, 2,* 507–515.

Welkowitz, L. A., Held, J. L., & Held, A. L. (1989). Management of neurotic scratching with behavioral therapy. *Journal of the American Academy of Dermatologists, 21,* 802–804.

Werth, G. R. (1978). The hives dilemma. *American Family Physician, 17,* 139–143.

Wilson, E. (1842). *A practical and theoretical treatise on the diagnosis, pathology, and treatment of diseases of the skin, arranged according to a natural system of classification and preceded by an outline of the anatomy and physiology of the skin.* London: J. Churchill.

Wittkower, E., & Russell, B. (1953). *Emotional factors in skin disease*. New York: Harper.

Wu, S. F., Kinder, B. N., Trunnel, T. N., & Fulton, J. E. (1988). Role of anxiety and anger in acne patients: A relationship with the severity of the disorder. *Journal of the American Academy of Dermatology, 18,* 325–332.

Zachariae, R., & Bjerring, P. (1990). The effect of hypnotically induced analgesia on flare reaction of the cutaneous histamine prick test. *Archives of Dermatological Research, 282,* 539–543.

Zachariae, R., Bjerring, P., & Arendt-Nielsen, L. (1989). Modulation of type I immediate and type IV delayed immunoreactivity using direct suggestion and guided imagery during hypnosis. *Allergy, 44,* 537–542.

Chapter 7

Raynaud's Disease and Phenomenon

Robert R. Freedman

R aynaud's phenomenon is characterized by episodic digital va-sospasms that are provoked by cold exposure, emotional stress, or both (Freedman & Ianni, 1983a). Estimates of its prevalence range from 4.3% and 2.7% of women and men, respectively, from a questionnaire study in South Carolina (Weinrich, Maricq, Keil, McGregor, & Diat, 1990) to 19% of women and 11% of men according to general practitioners in the United Kingdom (Simlan, Holligan, Brennan, & Maddison, 1990).

The term *Raynaud's disease* denotes the primary form of the disorder, in which the symptoms cannot be explained by an identifiable disease

---

The research described in this chapter was supported by National Institutes of Health grants HL-23828 and HL-30604.

process such as scleroderma or by other collagen vascular diseases. When the symptoms occur secondarily to another disease, the term *Raynaud's phenomenon* is used.

Psychological Control of Finger Blood Flow

Research on the pathophysiology of Raynaud's disease is most easily understood in the context of the mechanisms controlling finger blood flow. Blood flow in the human finger is almost entirely cutaneous and plays an important role in body temperature regulation. The palmar surface of the finger contains many arteriovenous shunts (anastomoses) that are capable of rapidly altering their rate of blood flow in response to changes in external temperature. This is mediated by the release of norepinephrine from sympathetic vasoconstrictor nerves (Figure 1). Body cooling produces reflex digital vasoconstriction through increased neuronal activity, and conversely, body heating causes peripheral vasodilation through withdrawal of this activity. Finger capillary blood flow is less affected by sympathetic nervous system activity than is arteriovenous shunt flow (Coffman, 1972). There are no known vasodilating nerves in the human finger.

Finger blood flow is also regulated through the actions of circulating vasoactive compounds with α- and β-adrenergic receptors to cause vasoconstriction and vasodilation, respectively. Epinephrine released from the adrenal medulla and norepinephrine released from nerve endings elsewhere in the body act at α-adrenergic receptors to cause vasoconstriction. These α-adrenergic receptors are inside the lumen of the blood vessel, whereas neuronal α-adrenergic receptors terminate within the blood vessel wall. Peripheral vascular α-adrenergic receptors are thermosensitive and serve as a means of local regulation of blood flow (Freedman, Sabharwal, Moten, & Migály, 1992). β-Adrenergic vasodilation has been demonstrated in the finger by arterial injection of isoproterenol, a synthetic β-adrenergic agonist, but a naturally occurring ligand that acts in this manner has not yet been found.

Etiology

Although the etiology of Raynaud's disease is not known, two main theories have been put forth to explain it. Raynaud (1888) thought

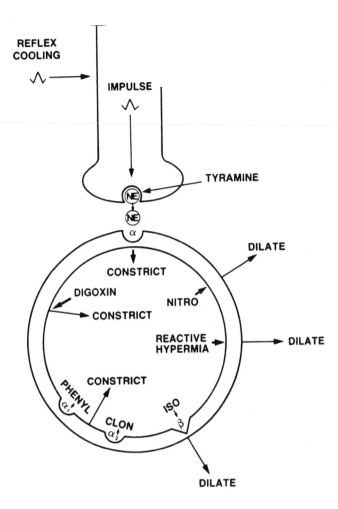

Figure 1.   Control of digital blood flow. Reflexive cooling causes digital vaso-constriction through the liberation of norepinephrine (NE) from sympathetic nerve endings, which can be reduced by indirect heating. Injection of tyra-mine causes vasoconstriction by displacing norepinephrine from the nerves. Vasoconstriction can also be caused by the interaction of circulating norepi-nephrine or synthetic agonists such as phenylephrine (PHENYL) or clonidine (CLON) with α1- and α2-adrenergic receptors. Synthetic β-adrenergic ago-nists such as isoproterenol (ISO) cause vasodilation through interaction with β receptors. Reactive hyperemia produces vasodilation through the accu-mulation of unknown compounds during ischemia. From "Raynaud's Dis-ease" by R. R. Freedman, in *Handbook of Clinical Psychophysiology* (p. 471) edited by G. Turpin, 1989, New York: Wiley. Copyright 1989 by Wiley.

that exaggerated sympathetic nervous system activity caused an increased vasoconstrictive response to cold, whereas Lewis (1929) felt that a "local fault" rendered small peripheral blood vessels hypersensitive to local cooling. Studies of plasma catecholamine levels in Raynaud's disease patients have generally not supported Raynaud's theory. Studies of plasma epinephrine and norepinephrine in Raynaud's disease patients have found levels that were higher than (Peacock, 1959), lower than (Surwit & Allen, 1983), or no different from (Kontos & Wasserman, 1969) those of normal persons. Moreover, microelectrode studies of skin nerve sympathetic activity found no differences between patients with primary Raynaud's disease and control subjects during cold pressor tests or tests with other sympathetic stimuli (Fagius & Blumberg, 1985).

Research has supported the theory of Lewis: There were no differences between patients with primary Raynaud's disease and control subjects in their responses to a variety of sympathetic stimuli, such as reflex cooling, indirect heating, or intra-arterial infusions of tyramine, a compound that causes the indirect release of norepinephrine from sympathetic nerve endings (Freedman, Sabharwal, Desai, Wenig, & Mayes, 1989). In the same investigation, it was demonstrated that patients had significantly greater digital vasoconstrictive responses to intra-arterial phenylephrine (an $\alpha1$-adrenergic agonist) and clonidine (an $\alpha2$-adrenergic agonist) than did normal control subjects. These results suggested that patients with primary Raynaud's disease have increased peripheral vascular $\alpha1$- and $\alpha2$-adrenergic receptor sensitivity or density, or both, compared with normal persons. Several studies of platelet $\alpha2$-adrenergic receptors also found increased receptor density in Raynaud's disease patients in relation to controls (Edwards, Phinney, Taylor, Keenan, & Porter, 1987; Graafsma et al., 1991; Keenan & Porter, 1983).

In a subsequent investigation, vasospastic attacks were induced in 9 of 11 patients with primary Raynaud's disease and in 8 of 10 patients with scleroderma (Freedman, Mayes, & Sabharwal, 1989). The attacks were photographed using an automatic camera and scored by three independent raters. Two fingers on one hand were anesthetized by local injection of lidocaine, and the effectiveness of the nerve blocks was demonstrated by plethysmography. The frequency of vasospastic attacks in nerve-blocked fingers was not significantly different from that in the corresponding intact fingers on the contralateral hand.

These findings clearly demonstrate that the vasospastic attacks of Raynaud's disease and phenomenon can occur without the involvement of efferent digital nerves and suggest there is no etiological role of sympathetic hyperactivity.

In vitro (Flavahan, Lindblad, Verebeuren, Shepherd, & Vanhoutte, 1985; Flavahan & Vanhoutte, 1986; Harker et al., 1990) and in vivo (Freedman et al., 1992) studies have shown that cooling modulates contractile responses mediated by α-adrenergic receptors, depending on the species and blood vessels involved. In a recent study, Freedman, Moten, Migály, and Mayes (1993) determine the effects of cooling on α1- and α2-adrenergic responses in Raynaud's disease patients using brachial artery infusions of α1- and α2-adrenergic agonists. This study examined 17 primary Raynaud's disease patients and 12 female normal volunteers. Clonidine HCl and phenylephrine HCl were administered through a brachial artery catheter while blood flow was measured by venous occlusion plethysmography in cooled and uncooled fingers. Cooling potentiated α2-adrenergic vasoconstriction in the patients ($p < .05$) but depressed this response in the controls ($p < .01$) (Figure 2). Vasoconstrictive responses to phenylephrine were not significantly affected by cooling but were significantly greater in the cooled and uncooled fingers of the patients than in the corresponding fingers of the controls ($p < .05$) (Figure 3). These results suggest that cold-induced sensitization of peripheral vascular α2-adrenergic receptors constitutes the local fault by which cooling triggers the vasospastic attacks of Raynaud's disease. Attacks that are induced by emotional stress can be explained by normal catecholamine elevations acting on hypersensitive vascular α1- and α2-adrenergic receptors.

Some studies have examined the physical properties of the blood in Raynaud's disease patients, but have been inconclusive. One investigation (Pringle, Walder, & Weaver, 1965) found increased blood viscosity and red blood cell aggregation in Raynaud's disease patients, but subsequent investigations have failed to confirm these findings (Johnsen, Nielsen, & Skovborg, 1977; McGrath, Peek, & Penny, 1978).

In summary, the most recent evidence strongly suggests that the vasospastic attacks of Raynaud's disease are locally triggered by peripheral vascular α2-adrenoceptors that are hypersensitive to cold. Moreover, because vascular α1- and α2-adrenoceptors are hypersensitive in Raynaud's disease patients in the basal state, normal cate-

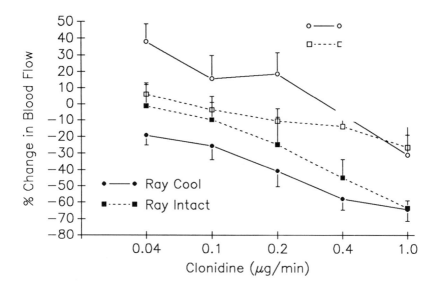

Figure 2. Finger blood flow responses to intra-arterial clonidine in cooled and intact fingers in 17 Raynaud's disease patients and 12 normal volunteers (*M* ± *SE*).

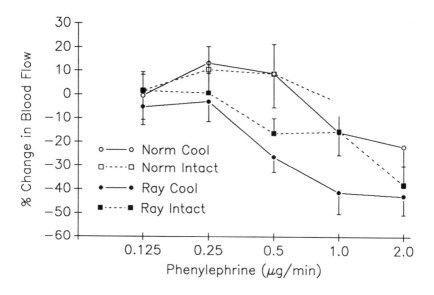

Figure 3. Finger blood flow responses to intra-arterial phenylephrine in cooled and intact fingers in 17 Raynaud's disease patients and 12 normal volunteers (*M* ± *SE*).

cholamine elevations that are produced by emotional stress or by reflex cooling can also trigger the vasospastic attacks.

Familial Aggregation of Idiopathic Raynaud's Disease

It has been demonstrated that α-adrenoceptor function is under considerable genetic control in humans (Propping & Friedl, 1983). As a first step toward identifying a genetic component in idiopathic Raynaud's disease, my colleagues and I sought to determine whether this syndrome showed significant familial aggregation. Thirty consecutive patients (26 women and 4 men) who were classified as having idiopathic Raynaud's disease served as probands in this investigation. All met the Allen and Brown (1932) criteria for primary Raynaud's disease and had negative antinuclear antibody tests; furthermore, their nailfold capillaries showed no evidence of connective tissue disease. Pedigrees were constructed for all probands. First-degree relatives of the probands and nonconsanguineous relatives were contacted by mail and by telephone and administered a questionnaire to determine the presence of Raynaud's symptoms and the absence of secondary disorders. They were medically examined when possible. The probands had 217 first-degree relatives of whom 46 (17 men and 29 women) were classified as having Raynaud's disease. This represents a prevalence of 21.2% (30.8% if the probands are included). There were 237 nonconsanguineous relatives who served as controls. Of these, 5 (3 men and 2 women) were considered to have Raynaud's disease (2.1%). A chi-square test showed that the prevalence of Raynaud's disease was significantly ($p < .0001$) higher in the probands' relatives than in the nonconsanguineous controls. This finding demonstrates significant familial aggregation of primary Raynaud's disease. Because the consanguineous and nonconsanguineous relatives presumably shared similar environments, this aggregation is most likely due to genetic factors.

Medical Treatments for Raynaud's Disease

Pharmacological treatments for Raynaud's disease have been previously reviewed (Coffman, 1991). Briefly, nifedipine is presently the drug of first choice for patients with primary Raynaud's disease. Nifedipine is a calcium slow-channel blocker that reduces the influx of calcium into cells, which thereby decreases vasoconstriction. Nifedipine has been demonstrated to decrease the frequency, duration, and intensity of vasospastic attacks in about two thirds of the primary and secondary Raynaud's patients treated (Coffman, 1991).

Because serotonergic vasoconstriction is also present in human fingers, ketanserin, a serotonergic S2 antagonist, has been used with primary and secondary Raynaud's patients. However, a large double-blind study of primary and secondary Raynaud's patients produced disappointing results (Coffman et al., 1989). The reduction in attack frequency with ketanserin was only 34%, compared with a placebo rate of 18%. There were no changes in the severity or duration of vasospastic attacks. Moreover, there were no changes in finger blood measurements during cold or warm conditions.

Surgical sympathectomies have been tried as a means of abolishing reflex sympathetic activity, but vascular tone generally recovers within a period of a few weeks (Robertson & Smithwick, 1951). The recent finding by my colleagues and me that vasospastic attacks can be induced in primary and secondary Raynaud's patients despite a digital nerve blockade raises serious questions regarding the physiological rationale for this procedure.

Effects of Temperature Biofeedback in Normal Persons

Toward the end of the development of nonpharmacological treatments for Raynaud's and other disorders, many investigators began to study the effects of temperature biofeedback in normal volunteers. The first controlled group studies of temperature biofeedback in normal subjects were performed by Keefe (Keefe, 1975; Keefe, 1978; Keefe & Gardner, 1979), who showed that various combinations of brief temperature feedback training and thermal suggestions produced significant increases in finger temperature, ranging from 0.8 to 1.3 °C. Subjects generally acquired the response early in training, and the magnitude of the response was not increased by additional training sessions. One study (Keefe, 1978) showed that the training effect was maintained at 1- and 2-week follow-up sessions.

For finger temperature self-control to be useful in the treatment of disease states, its effects must be replicable without instruments and outside the laboratory. The first study to examine this issue (Stoffer, Jensen, & Nesset, 1979) found that a group of normal subjects given contingent temperature feedback could significantly increase finger temperature after the removal of feedback, whereas a group given noncontingent feedback could not. Freedman and Ianni (1983b) extended this research to show that a group trained to vasodilate with temperature feedback could maintain this effect after the removal of feedback, both inside and outside the laboratory. These effects could not be explained by physiological relaxation and were not demonstrated by groups given frontalis electromyographic (EMG) feedback, autogenic training, or simple instructions to increase finger temperature. Another study has shown that a nonneural, β-adrenergic vasodilating mechanism is involved in vasodilation produced by temperature feedback (Freedman et al., 1988).

Behavioral Treatment of Raynaud's Disease

Despite the evidence that peripheral vascular α-adrenergic responsiveness is elevated in Raynaud's disease, it has not yet been possible to design pharmacological agents that specifically target the digital blood vessels. Thus, side effects such as hypotension, headaches, and flushing have limited the usefulness of some drugs. In contrast, behavioral treatments for Raynaud's disease have been promising and appear to have no adverse effects.

Behavioral treatments for Raynaud's disease have been designed to increase finger temperature or blood flow and ameliorate symptoms through relaxation procedures such as autogenic training (Surwit, Pilon, & Fenton, 1978) or through finger temperature biofeedback (Freedman & Ianni, 1983b; Freedman et al., 1988). In the first controlled study (Surwit et al., 1978), patients were randomly assigned to receive either autogenic training (self-suggestion of warm imagery) alone or in combination with temperature feedback. In addition, for a 1-month period, half of the subjects served as a waiting-list control group for the other half and then received treatment. Subjects as a whole showed improvement on a cold stress test and reported decreased attack frequencies (10–32%), but there were no group differences on these measures. Similar results were found in a subsequent study (Keefe, Surwit, & Pilon, 1980) that compared progressive relaxation, autogenic training, and a combination of both.

Because prior investigations used various combinations of behavioral procedures, another study (Freedman, Ianni, & Wenig, 1983) was conducted in which the effects of temperature feedback alone were compared with those of autogenic training or frontalis EMG feedback. In this same study a fourth procedure was also studied, in which temperature feedback was administered during mild cold stress to the finger. It was hypothesized that this procedure would enhance generalization of the feedback response to the natural environment, where it must be produced under cold conditions. Patients who received temperature feedback alone or under cold stress showed significant elevations in finger temperature (Figure 4) and significant

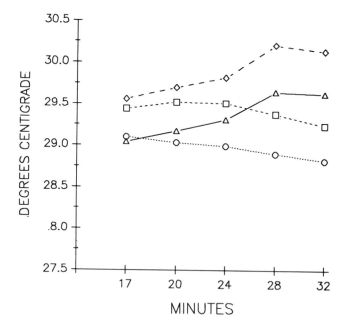

Figure 4. Finger temperatures of temperature feedback (△); temperature feedback under cold stress, left hand (◇); electromyographic feedback (□); and autogenic instructions (○) subjects averaged across training sessions. From "Behavioral Treatment of Raynaud's Disease" by R. R. Freedman, P. Ianni, and P. Wenig, 1983, *Journal of Consulting and Clinical Psychology, 51,* p. 543. Copyright 1983 by the American Psychological Association.

declines in reported symptom frequency (Figure 5) the following winter (66.8% and 92.5%, respectively). Those who received EMG feedback or autogenic training showed neither significant vasodilation nor symptomatic improvement but did demonstrate declines in muscle tension, heart rate, and reported stress levels. Patients in the temperature feedback groups did not show declines in the latter three measures but did maintain symptomatic improvement at 2- and 3-year follow-up periods (Freedman, Ianni, & Wenig, 1985).

Thus, the effects of finger temperature biofeedback are physiologically different from those of autogenic training, frontalis EMG feedback, or simple instructions to increase finger temperature. Temperature feedback produces digital vasodilation without bradycardia or decreased muscle tension, whereas the other techniques produce bradycardia and lower EMG levels but not increased finger temperature. Pharmacological research uncovered a β-adrenergic mechanism that may explain increased digital blood flow in the absence of decreased generalized physiological arousal (Cohen & Coffman, 1981). Therefore, my colleagues and I tested the involvement of this mechanism

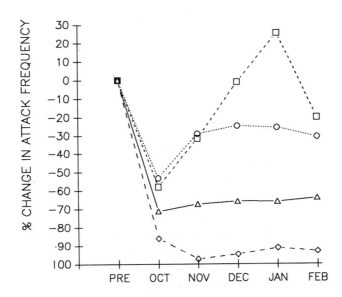

Figure 5. Reported attack frequencies of temperature feedback (△); temperature feedback under cold stress (◇); electromyographic feedback (□); and autogenic instructions (○) subjects during follow-up period, expressed as percentage change from pretreatment levels.

during temperature feedback in normal persons and Raynaud's disease patients by local beta blockade of the vasodilation with intra-arterial infusions of propranolol (Freedman et al., 1988).

In this study, 18 patients with idiopathic Raynaud's disease and 16 normal subjects were randomly assigned to receive 10 sessions of temperature feedback or autogenic training. After training, in a separate session, a catheter was placed in the right brachial artery using a local anesthetic and connected to two infusion pumps—one contained 0.9% saline solution whereas the other contained propranolol, a beta blocker. The pumps were housed in a soundproofed box and controlled remotely by the experimenter from a polygraph in a separate room. Finger blood flow was measured in both hands with venous occlusion plethysmography. After baseline recordings, the temperature-feedback signals or autogenic tapes were activated. After 6 min, the infusion was switched from saline to propranolol (0.5 mg/min) for 2 min, then saline for 4 min, propranolol (same dose) for 2 min, and saline for 4 min. These changes occurred without the subject's knowledge. Significant bilateral vasodilation occurred in the temperature-feedback subjects and was significantly reduced by propranolol in the infused hand but not in the control hand. The magnitudes of these effects were not significantly different in the Raynaud's disease and normal subjects. There were no significant blood flow changes in the patients or normal subjects who received autogenic training. There were no significant heart rate or blood pressure changes in the temperature-feedback group; the autogenic group showed a significant decline in heart rate during the autogenic instructions. Thus, a β-adrenergic mechanism is involved in feedback-induced vasodilation. Raynaud's patients who received temperature feedback showed significant increases in finger temperature and capillary blood flow and significant declines in attack frequency ($M = 81\%$), which were maintained at 1- and 2-year follow-up points.

The only known efferent vasomotor nerves in human fingers are adrenergic; neurogenic vasoconstriction is caused by the interaction of released norepinephrine with postjunctional α-adrenergic receptors. The finding by Freedman et al. (1988) of a β-adrenergic mechanism in temperature biofeedback thus raised the question of whether feedback-induced vasodilation is neurally mediated. Because it is possible to block the digital nerves by local injection of an anesthetic, we subsequently used this method to test the hypothesis that feedback-induced vasodilation is neurally mediated. Because digital nerve blockade raises finger blood flow to near ceiling levels, it was reduced to midrange levels by infusing norepinephrine (0.25 μg/min) in the right brachial artery. To control for all of the manipulations, blood flow was measured in three fingers: right, nerve-blocked with norepinephrine; right, no block with norepinephrine; left, no block without norepinephrine. The just-described propranolol infusion was then repeated (Figure 6). In two separate experiments of normal subjects ($N = 8$ and $N = 9$) and a subsequent experiment with Raynaud's disease patients ($N = 10$), it was found that vasodilation produced by temperature feedback was not attenuated by nerve blockade or by norepinephrine but was reduced by propranolol (Freedman et al., 1988). Thus, the β-adrenergic vasodilating mechanism of temperature feedback does not appear to be mediated through the digital nerves.

To examine further the possible changes in sympathetic nervous system activity during temperature feedback and autogenic training, Freedman et al. (1991) recently measured plasma levels of epinephrine and norepinephrine during these procedures. An intravenous needle was inserted into a vein on the back of the hand and connected to a Cormed blood withdrawal pump through nonthrombogenic tubing. The pump was located in an adjacent room, so that blood could be collected without observation by the subject. Plasma levels of epinephrine and norepinephrine were subsequently analyzed by high-performance liquid chromatography–exchange chromatography. Thirty-one patients with idiopathic Raynaud's disease were randomly assigned to receive eight 32-min sessions of finger temperature feedback ($n = 16$) or autogenic training ($n = 15$) over 28 days. During Sessions 1 and 8, blood was continuously drawn. During training, significant temperature and blood flow elevations were shown by feedback patients ($p < .001$), but not by autogenic patients. There were no significant effects for norepinephrine or epinephrine for either group. Virtually identical findings were obtained in a more recent study on normal subjects (Freedman, Keegan, Rodriguez, & Galloway, 1993).

These just-described investigations provided no evidence that sympathetic nervous system activation, as reflected by measures of plasma catecholamines, is reduced during behavioral treatments for primary Raynaud's disease. These results are consistent with previous findings that (a) catecholamine levels are not consistently elevated in these

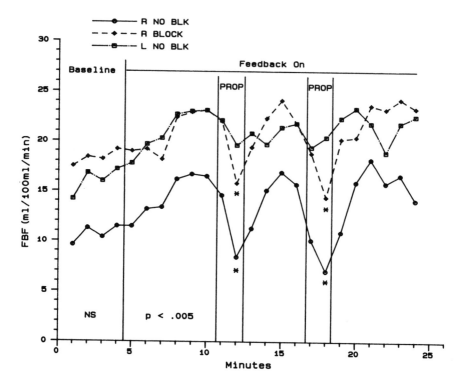

Figure 6. Blood flow (FBF) in three fingers during last 4 min of baseline period and subsequent temperature feedback period. Nerves in right second finger (R block) were anesthetized. During baseline period FBF did not significantly change (NS). When feedback was activated, FBF in all three fingers increased significantly ($p < .005$). Propranolol (PROP) infused in right brachial artery (0.5 mg for 2 min) caused significant ($p < .01$) reduction in FBF in infused hand (*) but not left hand. From "Nonneural Beta-Adrenergic Vasodilating Mechanism in Temperature Biofeedback" by R. R. Freedman et al., 1988, *Psychosomatic Medicine, 50*, p. 399. Copyright 1988 by Elsevier Science.

patients (Kontos & Wasserman, 1969; Surwit & Allen, 1983), (b) vasospastic attacks can be induced during sympathetic nerve blockade (Freedman, Sabharwal, et al., 1989), and (c) a sensitization of peripheral vascular α-adrenergic receptors is involved (Freedman, Mayes, & Sabharwal, 1989). Furthermore, the just-described findings are consistent with recent evidence that feedback-induced vasodilation is mediated, in part, through a nonneural β-adrenergic mechanism

(Freedman et al., 1988). Future research should attempt to identify the ligand responsible for this vasodilation and its precise mechanism of action.

Secondary Raynaud's Phenomenon

Behavioral and medical treatments for Raynaud's phenomenon have been less successful than those for the primary form of the disorder. In a case study, Freedman, Lynn, Ianni, and Hale (1981) showed that scleroderma patients who were treated with finger temperature feedback were able to increase digital temperature and show some symptomatic improvement. However, a subsequent controlled investigation produced disappointing results (Freedman, Ianni, & Wenig, 1984). In this study, 24 patients who met the American Rheumatism Association (now the American College of Rheumatology) classification criteria for systemic sclerosis were randomly assigned to receive 10 sessions of training in finger temperature feedback, EMG feedback, or autogenic training using the procedures of a previous study (Freedman et al., 1983). Subjects who received finger temperature feedback showed significant increases in finger temperature during training and during a posttraining voluntary control test, whereas those who received EMG feedback or autogenic training did not. After treatment, however, no group showed significant reductions in frequency of reported vasospastic attacks. There were no group differences in data obtained during ambulatory monitoring or laboratory cold stress tests. The reasons for the failure of temperature feedback to reduce symptoms in scleroderma patients are not known. However, it is likely that the underlying pathophysiology of secondary Raynaud's phenomenon is different from that of the primary disease.

Fewer pharmacological studies have been performed on secondary than on primary Raynaud's patients. Several small-scale studies (e.g., Belch et al., 1983) reported positive results of prostaglandin I2 and E1 infusions on secondary Raynaud's patients. However, it was necessary to administer the compounds by intravenous infusion. Most of the studies of nifedipine on Raynaud's disease also included secondary patients; although the results were generally positive, it was not always possible to distinguish between primary and secondary patients in some published reports (see Coffman, 1991).

Clinical and Methodological Recommendations

General Considerations

My colleagues and I have identified several procedural variables that seem to be important in the production of voluntary vasodilation with temperature feedback. Because temperature elevations often occur soon after the initiation of feedback, it is important that training sessions be brief to reduce subsequent frustration. Many subjects initially try too hard to perform the temperature feedback task, which results in vasoconstriction rather than vasodilation. Patients should therefore be dissuaded from focusing excessively on the feedback stimulus. Although biofeedback equipment manufacturers have developed elaborate and expensive feedback displays, the specific form of the feedback stimulus is probably not important. However, the stimulus should be neither startling nor intrusive, so that it can be maintained in the periphery of the patient's attention. Coaching the patient to avoid cold-related cognitions, in addition to reassuring him or her that most patients learn to master the task despite its difficulty, may facilitate vasodilation. Because finger temperature is affected by ambient temperature, it is important that training be conducted in a room with reasonably well-controlled temperature. Spurious fluctuations of room temperature only increase the difficulty of the temperature-feedback task. After the voluntary vasodilation skill has been acquired, the gradual introduction of cold stress during training should improve the robustness of the vasodilation response in cold situations outside the laboratory. Patients should be instructed to practice this response when opportune. However, my colleagues and I have not found rigid home practice requirements to be beneficial in training.

Training Environment

Because skin temperature is affected by ambient temperature, it is important that the evaluation and training of subjects be conducted in a temperature-controlled room. My colleagues and I have used an ambient temperature of 23 °C in our investigations. Subjects are typically seated in a large armchair with their hands and arms slightly above heart level. They are instructed to avoid physical maneuvers such as hand movements and respiratory changes during the recording period. It is important that subjects be physiologically adapted to the laboratory before the initiation of training to reduce spontaneous fluctuations in skin temperature and blood flow. However, if sessions are too long, subjects are likely to become bored. We have found that a resting baseline period of 16 min followed by a 16-min training period generally accommodates both factors. Ten sessions are generally administered on a biweekly basis.

Temperature Biofeedback

Although many temperature-biofeedback devices are commercially available, elaborate feedback displays are unnecessary. It is important, however, that the subject receive accurate and prompt physiological information. My colleagues and I at the C.S. Mott Center use Yellow Springs Thermivolt bridge circuits, with linear thermistors that have time constants from 0.3 s to 0.6 s. The output of one bridge drives a sinusoidal tone generator, the pitch of which varies inversely with temperature. We have also used a large zero-center meter to provide feedback.

Instructions for attending to the feedback stimulus are important. Specifically, excessive attention to the stimulation interferes with acquisition of the response. Therefore, subjects are instructed to focus on the production of digital pulsing sensations and to maintain the feedback stimulus in the periphery of their attention.

Temperature Feedback With Cold Stress

In this technique, subjects first receive five or six standard temperature-feedback sessions as described earlier. They then receive an equal number of sessions in which the finger controlling feedback stimulus is gradually externally cooled. The following is used: A 2.5-cm^2 thermoelectric device, the surface temperature of which is decreased from 30 °C to 20 °C at a rate of 1 °C/min and then maintained at 20 °C for 6 min. The middle phalanx of the subject's dominant third finger rests on the cooling surface, with the edge of this surface 1 cm from the feedback thermistor. Although the cooling stimulus is custom-made, similar devices are commercially available (e.g., from Cambion, Cambridge, Massachusetts, or Casleton, United Kingdom).

Symptom Reporting and Follow-up Procedures

The basic self-report instrument that is used to assess therapeutic change in the behavioral treatment of Raynaud's disease is the symptom report card. Patients are instructed to complete a card immediately after every attack. Symptom report cards are kept over a matter of months before, during, and after treatment. (The forms can be perforated and held in a binder.) Headings prompt the patient to record the specific circumstances of each attack, as well as the perceived cause and any methods that were used to inhibit or curtail the episode. Ratings of symptom severity and emotional stress are made from the scales provided, and the duration of the attack is recorded in minutes. Skin color changes that occur during the attack are also noted.

Weather is one factor in the constellation of symptom causes and must be taken into account in the recording process. It is necessary to establish the posttreatment recording period as one that is not warmer than the pretreatment period to provide a conservative measure of outcome. Ideally, follow-up data should be collected throughout an entire year of climate changes after termination of treatment. Few patients are willing to complete symptom report cards for this extended period of time. However, most are amenable to the use of a briefer reporting form over the interval. Because attack frequency has been regarded as the primary measure of therapeutic effectiveness, my colleagues and I have asked some patients to record nightly on a calendar the number of attacks they experienced during the day. The calendar page is mailed to the laboratory at the end of the month. Compliance with this procedure over extended time periods has generally been good, although reminders by telephone or letter are often helpful.

Approximately 1 year from the beginning of the pretreatment baseline, patients should complete full symptom report cards for 1 month. The weather during that month should be no warmer than that of the pretreatment month, to the extent that this is realistically possible. Comprehensive weather data for many locations in the United States are available from the U.S. Weather Service in Asheville, North Carolina, to aid in planning this process. At the end of the follow-up month, it is useful to interview the patient to review the symptom report data and to elucidate successful and unsuccessful implementation of therapeutic procedures.

Conclusions

Research on the pathophysiology of Raynaud's disease now shows that the attacks are caused not by sympathetic nervous system hyperactivity but probably by the hypersensitivity of peripheral vascular α2-adrenergic receptors to cooling. In addition, peripheral vascular α1-adrenoceptors are hypersensitive in Raynaud's disease patients in the basal state. Thus, normal catecholamine elevations produced by emotional stress or by reflex cooling can also trigger the vasospastic attacks. My colleagues and I recently found significant familial aggregation of Raynaud's disease, which suggests a genetic basis for this disorder. The pathophysiology of secondary Raynaud's phenomenon remains poorly understood.

The most efficacious treatment for primary Raynaud's disease now appears to be temperature biofeedback without other treatments. Several controlled group outcome studies (Freedman et al., 1983, 1988) have shown that primary Raynaud's patients who were given temperature biofeedback alone achieved symptom frequency reductions that ranged from 67% to 92%, which were maintained at 2- and 3-year follow-ups. The addition of other procedures, such as autogenic training or progressive relaxation, to temperature biofeedback produced less satisfactory results, as did the use of progressive relaxation and autogenic training alone. These results are superior to those of most pharmacological studies, and the biofeedback treatments do not have the concomitant side effects. The use of sympatholytic drugs and surgical sympathectomies is seriously challenged by findings that attacks can be induced by digital nerve blockade (Freedman, Mayes, & Sabharwal, 1989).

In research on the mechanisms of temperature biofeedback, my colleagues and I have shown that feedback-induced vasodilation is not achieved through reductions in sympathetic nervous system activation. Early studies in our laboratory did not find the expected reductions in heart rate, skin conductance level, or reported arousal in Raynaud's patients or normal subjects given temperature feedback (Freedman & Ianni, 1983a, 1983b; Freedman et al., 1983). We have subsequently demonstrated that feedback-induced vasodilation is not mediated through sympathetic nerves but rather through a β-adrenergic mechanism (Freedman et al., 1988). Consistent with these findings, we have most recently found that plasma levels of norepinephrine and epinephrine do not significantly change during temperature feedback or autogenic training in Raynaud's disease patients.

Research on the etiology and treatment of Raynaud's phenomenon has been less successful than research on the primary form of the disorder. Because of the difficulty of performing invasive procedures in patients with secondary Raynaud's phenomenon, less is known of the pathophysiology of their vasospastic attacks. However, histological studies have shown luminal narrowing because of intimal proliferation of connective tissue, thickening of the basement membrane, and fibrosis of the adventitia in these patients (e.g., Rodnan, 1979). In vivo observation of skin capillaries reveals consistent abnormalities in secondary patients (Maricq et al., 1980), and very low levels of finger capillary blood flow have been shown (Coffman & Cohen, 1971). In light of these findings, it may be difficult to achieve consistent vasodilation in secondary Raynaud's patients, although further research on this problem should be conducted.

In conclusion, knowledge of the pathophysiology of Raynaud's disease has grown considerably in the past decade. Temperature biofeedback has been shown to be an efficacious treatment for this disorder, and some aspects of its mechanism have been delineated. Further research should be conducted in this area and on the less understood problems of Raynaud's phenomenon.

REFERENCES

Allen, E., & Brown, G. (1932). A critical review of minimal requisites for diagnosis. *American Journal of Medical Science, 183,* 187–195.

Belch, J. J. F., Newman, P., Drury, J. K., McKenzie, F., Capell, H., Leiberman, P., Forbes, C. D., & Prentice, C. R. M. (1983). Intermittent epoprostenol (prostacyclin) infusion in patients with Raynaud's syndrome. *Lancet, i,* 313–315.

Coffman, J. D. (1972). Total and nutritional blood flow in the finger. *Clinical Science, 42,* 243–250.

Coffman, J. D. (1991). Raynaud's phenomenon. *Hypertension, 17,* 593–602.

Coffman, J. D., Clement, D. L., Creager, M. A., Dormady, J. A., Janssens, M. M.-L., McKedry, R. J. R., Murray, G. D., & Nielsen, S. L. (1989). International study of ketanserin in Raynaud's phenomenon. *American Journal of Medicine, 87,* 264–268.

Coffman, J. D., & Cohen, A. S. (1971). Total and capillary fingertip blood flow in Raynaud's phenomenon. *New England Journal of Medicine, 285,* 259–263.

Cohen, R., & Coffman, J. (1981). Beta-adrenergic vasodilator mechanism in the finger. *Circulation Research, 49,* 1196–1201.

Edwards, J. M., Phinney, E. S., Taylor, L. M., Keenan, E. J., & Porter, J. M. (1987). α_2-Adrenoceptor levels in obstructive and spastic Raynaud's syndrome. *Vascular Survey, 5,* 38–45.

Fagius, J., & Blumberg, H. (1985). Sympathetic outflow to the hand in patients with Raynaud's phenomenon. *Cardiovascular Research, 19,* 249–253.

Flavahan, N. A., Lindblad, L. E., Verebeuren, T. J., Shepherd, J. T., & Vanhoutte, P. M. (1985). Cooling and α_1- and α_2-adrenergic responses in cutaneous veins: Role of receptor reserve. *American Journal of Physiology, 249,* H950–H955.

Flavahan, N. A., & Vanhoutte, P. M. (1986). Effect of cooling on alpha$_1$- and alpha$_2$-adrenergic responses in canine saphenous and femoral veins. *Journal of Pharmacology and Experimental Therapeutics, 239,* 139–147.

Freedman, R. R. (1989). Raynaud's disease. In G. Turpin (Ed.), *Handbook of clinical psychophysiology* (pp. 469–495). New York: Wiley.

Freedman, R. R., & Ianni, P. (1983a). Role of cold and emotional stress in Raynaud's disease and scleroderma. *British Medical Journal, 287,* 1499–1502.

Freedman, R. R., & Ianni, P. (1983b). Self-control of digital temperature: Physiological factors and transfer effects. *Psychophysiology, 20,* 682–688.

Freedman, R. R., Ianni, P., & Wenig, P. (1983). Behavioral treatment of Raynaud's disease. *Journal of Consulting and Clinical Psychology, 151,* 539–549.

Freedman, R. R., Ianni, P., & Wenig, P. (1984). Behavioral treatment of Raynaud's phenomenon in scleroderma. *Journal of Behavioral Medicine, 7,* 343–353.

Freedman, R. R., Ianni, P., & Wenig, P. (1985). Behavioral treatment of Raynaud's disease: Long-term follow-up. *Journal of Consulting and Clinical Psychology, 53,* 136.

Freedman, R. R., Keegan, D., Migály, P., Galloway, M. P., & Mayes, M. (1991). Plasma catecholamines during behavioral treatments for Raynaud's disease. *Psychosomatic Medicine, 53,* 433–439.

Freedman, R. R., Keegan, D., Rodriguez, J., & Galloway, M. (1993). Plasma catecholamine levels during temperature biofeedback training in normal subjects. *Biofeedback and Self-Regulation, 18,* 107–114.

Freedman, R. R., Lynn, S., Ianni, P., & Hale, P. (1981). Biofeedback treatment of Raynaud's disease and phenomenon. *Biofeedback and Self-Regulation, 6,* 355–365.

Freedman, R. R., Mayes, M., & Sabharwal, S. (1989). Digital nerve blockade in Raynaud's disease. *Circulation, 80,* 1923–1924.

Freedman, R. R., Moten, M., Migály, P., & Mayes, M. (1993). Cold-induced potentiation of α_2-adrenergic vasoconstriction in idiopathic Raynaud's disease. *Arthritis and Rheumatism, 36,* 685–690.

Freedman, R. R., Sabharwal, S. C., Desai, N., Wenig, P., & Mayes, M. (1989). Increased α-adrenergic responsiveness in idiopathic Raynaud's disease. *Arthritis and Rheumatism, 32,* 61–65.

Freedman, R. R., Sabharwal, S. C., Ianni, P., Desai, N., Wenig, P., & Mayes, M. (1988). Nonneural beta-adrenergic vasodilating mechanism in temperature biofeedback. *Psychosomatic Medicine, 50,* 394–401.

Freedman, R. R., Sabharwal, S. C., Moten, M., & Migály, P. (1992). Local temperature modulates α_1- and α_2-adrenergic vasoconstriction in man. *American Journal of Physiology: Heart and Circulatory Physiology, 263,* H1197–H1200.

Graafsma, S. J., Wollersheim, H., Droste, H. T., ten Dam, M. A. G. J., van Tits, L. J. H., Reyenga, J., de Miranda, J. F. R., & Thien, T. (1991). Adrenoceptors on blood cells from patients with primary Raynaud's phenomenon. *Clinical Science, 80,* 325–331.

Harker, C. T. P., Ousley, E. J., Harris, J., Edwards, M., Taylor, L. M., & Porter, J. M. (1990). The effects of cooling on human saphenous vein reactivity to adrenergic agonists. *Journal of Vascular Surgery, 12,* 45–49.

Johnsen, T., Nielsen, S., & Skovborg, F. (1977). Blood viscosity and local response to cold in primary Raynaud's phenomenon. *Lancet, 2,* 1001–1002.

Keefe, F. (1975). Conditioning changes in differential skin temperature. *Perceptual and Motor Skills, 40,* 283–288.

Keefe, F. (1978). Biofeedback vs. instructional control of skin temperature. *Journal of Behavioral Medicine, 1,* 323–335.

Keefe, F., & Gardner, E. (1979). Learned control of skin temperature: Effects of short and long-term biofeedback training. *Behavior Therapy, 10,* 202–210.

Keefe, F., Surwit, R., & Pilon, R. (1980). Biofeedback, autogenic training, and progressive relaxation in the treatment of Raynaud's disease: A comparative study. *Journal of Applied Behavior Analysis, 13,* 3–11.

Keenan, E. J., & Porter, J. M. (1983). α_2-Adrenergic receptors in platelets from patients with Raynaud's syndrome. *Surgery, 94,* 204–209.

Kontos, H. A., & Wasserman, A. J. (1969). Effect of reserpine in Raynaud's phenomenon. *Circulation, 39,* 259–266.

Lewis, T. (1929). Experiments relating to the peripheral mechanism involved in spasmodic arrest of circulation in fingers, a variety of Raynaud's disease. *Heart, 15,* 7–101.

Maricq, H., LeRoy, E., D'Angelo, W., Medsger, T., Rodnan, G., Sharp, G., & Wolfe, J. (1980). Diagnostic potential of in vivo capillary microscopy in scleroderma and related disorders. *Arthritis and Rheumatism, 23,* 183–189.

McGrath, M., Peek, R., & Penny, R. (1978). Raynaud's disease: Reduced hand blood flows with normal blood viscosity. *Australian and New Zealand Journal of Medicine, 8,* 126–131.

Peacock, J. H. (1959). Peripheral venous blood concentration of epinephrine and norepinephrine in primary Raynaud's disease. *Circulation Research, 7,* 821–827.

Pringle, R., Walder, D., & Weaver, J. (1965). Blood viscosity and Raynaud's disease. *Lancet, 3,* 1085–1088.

Propping, P., & Friedl, W. (1983). Genetic control of adrenergic receptors on human platelets: A twin study. *Human Genetics, 64,* 105–109.

Raynaud, M. (1888). *New research on the nature and treatment of local asphyxia of the extremities* (T. Barlow, Trans.). London: New Syndenham Society.

Robertson, C., & Smithwick, R. (1951). The recurrence of vasoconstrictor activity after limb sympathectomy in Raynaud's disease and allied vasomotor states. *New England Journal of Medicine, 245,* 317–320.

Rodnan, G. (1979). Progressive systemic sclerosis (scleroderma). In D. McCarty (Ed.), *Arthritis and allied conditions* (pp. 762–810). Philadelphia: Lea & Febiger.

Simlan, A., Holligan, S., Brennan, P., & Maddison, P. (1990). Prevalence of symptoms of Raynaud's phenomenon in general practice. *British Medical Journal, 301,* 590–592.

Stoffer, G. R., Jensen, J. A. S., & Nesset, B. L. (1979). Effects of contingent versus yoked temperature feedback on voluntary temperature control and cold stress tolerance. *Biofeedback and Self-Regulation, 4,* 51–61.

Surwit, R. S., & Allen, L. M. (1983). Neuroendocrine response to cold in Raynaud's syndrome. *Life Sciences, 32,* 995–1000.

Surwit, R., Pilon, R., & Fenton, C. (1978). Behavioral treatment of Raynaud's disease. *Journal of Behavioral Medicine, 1,* 323–335.

Weinrich, M. C., Maricq, H. R., Keil, J. E., McGregor, A. R., & Diat, F. (1990). Prevalence of Raynaud's phenomenon in the adult population of South Carolina. *Journal of Clinical Epidemiology, 43,* 1343–1349.

Chapter

8

Rheumatoid Arthritis

Larry D. Young

Increased clinical and research collaboration between psychologists and rheumatologists in the past 15 years has enhanced the understanding of the psychological aspects of rheumatoid arthritis (RA). Historically, reports suggesting the involvement of psychological factors in RA have appeared in the literature as early as the early 20th century. Much of the clinical and research literature relating the two fields in the subsequent 6 decades has suffered from a variety of methodological weaknesses (Anderson, Bradley, Young, McDaniel,

I express my gratitude to Kim Barnes, Adela Larimore, and Wilson Somerville for their assistance in the preparation of this chapter. Also, I thank Jean Beckham, Edward Blanchard, and Jerry Parker for their helpful comments.

269

& Wise, 1985). These weaknesses include (a) the absence of appropriate control groups; (b) retrospective research focus; (c) failure to consider effects of patients' social and demographic characteristics; (d) inattention to medical factors; (e) unreliability of diagnosis, which contributed to increased heterogeneity of the sample; (f) overattention to negative traits and personality characteristics; and (g) theoretical diversity. Moreover, many of the attempts to identify characteristics of the "arthritic personality" were guided by psychoanalytic theory and used assessment procedures of questionable reliability or validity. In addition to becoming stronger and more sophisticated scientifically and conceptually, recent research has shifted its emphasis toward identifying the psychological variables that affect the clinical course of the disease or its symptoms as well as ascertaining the consequences of various disease variables on psychological or behavioral status. Consequently, the importance of psychological factors throughout the course of the disease has increasingly been recognized.

This chapter describes psychological research of clinical relevance in RA. Much of this research has been concerned with elucidating relationships between medical, functional, and psychological variables, although there is a growing body of research reporting psychological interventions to enhance patients' ability to cope with RA. A discussion of the relevant medical aspects of RA is presented to provide an understanding of the context within which the psychological and behavioral responses occur.

Medical Aspects of RA

RA is a chronic systemic inflammatory disorder characterized primarily by pain and destruction of peripheral joints. The term *arthritis* refers to joint disease, of which there are numerous subtypes. RA is a particularly severe subtype of arthritic disorder. Although the etiology of RA remains unknown, most evidence supports the concept that the pathological basis of RA is an inflammatory immune response, with some evidence implicating autoimmune mechanisms. Clinically, an inflammatory synovitis with associated immune reaction produces damage to the tissue lining the joint capsule (synovium) and cartilage. Progressive inflammation can accelerate the destruction of cartilage, bone, and tendon. These destructive changes, in conjunction with swelling and inflammation, alter the architecture of the joint as well as produce nociceptive stimulation.

This alteration in joint architecture, in turn, contributes to several additional changes. Changes in joint structure lead to altered joint function as individuals make behavioral adaptations to compensate for diminished strength and endurance or to decrease their pain. Such adjustments may place additional stress on noninvolved joints and induce symptoms, even though synovitis may be absent. Moreover, progressive disease in conjunction with these functional adjustments can contribute to joint deformities. The disease typically affects the joints in a bilateral and symmetric manner, with the joints of the feet, hands, and wrist most frequently involved. Other joints involved, in decreasing order of frequency, are knees, ankles, shoulders, and elbows. Because of the joints involved, patients commonly experience difficulty in carrying out many routine daily activities.

Although RA manifests itself predominately in the joints, systemic effects and nonspecific changes also occur. These include the development of disfiguring rheumatoid nodules in 10–15% of patients as well as the occurrence of clinically significant neuropathies and inflammatory responses in vascular, cardiac, pulmonary, muscular, and ocular tissues. Patients may experience fevers, fatigue, sleep disturbance, weakness, and loss of stamina in addition to pain and tenderness in nonarticular regions. It is not uncommon for these nonspecific symptoms to precede the onset of specific joint symptoms. In addition to these extra-articular systemic effects of RA, patients may also suffer from other chronic conditions that may affect physical or psychological function. The prevalence of comorbid conditions does not appear to be greater in RA than in other chronic conditions; however, their presence may pose an extra burden on patients and weaken research conclusions.

Although RA is not regarded as a fatal disease, numerous reports have documented increased mortality in RA patients in comparison with matched population norms (Pincus, Callahan, & Vaughn, 1987). Five-year mortality rates of 40% or greater have been reported in patients with extra-articular disease or in patients with severe functional disabilities.

The clinical course of RA is extremely variable from one patient to another. Approximately 10–20% of patients report mild symptoms that remit within 2 years and do not recur. Another 10–15% experience a steadily progressive and disabling course of their disease in spite of appropriate therapies. Most patients (approximately 70%), however, experience unpredictable exacerbations and remissions of disease activity with progressive deformity and disability (Weinblatt & Maier, 1989). Thus, at any point, patients exhibit the effects of both a variably active disease process and of the cumulative, progressive, negative impact of their disease.

The unpredictable, fluctuating clinical course of RA is accompanied by the absence of curative therapies. Because the etiology of the disease is unknown, medical intervention is largely palliative. Goals of therapy include relief of pain, modification of the disease process in an effort to minimize tissue damage, minimization of adverse drug effects, and preservation of function. Historically, pharmacological management has followed a "pyramidal" strategy, beginning with conservative therapies (including nonsteroidal anti-inflammatory drugs) and proceeding to more aggressive interventions (e.g., steroids or cytotoxic, disease-modifying antirheumatic drugs). The use of both inflammatory and disease-modifying agents is limited by their toxicity. Surgical replacement of severely degenerated joints has been required for some patients. The conservative medical approach has recently been challenged with recommendations that second-line agents be prescribed earlier and more aggressively (Wolfe, 1990). These disease-modifying drugs usually act relatively slowly, requiring from 2 to 6 months, and still require anti-inflammatory cotherapy.

In addition to pharmacotherapy, patients with RA commonly are treated with various other physical rehabilitation techniques such as splints, exercise, and rest (Liang & Logigian, 1992). Splinting provides an important means of joint protection and may aid in controlling pain and inflammation in the affected joint. Rest and pacing may reduce fatigue and improve function. Exercise is valuable but requires special consideration in RA patients. Exercise of actively inflamed joints can increase inflammation, enhance synovitis, increase intra-articular temperature, and exacerbate cartilage destruction. However, regular gradual physical exercise can maintain strength and range of motion, diminish fatigue, and improve general conditioning. There is even suggestive evidence that it may reduce the number of inflamed and swollen joints, retard radiographic changes, and improve overall functional capacity (Minor, 1991).

RA affects approximately 1% of the general population, with women almost three times as likely as men to be affected. Disease onset occurs most commonly between the ages of 20 and 50, with prevalence increasing with age. Thus, the disease is most likely to occur in early to middle adulthood, the years of greatest economic productivity. Approximately 60% of patients with RA become work disabled, and as a group, RA patients have been estimated to earn only 27–48% of the income of individuals without arthritis (Mitchell, Burkhauser, & Pincus, 1988). Furthermore, the fact that RA patients are preponderantly female has a qualitative influence on the way the disease alters family roles and function.

To briefly summarize, RA is a chronic, progressive disease that produces a number of specific stressors with which patients must cope. These include (a) a variety of physical symptoms and manifestations of the disease (joint and generalized pain, swelling, stiffness, fatigue, sleep disturbance, weakness, decreased range of motion, deformities, and various extra-articular manifestations); (b) medication side effects; (c) limitations of function; (d) financial hardship; (e) uncertainty over disease course and absence of a cure; (f) altered interpersonal, particularly marital and family, relationships; and (g) changes in a variety of cognitive variables (e.g., expectations for the future and self-perception). These stressors have consistently been related to measures of psychological function. It is important to note that these variables not only have an impact on psychological and behavioral status, but also may be affected by psychological and behavioral factors.

Recent Psychological Research

Psychological research on coping with RA has drawn from several conceptual traditions. The most general theoretical perspective, Lazarus and Folkman's (1984) conceptualization of appraisal and coping, has been applied to the entire spectrum of RA-related stress. A second research framework, the cognitive–behavioral approach to coping with chronic pain (Turk, Meichenbaum, & Genest, 1983), is somewhat more restrictive in its focus. The Vanderbilt Pain Management Inventory (VPMI; Brown & Nicassio, 1987), and the Coping Strategies Questionnaire (CSQ; Rosenstiel & Keefe, 1982) are among the most frequently used questionnaires from this tradition. Furthermore, the unpredictability and uncontrollability of many RA symptoms have encouraged investigators to consider learned helplessness (Garber & Seligman, 1980; Stein, Wallston, & Nicassio, 1988) or self-efficacy (Bandura, 1986; Lorig, Chastain, Ung, Shoor, & Holman, 1989) as theoretical perspectives from which to conduct their research. These two theoretical perspectives are quite similar conceptually, with the primary distinction being the broader, traitlike status of learned helplessness in contrast to the more situationally specific construct of self-efficacy.

As might be anticipated, these distinct but related theoretical frameworks have produced a body of research that is sometimes difficult to integrate. A recent review (Zautra & Manne, 1992) cited several factors that contribute to difficulty in formulating general conclusions regarding the efficacy of specific coping strategies. For example, a particular coping strategy may be beneficial in promoting positive coping with one set of RA-related stressors but ineffective or even maladaptive in coping with others. Future research may benefit from specifying the disease-related stressors under consideration. Second, descriptions of some coping strategies may be phrased in such general terms that a range of behaviors may be encompassed. For example, "making a plan of action and following it" might mean taking additional medication, practicing relaxation techniques, engaging in physical exercise, giving up plans for a desired activity, or going on with a planned activity in spite of pain. The understanding of the relative merits of particular coping strategies will be furthered when these sources of ambiguity are minimized.

Most psychological research efforts in RA have been devoted to investigations of pain, functional disability, and psychological adjustment. Each of these areas is briefly described.

Pain

Pain is regarded by RA patients as their principal stressor (Affleck, Pfeiffer, Tennen, & Fifield, 1988) and is the primary reason that they seek medical treatment (McKenna & Wright, 1985). It is associated with unauthorized analgesic use and a wide range of psychological and behavioral adjustments to reduce its intensity and aversiveness (Buckelew & Parker, 1989). Although several nociceptive mechanisms have been described (Utsinger, Zvaifler, & Ehrlich, 1985), the role of psychological variables in pain reports has consistently been demonstrated.

Greater pain has been associated with both anxiety and depression (Hawley & Wolfe, 1988), with interpersonal sensitivity and obsessive–compulsiveness on the SCL-90 (Parker, Frank, Beck, Finan, et al., 1988), and with neuroticism (Affleck, Tennen, Urrows, & Higgins, 1992). These results are congruent with RA patient perceptions of the qualitative aspects of their pain experience (Buckelew & Parker, 1989), research into which has consistently shown that the affective component of pain is greater than the sensory component. Furthermore, patients reporting more severe pain also report stronger perceptions of arthritis helplessness (Stein, Wallston, & Nicassio, 1988) and have lower self-efficacy ratings of their ability to manage pain, function, and other symptoms relating to their RA (Lorig et al., 1989). Although most of these results are based on cross-sectional research designs, Brown (1990) used causal modeling with data collected from a longitudinal research design to study prospectively the relationship between pain and depression. His results provide tentative support for the hypothesis that pain contributes to subsequent increases in depression, after controlling for prior levels of depression. Another report suggested that this causal relationship may be moderated by the use of passive coping strategies (Brown, Nicassio, & Wallston, 1989).

RA pain intensity is also influenced by patients' pain coping strategies. Patients who respond to their pain with negative, exaggerated, catastrophizing thoughts and perceptions of an inability to control or reduce their pain report much more severe and disabling pain (Keefe, Brown, Wallston, & Caldwell, 1989). In contrast, coping self-statements and perceptions of resourcefulness are associated with reports of less pain (Flor & Turk, 1988). Moreover, active pain coping strategies such as staying busy, ignoring pain, and using distraction are associated with less pain, whereas passive strategies such as restricting activities because of pain, engaging in wishful thinking, or depending on others for relief or assistance is related to more severe pain (Brown & Nicassio, 1987).

Research addressing the relative contributions of disease activity and psychological factors on pain has produced inconsistent results (Buckelew & Parker, 1989). Inasmuch as several studies have used variables that reflect stable aspects of the disease (e.g., disease duration or radiographic measures), it is possible that the weak relationships that have been found between disease activity, psychological factors, and pain simply reflect a failure to consider concurrent disease activity. However, Parker, Frank, Beck, Finan, et al. (1988) failed to find significant relationships between pain and parameters of current disease activity. Furthermore, a recent well-controlled study (Hagglund, Haley, Reveille, & Alarcón, 1989) found that, although the number of swollen joints and erythrocyte sedimentation rate were positively associated with pain intensity, the strongest predictors of pain ratings were measures of anxiety and depression. Similarly, a prospective study of daily pain (Affleck, Tennen, Urrows, & Higgins, 1991) found that depression was associated with more intense pain independent of disease activity.

Although various measures of anxiety and depression have been associated with self-reports of pain intensity, this is not the case with nonverbal pain behaviors such as guarded movements or rubbing painful joints. Two studies (Anderson et al., 1988; Buescher et al., 1991) that used an observation method that reliably and validly measures pain behaviors in RA patients indicated that these behaviors are related to disease activity but not to measures of depression, anxiety, or arthritis helplessness. Pain behavior is, however, inversely related to self-efficacy beliefs.

Functional Impairment

Progressive joint deterioration has long been recognized as a principal contributor to the disability of RA patients. Patients with RA are significantly more impaired in their ability to perform daily activities than are patients with other musculoskeletal diseases (Felts & Yelin, 1989). Almost 60% are forced to discontinue employment within 10 years of disease onset. Functional disability develops early in the course of RA and appears to worsen steadily, even when clinical variables remain unchanged or improve slightly (Wolfe, Hawley, & Cathey, 1991). Furthermore, pain is more strongly related to disability when patients with active disease initially consult a physician than it is subsequently, when disease activity is more stable (McFarlane & Brooks, 1988).

Functional impairment in RA patients reflects the influence of psychological as well as disease variables. Greater disability is reported by patients with greater hypochondriasis, depression, and denial of emotional problems (McFarlane & Brooks, 1988); state and trait anxiety and arthritis helplessness (Hagglund et al., 1989); disease-related cognitive distortions (Smith, Peck, Milano, & Ward, 1988); and catastrophization (Keefe et al., 1989). Patients who rely on passive coping strategies (Brown & Nicassio, 1987) or threat minimization, wish-fulfilling fantasy, and self-blame (Parker, McRae, et al., 1988), or who have low self-efficacy expectations (Lorig et al., 1989), also are more disabled. Most of these associations are based on concurrent assessment of psychological and disability measures, and there is evidence that they may vary depending on whether the assessment occurs during an interval of painful increased disease activity or when the disease is more stable (McFarlane & Brooks, 1988). However, a recent study (Lorish, Abraham, Austin, Bradley, & Alarcón, 1991) found that arthritis helplessness significantly predicted impairment 12 months later independent of disease activity.

Psychological and Behavioral Adjustment

As just described, the pain and progressive disability caused by RA are associated with psychological distress and a number of cognitive and behavioral changes. Depression, in particular, is frequently reported. Although approximately 40% of RA patients meet research diagnostic criteria for dysthymic disorder, this rate is not significantly greater than the rate observed in other severe, chronic medical conditions (Frank et al., 1988). One consideration in the assessment of depression in RA patients is the possibility that items manifesting disease activity (e.g., fatigue or sleep disturbance) might be interpreted spuriously as evidence of psychopathology.

Although Newman, Fitzpatrick, Lamb, and Shipley (1989) found that disability was the most important predictor of patients' depression, other studies have emphasized that the impact of pain or disease activity on depression may be mediated by reliance on passive coping strategies (Brown et al., 1989) or beliefs of arthritis helplessness (Smith, Peck, & Ward, 1990). A similar but more sophisticated causal model is discussed by Smith and Wallston (1992). A recent review

(Zautra & Manne, 1992) concluded that patients who rely on passive, avoidant, or emotion-focused strategies (e.g., self-blame, catastrophization, or fantasy) for coping with RA typically report lower self-esteem, poorer adjustment, and greater negative affect. The converse obtains for those patients who engage in active, problem-solving coping (e.g., information seeking, cognitive restructuring, rational thinking, and coping self-statements).

The importance of patient perceptions of personal control, helplessness, or self-efficacy for outcome has repeatedly been demonstrated. For example, Stein, Wallston, Nicassio, and Castner (1988) found that highly helpless patients were more likely to have analgesic, psychotropic, and anti-inflammatory medications prescribed for them than were patients who felt less helpless, even though their disease characteristics were not different. Moreover, the helpless patients were more likely to be nonadherent to their treatment regimen.

In view of the significant number of psychosocial changes experienced by patients with RA (Anderson et al., 1985), social support would be expected to be important in buffering the deleterious impact of these changes. Indeed, both social integration and qualitative aspects of social support are predictive of level of physical functioning (Goodenow, Reisine, & Grady, 1990). Quality of social support and satisfaction with level of social support are positively related to psychological adjustment (Smith & Wallston, 1992). Moreover, marital support has been demonstrated to influence coping attempts (Manne & Zautra, 1989). Specifically, patients who describe their spouse as supportive engage in more adaptive coping behaviors. Conversely, patients whose spouses are more critical are more likely to engage in maladaptive coping responses and to exhibit poor psychological adjustment.

Psychological Interventions

In view of the distress commonly reported by RA patients, it would be expected that psychological interventions would be considered. Nonetheless, the literature on outcome of traditional mental health approaches has been equivocal (Anderson et al., 1985). However, in the past 15 years a number of behavioral and cognitive–behavioral interventions directed toward assisting RA patients to cope more effectively with specific aspects of their disease have been reported

(McCracken, 1991; Young, 1992). These therapies generally have shared a self-management or coping skills training orientation that distinguished them from prior efforts.

Most cognitive–behavioral interventions have been directed at assisting patients to cope more effectively with specific aspects of their disease, especially pain. The result of the nine published controlled group outcome studies that are described in Table 1 provide convincing evidence of the efficacy of cognitive–behavioral interventions to decrease patients' pain. The two studies that did not obtain reductions in pain (Shearn & Fireman, 1985; Strauss et al., 1986) did not describe pain or RA symptom management as primary goals of therapy. In addition to noting methodological concerns with both studies, Young (1992) suggested that more traditional mental health approaches may not facilitate disease- or symptom-specific cognitive changes, such as self-efficacy, which have been shown to have positive impact on outcomes. Also, McCracken (1991) noted that the patients in the Shearn and Fireman study were recruited from a different patient population and may not be comparable to patients from other studies.

Improvements in measures of physical functioning and psychological adjustment were reported by these studies, albeit not as consistently as reductions in pain. Several studies have reported improvements in clinical (i.e., number of swollen joints or severity of swelling [Achterberg, McGraw, & Lawlis, 1981; O'Leary, Shoor, Lorig, & Holman, 1988; Radojevik, Nicassio, & Weisman, 1992]) or laboratory (i.e., erythrocyte sedimentation rate [Achterberg et al., 1981] or helper:suppressor T-cell ratio [O'Leary et al., 1988]) measures of disease activity. In addition, Bradley et al. (1987) reported improvement on the Rheumatoid Activity Index, a composite of rheumatoid factor titers, Westergren sedimentation rates, number of tender joints, grip strength, and patient's and physician's global estimates of disease activity. Furthermore, improvements in pain, functioning, and mood often were associated with relevant mediating variables such as enhanced self-efficacy, decreased catastrophizing, changes in coping strategies, or adherence to various treatment components.

Overall, these multicomponent cognitive–behavioral treatment programs have effected beneficial changes in a wide range of outcome variables. As McCracken (1991) cogently observed, the small sample sizes of these studies, in conjunction with large inter- and intrapatient

Table 1

Controlled Psychological Interventions in Rheumatoid Arthritis (RA)

Study	N	% Female	% Functional Class I/II/III[a]	Number of groups in experiment	Treatment duration	Therapy components	Outcome
Achterberg et al., 1981 Study 1	24	100	DNS[b]	2	12 sessions in 6 weeks	Relaxation and (a) BFB–temperature increase; (b) BFB–temperature decrease	Decreased pain; decreased EMG levels; reduced tension; improved sleep; and improved ADL in both BFB groups; each BFB group able to control temperature in desired direction
Study 2	23	DNS	DNS	2	Unspecified	Relaxation and temperature BFB	Decreased pain and joint count; improved functional ability; improved sleep
Shearn & Fireman, 1985	105	75	DNS	3	10 weekly sessions	Stress management	No between-group differences on any measure at posttreatment of FU; general improvement over time for all patients
Mitchell, 1986	18	DNS	DNS[c]	3	6 sessions in 2 weeks	Imagery and (a) BFB–temperature increase; (b) BFB–temperature decrease	At posttreatment, decreased pain and stiffness; improved overall condition in both BFB groups; each BFB group able to control temperature in desired direc-

Continued

						tion; at 4-week FU, decreased pain and increased overall condition for both BFB groups; decreased stiffness for BFB–temperature increase group
Strauss et al., 1986	57	81	DNS	3	Weekly for 3 months (assertiveness training) or 6 months (group therapy)	Group assertion–relaxation training	No change in composite self-reports at 3, 6, or 12 months; no change in physician estimate of disease activity at 3, 6, or 12 months; no between-group differences in NSAIDs at 3, 6, or 12 months
Bradley et al., 1987	53	81	9/53/38	3	10 group sessions and 5 individual BFB–temperature sessions in 15 weeks and monthly FU phone calls	Relaxation, imagery, goal setting, self-reinforcement, BFB–temperature	At posttreatment, decreased pain, pain behavior, anxiety, and objective and subjective disease activity; increased ability to control temperature with BFB; at 6-month FU, decreased anxiety, increased ability to control temperature with BFB; at 12-month FU, decreased pain, depression, disease activity, and health care utilization for RA; adherence rates affect results
Applebaum et al., 1988	18	11	0/33/67	2	10 sessions in 6 weeks	Relaxation, BFB–temperature, coping self-statements, problem solving, self-monitoring	At posttreatment, decreased pain and stiffness; increased functioning and joint ROM; at 18-month FU, no significant differences

Table 1 (continued)

Study	N	% Female	% Functional Class I/II/III[a]	Number of groups in experiment	Treatment duration	Therapy components	Outcome
O'Leary et al., 1988	33	100	DNS	2	5 weeks	Relaxation, imagery, goal setting, self-reinforcement, coping self-statements, distraction, relabeling	At posttreatment, decreased pain and joint impairment; increased self-efficacy; self-efficacy to manage pain associated with helper:suppressor T-cell ratios
Parker, Frank, Beck, Smarr, et al., 1988	83	4	7/77/16	3	1 week inpatient (approximately 25 h of therapy) and variable interval outpatient support group	Relaxation, attention diversion, problem solving, awareness of pain behavior, communication training	At 6-month FU, increased use of 4 coping strategies; no change in pain, disease activity, or self-report measures; at 12-month FU, increased use of 5 coping strategies; adherence rates affect results

Continued

| Radojevik et al., 1992 | 59 | 76 | DNS | 4 | 4 weekly sessions followed by 2 weeks for practice/skill consolidation | Relaxation, coping self-statements, pleasant imagery (plus instruction in reinforcement and extinction of pain behavior in some patients) | General improvement in pain and psychological status; reduced swelling and number of swollen joints at posttreatment and FU; no effects of family support; changes in coping behavior related to pain, number of painful joints, and psychological status; adherence affects results |

Note. DNS = did not specify; BFB = biofeedback; EMG = electromyographic activity; ADL = activities of daily living; NSAIDs = nonsteroidal anti-inflammatory drugs; ROM = range of motion; FU = follow-up.

[a]Functional Class I refers to minimal restriction in ability to perform activities; Class II reflects ability to conduct normal activities with moderate restriction of function; Class III refers to marked restriction in ability to perform normal activities of daily living; Class IV reflects functional incapacitation, which may require confinement to bed (Steinbrocker, Traeger, & Batterman, 1949). [b]Patients were described as Anatomic Stage II (slight bone destruction without deformation) or Stage III (cartilage and bone destruction with deformities). [c]Patients described as Anatomic Stage II.

variability on measures, make these positive outcomes more impressive and suggest significant clinical utility. Unfortunately, most studies report only the average improvement on particular measures for the entire group, a practice that precludes assessment of the proportion of patients who derive clinically significant benefit from the intervention. In the sole exception to this reporting practice, Radojevik et al. (1992) indicated that 59% of the patients in two treatment groups versus 24% of the patients in two control groups achieved at least a 50% reduction in pain.

Suggestions for Clinical Application

As previously noted, one of the principal conceptual traditions guiding research into RA has been the cognitive–behavioral approach to pain and pain management (Turk et al., 1983). Several assessment techniques and treatment components originally developed for chronic pain patients have been adapted for RA patients, considering the presence of a progressive, active disease process.

Assessment

By becoming familiar with assessment measures commonly used with RA patients, clinicians can have access to disease-specific data against which they can compare the results from individual patients. Methods for assessing pain, function, and depression have been applied to the RA population. An overview of these methods is presented.

The three most frequently used functional assessment instruments are the Arthritis Impact Measurement Scale (AIMS; Meenan, Gertman, & Mason, 1980), the Stanford Health Assessment Questionnaire (HAQ; Fries, Spitz, & Young, 1982), and the Sickness Impact Profile (SIP; Bergner, Bobbitt, Carter, & Gilson, 1981). Although each has several component scales that measure specific aspects of disease-related disability, these scale scores are usually combined to provide estimates of general dimensions of health status. For the AIMS, three summary scores are typically obtained: physical disability, psychological disability, and pain. The HAQ provides estimates of disability, discomfort, side effects, and medical costs. The SIP aggregates responses into summaries of physical and psychosocial dysfunction.

Reliable and valid measures of pain have been incorporated into the AIMS and HAQ and are often used in clinical assessments. Visual analogue scales (VAS; Downie et al., 1978) and the McGill Pain Questionnaire (Melzack, 1975) are also commonly used. There is evidence that these self-report measures of pain may be influenced by a patient's psychological distress, which does not appear to be the case for an observational method of assessing patient RA pain behaviors (Anderson et al., 1988). The pain behavior assessment methodology consists of observations by trained raters of the frequency of operationally defined pain behaviors (e.g., grimaces, guarded movements, and rubbing painful body parts) when patients are engaged in a structured sequence of sitting, standing, and walking activities. Furthermore, this observational method of pain behavior assessment has demonstrated sensitivity to change following cognitive–behavioral intervention (Bradley et al., 1987).

The assessment of psychological status, and especially depression, has been surrounded by controversy regarding the possibility that valid responses to symptoms of RA might spuriously inflate estimates of psychopathology. Pincus, Callahan, Bradley, Vaughn, and Wolfe (1986) identified five items from the Minnesota Multiphasic Personality Inventory that reflect not only the presence but also the severity of RA. These items are

9. I am about as able to work as I ever was.
51. I am in just as good physical health as most of my friends.
153. During the past few years I have been well.
163. I do not tire quickly.
243. I have few or no pains.

Each of the five items codes on both the Hypochondriasis (Hy) and Hysteria (Hs) scales, and three items also code on the Depression (D) scale. Failure to consider responses to these specific items could contribute to inappropriate interpretation of these three scales. The t scores for the Hy, D, and Hs scales have been reported in several studies (see Pincus et al., 1986) to average between 62 and 68 for RA patients. If positive responses to these five disease-related items are not counted, then the t scores for these three scales would decline 4–10 points. This would result in average t scores of about 57 for each of the three scales.

Two independent studies (Blalock, DeVellis, Brown, & Wallston, 1989; Callahan, Kaplan, & Pincus, 1991) identified three confounded items from the CES-D scales ("I felt that everything I did was an effort"; "my sleep was restless"; "I could not 'get going'"). The Beck Depression Inventory (BDI) likewise has been studied for possible criterion contamination of items. In two separate studies (Callahan et al., 1991; Peck, Smith, Ward, & Milano, 1989) there was agreement that seven items reflected RA disease processes ("I get as much satisfaction out of things as I used to"; "I can work about as well as before"; "I can sleep as well as usual"; "I don't get more tired than usual"; "my appetite is no worse than usual"; "I am no more worried about my health than usual"; "I have not noticed any recent changes in my interest in sex"). These items all loaded on a Somatic Complaints Factor that was significantly correlated with RA disease activity and disability (Peck et al., 1989). A second factor, Dysphoric Mood, was related to other measures of depression but only minimally to disease factors. More reliable assessment of depression in RA patients with the BDI may be achieved by relying on the Dysphoric Mood items.

The final psychological questionnaire that has been subjected to scrutiny regarding possible RA-related biasing of items in the direction of greater psychopathology is the SCL-90 (Parker et al., 1990). After eliminating the Somatization subscale from consideration, these investigators identified two items ("everything is an effort"; "feeling low in energy or slowed down") that reflected RA symptoms.

Thus, items from several commonly used psychological questionnaires have the capability to reflect RA independent of psychological status. This confounding is strongly exhibited in the BDI but is also reflected to a lesser extent in the Hs, D, and Hy scales of the MMPI.

Several other psychological constructs have been important in the evaluation of RA patients. These have included arthritis self-efficacy (Lorig et al., 1989), catastrophization from the CSQ (Rosenstiel & Keefe, 1982), arthritis helplessness (note that Stein, Wallston, & Nicassio, 1988, reported that a five-item subscale may be more reliable than the total score), active and passive coping strategies from the VPMI (Brown et al., 1989), and negative or distorted RA-related cognitions from the Cognitive Errors Questionnaire (Smith et al., 1988).

Psychological Treatment

Most of the interventions described in Table 1 followed an established protocol that determined treatment content and rate of progression.

The total number of sessions was relatively small, varying from 5 to 15, and these generally were conducted on an outpatient basis. Parker, Frank, Beck, Smarr, et al.'s (1988) inpatient program may have been an adaptation to the particular status of their population rather than a clinical requirement (the program was conducted at a U.S. Veterans Affairs Medical Center). The 24–28 hours of inpatient treatment is only slightly longer than the total time provided by other investigators. With the exception of four studies that used biofeedback (Achterberg et al., 1981; Mitchell, 1986; all of the Applebaum, Blanchard, Hickling, & Alfonso, 1988; and five sessions in Bradley et al., 1987), all treatment has been conducted in a group format. This format has several advantages. In addition to increasing efficiency, the group context allows for greater social support, modeling, and enhanced problem-solving. Patients benefit vicariously from observing other patients and also can apply problem-solving techniques to disease-related difficulties that they themselves may not currently be experiencing.

Instruction in relaxation techniques has been included in all reported behavioral interventions with RA patients. Specific relaxation techniques have included progressive muscle relaxation, autogenic training, controlled breathing, visual imagery, and both electromyographic and thermal biofeedback. Early successful studies incorporated only relaxation and biofeedback, whereas later studies provided a wider array of cognitive–behavioral techniques. The specified conceptual role of biofeedback has broadened from production of a specific psychophysiological effect (i.e., warmer hands) for its own sake to the multifaceted role of a self-regulatory skill associated with relaxation that can enhance motivation and confidence regarding additional behavioral change. In clinical practice, caution should be exercised in the muscle contraction phase of progressive muscle relaxation techniques with RA patients to avoid placing excessive stress on affected joints. Alternatively, clinicians may elect to omit muscle contraction altogether and select a more passive relaxation induction strategy.

A second important emphasis in cognitive–behavioral treatment studies with RA patients, particularly the more recent studies, has been on problem solving and goal setting (cf. Turk et al., 1983). Inasmuch as the disease course of RA is fluctuating and unpredictable, patients appear to benefit from explicit instruction and practice in adjusting to variations in symptoms and disease-related stressors. The diversity of coping challenges caused by RA makes it unlikely that a single coping strategy will be appropriate or effective in all situations. Thus, it is especially important that patients be attuned to the nature of the coping tasks required in a particular situation so that they can select the most appropriate responses for that circumstance, attempt them, and adjust their coping responses as necessary.

The third important emphasis explicitly included in several cognitive–behavioral interventions with RA patients is training in the increased use of self-reinforcement techniques or coping self-statements (cf. Turner & Romano, 1990). In addition to any benefits of strictly operant aspects of self-reinforcement, these techniques encourage patients to focus on specific behaviors within their capability and to respond deliberately and positively in producing these behaviors.

Theoretically, the practice of problem solving–goal setting combined with self-reinforcement–coping self-statements is expected to disrupt passive preoccupation with the negative aspects of the disease, substitute a more active involvement with positive self-generated coping responses, diminish pervasive appraisals of arthritis helplessness, reduce exaggerated catastrophizing thoughts, and enhance self-efficacy perceptions. Patients' appraisals of their disease-related limitations are more likely to be realistic and balanced with the recognition of alternative activities that remain within their capabilities.

Evidence is accumulating that patients' beliefs are important contributors to positive outcomes. Both O'Leary et al. (1988) and Parker et al. (1989) reported that treatment increased patients' self-efficacy beliefs or confidence in their ability to control and decrease their pain. These cognitive changes were associated with other therapeutic improvements. Similar results were reported with the Arthritis Self-Management Program (ASMP; Lorig & González, 1992). Specifically, although patients who completed the ASMP reported positive changes in exercise, relaxation, and a variety of positive coping efforts and also reported decreased disability, pain, and depression, the two sets of variables were only weakly related. Discovery of the moderating role of self-efficacy expectations in clinical improvement led to modifications in the ASMP designed to enhance self-efficacy beliefs. The consequence has been further improvement in outcomes for RA patients (Lorig & González, 1992).

The literature also mentions other treatment components, such as the use of distraction as a pain management strategy or training in communication skills. The rationale for including these other skills in multifaceted cognitive–behavioral treatment programs is plausible, but a component analysis has yet to be conducted with RA patients. As noted later, Parker, Frank, Beck, Smarr, et al. (1988) identified a subgroup of patients who reported both an increased use of several pain coping strategies and an improvement in their pain, but the relationship between these variables was not evaluated directly.

A final treatment parameter worthy of comment is the inclusion of a family member or significant other as a coparticipant. The negative impact of RA on interpersonal, particularly family, functioning in conjunction with the evidence that family criticism and lack of support promote dysfunctional coping (Manne & Zautra, 1989) provides a clear rationale for encouraging direct participation by a spouse or significant other. Bradley et al. (1987) and Radojevik et al. (1992) conducted the only studies to include family participation as a component of treatment, and only the latter study explicitly evaluated its impact. Failure to obtain enhancement of treatment effects as a result of increased adherence when a family member was a coparticipant may have been due to ceiling effects (overall adherence rates in this study were very high) or because the sample did not contain family members who promoted dysfunctional coping patterns. Family participation in treatment might be expected to improve outcomes when the family environment contributes to maladaptive coping efforts or when external contingent reinforcement may be necessary to increase adherence to treatment recommendations.

Results from the nine group outcome studies of cognitive–behavioral treatment with RA patients do not clearly delineate patient demographic characteristics that are associated with better outcomes. Investigators have attempted to ensure that groups within a study were generally equivalent in terms of age and socioeconomic characteristics, but have not examined whether these characteristics differentially affected treatment outcomes. Patient gender does not appear to be associated with outcome either within or between studies.

Similarly, several disease-related parameters do not appear to be related to treatment outcome. Applebaum et al.'s (1988) patients were more significantly disabled (67% Functional Class III) than were patients in the Bradley et al. (1987) and Parker, Frank, Beck, Smarr, et al. (1988) studies (38% and 16% Functional Class III, respectively). Nonetheless, the cognitive–behaviorally treated patients in the Applebaum et al. (1988) study exhibited post treatment results comparable to those of Bradley et al.'s (1987) patients and slightly better overall outcomes than similar patients in the Parker, Frank, Beck, Smarr, et al. (1988) study. Disease duration has not been associated with variations in treatment outcome either. However, most of the group studies have been of individuals with relatively established disease (average disease duration 8.0–14.9 years). In view of the evidence that patients with RA, in the initial 2–3 years of the disease as compared with later intervals, exhibit very different patterns of disease activity, pain, disability, and psychological distress (Fifield & Reisine, 1992; Hawley & Wolfe, 1992; Wolfe et al., 1991), cognitive–behavioral interventions might be even more effective with patients in the early stages of their disease, before expectations of helplessness are well established. Unfortunately, patients with early milder or less disabling disease have proven to be more difficult to recruit or retain in treatment (E. B. Blanchard, personal communication, January 1993). Finally, although it is intuitive that concurrent level of disease activity might alter the effectiveness of cognitive–behavioral treatment, there are no published reports that this is the case. However, Bradley and colleagues (Bradley et al., 1989) suggested that higher levels of disease activity may reduce the effectiveness of cognitive–behavioral strategies.

Therapists of patients with RA should remain mindful of the types of attributions that have been reported to be beneficial. These include attributing flares to the presence of stress or overactivity and facilitating patients' perceptions that they have personal control over their disease symptoms (rather than disease processes) (Affleck, Pfeiffer, Tennen, & Fifield, 1987; Affleck, Tennen, Pfeiffer, & Fifield, 1987). Furthermore, when a patient is having difficulty performing a task, comparison of the patient's performance with that of other RA patients rather than that of individuals without RA has been associated with enhanced psychological adjustment (Blalock, DeVellis, DeVellis, & Sauter, 1988).

The inclusion of a physical exercise component in a comprehensive treatment program is likely to confer benefits in multiple spheres of functioning. Indeed, physical inactivity by itself can cause many of the same symptoms as RA, including weakness, fatigue, decreased flexibility, sleep disturbance, reduced pain threshold, and depression.

In an excellent review, Minor (1991) reported that appropriate physical exercise routines with RA patients can produce significant increases in aerobic capacity, endurance, strength, flexibility, and physical activities; significant decreases in depression, anxiety, and pain; and improvements in various measures of disease (reduced joint involvement, greater grip strength, and faster walking time). Exercise programs should be modified in consideration of the unique needs of RA patients, which include (a) reduced biomechanical stress on the joints, (b) reduced impact loading, (c) control of stretching, (d) reduced compressive forces in the hip and knee, (e) avoidance of high repetition exercises, and (f) adaptation to changes in disease status. One practical implication of these suggestions for psychologists is that programmatic exercise for patients with RA should be directed by a trained therapist. However, behavioral strategies may enhance adherence or maintenance of an exercise program.

Because of the chronic and progressive nature of RA, it is especially important that any benefits derived from cognitive–behavioral treatments be as durable as possible. The coping skills–self-management framework used by the cognitive–behavioral therapies described in this chapter has as goals the acquisition and implementation of skills that will help the patient to adapt throughout the course of the disease. Evidence of durability of effects is weak but encouraging. Radojevik et al. (1992) and O'Leary et al. (1988) reported that posttreatment gains are maintained or improved at the 2- and 4-month follow-ups, respectively. Both Bradley et al. (1987) and Parker, Frank, Beck, Smarr, et al. (1988) reported the maintenance of treatment gains at the 12-month follow-up, although only a subset of Parker's patients maintained gains. Applebaum et al. (1988) reported no significant differences between groups at 18 months. Unfortunately, the reliability of this latter finding is weakened because almost half of the original sample could not be followed up.

Certainly, little enduring benefit is to be anticipated if patients fail to maintain potentially adaptive self-management techniques. Intuitively, patients who implement and maintain adaptive patterns of coping should have better long-term adjustment. This relationship was reported in the following three studies.

Parker, Frank, Beck, Smarr, et al. (1988) designated 13 patients as highly adherent on the basis of self-reported rate of adherence with 17 major components in the treatment program. These patients evidenced greater reductions in catastrophization, greater increases in belief that they could control and decrease their pain, and increased use of several coping strategies (e.g., ignoring pain sensations, coping self-statements, reinterpreting pain sensations, and increasing activities). These more highly adherent patients also reported less VAS pain, a smaller percentage of their body in pain, and lower appraisals of arthritis helplessness.

Radojevik et al. (1992) had patients self-monitor (a) postrelaxation peripheral temperature as an index of relaxation and (b) medical consumption. Patients who reported decreasing the frequency with which they engaged in various passive coping behaviors reported less joint exam pain and fewer painful joints. Increases in active coping strategies were associated with improvements in psychological status. Self-reported adherence to medication regimens was associated with posttreatment reductions in joint pain. Finally, patients' peripheral temperatures following home practice of relaxation were associated with decreased joint exam pain at both posttreatment and follow-up. Although this last finding is not strictly an effect of adherence, it is likely that relaxation efficacy is strongly affected by practice.

Finally, Bradley and his colleagues (Bradley et al., 1989) identified low-, moderate-, and high-adherence subgroups on the basis of self-report of the extent to which patients continued to use various treatment components during follow-up. The moderate-adherence subgroup produced significantly lower VAS pain intensity ratings and reported less arthritis helplessness than did patients in the low- and high-adherence subgroups. Similar patterns of results also obtained for ratings of pain unpleasantness and for a combined index of disease activity. Additional analyses confirmed that it was the moderate-adherence subgroup that accounted for the superiority of the entire cognitive–behavioral treatment group in measures of pain, pain behavior, disease activity, and arthritis helplessness. Two explanations for these results were suggested. First, the high-adherence patients may have provided an overly positive estimate of the degree of their adherence, and the subgroup labeled moderate-adherence may in fact have been the ones who actually continued to use the various coping strategies most frequently. The second explanation suggested by the data is slightly more complex and involves an interaction between disease activity and adherence. At both posttreatment and follow-up assessments, the moderate-adherence subgroup had relatively lower levels of disease activity, which may have permitted them to use their new coping behaviors more effectively. In contrast, the higher disease activity levels of the high-adherence subgroup may have reduced the effectiveness of their coping attempts in spite of their best efforts. It is also possible that the frequent use of adaptive coping skills by the high-adherence subgroup actually prevented them from experiencing even greater deleterious effects of their high disease activity.

Conclusion

RA is a painful, disabling, chronic disease that results in excessive suffering for many Americans. The pervasiveness of the psychological dimension of the disease is becoming increasingly apparent. Patients' disease-related appraisals, expectations, and behavioral competencies determine the strategies they use to cope with the disease and its impact on their lives. These cognitive and behavioral variables have been shown to influence patients' health status and quality of life. Moreover, these cognitive variables and specific coping strategies are modifiable with current interventional procedures, and their change contributes to improved health and quality of life for RA patients. Specific improvements have resulted in diminished pain, enhanced psychological adjustment, and improved physical functioning, and these benefits appear to be moderately durable. There is even weak evidence to suggest that psychological interventions might affect parameters of the disease process itself, although this conclusion remains speculative. Although many questions remain unanswered, the value of including cognitive–behavioral interventions in a comprehensive approach to managing RA seems clear. Psychologists clearly can make a positive contribution to the care of patients with RA. Opportunities for collaboration between psychologists and rheumatologists, both clinical and investigational, should continue to expand.

REFERENCES

Achterberg, J., McGraw, P., & Lawlis, G. F. (1981). Rheumatoid arthritis: A study of the relaxation and temperature biofeedback training as an adjunctive therapy. *Biofeedback and Self-Regulation, 6,* 207–233.

Affleck, G., Pfeiffer, C., Tennen, H., & Fifield, J. (1987). Attributional processes in rheumatoid arthritis patients. *Arthritis and Rheumatism, 30,* 927–931.

Affleck, G., Pfeiffer, C., Tennen, H., & Fifield, J. (1988). Social support and psychosocial adjustment to rheumatoid arthritis: Quantitative and qualitative findings. *Arthritis Care and Research, 1,* 71–77.

Affleck, G., Tennen, H., Pfeiffer, C., & Fifield, J. (1987). Appraisals of control and predictability in adapting to a chronic disease. *Journal of Personality and Social Psychology, 53,* 273–279.

Affleck, G., Tennen, H., Urrows, S., & Higgins, P. (1991). Individual differences in the day-to-day experience of chronic pain: A prospective daily study of rheumatoid arthritis patients. *Health Psychology, 10,* 419–426.

Affleck, G., Tennen, H., Urrows, S., & Higgins, P. (1992). Neuroticism and the pain-mood relation in rheumatoid arthritis: Insights from a prospective daily study. *Journal of Consulting and Clinical Psychology, 60,* 119–126.

Anderson, K. O., Bradley, L. A., Young, L. D., McDaniel, L. K., & Wise, C. M. (1985). Rheumatoid arthritis: Review of psychological factors related to etiology, effects, and treatment. *Psychological Bulletin, 98,* 358–387.

Anderson, K. O., Keefe, F. J., Bradley, L. A., McDaniel, L. K., Young, L. D., Turner, R. A., Agudelo, C. A., Semble, E. L., & Pisko, E. J. (1988). Predication of pain behavior and functional status of rheumatoid arthritis patients using medical status and psychological variables. *Pain, 33,* 25–32.

Applebaum, K. A., Blanchard, E. B., Hickling, E. J., & Alfonso, M. (1988). Cognitive behavioral treatment of a veteran population with moderate to severe rheumatoid arthritis. *Behavior Therapy, 19,* 489–502.

Bandura, A. (1986). *Social foundations of thought and action: A social cognitive theory.* Englewood Cliffs, NJ: Prentice-Hall.

Bergner, M., Bobbitt, R., Carter, W., & Gilson, B. (1981). The Sickness Impact Profile: Development and final revision of a health status measure. *Medical Care, 19,* 787–805.

Blalock, S., DeVellis, B., DeVellis, R., & Sauter, S. (1988). Self-evaluation processes and adjustment to rheumatoid arthritis. *Arthritis and Rheumatism, 31,* 1245–1251.

Blalock, S. J., DeVellis, R. F., Brown, G. K., & Wallston, K. A. (1989). Validity of the Center for Epidemiological Studies Depression Scale in arthritis populations. *Arthritis and Rheumatism, 32,* 991–997.

Bradley, L. A., Young, L. D., Anderson, K. O., Agudelo, C. A., Forbes, P. M., McDaniel, L. K., Williams, T., Pisko, E. J., Semble, E. L., & Turner, R. A. (1989). *Twelve-month follow-up of psychological therapy for rheumatoid arthritis patients: Relationship between reports of compliance and maintenance of treatment gains.* Unpublished manuscript.

Bradley, L. A., Young, L. D., Anderson, K. O., Turner, R. A., Agudelo, C. A., McDaniel, L. K., Pisko, E. J., Semble, E. L., & Morgan, T. M. (1987). Effects of psychological therapy on pain behavior of rheumatoid arthritis patients: Treatment outcome and six-month follow-up. *Arthritis and Rheumatism, 30,* 1105–1114.

Brown, G. K. (1990). A causal analysis of chronic pain and depression. *Journal of Abnormal Psychology, 99,* 127–137.

Brown, G. K., & Nicassio, P. M. (1987). Development of a questionnaire for the assessment of active and passive coping strategies in chronic pain patients. *Pain, 31,* 53–64.

Brown, G. K., Nicassio, P. M., & Wallston, K. A. (1989). Pain coping strategies and depression in rheumatoid arthritis. *Journal of Consulting and Clinical Psychology, 57,* 652–657.

Buckelew, S. P., & Parker, J. C. (1989). Coping with arthritis pain: A review of the literature. *Arthritis Care and Research, 2,* 136–145.

Buescher, K. L., Johnston, J. A., Parker, J. C., Smarr, K. L., Buckelew, S. P., Anderson, S. K., & Walker, S. E. (1991). Relationship of self-efficacy to pain behavior. *Journal of Rheumatology, 18,* 968–972.

Callahan, L., Kaplan, M., & Pincus, T. (1991). The Beck Depression Inventory, Center for Epidemiological Studies Depression Scale (CES-D), and General Well-Being Schedule depression subscale in rheumatoid arthritis. *Arthritis Care and Research, 4,* 3–11.

Downie, W. W., Leatham, P. A., Rhind, V. M., Wright, V., Branco, J. A., & Anderson, J. A. (1978). Studies with pain rating scales. *Annals of Rheumatoid Disease, 37,* 378–381.

Felts, W., & Yelin, E. (1989). The economic impact of the rheumatic diseases in the United States. *Journal of Rheumatology, 16,* 867–884.

Fifield, J., & Reisine, S. (1992). Characterizing the meaning of psychological distress in rheumatoid arthritis. *Arthritis Care and Research, 5,* 184–191.

Flor, H., & Turk, D. C. (1988). Chronic back pain and rheumatoid arthritis: Predicting pain and disability from cognitive variables. *Journal of Behavioral Medicine, 11,* 251–265.

Frank, R., Beck, N., Parker, J., Kashani, J., Elliott, T., Smith, A., Atwood, C., Brownlee-Duffeck, M., & Kay, D. (1988). Depression in rheumatoid arthritis. *Journal of Rheumatology, 15,* 920–925.

Fries, J., Spitz, P., & Young, D. (1982). The dimensions of health outcomes: The Health Assessment Questionnaire, disability and pain scales. *Journal of Rheumatology, 9,* 789–793.

Garber, J., & Seligman, M. E. P. (1980). *Human helplessness: Theory and applications.* New York: Academic Press.

Goodenow, C., Reisine, S. T., & Grady, K. E. (1990). Quality of social support and associated social and psychological functioning in women with rheumatoid arthritis. *Health Psychology, 9,* 266–284.

Hagglund, K. J., Haley, W. E., Reveille, J. D., & Alarcón, G. S. (1989). Predicting individual differences in pain and functional impairment among patients with rheumatoid arthritis. *Arthritis and Rheumatism, 32,* 851–858.

Hawley, D. J., & Wolfe, F. (1988). Anxiety and depression in patients with rheumatoid arthritis: A prospective study in 400 patients. *Journal of Rheumatology, 15,* 932–941.

Hawley, D. J., & Wolfe, F. (1992). Sensitivity to change of the Health Assessment Questionnaire (HAQ) and other clinical and health status measures in rheumatoid arthritis. *Arthritis Care and Research, 5,* 130–136.

Keefe, F. J., Brown, G. K., Wallston, K. A., & Caldwell, D. S. (1989). Coping with rheumatoid arthritis pain: Catastrophizing as a maladaptive strategy. *Pain, 37,* 51–56.

Lazarus, R. S., & Folkman, S. (1984). *Stress, appraisal, and coping.* New York: Springer.

Liang, M., & Logigian, M. (1992). *Rehabilitation of early rheumatoid arthritis.* Boston: Little, Brown.

Lorig, K., Chastain, R. L., Ung, E., Shoor, S., & Holman, H. R. (1989). Development and evaluation of a scale to measure perceived self-efficacy in people with arthritis. *Arthritis and Rheumatism, 32,* 37–44.

Lorig, K., & González, V. (1992). The integration of theory with practice: A 12-year case study. *Health Education Quarterly, 19,* 355–368.

Lorish, C. D., Abraham, N., Austin, J., Bradley, L. A., & Alarcón, G. S. (1991). Disease and psychosocial factors related to physical functioning in rheumatoid arthritis. *Journal of Rheumatology, 18,* 1150–1157.

Manne, S. L., & Zautra, A. J. (1989). Spouse criticism and support: Their association with coping and psychological adjustment among women with rheumatoid arthritis. *Journal of Personality and Social Psychology, 56,* 608–617.

McCracken, L. M. (1991). Cognitive–behavioral treatment of rheumatoid arthritis: A preliminary review of efficacy and methodology. *Annals of Behavioral Medicine, 13,* 57–65.

McFarlane, A. C., & Brooks, P. M. (1988). An analysis of the relationship between psychological morbidity and disease activity in rheumatoid arthritis. *Journal of Rheumatology, 15,* 926–931.

McKenna, F., & Wright, V. (1985). Pain and rheumatoid arthritis. *Annals of Rheumatic Disease, 44,* 805.

Meenan, R., Gertman, P., & Mason, J. (1980). Measuring health status in arthritis: The Arthritis Impact Measurement Scales. *Arthritis and Rheumatism, 23,* 146–152.

Melzack, R. (1975). The McGill Pain Questionnaire: Major properties and scoring methods. *Pain, 1,* 277–299.

Minor, M. A. (1991). Physical activity and management of arthritis. *Annals of Behavioral Medicine, 13,* 117–124.

Mitchell, J., Burkhauser, R., & Pincus, T. (1988). The importance of age, education, and comorbidity in the substantial earnings losses of individuals with symmetric polyarthritis. *Arthritis and Rheumatism, 31,* 348–357.

Mitchell, K. R. (1986). Peripheral temperature autoregulation and its effect on the symptoms of rheumatoid arthritis. *Scandinavian Journal of Behavioral Therapy, 15,* 55–64.

Newman, S. P., Fitzpatrick, R., Lamb, R., & Shipley, M. (1989). The origins of depressed mood in rheumatoid arthritis. *Journal of Rheumatology, 16,* 740–744.

O'Leary, A., Shoor, S., Lorig, K., & Holman, H. R. (1988). A cognitive–behavioral treatment for rheumatoid arthritis. *Health Psychology, 7,* 527–544.

Parker, J. C., Buckelew, S. P., Smarr, K. L., Buescher, K. L., Beck, N. C., Frank, R. G., Anderson, S., & Walker, S. E. (1990). Psychological screening in rheumatoid arthritis. *Journal of Rheumatology, 17,* 1016–1021.

Parker, J. C., Frank, R., Beck, N., Finan, M., Walker, S., Hewett, J. E., Broster, C., Smarr, K., Smith, E., & Kay, D. (1988). Pain in rheumatoid arthritis: Relationship to demographic, medical, and psychological factors. *Journal of Rheumatology, 15,* 433–437.

Parker, J. C., Frank, R. G., Beck, N. C., Smarr, K. L., Buescher, K. L., Phillips, L. R., Smith, E. I., Anderson, S. K., & Walker, S. E. (1988). Pain management in rheumatoid arthritis patients: A cognitive–behavioral approach. *Arthritis and Rheumatism, 31,* 593–601.

Parker, J. C., McRae, C., Smarr, K., Beck, N., Frank, F., Anderson, S., & Walker, S. (1988). Coping strategies in rheumatoid arthritis. *Journal of Rheumatology, 15,* 1376–1383.

Parker, J. C., Smarr, K. L., Buescher, K. L., Phillips, L. R., Frank, R. G., Beck, N. C., Anderson, S. K., & Walker, S. E. (1989). Pain control and rational thinking: Implications for rheumatoid arthritis. *Arthritis and Rheumatism, 32,* 984–990.

Peck, J. R., Smith, T. W., Ward, J. R., & Milano, R. (1989). Disability and depression in rheumatoid arthritis: A multi-trait, multi-method investigation. *Arthritis and Rheumatism, 32,* 1100–1106.

Pincus, T., Callahan, L. F., Bradley, L. A., Vaughn, W. K., & Wolfe, F. (1986). Elevated MMPI scores for hypochondriasis, depression, and hysteria in patients with rheumatoid arthritis reflect disease rather than psychological status. *Arthritis and Rheumatism, 29,* 1456–1466.

Pincus, T., Callahan, L., & Vaughn, W. K. (1987). Questionnaire, walking time, and button test measures of functional capacity as predictive markers for mortality in rheumatoid arthritis. *Journal of Rheumatology, 14,* 240–251.

Radojevik, V., Nicassio, P. M., & Weisman, M. H. (1992). Behavioral intervention with and without family support for rheumatoid arthritis. *Behavioral Therapy, 23,* 13–30.

Rosenstiel, A. K., & Keefe, F. J. (1982). The use of coping strategies in chronic low back pain patients: Relationship to patient characteristics and current adjustment. *Pain, 17,* 33–44.

Shearn, M. A., & Fireman, B. H. (1985). Stress management and mutual support groups in rheumatoid arthritis. *American Journal of Medicine, 78,* 771–775.

Smith, C. A., & Wallston, K. A. (1992). Adaptation in patients with chronic rheumatoid arthritis: Application of a general model. *Health Psychology, 11,* 151–162.

Smith, T. W., Peck, J. R., Milano, R. A., & Ward, J. R. (1988). Cognitive distortion in rheumatoid arthritis: Relation to depression and disability. *Journal of Consulting and Clinical Psychology, 56,* 412–416.

Smith, T. W., Peck, J. R., & Ward, J. R. (1990). Helplessness and depression in rheumatoid arthritis. *Health Psychology, 9,* 377–389.

Stein, M. J., Wallston, K. A., & Nicassio, P. M. (1988). Factor structure of the Arthritis Helplessness Index. *Journal of Rheumatology, 15,* 427–432.

Stein, M. J., Wallston, K. A., Nicassio, P. M., & Castner, N. M. (1988). Correlates of a clinical classification schema for the Arthritis Helplessness subscale. *Arthritis and Rheumatism, 31,* 876–881.

Steinbrocker, O., Traeger, C. H., & Batterman, R. C. (1949). Therapeutic criteria in rheumatoid arthritis. *Journal of the American Medical Association, 140,* 659–662.

Strauss, G. D., Spiegel, J. S., Daniels, M., Spiegel, T., Landsverk, J., Roy-Byrne, P., Edelstein, C., Ehlhardt, J., Falke, R., Hindin, L., & Zackler, L. (1986). Group therapies for rheumatoid arthritis. *Arthritis and Rheumatism, 29,* 1203–1209.

Turk, D. C., Meichenbaum, D., & Genest, M. (1983). *Pain and behavioral medicine.* New York: Guilford Press.

Turner, J. A., & Romano, J. M. (1990). Cognitive–behavioral therapy. In J. J. Bonica (Ed.), *The management of pain* (2nd ed., pp. 1711–1721). Philadelphia: Lea & Febiger.

Utsinger, P. D., Zvaifler, N. J., & Ehrlich, G. E. (Eds.). (1985). *Rheumatoid arthritis.* Philadelphia: Lippincott.

Weinblatt, M. E., & Maier, A. L. (1989). Treatment of rheumatoid arthritis. *Arthritis Care and Research, 2,* S23–S32.

Wolfe, F. (1990). 50 years of antirheumatic therapy: The prognosis of rheumatoid arthritis. *Journal of Rheumatology, 17*(Suppl. 22), 24–32.

Wolfe, F., Hawley, D., & Cathey, M. (1991). Clinical and health status measures over time: Prognosis and outcome assessment in rheumatoid arthritis. *Journal of Rheumatology, 18,* 1290–1297.

Young, L. D. (1992). Psychological factors in rheumatoid arthritis. *Journal of Consulting and Clinical Psychology, 60,* 619–627.

Zautra, A. J., & Manne, S. L. (1992). Coping with rheumatoid arthritis: A review of a decade of research. *Annals of Behavioral Medicine, 14,* 31–39.

Temporomandibular Disorders

Alan G. Glaros and Ernest G. Glass

Temporomandibular disorders (TMD) are a heterogeneous collection of disorders characterized by orofacial pain, masticatory dysfunction, or both. Temporomandibular disorders can be productively
organized into two broad diagnostic classes: (a) functional disorders
of the musculature of the face, head, neck, shoulders, and upper
back, and (b) disorders involving the hard structures and soft tissues
of the temporomandibular joint (TMJ). The two etiological classes are
not mutually exclusive, and patients who present at facial pain clinics
may be diagnosed as having disorders representative of both classes.

We thank Jerald Katz, Edward Mosby, and Stella Duong for their assistance
in the preparation of this chapter. We also thank Lois Hightower and Doug
Walter for their artistic talents in creating the figures.

The terminology for TMD has changed considerably since Costen's (1934) initial description of a "syndrome" involving the ear and TMJ, and the terminology used has often reflected particular perspectives on the etiology of the disorder (cf. Okeson, 1989). For example, *Costen's syndrome* originally referred to the loss of posterior teeth, which ostensibly produced increased ear pressure and pain. This conceptualization was shown to be incorrect, and terms such as *temporomandibular joint disturbance, temporomandibular joint dysfunction syndrome* (Shore, 1959), and *functional temporomandibular joint disturbances* (Ramfjord & Ash, 1971) came into use. As suggested by these terms, problems involving the TMJ were considered the primary etiological factors in the disorder. The importance of other etiological factors to the conceptualization of the problem is reflected in terms such as *occlusomandibular disturbance* (Gerber, 1971), emphasizing occlusion; *myoarthropathy of the temporomandibular joint* (Graber, 1971), emphasizing arthritides; and *pain–dysfunction syndrome* (Voss, 1964), *myofascial pain–dysfunction syndrome* (Laskin, 1969), and *temporomandibular pain–dysfunction syndrome* (Schwartz, 1959), emphasizing pain. Because TMD can be diagnosed in the absence of problems in the TMJ or in occlusion (cf. Truelove, Sommers, LeResche, Dworkin, & Von Korff, 1992), the more general terms *craniomandibular disorders* (McNeill et al., 1980) and *temporomandibular disorders* (Bell, 1982) have been proposed as alternatives. The American Dental Association has adopted the latter term, partly to facilitate communication and progress in research (Laskin et al., 1983).

The pain reported by TMD patients is typically located in the muscles of mastication, in the preauricular area, or in the TMJ (McNeill, Mohl, Rugh, & Tanaka, 1990). TMD patients may also report headache, other facial pains, earache, dizziness, and ringing in the ears, as well as neck, shoulder, and upper and lower back pain. TMD patients may report a variety of TMJ problems other than pain, including locking in the open or closed position and clicking, popping, and grating sounds. Patients may report difficulty opening their jaws wide as well as a sense that their occlusion (bite) feels "off."

Reports on the prevalence of TMD vary widely, depending on the definition of TMD used. In population studies that examined for clinical signs such as TMJ sounds, the prevalence rates tended to be high, with a median prevalence rate of 50–60% (Gale, 1992; Locker & Slade, 1988; Okeson, 1989). When reported symptoms of TMD are used as the criterion, the prevalence rate drops to a median of 32% (range = 16–59%). The prevalence rate drops to about 3–5% when the criterion is pain and dysfunction sufficiently severe to prompt the patient to seek help (De Kanter, Käyser, Battistuzzi, Truin, & Van 't Hof, 1992; Dworkin et al., 1990; LeResche, Dworkin, Sommers, & Truelove, 1991; Rugh & Solberg, 1985; Schiffman & Fricton, 1988; Schiffman, Fricton, Haley, & Shapiro, 1990; Solberg, 1983). These data suggest that the signs and symptoms of TMD are relatively common in the general population but are generally not of sufficient intensity to cause an individual to seek treatment.

The prevalence of TMD varies by age and gender. Prevalence studies that used signs, symptoms, and clinical samples indicate that TMD is more prevalent in those under age 45 (e.g., Duckro, Tait, Margolis, & Deshields, 1990; Glass, McGlynn, Glaros, Melton, & Romans, 1993). The data for gender show that the prevalence rates for men and women do not differ when nonclinical populations are assessed (Duckro et al., 1990; Helöe & Helöe, 1979; Swanljung & Rantanen, 1979). However, the ratio of females to males is at least 3:1 in patient samples (Reider, Martinoff, & Wilcox, 1983). The greater prevalence of women patients in clinical samples probably reflects social and psychological factors more than biological ones (Bush, Harkins, Harrington, & Price, 1993).

Our coverage of TMD begins with a brief discussion of the anatomy and biomechanics of the TMJ and facial musculature. In this section we also address normal and abnormal function. The nosological schemes for TMD are presented in the section that follows, with an emphasis on the recently published research diagnostic criteria for TMD. We then address factors that predispose, initiate, and maintain TMD. The principal treatment options for TMD patients, emphasizing dental and behavioral approaches, are then presented. Finally, we discuss controversies in TMD.

TMJ and Associated Musculature

The principal structures of the TMJ include the *condyle,* the *articular disc,* the *articular fossa,* and the associated membranes, fluids, and ligaments. These, together with the associated musculature, provide the basis for the normal function of the teeth and jaw.

The joint is unique in function in that it is capable of both a hinge (rotational) movement and a sliding (translational) movement. The rotational movement takes place in the lower compartment of the joint, and the translational movement takes place in the upper compartment. The joint is separated into these compartments by an articular disc.

Condyle

Arising from the U-shaped mandible, the condyle (Figures 1 and 2) is the portion of the mandible that articulates within the *glenoid fossa*

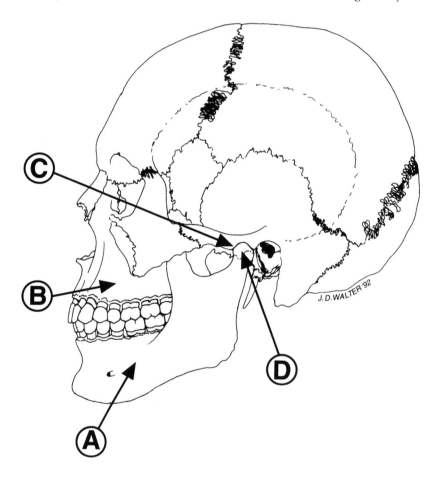

Figure 1. Gross anatomy of the skull and temporomandibular joint. A, Mandible; B, maxilla; C, articular eminence; D, condyle.

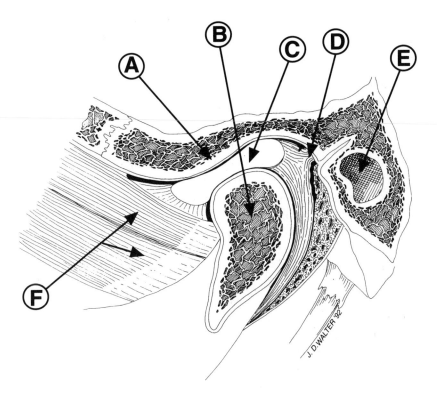

Figure 2.   Anatomy of the temporomandibular joint. A, Articular eminence; B, head of the condyle; C, articular disc; D, posterior attachment; E, external auditory meatus; F, lateral pterygoid muscle.

of the cranium (Hylander, 1992; Okeson, 1989). The condyles range in size from 15 to 20 mm in width mediolaterally and 8 to 10 mm in width anteroposteriorly. The medial and lateral projections of the condyles are termed *poles*. The articular surface of the condyle is the upper and superior portion of the condyle. It articulates indirectly through the articular disc against the articular eminence.

When the teeth are in a normal, intercuspal position, the condyle is "seated" in the glenoid fossa. When the teeth are separated and the mouth is opened, the condyle rotates within the fossa in the first 25 mm of interincisal opening and then translates to the midpoint of the articular eminence. The normal minimal opening ranges between 35 and 40 mm (LeResche, 1992).

A variety of conditions can affect the condyle. Degenerative disorders can lead to erosion and "flattening" of the condyle or the formation of undesirable growth or bone spurs. Both conditions may result in decreased function or pain.

Articular Disc

The articular disc facilitates condylar movement (see Figure 2). It is composed of dense fibrous connective tissue and is devoid of nerve and blood supply. The disc normally rests on the condyle and is attached to it medially and laterally by the discal ligaments (Ide, Nakazawa, & Kamimura, 1991). The dense fibrous connective tissue of the disc appears to tolerate the shearing forces involved in normal joint function better than the compressive forces associated with parafunctional behaviors such as clenching (Laskin, 1992).

In the closed position, the disc is "seated" with its posterior portion in the highest part of the fossa. In normal function (Figure 3), the condyle does not change its position in relation to the articular disc. The condyle–disc complex moves together as the condyle rotates within the fossa and translates to the eminence.

Alterations of normal disc function may be present in TMD. These can include the temporary or permanent displacement (derangement) of the disc from its normal position. In the most common derangement, the disc is displaced anteriorly with the jaw in a closed position (Figure 4). On opening and translation of the condyle, the disc is pulled posteriorly by the posterior ligament, and the disc "pops" or "clicks" back into normal position. With closing, the disc again pops or clicks out of normal position. If the disc is permanently out of place, then no sounds are heard on opening, and the individual generally cannot open his or her mouth more than about 25 mm.

Masticatory Musculature

The muscles that are most important to normal jaw function are the *masseter, temporalis,* and *lateral* and *medial pterygoids*. The masseter muscle (Figure 5) elevates the mandible during mastication. The masseter can be palpated by placing the fingers slightly above the angle of the mandible (the "point" of the jaw) and clenching. The temporalis muscle also closes the jaw and retracts the mandible. This muscle can be palpated by placing the fingers on the temples and clenching (Ide et al., 1991).

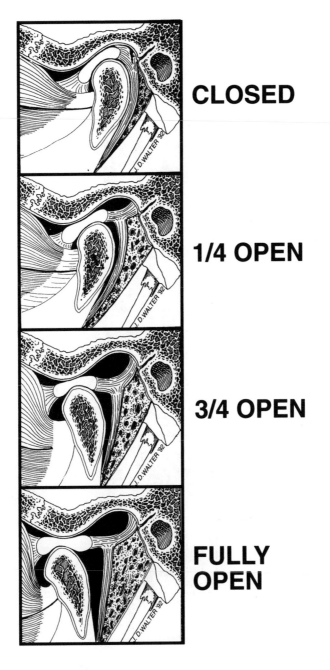

Figure 3.   Normal function of the temporomandibular joint.

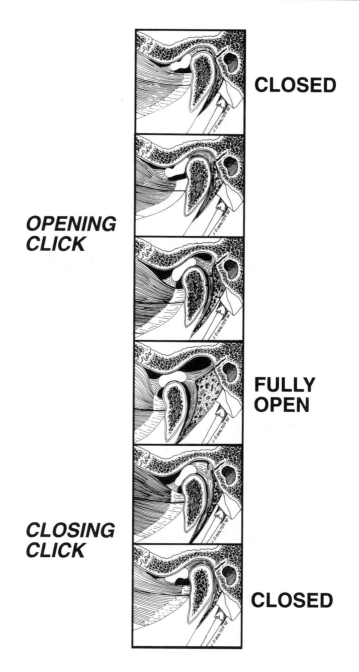

Figure 4.   Function of the temporomandibular joint in the presence of disc displacement.

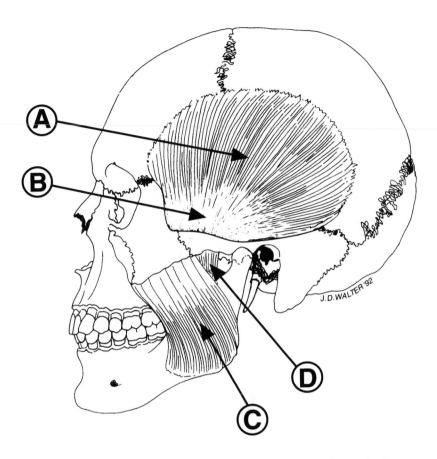

Figure 5. External masticatory musculature. A, Temporal muscle; B, temporalis tendon; C, superficial portion of the masseter muscle; D, deep portion of the masseter muscle.

The lateral (external) pterygoid muscle (Figure 6) helps to seat the condyle upward and forward on the posterior slope of the articular eminence. This muscle protrudes and depresses the mandible with lateral deviation to the opposite side and generally aids lateral movement to the opposite side (Miller, 1991). In addition, the lateral pterygoid helps position the foot of the disc under the crest of the eminence. This muscle is normally palpated from within the mouth. The medial (internal) pterygoid closes the jaw, produces lateral movement to the opposite side, and aids in protrusion. Like the external pterygoid, the muscle is normally palpated from inside the mouth.

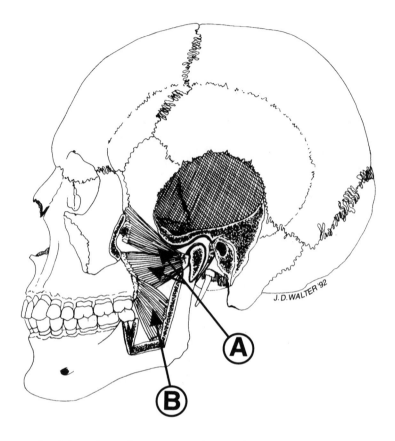

Figure 6. Internal masticatory musculature. A, Lateral pterygoid muscle; B, medial pterygoid muscle.

Additional muscles in which pain can be reported in a TMD patient include the *frontalis, sternocleidomastoid, anterior* and *posterior diagastric, splenius muscle group,* and *trapezius.*

The masticatory muscles are most active when chewing, biting, and swallowing. However, the muscles can also be active when various parafunctional habits and behaviors (e.g., chewing gum and clenching) are performed. Under the influence of these strong compressive forces, the articular disc space can narrow, the disc can "stick," and degenerative changes can occur (Laskin, 1992).

Summary

The hard and soft tissues of the TMJ and its associated musculature operate as a relatively stable, yet dynamically functioning whole. When the joint and its musculature operate normally, the joint is capable of smooth, pain-free movements in three planes of motion, affording an individual the ability to eat, laugh, yawn, chew, or engage in other activities involving the jaw.

Like other joints, however, the hard tissues of the TMJ are susceptible to degenerative changes, and displacement of the soft tissues can also result in pain or reduction in function. Furthermore, under the influence of abnormal loads placed on the joint by parafunctional events, the hard and soft tissues of the TMJ can change, producing chronic pain, discomfort, and other changes in function (Laskin, 1992).

Nosological Schemes for TMD

There is considerable agreement that most cases of TMD involve either muscle disorders, internal derangements of the TMJ, degenerative changes in the TMJ, or a combination of any of these. Studies suggest that about 23% of TMD patients have muscle disorders, 19% have either internal derangements or degenerative changes, and 27% have combined muscle–joint disorder (Schiffman et al., 1990).

Many of the diagnostic schemes developed to date to classify TMD patients have suffered from a variety of limitations (Ohrbach & Stohler, 1992). Some methodological issues include unknown interrater reliability for the methods used in patient assessment (Bergamini, Prayer-Galletti, & Tonelli, 1990; Talley, Murphy, Smith, Baylin, & Haden, 1990), poor specificity, and unknown interrater reliability for diagnosis. Clinically, some systems have only minimal biological plausibility and are not exhaustive (Bergamini et al., 1990). Some may not allow for multiple diagnoses (e.g., Farrar, 1972), and some do not facilitate decision making (American Academy of Craniomandibular Disorders, 1990; Bell, 1986; Block, 1980; Eversole & Machado, 1985).

Most systems also fail to assess psychological issues. Research suggests that TMD patients may suffer from a variety of psychological disorders. Kinney, Gatchel, Ellis, and Holt (1992), for example, assessed 50 chronic TMD patients using the Structured Clinical Interview for *DSM-III-R* (SCID; Spitzer, Williams, Gibbon, & First, 1990). Their results suggest that nearly half of the patients met the criteria for current Axis I disorders, excluding somatoform pain disorder, whereas 40% met diagnostic criteria for at least one personality disorder. These values appear to be well in excess of population prevalence rates (Regier et al., 1988).

Three nosological systems appear to have both clinical and research utility (Dworkin & LeResche, 1992; Fricton, Kroening, & Hathaway, 1988; Truelove et al., 1992). Of these three, the research diagnostic criteria (RDC) of Dworkin and LeResche (1992) are unique in that they require patients be assessed for psychological factors, including disability.

The RDC is a multiaxial system in which clinical disorders are assessed on Axis I, and pain-related disability and psychological factors are assessed on Axis II. The diagnoses within Axis I are illustrated in Table 1. Within Axis I, an individual may be diagnosed as having one of the muscle disorders (but not both), but each joint may be diagnosed as having one of the disc displacement diagnoses, one of the arthralgia/arthritis/arthrosis diagnoses, or both. Thus, a total of five diagnoses are possible within Axis I for each patient, although patients rarely have more than three (LeResche, 1992).

Under Axis II, patients are assessed in three domains: pain intensity and disability, depression, and nonspecific physical symptoms. These are described in Table 2. Characteristic pain intensity is assessed by taking the mean of three 10-point scales for assessing current, worst, and average pain (Von Korff, 1992), as reported in a patient history questionnaire. Disability scores are computed by taking the mean of three 10-point scales for assessing the effect of pain on daily, social, and work activities. In addition, the number of days in the past 6 months for which TMD pain kept the individual from normal activities is also counted. The disability scores and the disability days are both converted into "disability points" using a 4-point scale.

To obtain Grade 0, the patient must report no TMD pain in the past 6 months. In Grades I and II, the patient must receive fewer than three disability points and report low- or high-intensity pain (Grades I and II, respectively). Grade III patients must obtain 3 or 4 disability points, and Grade IV patients must obtain 5 or 6 disability points.

Depression is assessed using the depression scale from the revised, 90-item Symptom Checklist (SCL-90-R; Derogatis, 1983), supple-

Table 1

Research Diagnostic Criteria for Temporomandibular Disorders, Axis I

Diagnostic label	Description	Operational definition
Muscle diagnoses		
Myofascial pain	Pain of muscle origin	Patient report of orofacial pain Pain to palpation in 3 of 20 muscle sites
Myofascial pain with limited opening	Myofascial pain and limited movement and stiffness of the muscle during stretching	Myofascial pain Pain-free unassisted mandibular opening of less than 40 mm Mandibular opening with assistance of 5 mm or more greater than pain-free unassisted opening
Disc displacements		
Disc displacement with reduction	Displacement of disc from normal position, reducing on full opening, usually resulting in a noise	Reproducible click on both vertical opening and closing or reproducible click in both vertical range of motion and click during lateral excursion or protrusion
Disc displacement without reduction, with limited opening	Disc displacement associated with limited opening	History of limited opening Maximum unassisted opening ≤35 mm Passive stretch increases opening by 4 mm or less over maximum unassisted opening Contralateral excursion <7 mm and/or uncorrected deviation to the ipsilateral side on opening Absence of joint sounds or presence of joint sounds not meeting criteria for disc displacement with reduction

Table 1

Continued

Diagnostic label	Description	Operational definition
Disc displacement without reduction, without limited opening	Disc displacement not associated with limited opening	History of limitation of mandibular opening Maximum unassisted opening >35 mm Passive stretch increases opening by 5 mm or more over maximum unassisted opening Contralateral excursion ≥7 mm Presence of joint sounds not meeting criteria for disc displacement with reduction If imaging (arthrography or MRI) performed, evidence of displacement of disc without reduction

Arthralgia/arthritis/arthrosis

Diagnostic label	Description	Operational definition
Arthralgia	Pain and tenderness in the joint capsule and/or the synovial lining of the TMJ	Self-report of pain involving the TMJ Pain in one or both TMJs during palpation Absence of coarse crepitus
Osteoarthritis of the TMJ	Inflammatory condition within the TMJ resulting from degeneration of the joint structures	Arthralgia Either coarse crepitus in the joint or evidence of degeneration as seen in tomograms
Osteoarthrosis of the TMJ	Degenerative disorder of the joint in which joint form and structure are abnormal	No signs of arthralgia Either coarse crepitus in the joint or evidence of degeneration as seen in tomograms

Note. TMJ = temporomandibular joint.

Table 2

Research Diagnostic Criteria for Temporomandibular Disorders, Axis II

Criterion	Scoring
Pain intensity and disability	Grade 0, no temporomandibular pain in the prior 6 months Grade I, low disability–low-intensity pain Grade II, low disability–high-intensity pain Grade III, high disability–moderately limiting Grade IV, high disability–severely limiting
Depression	Normal Moderate (above 70th percentile) Severe (above 90th percentile)
Nonspecific physical symptoms	Normal Moderate (above 70th percentile) Severe (above 90th percentile)

mented by seven additional items. Nonspecific physical symptoms are assessed using the somatization scale of the SCL-90-R. The authors of the RDC take pains to point out the intent of the latter scale is to measure nonspecific physical symptoms, not the psychological construct of somatization (Von Korff, 1992). A Jaw Disability Scale is also included with the RDC History Questionnaire, but its reliability and validity have not been assessed (Von Korff, 1992), and it is likely that the scale will provide poor discrimination (Lund, 1992).

Summary

The RDC (Dworkin & LeResche, 1992) mark an important development in the assessment of TMD patients. The RDC diagnoses have operational definitions, and they address the most prevalent conditions found in TMD patients. The explicit recognition that psychological factors play a role in TMD should lead to better overall assessment of the typical TMD patient and facilitate research examining the role of psychological factors in TMD. However, research is still needed to establish the reliability, sensitivity, and specificity of the RDC as a whole (Widmer, 1992).

Predisposing, Initiating, and Perpetuating Factors in TMD

Considering the multiple diagnoses that constitute TMD, it is not surprising that a variety of factors are important in the disorder. One useful way to conceptualize these factors is to group them into three main groups: (a) predisposing factors, (b) initiating factors, and (c) perpetuating factors (Fricton & Chung, 1988; McNeill et al., 1980). These are not etiological factors. The variables that we describe are neither necessary nor sufficient to produce TMD. However, both research and clinical experience suggest that these variables may be related to TMD, although their impact on TMD is imperfectly understood and their interrelationships are likely to be complicated.

Predisposing Factors

The predisposing factors consist of the pathophysiological, psychological, and structural conditions that appear to enhance the likelihood that a TMD will occur.

Pathophysiological conditions.   A variety of pathophysiological conditions can predispose an individual to TMD. Some of these can include degenerative and rheumatological changes; infectious processes; neurological conditions; hormonal, nutritional, and metabolic conditions; neoplasms; and vascular problems (Fricton & Chung, 1988). In general, most of the pathophysiological conditions that predispose an individual to develop TMD involve systemic conditions.

Psychological conditions.   Our discussion of the psychological factors that predispose an individual to develop TMD focuses primarily on a psychophysiological model of TMD (Laskin, 1969). We review studies that deal with affective and other dispositional features of TMD patients in the section on perpetuating factors.

According to the psychophysiological model of TMD, people react to stress with different bodily systems. Some react via the head and neck muscles, and some of these become TMD patients (Kapel, Glaros, & McGlynn, 1989; Laskin, 1969; Rugh & Solberg, 1976; Zarb & Carlsson, 1979).

A number of studies have found that TMD patients (typically those with myofascial pain) show facial muscle activity responses to experimental stressors (Flor, Birbaumer, Schulte, & Roos, 1991; Kapel et al., 1989; Mercuri, Olson, & Laskin, 1979; Moss & Adams, 1984;

Rao & Glaros, 1979). Several have also reported that the muscular responsiveness occurred in the absence of cardiac or electrodermal changes in the TMD patients. However, not all studies have reported such psychophysiological responsiveness to experimental stressors (e.g., Montgomery & Rugh, 1987).

There is some evidence that TMD patients may also be characterized by increased levels of facial muscle activity at baseline as compared with non-TMD controls (Kapel et al., 1989; Rao & Glaros, 1979). However, the difference between the groups is generally of small magnitude (Montgomery & Rugh, 1990) and may be related to differences in the definition of the TMD group (Montgomery & Rugh, 1987) or insufficiently long adaptation and baseline measurement periods (Flor et al., 1991).

A recent report by Flor, Schugens, and Birbaumer (1992) raises the possibility that TMD patients have deficits in muscle discrimination abilities. In this study, 20 TMD patients (including patients with disc displacements, arthralgia/arthritis/arthrosis, as well as myofascial pain) were compared with 20 chronic low-back-pain patients and 20 normal controls. Each subject maximally tensed (but not to the point of pain) the muscle of interest, and each was then asked to relax the muscle maximally. This procedure provided reference points for the experimental task of producing eight different levels of masseter muscle and erector spinae muscle activity between the maximal and minimal levels. The results suggest that patients were less accurate on measures of accuracy and sensitivity than the controls. Additional analyses suggest that fatigue and attention could not account for the results.

Although Flor et al. (1992) interpreted their results in terms of deficits in muscular discrimination, other studies do not necessarily support the hypothesis of deficits in muscular discrimination (cf. Nemcovzsky & Gross, 1991). For example, Helkimo, Carlsson, and Carmeli (1975) reported a study showing that TMD patients can produce muscle tension levels reliably in response to verbal instructions. In this study, subjects were instructed to bite down on a bite-force measuring device at each of five different force levels: *very weak, weak, ordinary, strong,* and *maximum.* Patients performed the task using the left and right molars separately as well as the incisors. Patients also performed the force task on the device using their fingers. Each patient was tested twice, with an average of 1 week between sessions.

The results showed that test–retest reliabilities ranged from a low of 0.68 to a high of 0.95 for the tooth sites and from 0.62 to 0.85 for the fingers. The tooth forces produced by patients tended to increase as patients completed treatment for their TMD.

It is possible that differential task difficulty accounts for these apparently conflicting results. The Flor et al. (1992) tasks required subjects to produce muscle tension levels to match an external stimulus (a computer-generated display). In contrast, the Helkimo et al. (1975) tasks gave subjects greater latitude to set levels of muscle tension activity. As shown in a study by Glaros and Hanson (1990), the type of task required by Flor et al. (1992) is more difficult to perform at baseline than the type of task required by Helkimo et al. (1975).

TMD patients may also be predisposed to experience pain. Hagberg (1991), for example, found that TMD patients reported more musculoskeletal complaints, as assessed by experimentally induced electrical stimulation, than control subjects. TMD patients did not differ from controls in measures of pain tolerance; however, patients who had pain in many areas of the body also had the lowest tolerance to the experimentally induced pain.

These findings raise the intriguing possibility that certain classes of individuals may be biologically or psychologically predisposed to develop TMD. Unfortunately, the studies are not consistent in their findings, but this may reflect differences in the samples studied and in the experimental tasks. Alternatively, these findings may result from an adaptation to the disorder.

If the hypothesis that TMD patients have deficits in discrimination is correct, then it may be more likely to occur in the samples characterized by muscle disorders and less likely to occur in the samples characterized by disc displacements or degenerative changes. Furthermore, it would be useful to know whether these deficits also extend to other motor or sensory systems or are limited to the voluntary musculature.

Structural conditions. A variety of structural variables can predispose an individual to TMD. For example, genetic and developmental problems, such as severe skeletal malformations and inter- and intra-arch discrepancies, may increase the likelihood that an individual will develop TMD. Similarly, trauma to the face, head, and upper body such as that seen in motor vehicle accidents, home- or work-related accidents, or abuse can predispose a person to TMD (Fricton & Chung, 1988).

Prior dental treatment can also predispose a person to TMD. Occlusal factors, including ill-fitting crowns and bridgework and "high" restorations (i.e., amalgams that rise well above the normal occlusal surface of the tooth), may increase the probability that TMD will occur (Fricton & Chung, 1988).

The dental literature contains a large number of reports and studies on the role that occlusion plays in TMD. For example, some investigators have suggested that a wide variety of occlusal problems, both major and minor, can contribute to TMD (e.g., Geering, 1974; Ingervall, Mohlin, & Thilander, 1980). However, deviations from ideal occlusion are statistically normal in both child and adult populations (Kirveskari, Alanen, & Jämsä, 1992; Ramfjord & Ash, 1983). For example, the Kirveskari et al. (1992) study reported that over 95% of 5- and 10-year-old children showed occlusal interferences.

A number of investigators have reviewed the scientific literature on the role that occlusion plays in TMD. As predisposing factors, there is little credible, scientific evidence to link any of the various occlusal abnormalities to TMD (e.g., Glaros, Brockman, & Ackerman, 1992). Similarly, there is little evidence linking the presence or absence of orthodontic treatment with TMD (Egermark-Eriksson, Carlsson, Magnusson, & Thilander, 1990; Sadowsky, Theisen, & Sakols, 1991). However, gross defects brought on by trauma or by dental iatrogenesis may play a role.

Initiating Factors

Initiating factors including trauma to and repeated adverse loading on the joint may lead to the onset of symptoms.

Trauma. As suggested earlier, the types of injuries that can initiate TMD involve traumas to the head, neck, and upper torso as well as injuries associated with dental or medical procedures. Impact injuries and flexion–extension injuries, produced by motor vehicle accidents, work- and home-related accidents, physical abuse, and the like, can be the immediate precipitants of TMD (Burgess, 1991).

Dental and medical procedures can also precipitate TMD. Examples include prolonged mouth opening, which occurs with particular dental procedures, and general anesthesia intubation. Prolonged or excessive mouth opening may lead to muscle spasm or to discal problems.

Adverse loading.   Sustained or repetitive adverse loading can also initiate TMD. Adverse loading can occur via parafunctional habits and parafunctional behaviors. The parafunctional habits include chronic chewing of gum or pieces of ice. Biting on fingernails, cheeks, lips, and pencils also place adverse loads on the TMJ.

Parafunctional behaviors, on the other hand, typically involve clenching and grinding and appear to be strongly related to TMD (Sherman, 1985). Although both clenching and grinding are frequently subsumed under the rubric *bruxism*, the behaviors are quite different (cf. Glaros & Melamed, 1992). Clenching involves arrythmic, high-amplitude electromyographic (EMG) activity, typically of short duration; whereas grinding involves high-amplitude, brief, rhythmic EMG bursts that can vary in total duration (Ware & Rugh, 1988; Wruble, Lumley & McGlynn, 1989).

In the neurologically intact individual, grinding most commonly occurs at night, whereas clenching can occur both at night and during the day (FitzGerald, Jankovic, & Percy, 1990; Glaros & Rao, 1977). Both self-report data and sleep studies suggest that individuals can engage in both clenching and grinding behaviors, although the ratio between the behaviors appears to differ among individuals (Glaros, 1981; Wruble, 1988). Furthermore, at least some parafunctional tooth contact appears to be normal during sleep (Powell & Zander, 1965).

Some data suggest that clenching may be more responsive to stress than grinding (Olkinuora, 1972a, 1972b, 1972c). Unfortunately, most of the studies that examined the relationship between stress and these parafunctional behaviors did not distinguish between clenching and grinding, and this may account for the variability in the findings. Some studies showed a relationship between parafunctional behaviors and stress (e.g., Hicks, Conti, & Bragg, 1990) in a clear temporal fashion (Rugh & Robbins, 1982). The results of other studies suggest that the anticipation of stress may better predict parafunctional behaviors (e.g., Hopper, Gevirtz, Nigl, & Taddey, 1992).

Of course, parafunctional behaviors need not occur only in response to stress. TMD patients often report that they engage in clenching while reading, watching television, preparing meals, driving automobiles, and so forth. These reports suggest that clenching and other parafunctional behaviors are strongly learned behaviors.

Surprisingly, a considerable proportion of TMD patients do not appear to be aware of clenching or grinding on initial examination.

Our program, for example, routinely asks patients about clenching and grinding. About half of those who have some physical evidence of these behaviors (e.g., scalloping in the tongue; Sapiro, 1992) deny that they clench at their initial evaluation. Interestingly, the majority of these patients express surprise at the extent of their clenching at follow-up visits. This lack of awareness appears to be consistent with the discrimination deficits described earlier.

Perpetuating Factors

Perpetuating factors help sustain the disorder and also complicate its management. Many of the predisposing and initiating factors can also become perpetuating factors after the onset of the disorder. The perpetuating factors include behavioral, emotional, cognitive, and social elements.

Behavioral factors. We have already discussed the role that clenching, grinding, and other parafunctions can play in initiating TMD. As unlearned responses to the experience of pain, these behaviors can also perpetuate the disorder.

Prior research has suggested that chronic pain patients engage in bracing, guarding, and rigidity (Keefe & Williams, 1992) and that such behaviors can themselves ultimately result in pain. Similar processes may also exist for TMD patients. That is, they may react to the experience of pain by "bracing" (i.e., clenching) the muscles of mastication. Such behaviors create muscle and joint strain and subsequent pain.

The role that work-related behaviors and ergonomic variables play in maintaining TMD should be considered. Individuals who "hunch up" a shoulder to hold a telephone receiver to an ear can experience increased pain both because of pressure against the TMJ and increased muscle tension, primarily in the neck and shoulder. Similarly, ergonomic factors at work, especially related to computers, can maintain TMD. Poor positioning of a keyboard vertically (i.e., on the relatively high surface of a desk, rather than the lower surface of a typing table) and poor placement of the monitor (e.g., placement of the monitor to the side, requiring the operator to keep the head turned, placement of the monitor too high or low for visual comfort, or glare on the monitor from overhead lights) can increase or maintain pain in TMD patients.

Emotional factors. The emotional factors important in chronic pain patients are also important in TMD patients. Not only can these factors result from pain, they can also make the problem more difficult to tolerate and more difficult to manage.

The most important of the emotional factors is depression (Gamsa & Vikis-Freibergs, 1991; Magni, Caldieron, Rigatti-Luchini, & Merskey, 1990). A variety of studies have shown that TMD patients have significantly greater levels of depression than normal controls. The measures of depression have included the Beck Depression Inventory (BDI) (Wright, Deary, & Geissler, 1991), the Minnesota Multiphasic Personality Inventory (MMPI) (McCreary, Clark, Merril, Flack, & Oakley, 1991), and items derived from the Cornell Medical Index (Beaton, Egan, Nakagawa-Kogan, & Morrison, 1991). Although their levels of depression are significantly elevated compared with those of normal controls, most TMD patients do not show clinically significant depression. Wright et al. (1991), for example, reported that only 13.5% of TMD patients had clinically elevated depression scores on the BDI, whereas Kinney et al. (1992) reported that only 30% of TMD patients showed evidence of major depression on the SCID.

Comparisons between TMD patients and other chronic pain patients suggest that the two groups do not differ significantly on a variety of psychological measures, including depression, anxiety, somatization, hostility, or psychoticism (McKinney, Lundeen, Turner, & Levitt, 1990). However, TMD patients report lower levels of pain and dysfunction than other chronic pain patients (Keefe & Dolan, 1986; McKinney et al., 1990).

Comparisons among the subgroups of TMD patients show variability in pain and distress (Eversole, Stone, Matheson, & Kaplan, 1985). McCreary et al. (1991), for example, split TMD patients into three groups: (a) patients with primary myalgia, (b) patients with primary TMJ pain, and (c) patients with mixed myalgia and TMJ pain. As measured by a visual analogue scale of pain, the McGill Pain Questionnaire, the BDI, the State–Trait Anxiety Inventory, and the MMPI, patients with primary myalgia obtained the highest scores on the pain and distress measures. Following the primary myalgia group were, in order, the mixed myalgia–TMJ pain group and the TMJ pain group.

Anxiety may also play a role in TMD. There is some evidence that TMD patients show higher levels of anxiety than non-TMD individuals (McCreary et al., 1991; Southwell, Deary, & Geissler, 1990). However, the studies do not agree on whether state or trait anxiety is most characteristic of TMD patients.

Cognitive and social factors. The cognitive factors consist of thoughts or attitudes that, when negative or counterproductive, can make resolution of the problem more difficult. Perhaps the most important of these are unrealistic expectations of complete and immediate pain relief.

To manage their pain successfully, many TMD patients have to alter a well-ingrained set of behaviors involving eating and the mouth. For example, TMD patients may have to forego the pleasures associated with favorite, albeit hard and chewy, foods. Behaviors that are taken for granted by non-TMD individuals, such as the ability to laugh and sing or to kiss a loved one, may be associated with pain in the TMD patient. Understandably, TMD patients may not be willing to give up or reduce these behaviors. Instead, they may expect that practitioners will immediately, permanently, and completely take away the pain problem so that they can comfortably return to pleasurable behaviors. Because ethical practitioners cannot promise such an outcome, TMD patients may express dissatisfaction with their care.

Conflicting opinions, diagnoses, and recommendations can compound these unrealistic expectations. It is not unusual for TMD patients to consult otolaryngologists (for complaints involving the ears or sinus headaches) or neurologists (for headaches) before seeing a dentist. Unfortunately, research has shown that general dentists hold a broad range of opinions regarding diagnoses and appropriate treatments for individuals reporting facial pain (Glass et al., 1992; LeResche, Truelove, Dworkin, Whitney, & Harrison, 1991; Truelove, LeResche, Dworkin, & Whitney, 1991). In the presence of multiple attempts at diagnoses, multiple diagnoses (with the attendant possibilities of failed treatment), and conflicting treatment recommendations, it is not surprising that TMD patients have reported anger and frustration with their care. Furthermore, TMD patients may also experience a lack of motivation or reduced cooperation with treatment recommendations.

Unlike many low back pain patients, TMD patients typically do not receive compensation for their disorder. Accordingly, there is little monetary incentive to exaggerate or unnecessarily prolong complaints of pain. However, the role that other secondary gain issues, including concern from others and relief from responsibility, play in TMD is not well understood.

However, TMD patients often report greater irritability with loved ones and co-workers because of pain (Fricton & Chung, 1988). Thus, TMD can have social consequences in the family and workplace. Similarly, TMD patients may be less willing to engage in normal activities of daily living, particularly social and recreational ones, as a result of their pain.

Summary

The factors that predispose to, initiate, or perpetuate TMD are highly complex. Not surprisingly, a variety of medical conditions and traumas may be involved. Of equal interest, however, are findings suggesting that TMD patients may be predisposed to react to environmental stresses with increased activity in the facial musculature, that TMD patients have poor discriminative awareness of or control over muscles, and that the affective and dispositional correlates of TMD are similar to those of other chronic pain patients. Because TMD patients report lower levels of pain and disability than many other types of chronic pain patients, TMD can serve as a model for understanding the behavioral and psychological effects of chronic pain (cf. Kinney et al., 1992), independent of the complications of litigation, workers' compensation systems, and the like.

Comprehensive Assessment of TMD

An appropriate evaluation of a potential TMD patient relies on a thorough history, comprehensive physical examination, and thorough behavioral and psychological assessment. Without an adequate assessment, individuals may receive unnecessary or incorrect treatment that is based on cursory information.

The recommended minimum screening questions and examination procedures for TMD are presented in Tables 3 and 4 (American Academy of Orofacial Pain [AAOP], 1993). Although these may be sufficient for screening, they cannot substitute for a comprehensive evaluation of the TMD patient. According to the suggestions provided by the AAOP (1993), both the number of positive responses and the

Table 3

Recommended Screening Questions for Temporomandibular Disorders

1. Do you have difficulty or pain, or both, when opening your mouth, as for instance when yawning?
2. Does your jaw get "stuck," "locked," or "go out"?
3. Do you have difficulty or pain, or both, when chewing, talking, or using your jaws?
4. Are you aware of noises in the jaw joint?
5. Do your jaws regularly feel stiff, tight, or tired?
6. Do you have pain in or around the ears, temples, or cheeks?
7. Do you have frequent headaches and/or neckaches?
8. Have you had a recent injury to your head, neck, or jaw?
9. Have you been aware of any recent changes in your bite?
10. Have you previously been treated for jaw joint problems?

Note. From *Temporomandibular Disorders: Guidelines for Classification, Assessment, and Management* (p. 62) by the American Academy of Orofacial Pain, 1993, Chicago: Quintessence. Copyright 1993 by Quintessence. Adapted by permission.

apparent seriousness of the problem must be considered in the decision to refer a patient for a complete comprehensive history and examination. Thus, a positive response to a single question or a positive examination finding may be sufficient to warrant a comprehensive examination if the patient is highly concerned or if the problem is clinically significant. Currently, there are no recommendations for the psychological screening of potential TMD patients.

History

A comprehensive history of a facial pain patient provides a significant amount of information and is necessary for appropriate diagnosis. A good history of a TMD patient often contains the elements noted in Table 5.

Physical Examination

The physical examination of the TMD patient often begins with an inspection of the head, neck, dentition, and oral soft tissues to rule

Table 4

*Recommended Screening Examination Procedures
for Temporomandibular Disorders*

---

1. Measure range of motion of the mandible on opening and right and left laterotrusion.
2. Palpate for preauricular or intrameatal TMJ tenderness.
3. Auscultate and/or palpate for TMJ sounds.
4. Palpate for tenderness in the masseter and temporalis muscles.
5. Note excessive occlusal wear or tooth mobility, buccal mucosal ridging, or lateral tongue scalloping.
6. Inspect symmetry and alignment of the face, jaws, and dental arches.

Note. TMJ = temporomandibular joint. From *Temporomandibular Disorders: Guidelines for Classification, Assessment, and Management* (p. 63) by the American Academy of Orofacial Pain, 1993, Chicago: Quintessence. Copyright 1993 by Quintessence. Adapted by permission.

---

out tumors, infections, and other pathology that might account for the complaints in the patient's history. The function of the sensory and motor branches of the cranial nerves should be evaluated. Compression testing of temporal and carotid arteries for pain can provide clues to possible arteritis, carotodynia, or other vascular problems. Because many of the pains associated with TMD problems are felt in the ear, an otoscopic exam should also be included to rule out possible otic problems.

A variety of techniques are used to evaluate the TMJ and its function. Measurement of mandibular opening and of lateral and protrusive movements is easily accomplished with a small ruler. The opening, lateral, and protrusive movements are measured in millimeters. Minimal normal opening ranges between 35 and 40 mm (LeResche, 1992). The opening and closing patterns of the mandible are observed as the patient opens and closes. These movements are normally smooth and symmetrical, and movements that deviate to one side or have a serpentine pattern may indicate a soft or hard tissue problem within the TMJ (Fricton, Bromaghim, & Kroening, 1988). Range-of-motion measurements and observation of opening and closing patterns can be performed with and without assistance. Differences in

Table 5

Comprehensive History of the Patient With Temporomandibular Disorders

Chief complaint	Symptom most bothersome and the one most desired to be changed
History of present illness	Date of onset; onset event; character, intensity, duration, frequency, and location of the problem; remissions; change over time; modifying factors; previous treatment results
Medical history	Current or pre-existing diseases or disorders; prior surgeries and hospitalizations; trauma; use of prescribed and nonprescribed medications or substance abuse; allergies
Dental history	Current or pre-existing diseases or disorders; previous treatment and attitude toward treatment; trauma to jaw, teeth, or supporting tissues; parafunctional habits and behaviors
Personal history	Social, behavioral, and psychological; occupational, recreational, and family; litigation, disability, or other secondary gain issues

Note. From *Temporomandibular Disorders: Guidelines for Classification, Assessment, and Management* (p. 64) by the American Academy of Orofacial Pain, 1993, Chicago: Quintessence. Copyright 1993 by Quintessence. Adapted by permission.

range-of-motion measures may allow the health care provider to differentiate between a muscle or joint disorder. Similarly, certain manipulated or altered jaw positions that eliminate, alleviate, or aggravate joint pain, sounds, or incoordination can provide additional information about the hard and soft tissues of the TMJ (AAOP, 1993).

The TMJs are also palpated for tenderness and swelling. This is done by palpating the lateral poles of the condyles and also by having the examiner place his or her little fingers in the external auditory meatus while the patient closes his or her jaw from a maximally opened position (Laskin & Sarnat, 1992). This helps evaluate inflammation in the joints.

A comprehensive evaluation should also include palpation of the following muscles: frontalis, masseter, temporalis, sternocleidomastoid, trapezius, splenius group, anterior and posterior digastrics, temporalis tendon, and lateral and medial pterygoids. The recommended palpation pressure is 2 lb for extraoral muscles and 1 lb for the TMJ and intra-oral muscles. The pressure is applied with one or two fingertips, and the patient's response is scored as *none, mild, moderate,* or *severe* (LeResche, 1992).

An alternative to the use of finger palpation is the use of a pressure algometer. The algometer is applied at a steadily increasing pressure to the site until the patient reports pain or until a pressure threshold is reached. Preliminary research shows that the devices can be used with good reliability (Chung, Um, & Kim, 1992; List, Helkimo, & Falk, 1989; Ohrbach & Gale, 1989b). In addition, TMD patients tend to show lower thresholds for painful muscles than for nonpain sites (Ohrbach & Gale, 1989a).

Imaging of the TMJ

It may be necessary to image the TMJ and associated structures to rule out pathology. Imaging of the TMJ should be performed only when findings from a clinical examination will be significantly enhanced by the imaging process. Both hard and soft tissues can be imaged using the appropriate techniques (Dixon, 1991).

Hard tissue imaging

Panoramic and transcranial. Panoramic and transcranial views of the TMJ provide screening information but have limited value in definitive diagnosis. They can show only gross degenerative or traumatic changes (e.g., fractures and arthritis), and only in the lateral aspect of the joint. In addition, they can indicate the approximate degree to which the condyle translates to the articular eminence when the mouth is fully opened.

Conventional and computed tomography. Tomography of the TMJ involves imaging a single section through the condyle. The image produced by tomography is obtained when the X-ray beam and film (or detector) move in opposite directions from each other.

Conventional tomography can be used to image one or more sections through the condyle on radiographic film. Computed tomography, on the other hand, offers the added advantage of computer reconstruction of the image. With computed tomography, an operator can view multiple sections through the condyle, obtain three-dimensional views of the condyle, and view the image as it rotates on a computer screen.

Tomography is more accurate than panoramic or transcranial films for evaluating patients who are suspected to have degenerative changes in their TMJ (Kaplan & Helms, 1989). In addition, patients are generally exposed to greater levels of ionizing radiation with computed tomography than with conventional tomography. Computed tomography has been used to diagnose soft tissue abnormalities, but its utility as compared with other techniques is in dispute (Dixon, 1991; Westesson, Katzberg, Tallents, Sanchez-Woodworth, & Svensson, 1987).

Soft tissue imaging

Arthrography. In this technique, a radiopaque contrast medium is injected into the inferior joint space, the superior joint space, or both (Westesson & Bronstein, 1985). Tomography is then used to determine the position of the disc relative to the condyle. The functional dynamics of the disc and condyle can also be visualized using arthrography, fluoroscopy, and videotaping procedures. However, arthrography can also suggest soft tissue changes in otherwise asymptomatic joints (Kozeniauskas & Ralph, 1988). Arthrography is an invasive procedure, and it is potentially painful.

Magnetic resonance imaging (MRI). MRI can image malpositioned discs in the TMJ as well as soft tissues outside the capsule of the TMJ. MRI does not involve exposure to ionizing radiation, and the process per se is painless. However, the patient must hold still for about 15 min while one site is imaged, and holding open the mouth that long can cause pain (Kaplan & Helms, 1989). In addition, the scanner in which the patient must lie is small enough to cause some patients to experience claustrophobia (Westesson, 1992).

Behavioral and Psychological Evaluation

In this section, we will cover the four principal approaches to the behavioral and psychological evaluation of the TMD patient. These are (a) self-report and self-monitoring of pain, (b) behavioral indices of pain, (c) psychological instruments, and (d) psychophysiological monitoring. All of these supplement the information provided by a comprehensive clinical interview.

Self-report and self-monitoring of pain. A variety of self-report instruments have been used with TMD patients. These include visual analogue scales, numeric rating scales, the McGill Pain Questionnaire, verbal rating scales, and pain drawings (cf. Karoly & Jensen, 1987). All provide information about the TMD patient's perception of the intensity and quality of pain. Numerical rating scales can also be used to assess the pain-related disability associated with TMD (Von Korff, 1992).

Self-monitoring diaries are commonly used with TMD patients. As with other pain patients, the diaries provide information about the contexts in which pain occurs (or increases or decreases), the variability of pain, and the patient's and environment's response to the pain.

Behavioral indices of pain.   Two different kinds of pain are commonly reported by TMD patients. One type is characterized by chronic low-level aching, often in the muscles of mastication. The second is characterized by brief, intense, sharp or stabbing sensations of pain, often in the area of the TMJ. The former is generally not so severe that commonly used behavioral measures of pain, such as the UAB Pain Behavior Scale (Richards, Nepomuceno, Riles, & Suer, 1982), would reliably detect it. The second is so highly related to jaw function that behavioral measures may not add important diagnostic information.

However, a more subtle approach using facial expressions appears to hold promise. Research has shown cross-cultural similarities in facial expressions of such emotions as contempt (Ekman & Friesen, 1986), and facial expressions of pain should be equally similar across cultures (Craig, Prkachin, & Grunau, 1992). Use of the Facial Action Coding System (Ekman & Friesen, 1978) with TMD patients showed that the most frequently occurring pattern of facial expressions during painful palpation involved tightening of the skin around the eye, lowering the brow, and eye closing (LeResche & Dworkin, 1988). Furthermore, the correlations between such facial expression measures and pain report measures (such as the McGill Pain Questionnaire) are generally positive but only moderate in magnitude (usually 0.40–0.60) (McGlynn et al., 1990).

Psychological tests.   The tests typically used for assessing depression, anxiety, and psychopathology in chronic pain patients are also used for TMD patients. Commonly used tests of depression include the BDI (Beck, Rush, Shaw, & Emery, 1979) and the Zung Self-Rating Depression Scale (Zung, 1965). For anxiety, the State–Trait Anxiety Inventory (Spielberger, 1983) is frequently used. For general psychopathology, the revised MMPI for adults—the MMPI-2—may be used.

As noted earlier, the responses provided by TMD patients on these instruments are often significantly higher than the responses provided by nonpain individuals. Wright et al. (1991), for example, reported that a sample of 37 TMD patients obtained a mean BDI score of 5.5, as compared with a score of 3.6 obtained by 30 nonpain individuals. McCreary et al. (1991) reported that a sample of 27 myalgia patients, 42 TMJ pain patients, and 37 combined myalgia and TMJ pain patients obtained mean BDI scores of 11.6, 6.0, and 10.8, respectively. (The respective MMPI Scale 2 [Depression] scores were 66.5, 56.5, and 61.9.) As these values suggest, the responses provided by TMD patients are not necessarily clinically elevated.

Two instruments have been developed specifically for use with TMD patients: (a) the TMJ Scale, and (b) IMPATH:TMJ.

TMJ Scale. The TMJ Scale (Levitt, Lundeen, & McKinney, 1987) is a 97-item paper-and-pencil questionnaire developed to assess self-reported symptoms of TMD. It is designed primarily for use by dentists in general or specialty practices. Approximately 15 min is required to complete the test. The responses of the patient are computer scored, and the program generates scores for the Physical Domain scales, the Psychosocial Domain scales and the Global Scale of the test. An individual's responses on the scales are compared to scores and cut-off points derived from 1,215 dental patients, of which 742 were TMD patients.

The five Physical Domain scales are Pain Report, Palpation Pain, Perceived Malocclusion, Joint Dysfunction, and Range of Motion Limitation. A sixth scale, Non-TM Disorders, assesses the presence of painful conditions not involving the TMJ. The three Psychosocial Domain scales are Psychological Factors, Stress, and Chronicity. The Global Scale provides an overall assessment of the probability that the individual has a TMD. The issues assessed by these scales are noted in Table 6.

In the Physical Domain, clinician ratings were used as the external criteria. For example, clinician ratings of the presence of joint dysfunction were used to validate the items constituting the Joint Dysfunction Scale. A similar procedure was used for the Chronicity Scale in the Psychosocial Domain and for the Global Scale. For the two remaining scales in the Psychosocial Domain, a somewhat different technique was used. The Severity Index of the SCL-90-R Scale and the Total Stress score on the Derogatis Stress Profile were used to validate the items used in the Psychological Factors and Stress scales.

The scale scores appear to have good psychometric properties. The test–retest correlations for the individual scales ranged from 0.76 to

Table 6

Brief Description of the Scales Constituting the TMJ Scale

Scale	Description
Physical Domain	
Pain Report	Patient's perception of pain in the temporo-mandibular joints, muscles of mastication, and some of the neck muscles
Palpation Pain	Pain reported when patient presses on large facial muscles, as instructed by the test
Perceived Malocclusion	Patient reports that his or her bite feels "off," uncomfortable, or changing
Joint Dysfunction	Reports of TMJ locking in the open or closed positions and noises such as grating, grinding, or popping
Range of Motion Limitation	Limitations and difficulties in opening or moving the mandible
Non-TM Disorder	Reports of other painful conditions, including headache, neck pain, and general joint and muscle symptoms
Psychosocial Domain	
Psychological Factors	Reports of emotional distress, including anxiety, depression, and anger
Stress	Reports of perceived stress, stress-related symptoms, and stress-related behaviors, including clenching and grinding
Chronicity	Tendencies toward or the presence of a chronic disorder
Global Scale	Single predictor of the presence of a temporo-mandibular disorder

Note. TMJ = temporomandibular joint.

0.91. Correlations between scale scores and external criteria for a mixed group of TMD patients and non-TMD dental patients ranged from 0.20 to 0.72, with most of the correlations falling in the 0.33–0.56 range. The scales also appear to have appropriately high sensitivity and specificity (Levitt, 1990a, 1990b).

Cross-validation studies have reported coefficient alphas ranging from 0.81 to 0.95 in the test construction sample and from 0.81 to 0.94

in the cross-validation sample (Levitt, McKinney, & Lundeen, 1988). In both the test construction and cross-validation samples, the measures of internal consistency were greatest for the Global Scale.

Unfortunately, the scoring of the TMJ Scale is proprietary, and computer generation of a report involves a fee ranging from about $14–$18, not including the cost of the computer, printer, modem, or scanner. The TMJ Scale may also be scored and a report generated by mail, at a cost of $18–24 per scoring. However, this imposes a delay in the patient's evaluation.

IMPATH:TMJ. The IMPATH:TMJ uses a different approach than the TMJ Scale. The term *IMPATH* stands for Interactive Microcomputer Patient Assessment Tool for Health. A patient assessed by IMPATH:TMJ either sits in front of a computer screen while questions are presented on the monitor or fills out a computer-scanned pencil-and-paper instrument.

The IMPATH:TMJ functions as a screening instrument and can supplement a personal history. Used in this fashion, the IMPATH:TMJ is similar to the patient history questionnaires that are completed before comprehensive evaluations (cf. Von Korff, 1992). At the completion of the "interaction," the computer generates a report containing information on medical and illness history, a list of contributing factors, and indices to assess the severity of the illness and its impact on the patient's life (Fricton & Chung, 1988). The pretreatment data provided by the patient on the indices can be compared with values obtained at posttreatment intervals, data from other patients at the clinic site, or data from all patients using IMPATH:TMJ. Unfortunately, the psychometric characteristics of IMPATH:TMJ are not as well understood as those of the TMJ Scale.

Psychophysiological monitoring. Psychophysiological measures may be important in assessing TMD. For example, clenching and grinding place adverse stress on the TMJ and its musculature, and these behaviors may lead to pain. Because such parafunctional activities can occur without significant awareness on the patient's part, psychophysiological monitoring can serve a dual role of both assessing the prevalence of such activities and increasing patient awareness of their occurrence.

The commercially available devices for conducting ambulatory monitoring of TMD-relevant EMG activity do not yet have the desired sensitivity and specificity for discriminating parafunctional behaviors from functional behaviors. At their best, ambulatory devices can detect nocturnal EMG events associated with clenching and grinding (Cassisi, McGlynn, & Belles, 1987). Small, portable EMG monitoring devices can also provide additional information about EMG activities occurring during the day.

Current limitations on battery life make full-time, on-line monitoring difficult. Clinicians and researchers can select from among devices that sample EMG activity at fixed intervals, that "wake up" when EMG activity exceeds a given threshold, or that record continuously for limited periods of time (generally no more than a few hours). Typically, only one EMG site can be monitored by a single device, and the meaningfulness of the data obtained by such devices is difficult to assess. Nonetheless, the progress in miniaturization is impressive, and the capabilities of the devices have increased enormously in recent years. If the pace of improvement in these devices continues at its present rate, then researchers and clinicians should have useful devices for ambulatory monitoring within the next few years.

For those unwilling to wait, standard laboratory techniques for psychophysiological monitoring may provide some additional information. As noted earlier, certain types of TMD patients, particularly those with myofascial pain, may show increased levels of resting facial EMG activity, and differentially greater response to stress in those muscles, as compared with non-TMD individuals.

However, efforts to use these results for assessment purposes have had mixed results. Although some studies have shown modest utility for such approaches (e.g., Glaros, McGlynn, & Kapel, 1989), the relative unreliability of facial muscle EMG data (Biedermann, 1984; Burdette & Gale, 1990), even within a single session (cf. Hatch, Prihoda, & Moore, 1992), suggests that researchers and clinicians should be cautious in applying data obtained from psychophysiological approaches to diagnosis.

Summary

The behavioral and psychological techniques used to evaluate pain in TMD patients are essentially similar to those used for other chronic pain patients. Probably the most important and useful assessment technique is a comprehensive clinical interview. Self-report and self-monitoring measures such as visual analogue scales, numerical rating scales, and diaries also provide useful information at low cost. Psychological testing instruments such as the MMPI-2 may be useful for those patients in whom psychiatric disorders are suspected. However, practitioners should weigh the cost and time needed to administer these devices against the utility of the information received. As an alternative, practitioners may find that the use of specific tests for specific disorders is more cost-efficient.

Specialized instruments for evaluating TMD patients may be useful for screening purposes. However, evidence of psychologically significant findings detected by these tests must be followed up by careful interviewing or other psychological measures as needed.

Assessment of psychophysiological activity holds significant promise for understanding how environmental events, psychological stress, and psychophysiological activity interact in TMD patients. Although the technology for conducting such assessments is still in its infancy, the miniaturization of equipment and functional improvement of the circuits within the devices continue at a rapid pace. Perhaps in the not-too-distant future, clinicians will be able to perform sophisticated *in vivo* assessments of psychophysiological response in TMD patients.

Management of TMD

The management of TMD patients involves three goals: (a) decrease pain, (b) decrease adverse loading, and (c) improve function. To accomplish these goals, practitioners rely on patient education and palliative home care, interocclusal appliances, behavioral techniques, medications, and other management strategies.

Not all individuals who receive a diagnosis of TMD need active treatment. For example, individuals who experience disc displacement may not experience pain or suffer from functional limitations in the joint. For these individuals, patient education, home remedies, and instructions to limit parafunctional activities and exposure to stress may be sufficient.

On the other hand, if the problem progresses, if pain becomes bothersome, or if functional limitations occur, then a more active approach, including splints, behavioral techniques, and medications, can appropriately be used. For most TMD cases, conservative, reversible approaches should be attempted before irreversible techniques such as occlusal equilibration and surgery are used.

At all times, practitioners should keep in mind that patients are being treated, not diseases (AAOP, 1993). Although a biopsychosocial approach may be consistent with the training and experience of a health psychologist, individuals trained in a biomedical model may have more difficulty integrating psychosocial and behavioral knowledge and techniques into their management of a TMD patient (Glass et al., 1992; LeResche, Truelove, & Dworkin, 1993). Perhaps the optimal approach to the management of a TMD patient involves a conjoint, multidisciplinary model in which biomedical and psychological specialists integrate the assessment information and recommendations for management provided by each practitioner.

Patient Education and Palliative Home Care

Patient education and palliative home care involves instructing patients on the biomechanics of the TMJ and avoiding behaviors that can exacerbate the problem. Accordingly, patients are instructed not to chew gum, bite fingernails, or chew ice. They are asked to become aware of and minimize their clenching. They are asked to avoid problem foods, especially hard and chewy foods, known to increase their pain. They are instructed not to deliberately crack or pop their jaws.

A variety of home remedies can also benefit these patients. Applications of heat or cold packs can provide temporary reduction of pain. Over-the-counter analgesics can, when used appropriately, reduce pain to manageable levels. Stretching exercises can help increase range of motion and decrease pain levels (Clark & Merrill, 1992).

Although these techniques appear to have value, the degree to which they actively contribute to a reduction in pain, as compared with appropriate placebo treatments, is not well known. Similarly, the degree to which TMD patients are compliant with these instructions is not well understood.

Interocclusal Appliances (Splints)

The most common treatment for TMD involves interocclusal appliances (splints) (Glass, Glaros, & McGlynn, 1993). These devices, generally fabricated from a hard plastic or acrylic material, cover the occlusal and incisal surfaces of either the mandibular or maxillary teeth. Splints fabricated from soft materials tend to increase parafunctional behaviors (Okeson, 1987).

There is considerable variation in the type of splint used to treat TMD. The most commonly used splint (Glass, Glaros, & McGlynn, 1993) is termed a *flat plane* splint (also known as a muscle relaxation or stabilization splint), named for the generally flat surface presenting to the opposing teeth and its apparent effectiveness in reducing abnormal muscle tension (Figure 7) (Okeson, 1989). Other types of splints include a posterior or group function splint, an anterior repositioning splint, a pivot splint, a "neuromuscular" splint, and a soft splint. Except for the soft splint, the splints vary in the degree to which the mandible is forced into a particular position or to which the mandible is allowed to move freely in one or more of the three planes of motion.

Initially, TMD patients are instructed to wear the splint at night and at other times when they are clenching or in stressful situations. The splint is not worn when eating or drinking. As patients begin to

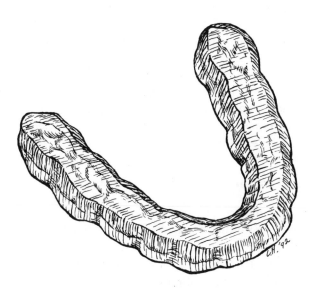

Figure 7.   Example of flat plane splint used to treat patients with temporomandibular disorders.

experience relief of their symptoms, the number of hours they wear the splint is gradually reduced. Many patients find that they cannot articulate clearly when the splint is first inserted, and the quality of their speech is thereby diminished. This tends to diminish as patients adapt to the splint.

Research suggests that splints are effective in reducing myofascial pain and some symptoms of internal derangement associated with TMD (Clark, 1984). Most TMD patients experience the benefits of splints within 1–4 weeks of their insertion.

The mechanism by which splints produce beneficial results is highly controversial. Some proposed mechanisms have included increased stability for the TMJ, improved functional position for the TMJ, improved occlusal conditions that reorganize neuromuscular activity and reduce abnormal muscle activity, and protection of the teeth and supportive structures from abnormal forces that promote breakdown or tooth wear (Okeson, 1989).

The reported effectiveness of splints may also be partially related to placebo factors and patient expectation for improvement. Greene and Laskin (1972), for example, examined the effectiveness of splints using a placebo-controlled design. In that study, a placebo splint covered the palate but did not cover the occlusal surfaces of the teeth. Results showed that 40% of patients that received the placebo splint improved, whereas 80% of patients that received a full coverage splint improved.

The treatment gains provided by splints are reversible if the problem is treated from only a physical standpoint. Under these circumstances, symptoms may reappear when patients stop using the splint, unless the patients are made aware of their parafunctional activities or self-induced muscle tension.

Behavioral Techniques

A considerable number of studies (many are summarized in Mealiea & McGlynn, 1987) indicate that EMG biofeedback training is an effective treatment modality for TMD. The most common sites for biofeedback training involve the masseter, temporalis, or frontalis areas of the face, and training is often accompanied by relaxation training or stress management training (cf. Glass, Glaros, & McGlynn, 1993). The typical length of treatment ranges from 6 to 12 sessions.

The early studies on biofeedback with TMD examined whether EMG biofeedback could prove useful in treament. In one study (Gessell, 1975), 23 patients with myofascial pain were given 3–14 sessions of biofeedback training for the masseter and temporalis areas. Fifteen of the 23 subjects showed a clinically positive response to this treatment. A number of studies that used group treatment designs followed (e.g., Carlsson & Gale, 1977), each generally reporting treatment success. Unfortunately, the follow-ups to these studies tended to be short or nonexistent. Furthermore, they relied mostly on patient self-report as the principal outcome variable.

Later studies used more sophisticated, control group designs. The dependent measures used were broadened to include dental examinations and reports of EMG activity, and the follow-ups were more likely to be reported. For example, Dalen, Ellertsen, Espelid, and Gronningsaeter (1986) compared EMG biofeedback to a waiting-list control. This study showed treatment success, which was somewhat maintained at 6-month follow-up.

Do biofeedback-based treatments for TMD offer a competitive alternative to regular dental or pharmacological approaches? Only a few studies have examined this possibility. In one early study, Dahlström, Carlsson, and Carlsson (1982) compared a group treated with EMG biofeedback with one treated with splints. Both groups appeared to improve with treatment, with maximal mouth opening improving only in the biofeedback group. Furthermore, a 1-year follow-up (Dahlström & Carlsson, 1984) showed that both groups maintained their gains.

A study by Crockett, Foreman, Alden, and Blasberg (1986) compared three treatments: bite splint and physiotherapy, EMG feedback and relaxation training, and transcutaneous nerve stimulation. The treatments all showed some success, but no one treatment was consistently superior to the others. Unfortunately, there was no follow-up to this study, and the sample sizes were small ($n = 7$ per group).

Hijzen, Slangen, and VanHouweligen (1986) also compared EMG feedback to splints. In addition, they used a no-treatment control group. Their EMG biofeedback treatment was, however, unusual. In most biofeedback studies, patients are asked to reduce masseter or temporalis activity during training. In the Hijzen et al. study, biofeedback training consisted of instructing patients to produce various levels of EMG activity in response to instructions. For example, subjects were asked to produce a particular voltage level and to hold that level for a brief time. Both treatments resulted in improvement, with the biofeedback showing superior results on joint dysfunction indices, pain, and mouth opening. In contrast, the splint group showed superior results in reducing joint sounds such as clicking and popping. Unfortunately, no follow-up was reported.

These comparative studies show that biofeedback training appears to provide levels of relief equivalent to that provided by bite splints. Initial evidence suggests that the gains produced by biofeedback are maintained over time.

The mechanism by which biofeedback training works is not clearly understood. Studies show that TMD patients who receive biofeedback typically show decreases in facial muscle activity and decreases in self-reported pain (e.g., Burdette & Gale, 1988). One hypothesis suggests that biofeedback works by promoting decreased EMG activity, which, in turn, is responsible for the reduction in self-reported pain. However, this hypothesis is challenged, albeit indirectly, by experimental studies showing that jaw pain subsides or is greatly reduced seconds after subjects cease sustained maximum clenching (Christensen, 1979).

In none of the studies reported to date were TMD patients specifically selected for high baseline levels of EMG activity, nor were any trained to attain a "normal" level of EMG activity (cf. Shellenberger & Green, 1986, 1987). If biofeedback works because it reduces EMG activity, then patients with elevated baseline levels of EMG activity would be most likely to benefit from biofeedback training, especially if the patients were trained to obtain and maintain a "normal" level of facial EMG activity.

An alternative hypothesis on the efficacy of biofeedback training suggests that biofeedback teaches patients general relaxation skills or better coping strategies. Many of the biofeedback studies incorporate relaxation training (Funch & Gale, 1984) or some type of cognitive awareness or stress management techniques into the treatment program (e.g., Burdette & Gale, 1988; Crockett et al., 1986). Biofeedback training may also increase the patient's awareness of tension (Dalen et al., 1986). For example, simple awareness of daytime clenching might be sufficient to produce desirable changes.

Further research is needed to specify more precisely the active elements of biofeedback treatment. Additional research is also needed to identify subsets of TMD patients likely to benefit from biofeedback training (cf. Funch & Gale, 1984; Gessell, 1975).

Nocturnal Alarms

For patients who engage in nocturnal clenching and grinding, a nocturnal alarm may be helpful. Typically, nocturnal alarms monitor EMG activity in a masticatory muscle (usually the masseter or temporalis) as the patient sleeps. An alarm sounds when EMG activity exceeds a threshold for some period of time or when a certain number of suprathreshold EMG events occur within a brief period of time.

During treatment with nocturnal alarms, patients typically show reductions in nocturnal EMG events, particularly when an arousal task is associated with the sounding of the alarm (Cassisi et al., 1987). Follow-up data suggest that the efficacy of nocturnal alarms may be limited to the active treatment period.

Medications

The medications that are typically used to treat TMD are analgesics (especially nonsteroidal anti-inflammatories and other nonopioid analgesics) and muscle relaxants (Glass, Glaros, & McGlynn, 1993). Other agents that are used by dentists, but at considerably lower levels, include opioid analgesics, local anesthetics, and antidepressants. The low rate with which dentists use antidepressants is puzzling, particularly in view of studies that show their efficacy in TMD and other chronic pain problems (cf. Kreisberg, 1988).

Other Management Techniques

Surgery, physical therapy, occlusal equilibration, and orthodontics are also used in the treatment of TMD patients. Surgery is typically recommended for patients with disc displacement without reduction or with severe degenerative conditions. For decreased mobility and pain that have not been resolved with nonsurgical therapy, arthroscopy appears to be the treatment of choice. In this procedure, a small incision is made anterior to the external auditory meatus, and a surgical instrument with optic fibers and surgical tools are inserted into the upper compartment of the TMJ. Any adhesions are broken up, and the joint is lavaged. This frequently results in improved range of motion for the patient (but often not to a normal range) and decreased pain. Follow-up studies suggest that these effects are maintained for at least several years following surgery (e.g., Clark, Moody, & Sanders, 1991; Indresano, 1989; Mosby, 1993).

More invasive open joint surgery is usually performed in cases of nonreducing discs or severe degenerative changes. The discs may be repositioned for more normal function, but they are unlikely to remain in the proper position (Montgomery, Gordon, Van Sickels, & Harms, 1992). The long-term effectiveness of open joint surgery appears to vary from good to problematic, depending on the specific procedure performed (Eriksson & Westesson, 1985; Hoffman, Moses, & Topper, 1991; Poker & Hopper, 1990).

Research has shown that the replacement of articular discs with artificial materials is problematic. Long-term follow-up studies using certain replacement materials indicate that the material may disintegrate over time or move from a proper position (Dolwick & Aufdemorte, 1985; Westesson, Eriksson, & Linström, 1987).

Physical therapy can be used both after and before surgery. The modalities used in physical therapy help improve the range of motion in the joint, especially after joint surgery, and reduce pain. Little is known about the long-term effectiveness of physical therapy techniques with TMD patients.

Occlusal equilibration and orthodontic treatment are reportedly used in a considerable proportion of TMD patients (Glass, Glaros, & McGlynn, 1993). Occlusal equilibration involves the spot grinding of teeth to eliminate discrepancies in the bite. Orthodontic treatments for TMD are designed to correct occlusal problems and purport to place the condyle in the proper position within the fossa.

Both occlusal equilibration and orthodontics assume that occlusal problems are the primary cause of TMD. As noted earlier, occlusal variables have not been reliably associated with TMD. Furthermore, there is no compelling evidence that either occlusal equilibration or orthodontic treatment alleviates (or causes) TMD (Clark & Adler, 1985; Greene, 1988).

Summary

The data suggest that conservative, reversible treatments consisting of a combination of patient education and home care; splints; behavioral techniques such as biofeedback, relaxation, and stress management; and medications provide excellent results in a substantial proportion of patients. The data show that behavioral techniques are competitive with dental and pharmacological techniques for managing TMD pain and may have long-term advantages over the other techniques.

Certain internal derangement and degenerative joint patients may benefit from surgery. But there is no evidence to support the use of this or other irreversible procedures with most muscle-related pain problems common to TMD patients.

Controversies in TMD Assessment and Management

There are a variety of devices available today that promise better diagnosis and management of TMD patients. These include electronic jaw-tracking devices, thermography, sonography, electrogalvanic stimulation (EGS), transcutaneous electrical nerve stimulation (TENS), ultrasound, iontophoresis, and acupuncture.

The electronic jaw-tracking device uses a miniature magnet that is placed on the lip surface of the lower front teeth, a sensor array held in place about the face, and a computer. The jaw is tracked as the magnet moves through the magnetic field generated by the sensor array. This is visualized on the computer monitor and compared with "normative" values prepared by the manufacturer of the device. On the basis of the deviation from these "norms," a diagnosis is made and treatment is rendered. However, the evidence in support of such devices in TMD diagnosis is sparse and unreplicated (Hsu, Palla, & Gallo, 1992; Mohl, McCall, Lund, & Plesh, 1990). For example, there are serious questions involving the accuracy of the equipment in tracking movement in the normal range of motion (Balkhi & Tallents, 1991).

There is also limited evidence of the diagnostic utility of thermography and sonography. Thermographic diagnosis is based on thermal asymmetry between normal and abnormal sites. Its reliability is technique-sensitive and requires excellent control of the test environment. Unfortunately, there is high within-patients and between-patients variability (Mohl, Ohrbach, Crow, & Gross, 1990).

Sonography uses ultrasound echoes, which are converted into amplified, audible sound waves as the echoes bounce off tissues in the

TMJ, to diagnose potential joint pathology. Comprehensive reviews have concluded that there is no clinical advantage of using sonography over a conventional stethoscope or direct auscultation to document joint sounds (Mohl, Lund, Widmer, & McCall, 1990; Widmer, 1989).

Several other treatment techniques with poor scientific support are in use today. One such technique, EGS, uses high-voltage, low-amperage monophasic current of varying frequencies to decrease muscle pain and activity and enhance healing. TENS uses low-voltage, low-amperage biphasic current at varying frequencies to relieve pain and decrease muscle hyperactivity. TENS is also purported to "balance" the alignment of the jaw musculature. There is little scientific evidence to support the use of EGS as a treatment modality or the use of TENS to balance the musculature (Mohl, McCall, Lund, & Plesh, 1990).

The efficacy of iontophoresis as a treatment modality is also poorly documented. In iontophoresis, medication can be driven through the skin to an affected area. The technique uses the polarity of the molecules to repel them away from the iontophoretic unit and push the molecules into the deep tissue. The depth of penetration is uncertain, and its usefulness with TMD is not well known (Laskin & Greene, 1990).

Several techniques for treatment of TMD patients may have promise. Because sensory counterstimulation is helpful in painful disorders, TENS may be helpful in reducing pain. However, if significant motor stimulation occurs concurrently, it may impair the analgesic effect and even exacerbate acute pain (Mohl, McCall, Lund, & Plesh, 1990). Ultrasound may also be useful in treating painful joints. However, the effect of treatment parameters such as duration of treatment, number of sessions, exposure time per session, and frequency and intensity of ultrasound need further systematic study (Mohl, Lund, Widmer, & McCall, 1990). Acupuncture may be used to reduce pain (Johansson, Wenneberg, Wagersten, & Haraldson, 1991), although patients prefer conventional treatments over acupuncture (Raustia, Pohjola, & Virtanen, 1985).

Summary

Although the just-noted techniques may ultimately be useful in diagnosing and treating TMD patients, there is weak or sparse evidence at present to support their use. As controlled research is performed, the utility of these techniques with TMD patients will be better known. Because most patients improve with reversible, noninvasive therapy using diagnostic and treatment techniques that are valid and reliable, conventional wisdom dictates that these be used first.

According to Mohl and Ohrbach (1992), the controversies noted earlier continue to affect the field for six reasons: (a) an insufficient amount of objective, scientifically derived clinical evidence; (b) a failure to communicate effectively the relevant existing evidence to dentists and other health care professionals; (c) a failure to use well-communicated scientific evidence; (d) an overdependence on clinical trial and error; (e) an overdependence on subjective reports of clinical success; and (f) a minimal appreciation that clinical successes, however noteworthy, are not scientific proof of cause and effect.

Perhaps a greater level of involvement by psychologists in TMD research will facilitate research in the field. Psychologists are generally well trained to design and conduct research, and they are sensitive to the psychological factors, including placebo effects, that can affect treatment outcomes.

Summary and Recommendations

Temporomandibular disorders are well within the purview of health psychology practice and research. The data currently available suggest that behavioral and psychological factors play a role in the predisposition to, initiation of, and maintenance of the disorder. The role of psychological factors in TMD has gained increased visibility with diagnostic criteria requiring psychological assessment of the patient. Both dental and psychological techniques can significantly diminish the pain of many TMD patients, and both sets of techniques appear to produce equivalent outcomes with selected patients.

The data suggest that most TMD patients will benefit from conservative, reversible treatments. Whether the treatment is provided by a psychologist or a dentist, the provider must consider the psychosocial characteristics of the patient, the patient's environment, the contributing factors, the illness behavior, and the physical processes necessary to establish a diagnosis and begin treatment. Furthermore, the patient must be involved in the physical and behavioral management of his or her pain problem.

Because most of the research on TMD, including research on the psychological aspects of the disorder, appears in dental journals, many psychologists may not be familiar with the considerable vitality of the field. Nonetheless, there is a great need for well-conducted studies examining the whole range of issues associated with TMD. Psychologists can assist in understanding better the ways in which TMD patients are similar to and different from other chronic pain patients and nonpatient samples. Psychologists can also assist in evaluating the treatments currently used for TMD, determining which subgroups of TMD patients are most likely to benefit from which treatments or combinations of treatments, establishing treatment parameters for the commonly used treatments, and evaluating new treatment (and diagnostic) methods as they become available.

REFERENCES

American Academy of Craniomandibular Disorders. (1990). *Craniomandibular disorders: Guidelines for the evaluation, diagnosis and management.* Chicago: Quintessence.

American Academy of Orofacial Pain. (1993). *Temporomandibular disorders: Guidelines for classification, assessment, and management.* Chicago: Quintessence.

Balkhi, K. M., & Tallents, R. H. (1991). Error analysis of a magnetic jaw tracking device. *Journal of Craniomandibular Disorders: Facial and Oral Pain, 5,* 51–56.

Beaton, R. D., Egan, K. J., Nakagawa-Kogan, H., & Morrison, K. N. (1991). Self-reported symptoms of stress with temporomandibular disorders: Comparisons to healthy men and women. *Journal of Prosthetic Dentistry, 65,* 289–293.

Beck, A. T., Rush, A. J., Shaw, B. F., & Emery, G. (1979). *Cognitive therapy of depression.* New York: Guilford Press.

Bell, W. E. (1982). *Clinical management of temporomandibular disorders.* Chicago: Year Book Medical Publishers.

Bell, W. E. (1986). *Temporomandibular disorders: Classification, diagnosis, management* (2nd ed.). Chicago: Year Book Medical Publishers.

Bergamini, M., Prayer-Galletti, S., & Tonelli, P. (1990). A classification of musculoskeletal disorders of the stomatognatic apparatus. *Frontiers of Oral Physiology, 7,* 185–190.

Biedermann, H.-J. (1984). Comments on the reliability of muscle activity comparisons in EMG biofeedback research with back pain patients. *Biofeedback and Self-Regulation, 9*, 451–458.

Block, S. L. (1980). Differential diagnosis of craniofacial-cervical pain. In B. G. Sarnat & D. M. Laskin (Eds.), *The temporomandibular joint* (3rd ed., pp. 348–421). Springfield, IL: Charles C Thomas.

Burdette, B. H., & Gale, E. N. (1988). The effects of treatment on masticatory muscle activity and mandibular posture in myofascial pain–dysfunction patients. *Journal of Dental Research, 67*, 1126–1130.

Burdette, B. H., & Gale, E. N. (1990). Reliability of surface electromyography of the masseteric and anterior temporal areas. *Archives of Oral Biology, 35*, 747–751.

Burgess, J. (1991). Symptom characteristics in TMD patients reporting blunt trauma and/or whiplash injury. *Journal of Craniomandibular Disorders: Facial and Oral Pain, 5*, 251–257.

Bush, F. M., Harkins, S. W., Harrington, W. G., & Price, D. D. (1993). Analysis of gender effects on pain perception and symptom presentation in temporomandibular pain. *Pain, 53*, 73–80.

Carlsson, S. G., & Gale, E. N. (1977). Biofeedback in the treatment of long-term temporomandibular joint pain: An outcome study. *Biofeedback and Self-Regulation, 2*, 161–171.

Cassisi, J. E., McGlynn, F. D., & Belles, D. R. (1987). EMG-activated feedback alarms for the treatment of nocturnal bruxism: Current status and future directions. *Biofeedback and Self-Regulation, 12*, 13–30.

Christensen, L. V. (1979). Some subjective-experimental parameters in experimental tooth clenching in man. *Journal of Oral Rehabilitation, 6*, 119–136.

Chung, S.-C., Um, B.-Y., & Kim, H.-S. (1992). Evaluation of pressure pain threshold in head and neck muscles by electronic algometer: Intrarater and interrater reliability. *Journal of Craniomandibular Practice, 10*, 28–34.

Clark, G. T. (1984). A critical evaluation of orthopedic interocclusal appliance therapy: Effective for specific symptoms. *Journal of the American Dental Association, 108*, 364–348.

Clark, G. T., & Adler, R. C. (1985). A critical evaluation of occlusal therapy: Occlusal adjustment procedures. *Journal of the American Dental Association, 110*, 743–750.

Clark, G. T., & Merril, R. L. (1992). Diagnosis and nonsurgical treatment of masticatory muscle pain and dysfunction. In B. G. Sarnat & D. M. Laskin (Eds.), *The temporomandibular joint: A biological basis for clinical practice* (4th ed., pp. 346–356). Philadelphia: W. B. Saunders.

Clark, G. T., Moody, D. G., & Sanders, B. (1991). Arthroscopic treatment of temporomandibular joint locking resulting from disc derangement: Two-year results. *Journal of Oral and Maxillofacial Surgery, 49*, 157–164.

Costen, J. B. (1934). Syndrome of ear and sinus symptoms dependent upon disturbed functions of the temporomandibular joint. *Annals of Otology, Rhinology, and Laryngology, 43,* 1–15.

Craig, K. D., Prkachin, K. M., & Grunau, R. V. E. (1992). The facial expression of pain. In D. C. Turk & R. Melzack (Eds.), *Handbook of pain assessment* (pp. 257–276). New York: Guilford Press.

Crockett, D. J., Foreman, M. E., Alden, L., & Blasberg, B. (1986). A comparison of treatment modes in the management of myofascial pain dysfunction syndrome. *Biofeedback and Self-Regulation, 11,* 279–291.

Dahlström, L., Carlsson, G. E., & Carlsson, S. G. (1982). Comparison of effects of electromyographic biofeedback and occlusal splint therapy on mandibular dysfunction. *Scandinavian Journal of Dental Research, 90,* 151–156.

Dahlström, L., & Carlsson, S. G. (1984). Treatment of mandibular dysfunction: The clinical usefulness of biofeedback in relation to splint therapy. *Journal of Oral Rehabilitation, 11,* 277–284.

Dalen, K., Ellertsen, B., Espelid, I., & Gronningsaeter, A. G. (1986). EMG feedback in the treatment of myofascial pain dysfunction syndrome. *Acta Odontologica Scandinavica, 44,* 279–284.

De Kanter, R. J. A. M., Käyser, A. F., Battistuzzi, P. G. F. C. M., Truin, G. J., & Van 't Hof, M. A. (1992). Demand and need for treatment of craniomandibular dysfunction in the Dutch adult population. *Journal of Dental Research, 71,* 1607–1612.

Derogatis, L. (1983). *SCL-90-R: Administration, scoring and procedures manual—II for the revised version.* Towson, MD: Clinical Psychometric Research.

Dixon, D. C. (1991). Diagnostic imaging of the temporomandibular joint. *Dental Clinics of North America, 35,* 53–74.

Dolwick, M. F., & Aufdemorte, T. B. (1985). Silicone-induced foreign body reaction and lymphadenopathy after temporomandibular joint arthroplasty. *Oral Surgery, Oral Medicine, and Oral Pathology, 59,* 449–452.

Duckro, P. N., Tait, R. C., Margolis, R. B., & Deshields, T. L. (1990). Prevalence of temporomandibular symptoms in a large United States metropolitan area. *Journal of Craniomandibular Practice, 8,* 131–138.

Dworkin, S. F., Huggins, K. H., LeResche, L., Von Korff, M., Howard, J., Truelove, E., & Sommers, E. (1990). Epidemiology of signs and symptoms in temporomandibular disorders: I. Clinical signs in cases and controls. *Journal of the American Dental Association, 120,* 273–281.

Dworkin, S. F., & LeResche, L. (Eds.). (1992). Research diagnostic criteria for temporomandibular disorders: Review, criteria, examinations and specifications, critique. *Journal of Craniomandibular Disorders: Facial and Oral Pain, 6,* 301–355.

Egermark-Eriksson, I., Carlsson, G. E., Magnusson, T., & Thilander, B. (1990). A longitudinal study on malocclusion in relation to signs and symptoms of craniomandibular disorders in children and adolescents. *European Journal of Orthodontics, 12,* 399–407.

Ekman, P., & Friesen, W. V. (1978). *Facial action coding system: Investigator's guide.* Palo Alto, CA: Consulting Psychologists Press.

Ekman, P., & Friesen, W. V. (1986). A new pan-cultural facial expression of emotion. *Motivation and Emotion, 10,* 159–168.

Eriksson, L., & Westesson, P. L. (1985). Long-term evaluation of meniscectomy of the temporomandibular joint. *Journal of Oral and Maxillofacial Surgery, 43,* 263–269.

Eversole, L. R., & Machado, L. (1985). Temporomandibular joint internal derangements and associated neuromuscular disorders. *Journal of the American Dental Association, 110,* 69–79.

Eversole, L. R., Stone, C. E., Matheson, D., & Kaplan, H. (1985). Psychometric profiles and facial pain. *Oral Surgery, Oral Medicine, and Oral Pathology, 60,* 269–274.

Farrar, W. B. (1972). Differentiation of temporomandibular joint dysfunction to simplify treatment. *Journal of Prosthetic Dentistry, 28,* 629–636.

FitzGerald, P. M., Jankovic, J., & Percy, A. K. (1990). Rett syndrome and associated movement disorders. *Movement Disorders, 5,* 195–202.

Flor, H., Birbaumer, N., Schulte, W., & Roos, R. (1991). Stress-related electromyographic responses in patients with chronic temporomandibular pain. *Pain, 46,* 145–152.

Flor, H., Schugens, M. M., & Birbaumer, N. (1992). Discrimination of muscle tension in chronic pain patients and healthy controls. *Biofeedback and Self-Regulation, 17,* 165–177.

Fricton, J. R., Bromaghim, C., & Kroening, R. J. (1988). Physical evaluation: The need for a standardized examination. In J. R. Fricton, R. J. Kroening, & K. M. Hathaway (Eds.), *TMJ and craniofacial pain: Diagnosis and management* (pp. 39–52). St. Louis, MO: Ishiyaku EuroAmerica.

Fricton, J. R., & Chung, S. C. (1988). Contributing factors: A key to chronic pain. In J. R. Fricton, R. J. Kroening, & K. M. Hathaway (Eds.), *TMJ and craniofacial pain: Diagnosis and management* (pp. 27–37). St. Louis, MO: Ishiyaku EuroAmerica.

Funch, D. P., & Gale, E. N. (1984). Biofeedback and relaxation therapy for chronic temporomandibular joint pain: Predicting successful outcomes. *Journal of Consulting and Clinical Psychology, 52,* 928–935.

Gale, E. N. (1992). Epidemiology. In B. G. Sarnat & D. M. Laskin (Eds.), *The temporomandibular joint: A biological basis for clinical practice* (4th ed., pp. 237–248). Philadelphia: W. B. Saunders.

Gamsa, A., & Vikis-Freibergs, V. (1991). Psychological events are both risk factors in, and consequences of, chronic pain. *Pain, 44,* 271–277.

Geering, A. H. (1974). Occlusal interferences and functional disturbances of the masticatory system. *Journal of Clinical Periodontology, 1,* 112–119.

Gerber, A. (1971). Kiefergelenk und Zahnokklusion [Temporomandibular joint and dental occlusion]. *Deutsch Zahnerztliche Zeitschrift, 26,* 119–141.

Gessell, A. H. (1975). Electromyographic biofeedback and tricyclic antidepressants in myofascial pain–dysfunction syndrome: Psychological predictors of outcome. *Journal of the American Dental Association, 91,* 1048–1052.

Glaros, A. G. (1981). Incidence of diurnal and nocturnal bruxism. *Journal of Prosthetic Dentistry, 45,* 545–549.

Glaros, A. G., Brockman, D. L., & Ackerman, R. J. (1992). Impact of overbite on indicators of temporomandibular joint dysfunction. *Journal of Craniomandibular Practice, 10,* 277–281.

Glaros, A. G., & Hanson, K. (1990). EMG biofeedback and discriminative muscle control. *Biofeedback and Self-Regulation, 15,* 135–143.

Glaros, A. G., McGlynn, F. D., & Kapel, L. (1989). Sensitivity, specificity, and the predictive value of facial electromyographic data in diagnosing myofascial pain dysfunction. *Journal of Craniomandibular Practice, 7,* 189–193.

Glaros, A. G., & Melamed, B. G. (1992). Bruxism in children: Etiology and treatment. *Applied and Preventive Psychology, 1,* 191–199.

Glaros, A. G., & Rao, S. M. (1977). Bruxism: A critical review. *Psychological Bulletin, 84,* 767–781.

Glass, E., Glaros, A., LeResche, L., Truelove, E. L., Dworkin, S. F., & McLaughlin, L. (1992). Dentists' understanding of temporomandibular disorders and chronic pain. *Journal of Dental Research, 71,* 150.

Glass, E. G., Glaros, A. G., & McGlynn, F. D. (1993). Myofascial pain dysfunction: Treatments used by ADA members. *Journal of Craniomandibular Practice, 11,* 25–29.

Glass, E. G., McGlynn, F. D., Glaros, A. G., Melton, K., & Romans, K. (1993). Prevalence of temporomandibular disorder symptoms in a major metropolitan area. *Journal of Craniomandibular Practice, 11,* 217–220.

Graber, G. (1971). Neurologische und psychosomatische Aspekte der Myoarthropathien des Kauorgans [Neurologic and psychosomatic aspects of myoarthropathies of the masticatory apparatus]. *ZWR, 80,* 997–1000.

Greene, C. S. (1988). Orthodontics and temporomandibular disorders. *Dental Clinics of North America, 32,* 529–538.

Greene, C. S., & Laskin, D. M. (1972). Splint therapy for the myofascial pain–dysfunction (MPD) syndrome: A comparative study. *Journal of the American Dental Association, 84,* 624–628.

Hagberg, C. (1991). General musculoskeletal complaints in a group of patients with craniomandibular disorders (CMD): A case control study. *Swedish Dental Journal, 15,* 179–185.

Hatch, J. P., Prihoda, T. J., & Moore, P. J. (1992). The application of generalizability theory to surface electromyographic measurements during psychophysiological stress testing: How many measurements are needed? *Biofeedback and Self-Regulation, 17,* 17–39.

Helkimo, E., Carlsson, G. E., & Carmeli, Y. (1975). Bite force in patients with functional disturbances of the masticatory system. *Journal of Oral Rehabilitation, 2*, 397–406.

Helöe, B., & Helöe, L. A. (1979). Frequency and distribution of myofascial pain–dysfunction syndrome in a population of 25-year-olds. *Community Dentistry and Oral Epidemiology, 7*, 357–360.

Hicks, R. A., Conti, R. A., & Bragg, H. R. (1990). Increases in nocturnal bruxism among college students implicate stress. *Medical Hypotheses, 33*, 239–240.

Hijzen, T. H., Slangen, J. L., & VanHouweligen, H. C. (1986). Subjective, clinical and EMG effects of biofeedback and splint treatment. *Journal of Oral Rehabilitation, 13*, 529–539.

Hoffman, D., Moses, J., & Topper, D. (1991). Temporomandibular joint surgery. *Dental Clinics of North America, 35*, 89–107.

Hopper, D. K., Gevirtz, R. N., Nigl, A. J., & Taddey, J. (1992). Relationship between daily stress and nocturnal bruxism. *Biofeedback and Self-Regulation, 17*, 309.

Hsu, M.-L., Palla, S., & Gallo, L. M. (1992). Sensitivity and reliability of the T-scan system for occlusal analysis. *Journal of Craniomandibular Disorders: Facial and Oral Pain, 6*, 17–23.

Hylander, W. L. (1992). Functional anatomy. In B. G. Sarnat & D. M. Laskin (Eds.), *The temporomandibular joint: A biological basis for clinical practice* (4th ed., pp. 60–92). Philadelphia: W. B. Saunders.

Ide, Y., Nakazawa, K., & Kamimura, K. (1991). *Anatomical atlas of the temporomandibular joint.* Chicago: Quintessence.

Indresano, A. G. (1989). Arthroscopic surgery of the temporomandibular joint: Report of 64 patients with long-term follow-up. *Journal of Oral and Maxillofacial Surgery, 47*, 439–441.

Ingervall, B., Mohlin, B., & Thilander, B. (1980). Prevalence of symptoms of functional disturbances of the masticatory system in Swedish men. *Journal of Oral Rehabilitation, 7*, 185–197.

Johansson, A., Wenneberg, B., Wagersten, C., & Haraldson, T. (1991). Acupuncture in treatment of facial muscular pain. *Acta Odontologica Scandinavica, 49*, 53–58.

Kapel, L., Glaros, A. G., & McGlynn, F. D. (1989). Psychophysiological responses to stress in patients with myofascial pain–dysfunction syndrome. *Journal of Behavioral Medicine, 12*, 397–406.

Kaplan, P. A., & Helms, C. A. (1989). Current status of temporomandibular joint imaging for the diagnosis of internal derangements. *American Journal of Roentgenology, 152*, 697–705.

Karoly, P., & Jensen, M. P. (1987). *Multimethod assessment of chronic pain.* Elmsford, NY: Pergamon Press.

Keefe, F. J., & Dolan, E. (1986). Pain behavior and pain coping strategies in low back pain and myofascial pain dysfunction syndrome patients. *Pain, 24*, 49–56.

Keefe, F. J., & Williams, D. A. (1992). Assessment of pain behaviors. In D. C. Turk & R. Melzack (Eds.), *Handbook of pain assessment* (pp. 277–292). New York: Guilford Press.

Kinney, R. K., Gatchel, R. J., Ellis, E., & Holt, C. (1992). Major psychological disorders in chronic TMD patients: Implications for successful management. *Journal of the American Dental Association, 123,* 49–54.

Kirveskari, P., Alanen, P., & Jämsä, T. (1992). Association between craniomandibular disorders and occlusal interferences in children. *Journal of Prosthetic Dentistry, 67,* 692–696.

Kozeniauskas, J. J., & Ralph, W. J. (1988). Bilateral arthrographic evaluation of unilateral TMJ pain and dysfunction. *Journal of Prosthetic Dentistry, 60,* 98–105.

Kreisberg, M. K. (1988). Tricyclic antidepressants: Analgesic effect and indications in orofacial pain. *Journal of Craniomandibular Disorders: Facial and Oral Pain, 2,* 171–177.

Laskin, D. M. (1969). Etiology of the pain–dysfunction syndrome. *Journal of the American Dental Association, 79,* 147–153.

Laskin, D. M. (1992). Temporomandibular disorders: Diagnosis and etiology. In B. G. Sarnat & D. M. Laskin (Eds.), *The temporomandibular joint: A biological basis for clinical practice* (4th ed., pp. 316–328). Philadelphia: W. B. Saunders.

Laskin, D. M., & Greene, C. S. (1990). Technological methods in the diagnosis and treatment of temporomandibular disorders. *International Journal of Technology Assessment in Health Care, 6,* 558–568.

Laskin, D., Greenfield, W., Gale, E., Rugh, J., Neff, P., Alling, C., & Ayer, W. A. (Eds.). (1983). *The president's conference on the examination, diagnosis, and management of temporomandibular disorders.* Chicago: American Dental Association.

Laskin, D. M., & Sarnat, B. G. (1992). History and physical examination. In B. G. Sarnat & D. M. Laskin (Eds.), *The temporomandibular joint: A biological basis for clinical practice* (4th ed., pp. 249–256). Philadelphia: W. B. Saunders.

LeResche, L. (Ed.). (1992). Research diagnostic criteria: Axis I. Clinical TMD conditions (Part II. A, pp. 327–330). In S. F. Dworkin & L. LeResche (Eds.), Research diagnostic criteria for temporomandibular disorders: Review, criteria, examinations and specifications, critique. *Journal of Craniomandibular Disorders: Facial and Oral Pain, 6,* 301–355.

LeResche, L., & Dworkin, S. F. (1988). Facial expressions of pain and emotion in chronic TMD patients. *Pain, 35,* 71–78.

LeResche, L., Dworkin, S. F., Sommers, E. E., & Truelove, E. L. (1991). An epidemiologic evaluation of two diagnostic classification schemes for temporomandibular disorders. *Journal of Prosthetic Dentistry, 65,* 131–137.

LeResche, L., Truelove, E. L., & Dworkin, S. F. (1993). Dentists' knowledge and beliefs concerning temporomandibular disorders. *Journal of the American Dental Association, 124*(5), 90–106.

LeResche, L., Truelove, E. L., Dworkin, S. F., Whitney, C. W., & Harrison, R. (1991). Dentists' understanding of temporomandibular disorders. *Journal of Dental Research, 70*, 338.

Levitt, S. R. (1990a). Predictive value of the TMJ Scale in detecting clinically significant symptoms of temporomandibular disorders. *Journal of Craniomandibular Disorders: Facial and Oral Pain, 4*, 177–185.

Levitt, S. R. (1990b). The predictive value of the TMJ Scale in detecting psychological factors and non-TM disorders in patients with temporomandibular disorders. *Journal of Craniomandibular Practice, 8*, 225–233.

Levitt, S. R., Lundeen, T. F., & McKinney, M. W. (1987). *The TMJ Scale manual.* Durham, NC: Pain Resource Center.

Levitt, S. R., McKinney, M., & Lundeen, T. (1988). The TMJ Scale: Cross-validation and reliability studies. *Journal of Craniomandibular Practice, 6*, 17–25.

List, T., Helkimo, M., & Falk, G. (1989). Reliability and validity of a pressure threshold meter in recording tenderness in the masseter muscle and the anterior temporalis muscle. *Journal of Craniomandibular Practice, 7*, 223–229.

Locker, D., & Slade, G. (1988). Prevalence of symptoms associated with temporomandibular disorders in a Canadian population. *Community Dentistry and Oral Epidemiology, 16*, 310–313.

Lund, J. P. (Ed.). (1992). Review and commentary: Basic sciences (Part IV. A, pp. 346–350). In S. F. Dworkin & L. LeResche (Eds.), Research diagnostic criteria for temporomandibular disorders: Review, criteria, examinations and specifications, critique. *Journal of Craniomandibular Disorders: Facial and Oral Pain, 6*, 301–355.

Magni, G., Caldieron, C., Rigatti-Luchini, S., & Merskey, H. (1990). Chronic musculoskeletal pain and depressive symptoms in the general population: An analysis of the 1st National Health and Nutrition Examination Survey data. *Pain, 43*, 299–307.

McCreary, C. P., Clark, G. T., Merril, R. L., Flack, V., & Oakley, M. E. (1991). Psychological distress and diagnostic subgroups of temporomandibular disorder patients. *Pain, 44*, 29–34.

McGlynn, F. D., Gale, E. N., Glaros, A. G., LeResche, L., Massoth, D. L., & Weiffenbach, J. M. (1990). Biobehavioral research in dentistry: Some directions for the 1990s. *Annals of Behavioral Medicine, 12*, 133–140.

McKinney, M. W., Lundeen, T. F., Turner, S. P., & Levitt, S. R. (1990). Chronic TM disorder and non-TM disorder pain: A comparison of behavioral and psychological characteristics. *Journal of Craniomandibular Practice, 8*, 40–46.

McNeill, C., Danzig, W. M., Farrar, W. B., Gelb, H., Lerman, M. D., Moffett, B. C., Pertes, R., Solberg, W. K., & Weinberg, L. A. (1980). Craniomandibular (TMJ) disorders: The state of the art. *Journal of Prosthetic Dentistry, 44*, 434–437.

McNeill, C., Mohl, N. D., Rugh, J. D., & Tanaka, T. T. (1990). Temporo-mandibular disorders: Diagnosis, management, education, and research. *Journal of the American Dental Association, 120,* 253–263.

Mealiea, W. L., & McGlynn, F. D. (1987). Temporomandibular disorders and bruxism. In J. P. Hatch, J. G. Fisher, & J. D. Rugh (Eds.), *Biofeedback: Studies in clinical efficacy* (pp. 123–151). New York: Plenum.

Mercuri, L. G., Olson, R. E., & Laskin, D. M. (1979). The specificity of response to experimental stress in patients with myofascial pain dys-function syndrome. *Journal of Dental Research 58,* 1866–1871.

Miller, A. J. (1991). *Craniomandibular muscles: Their role in function and form.* Boca Raton, FL: CRC Press.

Mohl, N. D., Lund, J. P., Widmer, C. G., & McCall, W. D., Jr. (1990). Devices for the diagnosis and treatment of temporomandibular disorders: Part II. Electromyography and sonography. *Journal of Prosthetic Dentistry, 63,* 332–336.

Mohl, N. D., McCall, W. D., Jr., Lund, J. P., & Plesh, O. (1990). Devices for the diagnosis and treatment of temporomandibular disorders: Part I. Introduction, scientific evidence, and jaw tracking. *Journal of Prosthetic Dentistry, 63,* 198–201.

Mohl, N. D., & Ohrbach, R. (1992). The dilemma of scientific knowledge versus clinical management of temporomandibular disorders. *Journal of Prosthetic Dentistry, 67,* 113–120.

Mohl, N. D., Ohrbach, R. K., Crow, H. C., & Gross, A. J. (1990). Devices for the diagnosis and treatment of temporomandibular disorders: Part III. Thermography, ultrasound, electrical stimulation, and electromy-ographic biofeedback. *Journal of Prosthetic Dentistry, 63,* 472–477.

Montgomery, G. T., & Rugh, J. D. (1987). Physiological reactions of patients with TM disorders vs. symptom-free controls on a physical stress task. *Journal of Craniomandibular Disorders: Facial and Oral Pain, 1,* 243–250.

Montgomery, G. T., & Rugh, J. D. (1990). Psychophysiological responsibility on a laboratory stress task: Methodological implications for a stress-muscle hyperactivity pain model. *Biofeedback and Self-Regulation, 15,* 121–134.

Montgomery, M. T., Gordon, S. M., Van Sickels, J. E., & Harms, S. E. (1992). Changes in signs and symptoms following temporomandibular joint disc repositioning surgery. *Journal of Oral and Maxillofacial Surgery, 50,* 320–328.

Mosby, E. L. (1993). Efficacy of temporomandibular joint arthroscopy: A retrospective study. *Journal of Oral and Maxillofacial Surgery, 51,* 17–21.

Moss, R. A., & Adams, H. E. (1984). Physiological reactions to stress in subjects with and without myofascial pain dysfunction symptoms. *Journal of Oral Rehabilitation, 11,* 219–232.

Nemcovsky, C. E., & Gross, M. D. (1991). A comparative study of the ster-eognathic ability between patients with myofascial pain dysfunction syn-drome and a control group. *Journal of Craniomandibular Practice, 9,* 35–38.

Ohrbach, R., & Gale, E. N. (1989a). Pressure pain thresholds, clinical assessment, and differential diagnosis: Reliability and validity in patients with myogenic pain. *Pain, 39,* 157–169.

Ohrbach, R., & Gale, E. N. (1989b). Pressure pain thresholds in normal muscles: Reliability, measurement effects, and topographic differences. *Pain, 37,* 257–263.

Ohrbach, R., & Stohler, C. (Eds.). (1992). Review of the literature: Current diagnostic systems (Part I. B, pp. 307–317). In S. F. Dworkin & L. LeResche (Eds.), Research diagnostic criteria for temporomandibular disorders: Review, criteria, examinations and specifications, critique. *Journal of Craniomandibular Disorders: Facial and Oral Pain, 6,* 301–355.

Okeson, J. P. (1987). The effects of hard and soft occlusal splints on nocturnal bruxism. *Journal of the American Dental Association, 114,* 788–791.

Okeson, J. P. (1989). *Management of temporomandibular disorders and occlusion* (2nd ed.). St. Louis, MO: Mosby.

Olkinuora, M. (1972a). Bruxism: A review of the literature on, and a discussion of studies of bruxism and its psychogenesis and some new psychological hypotheses. *Suomen Hammaslääkäriseuran Toimituksia, 68,* 110–123.

Olkinuora, M. (1972b). A factor-analytic study of psychosocial background in bruxism. *Suomen Hammaslääkäriseuran Toimituksia, 68,* 184–199.

Olkinuora, M. (1972c). Psychosocial aspects in a series of bruxists compared with a group of non-bruxists. *Suomen Hammaslääkäriseuran Toimituksia, 68,* 200–208.

Poker, I. D., & Hopper, C. (1990). Surgery for temporomandibular joint pain. *Dental Update, 17,* 291–297.

Powell, R. N., & Zander, H. A. (1965). The frequency and distribution of tooth contact during sleep. *Journal of Dental Research, 44,* 713–717.

Ramfjord, S. P., & Ash, M. M. (1971). *Occlusion* (2nd ed.). Philadelphia: W. B. Saunders.

Ramfjord, S. P., & Ash, M. M. (1983). *Occlusion* (3rd ed.). Philadelphia: W. B. Saunders.

Rao, S. M., & Glaros, A. G. (1979). Electromyographic correlates of experimentally induced stress in diurnal bruxists and normals. *Journal of Dental Research, 58,* 1872–1878.

Raustia, A. M., Pohjola, R. T., & Virtanen, K. K. (1985). Acupuncture compared with stomatognathic treatment for TMJ dysfunction: Part I. A randomized study. *Journal of Prosthetic Dentistry, 54,* 581–585.

Regier, D. A., Boyd, J. H., Burke, J. D., Jr., Rae, D. S., Myers, J. K., Kramer, M., Robins, L. N., George, L. K., Karno, M., & Locke, B. Z. (1988). One-month prevalence of mental disorders in the United States. *Archives of General Psychiatry, 45,* 977–986.

Richards, J. S., Nepomuceno, C., Riles, M., & Suer, Z. (1982). Assessing pain behavior: The UAB Pain Behavior Scale. *Pain, 14,* 393–398.

Rieder, C. E., Martinoff, J. T., & Wilcox, S. A. (1983). The prevalence of mandibular dysfunction: Part I. Sex and age distribution of related signs and symptoms. *Journal of Prosthetic Dentistry, 50,* 81–88.

Rugh, J. D., & Solberg, W. K. (1976). Psychological implications of tempo-romandibular pain and dysfunction. *Oral Science Review, 7,* 3–30.

Rugh, J. D., & Solberg, W. K. (1985). Oral health status in the United States: Temporomandibular disorders. *Journal of Dental Education, 49,* 398–404.

Rugh, J. D., & Robbins, J. W. (1982). Oral habit disorders. In B. D. Ingersoll (Ed.), *Behavioral aspects in dentistry* (pp. 179–202). New York: Appleton-Century-Crofts.

Sadowsky, C., Theisen, T. A., & Sakols, E. I. (1991). Orthodontics and TMJ sounds: A longitudinal study. *American Journal of Orthodontics and Dentofacial Orthopedics, 101,* 13–20.

Sapiro, S. M. (1992). Tongue indentations as an indicator of clenching. *Clinical Preventive Dentistry, 14*(2), 21–24.

Schiffman, E., & Fricton, J. R. (1988). Epidemiology of TMJ and craniofacial pain. In J. R. Fricton, R. J. Kroening, & K. M. Hathaway (Eds.), *TMJ and craniofacial pain: Diagnosis and management* (pp. 1–10). St. Louis, MO: Ishiyaku EuroAmerica.

Schiffman, E. L., Fricton, J. R., Haley, D. P., & Shapiro, B. L. (1990). The prevalence and treatment needs of subjects with temporomandibular disorders. *Journal of the American Dental Association, 120,* 295–303.

Schwartz, L. (1959). *Disorders of the temporomandibular joint.* Philadelphia: W. B. Saunders.

Shellenberger, R., & Green, J. (1986). *From the ghost in the box to successful biofeedback training.* Greeley, CO: Health Psychology Publications.

Shellenberger, R., & Green, J. (1987). Specific effects and biofeedback versus biofeedback-assisted self-regulation training. *Biofeedback and Self-Regulation, 12,* 185–209.

Sherman, R. A. (1985). Relationships between jaw pain and jaw muscle contraction level: Underlying factors and treatment effectiveness. *Journal of Prosthetic Dentistry, 54,* 114–118.

Shore, N. A. (1959). *Occlusal equilibration and temporomandibular joint dysfunction.* Philadelphia: W. B. Saunders.

Solberg, W. K. (1983). Epidemiology, incidence and prevalence of temporomandibular disorders: A review. In D. Laskin, W. Greenfield, E. Gale, J. Rugh, P. Neff, C. Alling, & W. A. Ayer (Eds.), *The president's conference on the examination, diagnosis, and management of temporomandibular disorders* (pp. 30–39). Chicago: American Dental Association.

Southwell, J., Deary, I. J., & Geissler, P. (1990). Personality and anxiety in temporomandibular joint syndrome patients. *Journal of Oral Rehabilitation, 17,* 239–243.

Spielberger, C. D. (1983). *Manual for the State–Trait Anxiety Inventory (Form Y).* Palo Alto, CA: Consulting Psychologists Press.

Spitzer, R. L., Williams, J. B. W., Gibbon, M., & First, M. B. (1990). *User's guide for the Structured Clinical Interview for DSM-III-R.* Washington, DC: American Psychiatric Press.

Swanljung, O., & Rantanen, T. (1979). Functional disorders of the masticatory system in southwest Finland. *Community Dentistry and Oral Epidemiology*, 7, 177–182.

Talley, R. L., Murphy, G. J., Smith, S. D., Baylin, M. A., & Haden, J. L. (1990). Standards for the history, examination, diagnosis, and treatment of temporomandibular disorders (TMD): A position paper. *Journal of Craniomandibular Practice*, 8, 60–77.

Truelove, E. L., LeResche, L., Dworkin, S. F., & Whitney, C. W. (1991). Dentists' diagnosis and treatment of temporomandibular disorders. *Journal of Dental Research*, 70, 372.

Truelove, E. L., Sommers, E. E., LeResche, L., Dworkin, S. F., & Von Korff, M. (1992). Clinical diagnostic criteria for TMD: New classification permits multiple diagnoses. *Journal of the American Dental Association*, 123, 47–54.

Von Korff, M. R. (Ed.). (1992). Research diagnostic criteria: Axis II. Pain related disability and psychological status (Part II. B, pp. 330–334). In S. F. Dworkin & L. LeResche (Eds.), Research diagnostic criteria for temporomandibular disorders: Review, criteria, examinations and specifications, critique. *Journal of Craniomandibular Disorders: Facial and Oral Pain*, 6, 301–355.

Voss, V. R. (1964). Die Behandlung von Beschwerden des Kiefergelenkes mit Aufbißplatten [The treatment of temporomandibular joint pain with bite plates]. *Deutsch Zahnaerztliche Zeitschrift*, 19, 545–549.

Ware, J. C., & Rugh, J. D. (1988). Destructive bruxism: Sleep stage relationship. *Sleep*, 11, 172–181.

Westesson, P.-L. (1992). Imaging. In B. G. Sarnat & D. M. Laskin (Eds.), *The temporomandibular joint: A biological basis for clinical practice* (4th ed., pp. 257–288). Philadelphia: W. B. Saunders.

Westesson, P.-L., & Bronstein, S. L. (1985). Temporomandibular joint: Comparison of single- and double-contrast arthrography. *Radiology*, 160, 65–70.

Westesson, P.-L., Eriksson, L., & Linström, C. (1987). Destructive lesions of the mandibular condyle following diskectomy with temporary silicone implant. *Oral Surgery, Oral Medicine, and Oral Pathology*, 63, 143–150.

Westesson, P.-L., Katzberg, R. W., Tallents, R. H., Sanchez-Woodworth, R. E., & Svensson, S. A. (1987). CT and MR of the temporomandibular joint: Comparison with autopsy specimens. *American Journal of Roentgenology*, 148, 1165–1171.

Widmer, C. G. (1989). Temporomandibular joint sounds: A critique of techniques for recording and analysis. *Journal of Craniomandibular Disorders: Facial and Oral Pain*, 3, 213–217.

Widmer, C. G. (Ed.). (1992). Review of the literature: Reliability and validation of examination methods (Part I. B, pp. 318–326). In S. F. Dworkin & L. LeResche (Eds.), Research diagnostic criteria for temporomandibular disorders: Review, criteria, examinations and specifications, critique. *Journal of Craniomandibular Disorders: Facial and Oral Pain*, 6, 301–355.

Wright, J., Deary, I. J., & Geissler, P. R. (1991). Depression, hassles and somatic symptoms in mandibular dysfunction syndrome patients. *Journal of Dentistry, 19*, 352–356.

Wruble, M. K. (1988). *Sleep posture and sleep related bruxism.* Unpublished master's thesis, University of Florida, Gainesville.

Wruble, M. K., Lumley, M. A., & McGlynn, F. D. (1989). Sleep-related bruxism and sleep variables: A critical review. *Journal of Craniomandibular Disorders: Facial and Oral Pain, 3*, 152–158.

Zarb, G. A., & Carlsson, G. E. (1979). *Temporomandibular joint function and dysfunction.* Copenhagen, Denmark: Munksgaard.

Zung, W. W. K. (1965). A self-rating depression scale. *Archives of General Psychiatry, 12*, 63–70.

10

Psychosocial Issues in Diabetes Mellitus

William H. Polonsky

Approximately 5.5 million people in the United States are currently living with diabetes mellitus, and it is suspected that an equivalent number of cases have not yet been diagnosed (Herman, Teutsch, & Geiss, 1987). There is as yet no cure, and diabetes remains one of the leading causes of morbidity and mortality in the U.S. There are two primary forms of the disease, both characterized by chronic hyperglycemia (abnormally high levels of blood glucose). *Type I diabetes* (insulin-dependent diabetes mellitus, or IDDM) typically occurs during childhood or adolescence, when genetic and autoimmune processes prompt the destruction of the pancreatic beta cells, the primary source of insulin (Lefebvre, 1986). Without sufficient insulin, glucose cannot be properly absorbed into the tissues, which leads to hyperglycemia and compensatory metabolic breakdown of fats (which, if unchecked, leads to ketoacidosis, coma, and eventually death). *Type*

II diabetes (non-insulin-dependent diabetes mellitus, or NIDDM) typically occurs after age 40. It is believed that chronic hyperglycemia results from pervasive insulin resistance in combination with beta cell dysfunction. Ketoacidosis rarely occurs. Most NIDDM patients are obese (approximately 80%), and obesity is a main contributor to insulin resistance. It is estimated that NIDDM is 7–10 times more prevalent than IDDM.

Both forms of diabetes are associated with the development of long-term complications, including increased risk of renal failure, blindness, and cardiovascular disease. Diabetes is the third leading cause of death in the U.S. and is the leading cause of lower extremity amputations, blindness, and kidney transplants. In total, approximately 50–75% of diabetic patients develop serious complications (Strowig & Raskin, 1992).

There is strong evidence that chronic hyperglycemia, in combination with genetic factors, plays a principal role in the development of long-term complications (Strowig & Raskin, 1992). Thus, the primary goal of treatment is to avoid hyperglycemia by maintaining blood glucose levels as close to the normal range as possible (80–120 mg/dl). Effective diabetes management requires a careful balancing of self-care behaviors that focus on diet, exercise, self-monitoring of blood glucose (SMBG), and medication.

Medication regimens vary greatly. NIDDM patients may be treated with diet alone (often focusing on weight reduction), oral hypoglycemic agents, or insulin. Because weight reduction may lead to the normalization of blood glucose levels in many NIDDM patients, diet and exercise are often the focus of treatment. IDDM patients, for whom insulin is essential for survival, may take one or more injections each day, depending on blood glucose goals. Many patients are given intensive insulin regimens, which are designed to restrict blood glucose levels to near-normal levels (Hirsch, Farkas-Hirsch, & Skyler, 1990). These regimens involve three or more injections each day or an insulin pump (for continuous infusion of insulin).

This chapter focuses primarily on IDDM and insulin-managed NIDDM patients and reviews the principal psychosocial factors in diabetes self-management, stress and distress in diabetes, and psychosocial treatment approaches. For the insulin-managed patient, the balancing of food, exercise, and insulin over time while constantly monitoring blood glucose levels is a particularly complex, demanding, and often frustrating effort. Strategies for avoiding hyperglycemia, for example, often promote hypoglycemic (abnormally low blood glucose) episodes. Hypoglycemia commonly causes unpleasant physical symptoms and can be quite frightening (Gonder-Frederick, Cox, Bobbitt, & Pennebaker, 1989); if hypoglycemia becomes severe, marked cognitive or motor dysfunction, coma, or even death may result. Patients are therefore required to walk a difficult tightrope each day, avoiding the dangers of hyperglycemia (by promoting hypoglycemic strategies) while simultaneously guarding against hypoglycemia (by promoting hyperglycemic strategies).

Adherence in Diabetes Self-Management

The burdensome nature of diabetes self-care cannot be underestimated. Patients confront a difficult set of behavioral and emotional challenges. Regimen activities must be performed accurately and frequently (e.g., SMBG), life-style restrictions must be carefully followed (e.g., food selections), and frequent decisions must be made (e.g., estimating whether a planned sports activity may lead to a hypoglycemic episode). Such complex work must continue daily, without break, for the rest of the patient's life. Meanwhile, there is the ongoing emotional struggle of adapting to life with a chronic illness as well as coping with the grim possibility of long-term complications.

Not surprisingly, diabetes regimen adherence is often problematic (Glasgow, 1991). Physicians' recommendations for self-care are frequently not followed, patients' blood glucose data are often falsified, and dropout from medical care is common. Early studies reported high levels of nonadherence, with 80% of patients failing to administer insulin regularly in an acceptable manner, 35–75% failing to follow their diet properly, and 43% failing to test regularly for urine glucose (Kurtz, 1990). Diet and exercise requirements are reported to be the most difficult components of treatment to meet (Glasgow, McCaul, & Schafer, 1986, 1987). For example, Christensen and colleagues found that 78% of patients deviated significantly from their recommended dietary regimens at least weekly (Christensen, Terry, Wyatt, Pichert, & Lorenz, 1983). In a recent survey of 456 insulin-managed women, 83% of the patients agreed with the statement, "I am supposed to follow a certain meal plan, but it is impossible" (Polonsky,

Anderson, & Lohrer, 1991). In a 1-year follow-up of an outpatient diabetes education program, diet and exercise behaviors, which were significantly improved immediately following the program, had regressed to baseline levels (Rubin, Peyrot, & Saudek, 1991). Interestingly, reported improvements in SMBG and self-adjustment of insulin dosages were maintained. This is consistent with the findings of Glasgow, McCaul, and Schafer (1987), who found that patients had more difficulty adhering to diet and exercise prescriptions (those tasks requiring the greatest modifications in life-style) than to medication and testing prescriptions.

Adherence difficulties, however, are not restricted to diet and exercise behaviors. Recent research suggests that 10–40% of women with IDDM intentionally omit insulin doses regularly (Birk & Spencer, 1989; Fairburn, Peveler, Davies, Mann, & Mayou, 1991; LaGreca, Schwarz, & Satin, 1987; Marcus & Wing, 1990; Rodin, Craven, Littlefield, Murray, & Daneman, 1991; Rodin, Johnson, Garfinkel, Daneman, & Kenshole, 1986; Stancin, Link, & Reuter, 1989). Patients may also fabricate their blood glucose monitoring results. Several studies have shown that patients reported and recorded 30–40% more blood glucose tests than were verified by patients' glucometers (patients were not aware of the meter's memory capacity) (Mazze et al., 1984; Wilson & Endres, 1986). In addition, dropout from medical care is common. A recent study of an office-based private endocrinology practice indicated that 12% of diabetic patients dropped out after the initial visit, and 33% of the remaining cohort dropped out during each subsequent 6-month period (Graber, Davidson, Brown, McRae, & Wooldridge, 1992).

These data indicate that poor adherence to the diabetes regimen is relatively widespread. Given the risks of diabetic complications, it is essential that the factors that underlie poor adherence be investigated. In this manner, more comprehensive psychosocial strategies can be developed to promote regimen adherence.

Problems in the Measurement of Regimen Adherence

Unfortunately, the ability to measure adherence is severely compromised in four main ways. First, as just discussed, falsification of self-reported adherence data is all too common. Falsification may occur because patients deny that they are struggling emotionally with self-management (Edelwich & Brodsky, 1986) because they wish to avoid a confrontation with a physician perceived to be overly critical or because they wish to please a physician whose positive regard is important. Moreover, it must be remembered that some patients have difficulty accurately recalling their adherence behaviors (Lichtman et al., 1992).

Second, even in situations in which accuracy of self-reported data can be assured, such data can be difficult to evaluate because patients typically have not received explicit instructions from their physicians. Patients may be advised to "try to follow your meal plan better," "start exercising," or "test your blood sugars more frequently." When such patients then describe that they are, for example, practicing SMBG twice daily, how can an observer decide whether this is appropriately "adherent"? Because of this dilemma, self-report instruments such as the Self-Care Inventory have been developed (Greco et al., 1990). In it, patients are asked to indicate the degree to which they have followed their physician's recommendations for 14 different regimen behaviors. Although this avoids the difficulty of interpreting actual behaviors, data concerning actual behaviors and actual recommendations are not identified. Patients may perceive themselves as adherent to physician recommendations (e.g., to start exercising), but this does not mean that their behaviors are, in fact, efficacious.

Third, recent evidence suggests that regimen adherence is not unidimensional, with correlations between the various regimen components typically being low ($rs < 0.20$) (Glasgow, 1991; Glasgow et al., 1987). Patients are thus selectively adherent; one patient may follow the medication regimen faithfully and simultaneously ignore dietary recommendations, whereas another patient may avoid exercise and yet practice SMBG on a regular basis. These data indicate that there is no underlying personality or attitude dimension that globally determines responses to all treatment demands. Thus, a global measure of adherence may be inadequate. A variety of factors may differentially promote adherence to the various regimen components.

Fourth, to avoid the difficulties of self-reported data, many researchers focus on glycosylated hemoglobin (HbA1) as a more appropriate outcome measure. The level of HbA1, which provides an accurate biological marker of blood glucose control over a 6–8-week period, is often viewed as a final common pathway for the various adherence behaviors. However, glycemic control is also influenced by many other factors, including insulin sensitivity (e.g., pubertal changes or hormonal changes during pregnancy), illness severity, and the efficacy of the recommended regimen. Indeed, most studies have demonstrated only weak correlations between adherence measures and HbA1, which points to the importance of not equating adherence with glycemic control (Glasgow et al., 1987, 1989; Hanson, Henggeler, & Burghen, 1987a).

Despite these methodological limitations, a growing number of psychosocial variables have been found to be associated with self-management behaviors and with glycemic control. These include intrapersonal, interpersonal, and environmental factors.

Psychosocial Factors in Diabetes Self-Management

Patients who evidence poor regimen adherence are commonly accused of lacking willpower; being stupid, crazy, or uneducated about diabetes self-management; or being insufficiently frightened (of potential long-term complications). These suppositions, however, have rarely been supported by research. Level of glycemic control, for example, has not been found to be associated with diabetes knowledge (Jacobson, Adler, Wolfsdorf, Anderson, & Derby, 1990). Indeed, it has been a relatively consistent finding that diabetes education programs are successful in increasing knowledge about diabetes self-management but do not lead to significant improvements in glycemic control (see Goodall & Halford, 1991). In addition, both HbA1 and self-reported adherence were recently found to be positively associated with fear of long-term complications (for HbA1, $r = 0.17$, $p < .0005$; for self-reported adherence, $r = 0.27$, $p < .0001$), which suggests that those adhering poorly were the most fearful (Polonsky, Anderson, Lohrer, & Schwartz, 1991).

Poor adherence is, in fact, commonly rational and strategically sound (Becker & Janz, 1985; Surwit, Feinglos, & Scovern, 1983). In response to the perceived costs and benefits of self-management (as determined by an array of personal, social, and environmental reinforcers, mostly diabetes-specific), patients achieve levels of regimen adherence that are subjectively appropriate for their situation (although not necessarily satisfactory for their long-term health).

Intrapersonal Factors

Psychological disorders, especially affective illness (Lustman, Griffith, & Clouse, 1988; Lustman, Griffith, Clouse, & Cryer, 1986; Mazze et al., 1984) and eating disorders (Marcus & Wing, 1990; Polonsky et al., 1991) have been associated with poor diabetes regimen adherence. Although most findings have been correlational in nature, it is reasonable to speculate that such syndromes as chronic depression and bulimia may interfere with a patient's motivation to follow, for example, a prescribed diet regimen, which thereby leads to poorer glycemic control. Especially in adolescents and young adults, such syndromes and behaviors have been linked to repeated episodes of diabetic ketoacidosis (Schade, Drumm, Duckworth, & Eaton, 1985). Generalizations from these data to less severe forms of distress may be unwise. Although affective illness, for example, is linked to poor adherence, related subclinical conditions such as depressed mood have not been found to be associated with self-reported adherence or with long-term blood glucose control (Jacobson et al., 1990; Polonsky, Anderson, Lohrer, Aponte, & Jacobson, 1993).

Patient coping skills have also been linked to regimen adherence, especially in IDDM adolescents. Two problematic forms of coping, avoidance and inappropriate ventilation of feelings, have been found to be associated with poor regimen adherence (Hanson et al., 1989). Avoidance and wishful thinking have also been linked to poor glycemic control (Delamater, Kurtz, Bubb, White, & Santiago, 1987).

Recent research has increasingly focused on the influence of diabetes-specific attitudes on regimen adherence, including health beliefs about diabetes and fear of hypoglycemia. Applying the health belief model to diabetes (Becker & Janz, 1985), investigators have examined patients' beliefs about illness severity, vulnerability to negative outcomes, costs and benefits of adherence behaviors, and ability to successfully complete self-management behaviors (i.e., self-efficacy). Using a variety of different instruments, investigators have frequently observed positive associations between specific health beliefs and measures of adherence, although there are no consistent patterns across studies (Brownlee-Duffeck et al., 1987; Cerkoney & Hart, 1980;

Hampson, Glasgow, & Toobert, 1990). Future investigations are likely to focus on interactions among different health beliefs, which may prove to be more potent determinants of adherence. Bond, Aiken, and Somerville (1992), for example, found that self-reported regimen adherence was highest in those patients who perceived the greatest potential benefits from treatment and felt the least threatened by the disease process. Interestingly, this suggests that threatening patients with the consequences of their actions (i.e., long-term complications) may actually undermine adherence.

As noted earlier, hypoglycemia is often perceived and experienced as frightening, is usually associated with unpleasant physical symptoms, and can become life threatening. Not surprisingly, patients may develop a pronounced and chronic fear of hypoglycemia. Researchers have speculated that such fear, especially in IDDM patients, may result in a phobic avoidance of near-normal blood glucose levels. According to this hypothesis, such fear leads to difficulty adhering to the diabetic regimen (Weiner & Skipper, 1979) and to behaviors promoting the maintenance of elevated blood glucose levels (Cox, Irvine, Gonder-Frederick, Nowacek, & Butterfield, 1987; Polonsky, Davis, Jacobson, & Anderson, 1992a; Surwit et al., 1983), which thereby markedly reduces the risk of hypoglycemia. Using the Hypoglycemic Fear Survey (Cox et al., 1987), recent studies of IDDM patients have not corroborated this hypothesis (Cox et al., 1987; Green, Wysocki, & Reineck, 1990; Irvine, Cox, & Gonder-Frederick, 1992). In one study, a significant positive association between hypoglycemic fear and HbA1 was found in insulin-managed Type II patients but not in Type I patients (Polonsky, Davis, Jacobson, & Anderson, 1993). Anecdotal data suggest that fear of hypoglycemia may lead to the intentional elevation of blood glucose levels in IDDM patients but probably in only certain subgroups of patients, which have not yet been identified.

Interpersonal Factors

Social support may be one of the most important contributors to regimen adherence (Rubin, Biermann, & Toohey, 1992). In a recent survey (Polonsky et al., 1991), feeling alone with one's diabetes was linked to poorer glycemic control ($r = 0.26$, $p < .0001$) and poorer regimen adherence ($r = 0.30$, $p < .0001$). In children and adolescents, high levels of family support and cohesion and low levels of family conflict have been associated with better glycemic control and regimen adherence (Anderson, 1990). Family cohesiveness at disease onset has also been found to be predictive of regimen adherence at 4 years after onset (Hauser et al., 1990). Using the Diabetes Family-Behavior Checklist (Schafer, McCaul, & Glasgow, 1986), several studies have shown that regimen adherence is linked to the frequency of diabetes-specific supportive and nonsupportive behaviors among adolescents (Hanson, Henggeler, & Burghen, 1987b; Schafer et al., 1986) and adults (Glasgow & Toobert, 1988). Inconsistencies, however, are apparent in these results, with some evidence suggesting that regimen adherence is exclusively linked to positive, supportive behaviors (Glasgow & Toobert, 1988; Hanson et al., 1987b) and other evidence pointing to an exclusive (although negative) contribution of negative, hindering behaviors (Schafer et al., 1986).

The latter results point to the complex, multidimensional nature of social support in diabetes. Although certain social actions may support adherence (e.g., one patient asked her college roommate to sit with her each morning while she tested her blood glucose, which led to more regular testing), other types of "support" may actually undermine adherence (e.g., patients often find that their spouses become "diabetes policemen," criticizing everything they consume, which often leads to secretive eating). Gender differences may also be important. Kaplan and Hartwell (1987) found that satisfaction with social support was associated with glycemic control in NIDDM, although oppositely for women and men. The women who were most satisfied with their social support evidenced better glycemic control than those who were least satisfied. Among men, those most satisfied with their social support evidenced poorer glycemic control than those who were least satisfied. These findings may indicate that the support systems of men and women differentially influence regimen behaviors (see Wing, Marcus, Epstein, & Jawad, 1991), with women's networks more likely to support adherence behaviors (e.g., appropriate eating) and with men's networks more likely to promote nonadherence (e.g., excessive drinking).

The quality of the patient–provider relationship may also be an important social contributor to regimen adherence (Jacobson, Hauser, Anderson, & Polonsky, in press). To date, however, there has been little study in this area. Anecdotal data suggest that when the physician fails to examine and discuss the patient's blood glucose test records, the patient is less motivated to continue with testing and recording. Furthermore, there may be substantial (although often uncommunicated) differences between patient and physician expectations for treatment adherence. When provider expectations are perceived to be too high, patients may begin to falsify their treatment records (Delamater, Kurtz, White, & Santiago, 1988), become "burned out" and subsequently less adherent (Hoover, 1988), and drop out of treatment altogether (Jacobson, Adler, Derby, Anderson, & Wolfsdorf, 1991). Of greatest interest, recent evidence suggests that modifying the patient–provider relationship leads to improved glycemic control (Greenfield, Kaplan, Ware, Yano, & Frank, 1988). In a randomized trial design, patients were trained and prompted in a brief session immediately preceding their physician visit to participate more effectively in their own medical care. Experimental patients learned to clarify their particular needs during the upcoming visit, question their physicians more precisely, and negotiate specific medical decisions. After two physician visits, experimental subjects evidenced significant improvement in glycemic control, whereas control subjects remained unchanged.

Environmental Factors

A number of treatment-associated contingencies may contribute to negative reinforcement of regimen adherence. Intensive insulin programs have been successful in promoting improved (i.e., near-normal) glycemic control but have also led to marked increases in severe hypoglycemia (Diabetes Control and Complications Trial [DCCT] Research Group, 1987) and significant weight gain (DCCT Research Group, 1988). Similarly, Wing, Klein, and Moss (1990) found that improved glycemic control in a population-based sample was associated with significant weight gain. Especially among women with diabetes, weight gain is widely perceived as strongly negative (Polonsky, Anderson, et al., 1993).

In addition, recent evidence suggests that elevated blood glucose levels are often not negatively reinforced by patient symptoms. Type I patients with poor glycemic control report feeling physically best at a blood glucose level significantly higher than the level at which those with good control report feeling their best. In addition, those with poor control report first perceiving hyperglycemic symptoms at a blood glucose level significantly higher than that reported by those in good control (Jacobson et al., 1990; Polonsky, Davis, Jacobson, & Anderson, 1992b). These data suggest that attempts to improve regimen adherence may be thwarted in those patients for whom hyperglycemia is not negatively reinforced (i.e., who feel best when blood glucose levels are too high).

Although treatment regimen goals may be prescribed imprecisely (e.g., "try to follow your meal plan more closely"), patients may develop unreasonably high self-expectations (e.g., "I must never 'cheat' on my diet," or "A blood glucose result of greater than 200 mg/dl means that I have done something wrong or bad"). Self-criticism may frequently occur in response to entirely reasonable diet excursions or uncontrollable blood glucose elevations. Such negative reinforcement may lead to markedly poorer regimen adherence or burnout. As Hoover (1988) described it, "few things generate burnout like the awful frustration of having followed instructions and done everything just right and still be failing to get the diabetes into control. At those times it seems no use to continue to try" (p. 322).

More common barriers to adherence have been studied, including such diabetes-specific treatment problems as time demands, expense, treatment complexity, inconvenience, and competing priorities. Using self-report scales designed to assess these barriers for each component of the treatment regimen, researchers have found that, for each specific treatment task, more self-reported barriers are associated with poorer adherence for the corresponding treatment task (Glasgow et al., 1986; Irvine, Saunders, Blank, & Carter, 1990).

Improved regimen adherence may lead to more frequent hypoglycemia, unwanted weight gain, and maintenance of blood glucose at a level lower than at which the patient feels best. With imprecise treatment goals, self-criticism may continue unabated. Moreover, as noted earlier, improved adherence does not necessarily lead to improved glycemic control. Although regimen adherence may reduce the likelihood of long-term complications, immediate reinforcers (commonly more potent) are likely to be decidedly negative, positive reinforcers rare, and environmental barriers plentiful. It is not surprising that difficulties with adherence are widespread.

Stress and Distress in Diabetes

Recent research has suggested that psychosocial stress may affect glycemic control in IDDM indirectly (through regimen behaviors) or directly (through psychophysiological pathways). It is evident that chronic stress can interfere with routine treatment tasks (e.g., stressful demands at work can lead to less regular exercise) or promote deleterious behaviors (e.g., binge eating or excessive alcohol intake). Indeed, significant associations between poor regimen adherence, especially in meal plan deviations, and chronic stress have been documented (Frenzel, McCaul, Glasgow, & Schafer, 1988; Hanson & Pritchert, 1986).

Descriptive studies have also indicated that chronic psychosocial stress may be directly linked to poor glycemic control in adults and adolescents with IDDM (i.e., statistically controlling for adherence behaviors; Cox et al., 1984; Hanson et al., 1987a; Hanson & Pritchert, 1986). However, laboratory studies have consistently failed to support such an association (Delamater et al., 1988; Edwards & Yates, 1985; Gilbert, Johnson, Silverstein, & Malone, 1989; Kemmer et al., 1986). Marked changes in autonomic and hormonal responses have been observed following experimental induction of acute stress in IDDM patients (Kemmer et al., 1986), but corresponding changes in blood glucose have not been observed. Similarly, results have been largely equivocal in several studies that examined the effects of relaxation training on blood glucose levels (Feinglos, Hastedt, & Surwit, 1987; McGrady, Bailey, & Good, 1991; Surwit & Feinglos, 1983). These data suggest that relaxation may be of value to NIDDM patients (Surwit & Feinglos, 1983), but the evidence for glycemic effects in IDDM patients is mixed (Feinglos et al., 1987; McGrady et al., 1991). In general, these findings are in marked contrast to patients' reports, in which the belief is common that acute and chronic stress strongly and directly influence blood glucose levels (Cox et al., 1984).

Recent evidence has pointed to additional levels of complexity, which suggests that there may be individual differences in glycemic responses to stress. It is possible that some patients typically respond to stress with elevations in blood glucose, whereas other patients characteristically respond with a lowering of blood glucose and others do not respond at all (Gonder-Frederick, Carter, Cox, & Clarke, 1990). In addition, a glycemic response to stress may occur only when particular styles of coping, including anger (Peyrot & McMurray, 1992), Type A behavior (Stabler et al., 1987), and poor social competence (Hanson et al., 1987b), are engaged. Differences in stressor charac- teristics (Gonder-Frederick et al., 1990) and antecedent glycemic status (Cox & Gonder-Frederick, 1991) may also moderate the effects of stress on blood glucose levels. These data suggest that psychosocial stress may directly interfere with regimen adherence, potentially leading to poorer glycemic control. It is also plausible that stress may directly influence glycemic control, although research findings are inconsist- ent. In both cases, psychosocial moderator variables, especially dif- ferences in coping styles, are likely to figure strongly.

Links between glycemic control and diabetes-specific distress have also been reported (Polonsky et al., 1991). Such distress may occur in response to any of a variety of personal, social, and environmental contingencies (see Table 1), resulting in feelings of depression, anger, being overwhelmed, or denial. The Problem Areas in Diabetes Survey (Polonsky et al., 1991), which comprises 24 items, each representing an area of diabetes-specific distress, was developed to assess diabetes- specific distress. These areas of distress include difficult feelings about diabetes (e.g., "feeling angry when you think about having and living with diabetes"), interpersonal distress (e.g., "feeling that your friends and family are not supportive of your diabetes management efforts"), and frustration with aspects of the regimen (e.g., "not having clear and concrete goals for your diabetes care"). On a 6-point Likert scale, 450 insulin-managed women rated the degree to which each item was currently problematic for them, from 1 (*no problem*) to 6 (*serious problem*). A total scale score was computed by averaging the item responses.

As shown in Table 1, patients reported significant levels of diabetes- specific distress. For example, 42% indicated that "worrying about the future and the possibility of serious complications" was a serious problem for them, and 30% reported that "feeling guilty or anxious when you get off track with your diabetes management" was of great concern. High levels of reported distress were associated with poor regimen adherence ($r = 0.44$, $p < .0001$) and poor glycemic control ($r = 0.32$, $p < .0001$). Although cause and effect cannot be determined, these data suggest that diabetes-specific distress may affect glycemic control, with patient burnout leading to impaired regimen adherence (see Cox & Gonder-Frederick, 1992).

Table 1

Distribution of Problem Areas in Diabetes Survey Items Scores

Item	No problem (% scoring < 2)	Serious problem (% scoring > 5)
Worrying about the future and the possibility of serious complications	20.9	42.0
Feeling guilty or anxious when you get off track with your DM management	31.3	30.3
Now following your meal plan successfully	40.3	27.2
Feeling scared when you think about having/living with DM	45.3	25.7
Feeling discouraged with your DM regimen	39.1	24.3
Feeling depressed when you think about having/living with DM	48.2	24.0
Poor BG control	40.3	22.8
Feeling constantly concerned about food and eating	44.9	22.4
Feeling "burned out" by the constant effort to manage DM	50.2	22.2
Feeling angry when you think about having/living with DM	53.6	22.2
Not testing BG frequently enough	50.7	21.7
Coping with complications of DM	48.7	20.0
Feeling that DM is taking up too much mental and physical energy	57.6	18.2
Worrying about reactions	56.0	17.4
Not knowing if the mood or feelings you are experiencing are related to your BG levels	45.5	17.3
Feeling overwhelmed by your DM regimen	53.4	16.7
Feeling alone with DM	58.0	15.4
Feelings of deprivation regarding food and meals	52.6	15.0
Not "accepting" DM	64.9	14.7
Not having clear and concrete goals for your DM care	60.7	10.9
Uncomfortable interactions around DM with family/friends who do not have DM	69.3	10.5
Not doing insulin injections in a timely fashion	77.2	9.4
Feeling that friends/family are not supportive of DM management efforts	71.7	8.0
Feeling unsatisfied with your DM physician	85.5	4.9

Note. DM = diabetes mellitus; BG = blood sugar.

In summary, numerous psychosocial factors may influence diabetes self-management and glycemic control. Most studies, however, have been cross-sectional and correlational in design; few studies have examined regimen behaviors over time (see Rubin et al., 1989). This makes it difficult to distinguish factors that may be direct contributors to self-care from those that may have resulted from poor self-care. In fact, it may be that a significant number of these variables function in a cyclical fashion, serving as both causes and effects. For example, the cause of observed associations between family conflict and poor glycemic control in IDDM adolescents (Anderson, 1990) may begin with impairment of glycemic control (perhaps, unknown to the family, due to pubertal changes, not impaired regimen adherence; see Amiel, Sherwin, Simonson, Lauritano, & Tamborlane, 1986), which leads to widespread family disagreements. In time, the ongoing conflict may lead to feelings of frustration and hopelessness in family members, which thereby results in an abdication of regimen responsibilities and worsening of glycemic control.

Psychosocial Assessment and Treatment

A primary concern for researchers is the development of appropriate assessment protocols for the identification of those patients who are at highest risk for self-management problems and the construction of effective psychosocial interventions. It is important to remember that difficulties with adherence are usually strategic. Coping with diabetes and diabetes treatment is a process of behavioral self-regulation (Surwit et al., 1983). Patients respond in a rational fashion to a bewildering array of diabetes-specific positive and negative reinforcers, social and emotional pressures, and diabetes-related attitudes. The just-presented data suggest that diabetes-specific factors may play as large a role in determining adherence as do nonspecific factors, such as stress and depression (Glasgow, 1991; Lustman, Griffith, Gavard, & Clouse, 1992). Although nonspecific factors must be examined, a psychosocial evaluation should focus on the following: (a) diabetes-relevant attitudes (health beliefs, Brownlee-Duffeck et al., 1987; hypoglycemic fear, Cox et al., 1987; attitudes toward euglycemia and hyperglycemia, Polonsky et al., 1992b), (b) diabetes-focused social support (family behavior, Schafer et al., 1986), (c) diabetes-specific emotional distress

(Polonsky et al., 1991), and (d) diabetes-associated environmental barriers (Irvine et al., 1990). Special attention should be given to patients' self-management struggles around food and eating (Glasgow, 1991; Polonsky et al., 1991). In each case, brief psychometric instruments are available, although test development is still preliminary.

Few comprehensive psychosocial interventions in diabetes have been reported. Psychoeducational programs to promote coping and problem-solving training relevant to diabetes treatment issues have been found to affect regimen adherence and consequent glycemic control positively (Anderson, Wolf, Burkhardt, Cornell, & Bacon, 1989; Rubin, Peyrot, & Saudek, 1989, 1991, 1993; Satin, LaGreca, Zigo, & Skyler, 1989). Psychoeducational intervention has also been directed toward improving patients' accuracy in estimating blood glucose levels (Cox et al., 1991). Preliminary data indicate that patients can significantly improve their ability to detect hypoglycemia and hyperglycemia (Cox et al., 1989; Nurick & Johnson, 1991), thereby leading to improved glycemic control (Cox et al., 1991). Psychosocial treatment intervention for regimen adherence problems should center on the following four strategies.

Normalize the Experience of Diabetes-Associated Distress

It must be acknowledged to the patient that living with diabetes is commonly frustrating and overwhelming. Feelings of burnout are an understandable response to coping with a remarkably difficult illness (Hoover, 1988; Polonsky et al., 1991). Aspects of distress should be carefully evaluated. From this base of understanding, problem-solving strategies may be used to ameliorate such distress and promote more effective motivation for treatment adherence.

Concretize the Treatment Regimen

As just discussed, treatment directions and expectations may be imprecise, leaving patients unable to congratulate themselves when they have satisfactorily completed their appropriate regimen behaviors. Over a 1-week period, for example, exactly what frequency of SMBG should be considered successful? It is important that treatment behavior recommendations be clearly detailed and written. In addition, recommendations must be tailored to the patient's life-style and abilities (Glasgow, 1991), with gradual regimen changes being instituted one at a time. Regimen behavior goals must be reasonable as well as concrete. In this manner, the likelihood of less-than-perfect adherence is normalized for the patient, leading to fewer feelings of personal failure and the possibility of a more honest alliance between the patient and health care providers (see Delameter et al., 1988). As Kurtz (1990) noted, "one should explicitly state that perfect adherence is not expected and acknowledge the magnitude of the tasks at hand" (p. 54). With clear target goals for treatment, it is easier to self-generate positive reinforcement. Patients should be encouraged to clarify (and negotiate) target goals with their physician (using the model of Greenfield et al., 1988) and to independently develop problem-solving skills for concretizing their own regimen expectations.

Modify Health Beliefs

Open-ended discussion with the patient regarding his or her beliefs about the utility of regimen adherence is essential. High levels of perceived threat (e.g., "severe complications are inevitable") as well as low levels (e.g., "diabetes is no big deal") may be associated with poor adherence. Benefits and costs of treatment behaviors must be thoroughly examined and consciously weighed. Patients' confidence in their ability to complete all regimen tasks (diabetes self-efficacy) should also be reviewed. In subsequent problem-solving discussions, negotiated behavioral changes can then lead to marked shifts in perceived treatment costs and subsequent adherence. One young woman, for example, tended to skip her evening insulin injection at home because she was anxious to get to her boyfriend's house as quickly as possible each evening. Following the psychosocial evaluation, she agreed to leave extra insulin and syringes at her boyfriend's house and began to take her evening injection there. The perceived treatment cost ("too many minutes away from my boyfriend") had been significantly reduced, and episodes of insulin omission soon ceased.

Maximize Social Support

There are likely to be large individual differences in diabetes-related social support needs. For most patients, however, enhancing appropriate support may be the most powerful means for promoting greater adherence. Recent evidence suggests that isolation and secretiveness about diabetes issues are strongly associated with poor regimen adherence (Polonsky et al., 1991). Careful evaluation is vital; anecdotal evidence suggests that patients are commonly confused and frustrated with diabetes-related support from friends and family. For example, seemingly supportive comments, such as "Should you be eating that?" or "You seem upset, maybe you should check your blood sugars!" are rarely perceived as supportive by the patient. Open-ended discussion may help patients to clarify and detail the particular forms of support that would be most beneficial for them (e.g., "inviting my neighbor over for dinner may help me to manage my eating during the evening"). Patients should be encouraged to approach members of their support network, including their health care providers, and negotiate for the specific types of support they may need.

Conclusion

Living with diabetes can be difficult, and the daily self-management tasks of diabetes can lead to significant frustration. Poor adherence to the self-management regimen is surprisingly common. There is a growing body of research data that points to the strategic influence of intrapersonal (e.g., diabetes-specific health beliefs), interpersonal (e.g., diabetes-specific social support), and environmental factors (e.g., treatment-associated weight gain) on adherence. Although psychopathology and life stress may contribute to poor adherence, these data suggest that the most influential psychosocial factors are diabetes-specific.

It is also apparent that diabetes-specific distress occurs frequently. For example, patients may develop disordered eating patterns, fear of hypoglycemia, or feelings of loneliness and isolation with their illness. They may become preoccupied with the fear of severe diabetic complications developing and feel overwhelmed or burned out by an illness and regimen that continually frustrate them. Distress may result from frustrations with self-management, but it may also promote poor adherence, leading to a reinforcing cycle of worsening blood glucose control and greater diabetes-specific distress.

Comprehensive psychosocial and behavioral intervention in diabetes is greatly needed, yet few programs have been developed. Although generic treatment approaches (e.g., stress management) may be of some value in promoting adherence, truly effective intervention should be diabetes-focused, emphasizing careful assessment and a problem-solving approach toward self-management and diabetes-specific distress. The most important elements of treatment are (a) normalizing diabetes-specific distress, (b) concretizing the self-management regimen (including the establishment of reasonable treatment goals), (c) identifying and modifying diabetes-specific health beliefs, and (d) maximizing diabetes-specific social support.

REFERENCES

Amiel, S. A., Sherwin, R. S., Simonson, D. C., Lauritano, A. A., & Tamborlane, W. V. (1986). Impaired insulin action in puberty: A contributing factor to poor glycemic control in adolescents with diabetes. *New England Journal of Medicine, 315,* 215–219.

Anderson, B. J. (1990). Diabetes and adaptation in family systems. In C. S. Holmes (Ed.), *Neuropsychological and behavioral aspects of diabetes* (pp. 85–101). New York: Springer-Verlag.

Anderson, B. J., Wolf, F. M., Burkhardt, M. T., Cornell, R. G., & Bacon, G. E. (1989). Effects of peer-group intervention on metabolic control of adolescents with IDDM: A randomized outpatient study. *Diabetes Care, 12,* 179–183.

Becker, M. H., & Janz, N. K. (1985). The health belief model applied to understanding diabetes regimen compliance. *Diabetes Educator, 11,* 41–47.

Birk, R., & Spencer, M. (1987). The prevalence of anorexia nervosa, bulimia, and induced glycosuria in diabetic females [abstract]. *Diabetes, 36*(Suppl. 1), 88.

Bond, G. G., Aiken, L. S., & Somerville, S. C. (1992). The health belief model and adolescents with insulin-dependent diabetes mellitus. *Health Psychology, 11,* 190–198.

Brownlee-Duffeck, M., Peterson, L., Simonds, J. F., Goldstein, J. F., Kilo, C., & Hoette, S. (1987). The role of health beliefs in the regimen adherence and metabolic control of adolescents and adults with diabetes mellitus. *Journal of Consulting and Clinical Psychology, 55,* 139–144.

Cerkoney, K. A. B., & Hart, L. K. (1980). The relationship between the health belief model and compliance of persons with diabetes mellitus. *Diabetes Care, 3,* 594–598.

Christensen, N. K., Terry, R. D., Wyatt, S., Pichert, J. W., & Lorenz, R. A. (1983). Quantitative assessment of dietary adherence in patients with insulin-dependent diabetes mellitus. *Diabetes Care, 6,* 245–250.

Cox, D. J., & Gonder-Frederick, L. A. (1991). The role of stress in diabetes mellitus. In P. McCabe, N. Schneiderman, T. Field, & J. Skyler (Eds.), *Stress and coping* (pp. 119–134). Hillsdale, NJ: Erlbaum.

Cox, D. J., & Gonder-Frederick, L. A. (1992). Major developments in behavioral diabetes research. *Journal of Consulting and Clinical Psychology, 60,* 628–638.

Cox, D. J., Gonder-Frederick, L. A., Julian, D., Cryer, P., Lee, J. H., Richards, F. E., & Clarke, W. (1991). Intensive versus standard blood glucose awareness training (BGAT) with insulin-dependent diabetes: Mechanisms and ancillary effects. *Psychosomatic Medicine, 53,* 453–462.

Cox, D. J., Gonder-Frederick, L. A., Lee, J. H., Julian, D., Carter, W. R., & Clarke, W. (1989). Effects and correlates of blood glucose awareness training among patients with IDDM. *Diabetes Care, 12,* 313–318.

Cox, D. J., Irvine, A., Gonder-Frederick, L., Nowacek, G., & Butterfield, J. (1987). Fear of hypoglycemia: Quantification, validation, and utilization. *Diabetes Care, 10,* 617–621.

Cox, D. J., Taylor, A. G., Nowacek, G., Holley-Wilcox, P., Pohl, S. L., & Guthrow, E. (1984). The relationship between psychological stress and insulin-dependent diabetic blood glucose control: Preliminary investigations. *Health Psychology, 3,* 63–75.

Delamater, A. M., Kurtz, S. M., Bubb, J., White, N. H., & Santiago, J. V. (1987). Stress and coping in relation to metabolic control of adolescents with Type 1 diabetes. *Developmental and Behavioral Pediatrics, 8,* 136–140.

Delamater, A. M., Kurtz, S. M., White, N. H., & Santiago, J. V. (1988). Effects of social demand on reports of self-monitored blood glucose in adolescents with Type I diabetes mellitus. *Journal of Applied Social Psychology, 18,* 491–502.

Diabetes Control and Complications Trial Research Group. (1987). Diabetes control and complications trial (DCCT): Results of a feasibility study. *Diabetes Care, 10,* 1–19.

Diabetes Control and Complications Trial Research Group. (1988). Weight gain associated with intensive therapy in the diabetes control and complications trial. *Diabetes Care, 11,* 567–573.

Edelwich, J., & Brodsky, A. (1986). *Diabetes: Caring for your emotions as well as your health.* Reading, MA: Addison-Wesley.

Edwards, C., & Yates, A. J. (1985). The effects of cognitive task demand on subjective stress and blood glucose levels in diabetics and nondiabetics. *Journal of Psychosomatic Research, 29,* 59–69.

Fairburn, C. G., Peveler, R. C., Davies, B., Mann, J. I., & Mayou, R. A. (1991). Eating disorders in young adults with insulin-dependent diabetes mellitus: A controlled study. *British Medical Journal, 303,* 17–20.

Feinglos, M. N., Hastedt, P., & Surwit, R. S. (1987). Effects of relaxation therapy on patients with Type I diabetes mellitus. *Diabetes Care, 10,* 72–75.

Frenzel, M. P., McCaul, K. D., Glasgow, R. E., & Schafer, L. C. (1988). The relationship of stress and coping to regimen adherence and glycemic control of diabetes. *Journal of Social and Clinical Psychology, 6,* 77–87.

Gilbert, B. O., Johnson, S. B., Silverstein, J., & Malone, J. (1989). Psychological and physiological responses to acute laboratory stressors in insulin-dependent diabetes mellitus adolescents and nondiabetic controls. *Journal of Pediatric Psychology, 14,* 577–591.

Glasgow, R. E. (1991). Compliance to diabetes regimens: Conceptualization, complexity, and determinants. In J. A. Cramer & B. Spiker (Eds.), *Patient compliance in medical practice and clinical trials* (pp. 209–224). New York: Raven Press.

Glasgow, R. E., McCaul, K. D., & Schafer, L. C. (1986). Barriers to regimen adherence among persons with insulin-dependent diabetes. *Journal of Behavioral Medicine, 9,* 65–77.

Glasgow, R. E., McCaul, K. D., & Schafer, L. C. (1987). Self-care behaviors and glycemic control in Type I diabetes. *Journal of Chronic Diseases, 40,* 399–412.

Glasgow, R. E., & Toobert, D. J. (1988). Social environment and regimen adherence among Type II diabetic patients. *Diabetes Care, 11,* 377–386.

Glasgow, R. E., Toobert, D. J., Riddle, M., Donnelly, J., Mitchell, D. L., & Calder, D. (1989). Diabetes-specific social learning variables and self-care behaviors among persons with Type II diabetes. *Health Psychology, 8,* 285–303.

Gonder-Frederick, L. A., Carter, W. R., Cox, D. J., & Clarke, W. L. (1990). Environmental stress and blood glucose change in insulin-dependent diabetes mellitus. *Health Psychology, 9,* 503–515.

Gonder-Frederick, L. A., Cox, D. J., Bobbitt, S. A., & Pennebaker, J. W. (1989). Mood changes associated with blood glucose fluctuations in insulin-dependent diabetes mellitus. *Health Psychology, 8,* 45–59.

Goodall, T. A., & Halford, W. K. (1991). Self-management of diabetes mellitus: A critical review. *Health Psychology, 10,* 1–8.

Graber, A. L., Davidson, P., Brown, A. W., McRae, J. R., & Wooldridge, K. (1992). Dropout and relapse during diabetes care. *Diabetes Care, 15,* 1477–1483.

Greco, P., LaGreca, A. M., Ireland, S., Wick, P., Freeman, C., Agramonte, R., Gutt, M., & Skyler, J. S. (1990). Assessing adherence in IDDM: A comparison of two methods. *Diabetes, 39*(Suppl. 1), 165A.

Green, L., Wysocki, T., & Reineck, B. (1990). Fear of hypoglycemia in children and adolescents with diabetes. *Journal of Pediatric Psychology, 15,* 633–641.

Greenfield, S., Kaplan, S. H., Ware, J. E., Yano, E. M., & Frank, H. J. L. (1988). Patients' participation in medical care: Effects on blood sugar control and quality of life in diabetes. *Journal of General Internal Medicine, 3,* 448–457.

Hampson, S. E., Glasgow, R. E., & Toobert, D. J. (1990). Personal models of diabetes and their relation to self-care activities. *Health Psychology, 9,* 632–646.

Hanson, C. L., Cigrang, J. A., Harris, M. A., Carle, D. L., Relyea, G., & Burghen, G. A. (1989). Coping styles in youth with insulin-dependent diabetes mellitus. *Journal of Consulting and Clinical Psychology, 57,* 644–651.

Hanson, C. L., Henggeler, S. W., & Burghen, G. A. (1987a). Model of associations between psychosocial variables and health-outcome measures of adolescents with IDDM. *Diabetes Care, 10,* 752–758.

Hanson, C. L., Henggeler, S. W., & Burghen, G. A. (1987b). Social competence and parental support as mediators of the link between stress and metabolic control in adolescents with insulin-dependent diabetes mellitus. *Journal of Consulting and Clinical Psychology, 55,* 529–533.

Hanson, C. L., & Pritchert, J. W. (1986). Perceived stress and diabetes control in adolescents. *Health Psychology, 5,* 439–452.

Hauser, S. T., Jacobson, A. M., Lavori, P., Wolfsdorf, J., Herskowitz, R., Milley, J., Bliss, R., Gelfand, E., & Wertlieb, D. (1990). Adherence among children and adolescents with insulin-dependent diabetes mellitus over a four-year longitudinal follow-up: II. Immediate and long-term linkages with the family milieu. *Journal of Pediatric Psychology, 15,* 527–542.

Herman, W. H., Teutsch, S. M., & Geiss, L. S. (1987). Diabetes mellitus. In R. W. Amler & H. B. Dull (Eds.), *Closing the gap: The burden of unnecessary illness* (pp. 72–82). New York: Oxford University Press.

Hirsch, I. B., Farkas-Hirsch, R., & Skyler, J. S. (1990). Intensive insulin therapy for treatment of Type I diabetes mellitus. *Diabetes Care, 13,* 1265–1283.

Hoover, J. W. (1988). Patient 'burnout' can explain noncompliance. In L. P. Krall (Ed.), *World book of diabetes in practice* (Vol. 3, pp. 321–324). New York: Elsevier Science.

Irvine, A. A., Cox, D. J., & Gonder-Frederick, L. A. (1992). Fear of hypoglycemia: Relationship to physical and psychological symptoms in patients with insulin-dependent diabetes mellitus. *Health Psychology, 11,* 135–138.

Irvine, A. A., Saunders, J. T., Blank, M. B., & Carter, W. R. (1990). Validation of scale measuring environmental barriers to diabetes-regimen adherence. *Diabetes Care, 13,* 705–711.

Jacobson, A. M., Adler, A. G., Derby, L., Anderson, B. J., & Wolfsdorf, J. I. (1991). Clinic attendance and glycemic control: Study of contrasting groups of patients with IDDM. *Diabetes Care, 14,* 599–601.

Jacobson, A. M., Adler, A. G., Wolfsdorf, J. I., Anderson, B. J., & Derby, L. (1990). Psychological characteristics of adults with IDDM: Comparison of patients in poor and good glycemic control. *Diabetes Care, 13,* 375–381.

Jacobson, A. M., Hauser, S., Anderson, B. J., & Polonsky, W. H. (in press). Psychosocial aspects of diabetes. In C. Kahn & G. Weir (Eds.), *Joslin's diabetes mellitus* (13th ed.). Philadelphia: Lea & Febiger.

Kaplan, R. M., & Hartwell, S. L. (1987). Differential effects of social support and social network on physiological and social outcomes in men and women with Type II diabetes mellitus. *Health Psychology, 6,* 387–398.

Kemmer, F. W., Bisping, R., Steingruber, H. J., Baar, H., Hardtmann, F., Schlaghecke, R., & Berger, M. (1986). Psychological stress and metabolic control in patients with Type I diabetes mellitus. *New England Journal of Medicine, 314,* 1078–1086.

Kurtz, S. M. S. (1990). Adherence to diabetes regimens: Empirical status and clinical applications. *Diabetes Educator, 16,* 50–56.

LaGreca, A. M., Schwarz, L. T., & Satin, W. (1987). Eating patterns in young women with IDDM: Another look. *Diabetes Care, 10,* 659–660.

Lefebvre, P. (1986). Clinical diabetes mellitus—An update. In L. P. Krall (Ed.), *World book of diabetes in practice* (Vol. 2, pp. 1–2). New York: Elsevier Science.

Lichtman, S. W., Pisarska, K., Berman, E. R., Pestone, M., Dowling, H., Offenbacher, E., Weisel, H., Heshka, S., Matthews, D. E., & Heymsfield, S. B. (1992). Discrepancy between self-reported and actual caloric intake and exercise in obese subjects. *New England Journal of Medicine, 327,* 1893–1898.

Lustman, P. J., Griffith, L. S., & Clouse, R. E. (1988). Depression in adults with diabetes: Results of 5-year follow-up study. *Diabetes Care, 11,* 605–612.

Lustman, P. J., Griffith, L. S., Clouse, R. E., & Cryer, P. E. (1986). Psychiatric illness in diabetes mellitus: Relationship to symptoms and glucose control. *Journal of Nervous and Mental Disease, 174,* 736–742.

Lustman, P. J., Griffith, L. S., Gavard, J. A., & Clouse, R. E. (1992). Depression in adults with diabetes. *Diabetes Care, 15,* 1631–1639.

Marcus, M. D., & Wing, R. R. (1990). Eating disorders and diabetes. In C. S. Holmes (Ed.), *Neuropsychological and behavioral aspects of diabetes* (pp. 102–121). New York: Springer-Verlag.

Mazze, R. S., Shamoon, H., Pasmantier, R., Lucido, D., Murphy, J., Hartman, K., Kuykendall, V., & Lopatin, W. (1984). Reliability of blood glucose monitoring by patients with diabetes mellitus. *American Journal of Medicine, 77,* 211–217.

McGrady, A., Bailey, B. K., & Good, M. P. (1991). Controlled study of biofeedback-assisted relaxation in Type I diabetes. *Diabetes Care, 14,* 360–365.

Nurick, M. A., & Johnson, S. B. (1991). Enhancing blood glucose awareness in adolescents and young adults with IDDM. *Diabetes Care, 14,* 1–7.

Peyrot, M. F., & McMurray, J. F. (1992). Stress buffering and glycemic control. *Diabetes Care, 15,* 842–846.

Polonsky, W. H., Anderson, B. J., & Lohrer, P. A. (1991). Disordered eating and regimen manipulation in women with diabetes: Relationships to glycemic control. *Diabetes, 40*(Suppl. 1), 540A.

Polonsky, W. H., Anderson, B. J., Lohrer, P. A., Aponte, J. E., & Jacobson, A. M. (1993). *Insulin omission in women with IDDM.* Unpublished manuscript.

Polonsky, W. H., Anderson, B. J., Lohrer, P. A., & Schwartz, C. (1991, February). *Assessment of diabetes-specific distress.* Paper presented at the Invitational Conference for Behavioral Research in Diabetes, Miami, FL.

Polonsky, W. H., Davis, C. L., Jacobson, A. M., & Anderson, B. J. (1992a). Correlates of hypoglycemic fear in diabetes mellitus. *Health Psychology, 11,* 199–202.

Polonsky, W. H., Davis, C. L., Jacobson, A. M., & Anderson, B. J. (1992b). Hyperglycaemia, hypoglycaemia, and blood glucose control in diabetes: Symptom perceptions and treatment strategies. *Diabetic Medicine, 9,* 120–125.

Polonsky, W. H., Davis, C. L., Jacobson, A. M., & Anderson, B. J. (1993). *Hypoglycemic fear and glycemic control in diabetes mellitus.* Unpublished manuscript.

Rodin, G. M., Craven, J., Littlefield, C., Murray, M., & Daneman, D. (1991). Eating disorders and intentional insulin undertreatment in adolescent females with diabetes. *Psychosomatics, 32,* 171–176.

Rodin, G. M., Johnson, L. E., Garfinkel, P. E., Daneman, D., & Kenshole, A. B. (1986). Eating disorders in female adolescents with insulin-dependent diabetes mellitus. *International Journal of Psychiatry in Medicine, 16,* 49–57.

Rubin, R. R., Biermann, J., & Toohey, B. (1992). *Psyching out diabetes.* Los Angeles: Lowell House.

Rubin, R. R., Peyrot, M., & Saudek, C. D. (1989). Effect of diabetes education on self-care, metabolic control, and emotional well-being. *Diabetes Care, 12,* 673–679.

Rubin, R. R., Peyrot, M., & Saudek, C. D. (1991). Differential effects of diabetes education on self-regulation and life-style behaviors. *Diabetes Care, 14,* 335–338.

Rubin, R. R., Peyrot, M., & Saudek, C. D. (1993). The effect of a diabetes education program incorporating coping skills training on emotional well-being and diabetes self-efficacy. *Diabetes Educator, 19,* 210–214.

Satin, W., LaGreca, A. M., Zigo, M. A., & Skyler, J. S. (1989). Diabetes in adolescence: Effects of multifamily group intervention and parental simulation of diabetes. *Journal of Pediatric Psychology, 14,* 259–275.

Schade, D. S., Drumm, D. A., Duckworth, W. C., & Eaton, R. P. (1985). The etiology of incapacitating, brittle diabetes. *Diabetes Care, 8,* 12–20.

Schafer, L. C., McCaul, K. D., & Glasgow, R. E. (1986). Supportive and nonsupportive family behaviors: Relationships to adherence and metabolic control in persons with Type I diabetes. *Diabetes Care, 9,* 179–185.

Stabler, B., Surwit, R. S., Lane, J. D., Morris, M. A., Litton, J., & Feinglos, M. N. (1987). Type A behavior pattern and blood glucose control in diabetic children. *Psychosomatic Medicine, 49,* 313–316.

Stancin, L., Link, D. L., & Reuter, J. M. (1989). Binge eating and purging in young women with IDDM. *Diabetes Care, 12,* 601–603.

Strowig, S., & Raskin, P. (1992). Glycemic control and diabetic complications. *Diabetes Care, 15,* 1126–1140.

Surwit, R. S., & Feinglos, M. N. (1983). The effects of relaxation in glucose tolerance in non-insulin-dependent diabetes. *Diabetes Care, 6,* 176–179.

Surwit, R. S., Feinglos, M. N., & Scovern, A. W. (1983). Diabetes and behavior: A paradigm for health psychology. *American Psychologist, 38,* 255–262.

Weiner, M. F., & Skipper, F. (1979). Euglycemia: A psychological study. *International Journal of Psychiatry in Medicine, 9,* 281–288.

Wilson, D. P., & Endres, R. K. (1986). Compliance with blood glucose monitoring in children with Type I diabetes mellitus. *Journal of Paediatrics, 108,* 1022–1024.

Wing, R. R., Klein, R., & Moss, S. E., (1990). Weight gain associated with improved glycemic control in population-based sample of subjects with Type I diabetes. *Diabetes Care, 13,* 1106–1109.

Wing, R. R., Marcus, M. D., Epstein, L. H., & Jawad, A. (1991). A "family-based" approach to the treatment of obese Type II diabetic patients. *Journal of Consulting and Clinical Psychology, 59,* 156–162.

Premenstrual Syndromes: A Health Psychology Critique of Biomedically Oriented Research

Jean A. Hamilton and Sheryle Gallant

A substantial number of women in the United States and else-where report mood and behavior changes that are linked in timing with the menstrual cycle. Psychiatric researchers have been especially interested in premenstrual dysphoric moods, as evidenced by the psychiatric diagnosis *late luteal phase dysphoric disorder* (LLPDD), which first appeared in the psychiatric nomenclature in an appendix to the revised third edition of the *Diagnostic and Statistical Manual of Mental Disorders* (*DSM-III-R*, American Psychiatric Association, 1987; however, an interim draft of the fourth edition of the *DSM* [*DSM-IV*; American Psychiatric Association, in press], dated March 1, 1993, renames LLPDD *premenstrual dysphoric disorder*, pp. j:5, w:1). The proposed diagnosis was meant, in part, to advance research by making criteria for the selection of research subjects more uniform, thereby increasing comparability of studies. In this chapter, we generally refer to premenstrual syndromes (PMS)/LLPDD, specifying whenever possible when criteria for LLPDD have been met.

As shown in Figure 1, the menstrual cycle has been defined by endocrine physiologists in terms of cyclic sex steroid hormone (e.g., estradiol and progesterone) changes. Postmenstrually (i.e., in the follicular cycle phase), these hormone levels are low in magnitude and relatively unvarying over time. Premenstrually (e.g., in the luteal phase), the hormone levels are higher in magnitude and levels vary considerably over time; with the decline in progesterone premen-

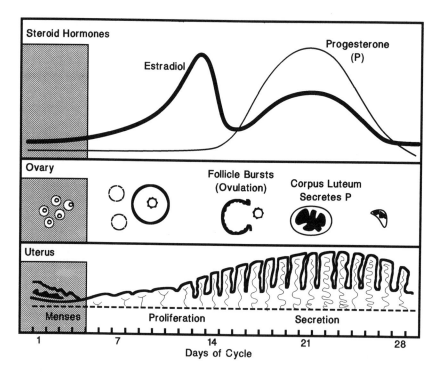

Figure 1. The top panel shows fluctuations in plasma estradiol and progesterone (P), which are regulated centrally, for example, by hypothalamic gonadotropin releasing hormone (GNRH, also known as LHRH), which stimulates release of luteinizing hormone from the pituitary, mediating ovulation; also released from the pituitary is follicle stimulating hormone. The middle panel shows corresponding events in the ovary, and the bottom panel shows events in the uterus. From *Harrison's Principles of Internal Medicine* (12th ed., p. 1781) edited by J. D. Wilson, E. Braunwald, K. J. Isselbacher, R. G. Petersdorf, J. B. Martin, A. S. Fauci, and R. K. Root, 1991, New York: McGraw-Hill. Copyright 1991 by McGraw-Hill. Adapted by permission.

strually, the proliferation of blood vessels lining the uterus can no longer be supported and menstruation begins. Changes in steroid hormones are in turn linked to the activity of central releasing hormones. The endocrine definition of the cycle has led some to the mistaken impression that the cycle is purely a biological phenomenon. After all, the correlation between cycles of hormonal changes and cycles of symptoms seems compelling, at least at first glance.

We argue, however, that the observed correlation in timing fails to support the implicit biomedical theory that menstrual-linked symptoms or syndromes are essentially, if not exclusively, biologically driven. Instead, empirical data strongly support an alternative hypothesis suggested by health psychology: The mind plays an important role in shaping the formation and expression of physical and mental symptoms in humans in general, including women's menstrual-linked symptoms in particular.

We begin with a synopsis of menstrual cycle research from the biomedical perspective. Next, we provide a health psychology critique of this research, documenting that symptoms and syndromes described with reference to the menstrual cycle lend themselves to a psychological conceptualization. Finally, we address clinical advances of interest to health psychologists and future directions for research.

Methodological innovations that were introduced in the 1980s, including the LLPDD diagnosis and other assessment procedures, heralded a new generation of research. In view of these methodological refinements, in this chapter we highlight only the past decade of research. In particular, we focus on three main types of studies: those that used the LLPDD criteria (along with some procedure to confirm subjects' perceptions of having increased symptoms premenstrually); those that assessed large groups of women living in the community, using epidemiological methods; and those that experimentally tested specific hypotheses. Previous reviews should be consulted for more detailed discussion of earlier research (Logue & Moos, 1986; Parlee, 1973; Rubinow & Roy-Byrne, 1984).

Synopsis of Research From the Biomedical Perspective

Biomedically oriented research appears to be powerfully straightforward and efficient. As we later demonstrate, however, its simplicity and apparent clarity come at a high price. For example, such research too often sidesteps important aspects of research design, such as the appropriate use of control groups, attention to the use of blind procedures (or other methods for addressing demand characteristics, expectancies, or attributional biases), and development of empirically based cutoff scores.

Assessment

The most commonly used method of assessment in biomedical research over the past decade has been the use of so-called prospective (although *concurrent* is a better term; e.g., Rubinow, Roy-Byrne, Hoban, Gold, & Post, 1984) daily ratings to "confirm" global, retrospective self-reports of menstrual-related symptoms. The addition of daily measures was meant to refine assessments because only about half of the women who identified themselves as having PMS demonstrated such changes on daily ratings (Endicott & Halbreich, 1982). Furthermore, many studies had shown that the increases in symptoms reported premenstrually on retrospective measures were often much greater than those observed when prospective measures were used (Englander-Golden, Whitmore, & Dienstbier, 1978; Rapkin, Chang, & Reading, 1988). Hence, prospective methods were meant to correct weaknesses in retrospective ratings, and this refinement ushered in a new generation of research.

Investigators at the National Institute of Mental Health (NIMH), most prominently Rubinow et al. (1984), took the lead in the U.S. in establishing methods of assessment. These investigators confirmed cases in which a 30% increase was observed in symptoms premenstrually compared with a postmenstrual baseline. As shown in Figure 2, the rating instrument used was a bipolar visual analogue scale for depression, for which zero is *most happy ever* and 100 is *most sad or depressed ever;* the midpoint is undefined, however, and severity cannot be defined in absolute terms or compared across subjects. Apparently, in some cases the difference was divided by the range of ratings over all cycle days, a method that has been labeled the "modified 30% change" rule (Gallant, Popiel, Hoffman, Chakraborty, & Hamilton, 1992b).

Rubinow's confirmation criterion acquired special importance because it was adopted by an NIMH Conference that he co-chaired in

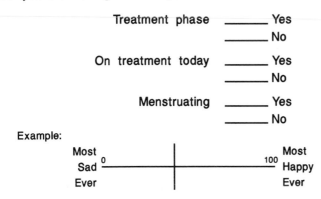

Name   Date

Please rate the way you feel **RIGHT NOW** on the following scales. Place a line through the scale line at a point that best describes how you are feeling on that particular item.

Treatment phase _____ Yes
_____ No

On treatment today _____ Yes
_____ No

Menstruating _____ Yes
_____ No

Example:

Most   0   100   Most
Sad ————————————|———————————— Happy
Ever   Ever

Figure 2. A bipolar daily rating form. From "Prospective Assessment of Menstrually Related Mood Disorders" by D. R. Rubinow, P. Roy-Byrne, M. C. Hoban, P. W. Gold, and R. M. Post, 1984, *American Journal of Psychiatry, 141,* p. 685. Copyright 1984 by the American Psychiatric Association. Reprinted by permission.

the early 1980s (Blume, 1983). Combined with early drafts for the LLPDD diagnosis (which appeared by about 1985), the 30% change rule has come to dominate biomedically oriented research over the past 7 years. Rubinow and Roy-Byrne (1984) suggested that the new criteria were so important in advancing research that previous studies were, in essence, obsolete.

An important new method of assessment was developed by Mitchell, Woods, and Lentz (1991). In a large, randomly selected community-based sample of nonpatient women, they used specific severity level and change criteria to define standardized cutoffs for establishing the diagnosis of PMS and for distinguishing between PMS and the premenstrual exacerbation of symptoms present over the cycle. One advantage of this method over the 30% change criterion is that the latter uses only percentage change without a baseline minimum severity level against which the percentage change is evaluated. Unfortunately, this can result in confirming PMS/LLPDD in women who have a small absolute level of and increase in symptoms premenstrually. The cutoffs established in the population study can be used in future research provided that the same daily symptom scale is used.

Another popular method in the U.S. is the Premenstrual Assessment Form (PAF), which consists of 95 items, each rated on a 6-point scale (Endicott, Halbreich, Schacht, & Nee, 1981). Using cluster analysis, this method has been useful in documenting subtypes of PMS. There is substantial overlap for various subtypes, however, because the clusters are not orthogonal. A daily rating form that is based on the PAF can also be used to confirm retrospective ratings.

Diagnosis

As previously summarized (Gallant (Alagna) & Hamilton, 1988, p. 273), LLPDD can be provisionally diagnosed using retrospective self-reports obtained by clinical interview. The criteria include reports of at least 5 of 10 mood, behavioral, or somatic symptoms (e.g., marked affective lability, anger or irritability, anxiety or tension, depressed mood, decreased interest in usual activities, fatigue or lack of energy, sense of difficulty concentrating, change in appetite, change in sleep, or other physical symptoms such as breast tenderness, with at least one symptom being affective) occurring for most menstrual cycles "during the last week of the luteal phase and remitted within a few days after onset of the follicular phase" (American Psychiatric Association, 1987, p. 369). Severity is indicated by description of symptoms as "marked" or "persistent" and by reports that the "disturbance seriously interferes with work or with usual social activities or relationships with others" (American Psychiatric Association, 1987, p. 369). In recognition of problems with retrospective reports of premenstrual symptoms, however, the diagnosis requires confirmation "by prospective daily self-ratings during at least two symptomatic cycles" (American Psychiatric Association, 1987, p. 369).

It is important to note that the LLPDD diagnosis, which Rubinow and other leaders in the field supported (Rovner, 1986, 1987; Severino & Moline, 1989, p. 21), focuses attention on only one syndrome, dysphoria, of many that are reported premenstrually (Halbreich, Endicott, Schacht, & Nee, 1982; Woods, 1987). Among the other psychiatric syndromes that can be linked in timing to the cycle are psychoses and mania (Altschule & Brem, 1963; Berlin, Bergey, & Money,

1982; Conrad & Hamilton, 1986; Endo, Daiguji, Asano, Yamashita, & Takahashi, 1978; Glick & Stewart, 1980; Teja, 1976; Williams & Weekes, 1952). In addition, a number of well-recognized medical illnesses are exacerbated in some women premenstrually. Of special interest are neurological disorders having a unique course in females, for example, premenstrually occurring migraine headaches (MacGregor, Chia, Vohrah, & Wilkinson, 1990) and seizures (Labbate, Shearer, & Waldrep, 1991; Newmark & Penry, 1980; Price, 1980; Schacter, 1988).

Moreover, the LLPDD diagnosis arbitrarily restricts attention to symptoms occurring premenstrually, despite the fact that menstrually linked symptoms are not confined to the premenstruum but occur during menses as well (Woods, 1987). Overall, women are most severely symptomatic during menses, not during the premenses. It is also well known that symptoms can be linked in timing with ovulation, so there are two peaks in symptoms, as shown in Figure 3 (Metcalf, Livesey, & Wells, 1989, Figure 2c; Rubinow et al., 1984, Figure 2, Patient 5).

By requiring the remission of symptoms at baseline, the definition of LLPDD focuses attention on "pure" premenstrual dysphoria, as

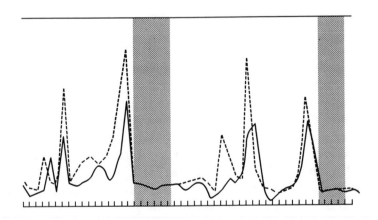

Figure 3. The shaded areas designate menstruation. Two peaks in daily symptom ratings are shown: one occurring premenstrually and the other around the time of ovulation, at midcycle. Solid line indicates morning ratings of depression, and broken line indicates evening ratings of depression. From "Prospective Assessment of Menstrually Related Mood Disorders" by D. R. Rubinow, P. Roy-Byrne, M. C. Hoban, P. W. Gold, and R. M. Post, 1984, *American Journal of Psychiatry, 141,* p. 686. Copyright 1984 by the American Psychiatric Association. Reprinted by permission.

opposed to dysphoric syndromes characterized by a premenstrual exacerbation of mild depressive symptoms that are present throughout the cycle (Jensvold, Reed, Jarrett, & Hamilton, 1992). The need to differentiate women with PMS/LLPDD from women with a premenstrual exacerbation of chronic symptoms highlights the importance of prospective ratings over the cycle because the two groups are often indistinguishable on the basis of premenstrual symptoms alone.

Epidemiology

Women of many cultures (including Turks, Nigerians, Americans, Apaches, Greeks, and Japanese) have retrospectively reported varying degrees of premenstrual symptoms (Janiger, Riffenburgh, & Karsh, 1972). Cross-culturally, there are consistencies in reports of premenstrual cramps, perceptions of lowered work or school performance, and anxiety, as assessed by randomized sampling of American, Italian, and Bahrainian women (Monagle, Al-Gasser, Woods, & Dan, 1992).

The prevalence of PMS depends on the symptoms assessed, the procedures used to assess symptoms (e.g., concurrent vs. retrospective ratings), the definition of premenstrual, and the severity criterion (Hamilton & Gallant, 1990). Despite variations in methods of assessment, Logue and Moos (1986) found that approximately 40% of women report symptoms of mild to moderate severity, and that 2–10% experience severe and sometimes incapacitating symptoms.

Although not specific to LLPDD, one of the better estimates of premenstrual affective symptoms comes from a large population-based sample of 2,650 urban women in Canada (Ramcharan, Love, Fick, & Goldfien, 1992). The study used the Moos Menstrual Distress Questionnaire (MDQ; Moos, 1985) cross-sectionally but decreased retrospective biases by limiting recall to the past 24 hours. Symptom severity was arbitrarily defined by scores at or above the 95th percentile, so that the overall percentage of women with self-rated severe scores on individual symptoms was about 5%. Using the MDQ "negative affect" scale, however, the proportion of naturally cycling women who experienced distressing affective symptoms premenstrually was found to be 1%.

In another community-based study that used daily diaries, Woods (1987) found that 13% of women exhibited a pattern of increased symptom severity in the premenses. Only 8% showed the classic PMS pattern of low severity postmenstrually and high severity premenstrually. More recently, Mitchell et al. (1991), also using daily diaries, found that 2.7–9.8% of women in a community sample demonstrated evidence of PMS.

Using *DSM-III-R* criteria and prospective ratings in a community survey, Haskett found that 3.4% of women of reproductive age had LLPDD (Haskett, unpublished raw data, 1987, cited in Rivera-Tovar & Frank, 1990). Similarly, a study of LLPDD that used a 30% change criterion in a sample of university women found a prevalence of 4.6% (Rivera-Tovar & Frank, 1990).

Comorbidity and Lifetime Psychiatric Diagnoses

The co-occurrence of PMS/LLPDD and other psychiatric diagnoses has drawn a great deal of interest. Three types of studies are discussed: (a) those that assessed rates of psychiatric comorbidity in PMS/LLPDD patients, (b) those that assessed lifetime psychiatric illness in PMS/LLPDD patients, and (c) those that assessed rates of premenstrual exacerbations of symptoms of a target syndrome in patients with other psychiatric diagnoses. Although earlier studies were suggestive of similar trends (Endicott et al., 1981; Stout, Steege, Blazer, & George, 1986), the present discussion is limited to studies of self-identified, treatment-seeking, and confirmed LLPDD patients, as documented by at least the 30% change criterion using daily measures, and to those that used standardized psychiatric interview schedules or other structured instruments.

LLPDD patients and comorbidity.   It is now well documented that LLPDD patients have substantial rates of psychiatric comorbidity. For *DSM-III-R* Axis I diagnoses, comorbidity rates vary from 34% for an anxiety or depressive disorder (Severino, Hurt, & Shindledecker, 1989) to 42% for affective disorders and 46% for adjustment disorders (Gise, Lebovits, Paddison, & Strain, 1990). In comparison, 1-month prevalence rates for anxiety and affective disorders combined in the Epidemiologic Catchment Area Survey (Regier et al., 1988) were approximately 18% for women of reproductive years (18–44 years).

Hence, it appears that prevalence rates for certain concurrent Axis I diagnoses are considerably higher among PMS/LLPDD patients than among the general population of women of reproductive years (e.g., the rate for anxiety and affective disorders is about twofold higher).

Lifetime psychiatric diagnoses. Confirmed LLPDD patients also have higher rates of lifetime psychiatric illness than expected in the general population. Rates of lifetime diagnosis in PMS patients vary from 30% (DeJong et al., 1985) to 46% (Pearlstein et al., 1990) for major depressive disorder, to 62% for an anxiety or depressive disorder (Severino et al., 1989), to as high as 44% for posttraumatic stress disorder (PTSD) (Jensvold & Putnam, 1990), to 78% for all Axis I disorders (Pearlstein et al., 1990). In comparison, the lifetime prevalence of major depressive episodes is about 7% for women, the lifetime prevalence of PTSD in young females is generally about 11% (Breslau, Davis, Andreski, & Peterson, 1991, who also reported higher rates of PTSD among females than among males, although Helzer, Robins, & McEvoy, 1987, reported a much lower overall rate of 1%), and the point prevalence for lifetime diagnosis overall (including a present episode) ranges from 28% to 38% (Robins et al., 1984). Hence, among LLPDD patients lifetime rates are 4 to nearly 7 times higher for depressive disorder, as much as 4 times higher for PTSD, and about 2.4 times higher for all Axis I disorders.

Differentiation of LLPDD and depressive disorders: Distinct entities? Given the high degree of overlap with depressive disorders, a final issue is whether LLPDD can in fact be distinguished from mood disorders. The LLPDD diagnosis assumes that premenstrual dysphoria can be distinguished from exacerbations of affective disorders, although it is silent on methods for doing so. The implication, however, is that LLPDD is a distinct entity. This conceptualization is supported by studies that documented the following: (a) Confirmed LLPDD (albeit with mood scores averaging only a 20% change) can exist even when current Axis I disorders are excluded (Beck, Gevirtz, & Mortola, 1990); (b) premenstrual episodes are distinct from major (endogenous) depression, as assessed by both psychological and cortisol secretory measures (Mortola, Girton, & Yen, 1989); (c) both a pure LLPDD group and an "intermittently depressed" (McMillan & Pihl, 1987) group having premenstrual exacerbations of subclinical depression (Chisholm, Jung, Cumming, Fox, & Cumming, 1990; Warner, Bancroft, Dixson, & Hampson, 1991) can be identified using self-reports, and these groups can be further distinguished using a dichotic listening task (McMillan & Pihl, 1987); (d) women with LLPDD fail to show changes that are characteristic of depression on measures of selective and incidental recall, perceptual speed, mental arithmetic, and tolerance for frustration (Rapkin, Chang, & Reading, 1989); (e) premenstrual dysphoria can become more pronounced after major depression is treated (Jensvold et al., 1992; Yonkers & White, 1992); and (f) in a follow-up study, a history of premenstrual depression (whether or not it is confirmed) is independently predictive of future risk of major depressive disorder, even when personal, lifetime, and family history are considered (Graze, Nee, & Endicott, 1990).

On the other hand, there is some evidence that suggests a menstrual artifact in determining rates of major depression (Hamilton, Gallant (Alagna), & Lloyd, 1989); although they remain to be replicated, the results of this study suggest that at least part of the excess of depression observed in women may result from premenstrual elevations in symptoms ratings as opposed to true differences in rates of major depression.

Other psychiatric disorders: Premenstrual exacerbations.   Data on the possible effects of the menstrual cycle on anxiety-related symptoms and syndromes are mixed. Brier, Charney, and Heninger (1986) found that 51% of agoraphobics experienced premenstrual exacerbations of anxiety symptoms. However, three other studies failed to find premenstrual exacerbations in patients with panic disorder (Cameron, Kuttesch, McPhee, & Curtis, 1988; Cook et al., 1990; Stein, Schmidt, Rubinow, & Uhde, 1989). A study of bulimics showed no relationship between food consumption and the menstrual cycle (Leon, Phelan, Kelly, & Patten, 1986). However, two other studies (Gladis & Walsh, 1987; Price, Torem, & DiMarzio, 1987) found an increase in binge frequency premenstrually; so indeed, the data are mixed.

Anecdotally, premenstrual exacerbations of dissociative experiences were reported by a woman with multiple personality disorder who was intensively studied at NIMH (Loewenstein, Hamilton, Alagna, Reid, & deVries, 1987). As shown in Figure 4, Jensvold and Putnam (1990) found that dissociative symptoms increased significantly—by nearly 30%—premenstrually compared with postmenstrually in the confirmed LLPDD patients but not in controls.

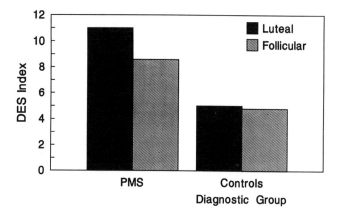

Figure 4. Dissociative experiences (DES) are plotted for two groups: PMS/LLPDD patients and controls. Ratings were summed for two time periods, with solid bars indicating luteal ratings (premenstrually) and shaded bars indicating follicular ratings (postmenstrually). From *Postabuse Syndromes in Premenstrual Syndrome Patients and Controls* (p. 16) by M. Jensvold and F. Putnam, 1990. Adapted by permission.

Etiology and Risk Factors

The etiology of premenstrual changes, including LLPDD, is unknown. A plethora of biological causes have been proposed and investigated, but the data remain inconclusive (Rubinow & Roy-Byrne, 1984; Severino & Moline, 1989).[1] It is clear, however, that basal measures of plasma hormones are insufficient to demonstrate differences between symptomatic and nonsymptomatic women. Further dis-

---

[1] Biological hypotheses include the hypotheses that premenstrual changes are caused directly by sex steroid hormones (progesterone deficiency, excess estrogen, reduced progesterone:estrogen ratio, biogenically active progesterone metabolites, and androgens) or by other hormones (prolactin, mineralocorticoids, thyroid, insulin and glucose metabolism, and melatonin), or that premenstrual changes are indirect effects that are neurotransmitter (biogenic amines such as catecholamines, serotonin, neurotensin, and acetylcholine) or peptide (endogenous opiate) mediated, or are indirectly caused by circadian rhythms, other substances with biological activity (prostaglandins, pyridoxine, or diet), allergic reactions, yeast infection, impaired capillary blood flow, genetic factors, or some combination of these.

cussed in following sections are risk factors, including results of genetic and twin studies, and biological findings that appear especially promising.

Risk factors.   Studies of confirmed LLPDD patients suggest that higher symptom ratings are modestly associated with the following: younger ages (i.e., in a sample of adults 25–45 years old, with a mean age of about 34 years, the correlation between age and symptom severity was − 0.24; Freeman, Sondheimer, & Rickels, 1988), low level of exercise ($r = -0.27$; Freeman et al., 1988), more children ($r = 0.25$; Freeman et al., 1988), and a psychiatric history, including a history of postnatal (postpartum) depression (Dinnerstein, Morse, & Gotts, 1988; Pearlstein et al., 1990; Warner et al., 1991).[2]

Possible risk factors related to reproductive and other medical history have been previously summarized in more detail (Hamilton, Parry, & Blumenthal, 1988). As examples, there is some evidence that "morning sickness" (nausea) during pregnancy may be related to vulnerability to psychiatric side effects, such as depressive symptoms induced by oral contraceptives (OCs), and women who experience difficulty in tolerating OCs typically report more severe premenstrual symptoms. Premenstrual symptoms may also be related to risk for severe postpartum "blues," although it is not clear whether PMS operates independently from other risk factors such as personal or family history of mood disorders. Such data are inconclusive, however, because history of PMS was assessed retrospectively.

Several studies have examined retrospective reports of PMS in monozygotic and dizygotic twin pairs (Dalton, Dalton, & Guthrie, 1987; Kendler et al., 1992; van den Akker, Stein, Neale, & Murray, 1987), although data were not necessarily available on twins reared together compared with those reared apart (Dalton et al., 1987). Using mathematical models to partition familial and genetic effects, it has been suggested that PMS may have a genetic component, estimated to account for 30–80% of the influencing factors in various samples. In

---

[2] The negative correlation with age among adults is supported by the linear trend observed in a community-based survey using retrospective assessment of PMS. That is, in a sample with ages ranging from 20 years to 49 years, extreme symptom ratings occurred most frequently among women aged 20–24 years and least frequently among those aged 45–49 years (Ramcharan et al., 1992).

the Kendler study, familial similarity of premenstrual symptoms was considered due solely to genetic factors, although familial environmental effects accounting for as much as 10% of the variance may have been undetected.

Biological findings that appear especially promising. Three areas of inquiry are especially promising: (a) increased sensitivity to induction of panic attacks, (b) elucidation of pathways for progesterone metabolism and individual differences in levels of biogenically active progesterone metabolites, and (c) recognition of cyclic effects for other medically recognized conditions.

Several groups of patients with LLPDD have been observed to show increased sensitivity to induction of panic attacks. Both carbon dioxide inhalation and lactate infusion are anxiogenic, in some cases inducing paniclike attacks. Carbon dioxide inhalation induced panic in 64% of women with confirmed LLPDD, compared with none in a control group (Harrison et al., 1989), and lactate infusion induced panic in 63% of women with LLPDD compared with 13% of a control group (Facchinetti, Romano, Fava, & Genazzani, 1992). In these studies, panic was not accounted for by comorbid panic disorder. It appears that LLPDD may be associated with increased sensitivity to panic-inducing agents.

MacDonald, Dombroski, and Casey (1991) proposed the progesterone metabolite theory of PMS. There are large (30-fold) interindividual variations in the pathways used to metabolize progesterone. Because progesterone metabolites are known to be biogenically active, different routes of metabolism may help explain differing subtypes of PMS. In particular, progesterone metabolites are known to affect GABAergic systems in the central nervous system. Various progesterone metabolites have effects that facilitate or inhibit the actions of GABAergic systems in a manner similar to that of the benzodiazepine (e.g., Valium-like) class of drugs, which have both antiseizure and antianxiety effects. These findings are suggestive of polymorphism in the genes that encode the enzymes that metabolize progesterone.

Several lines of evidence suggest that an underlying cyclic process may contribute to a wide variety of periodic illnesses (Jenner, 1968; Morley, 1970), ranging from asthma (Eliasson & DeGraff, 1987; Eliasson, Scherzer, & DeGraff, 1986; Gibbs, Coutts, Lock, Finnegan, & White, 1984), to rheumatoid arthritis (Goldstein, Duff, & Karsh, 1987; Latman, 1983), to neutropenia (a rare, cyclic blood disease characterized by 21-day cycles in numbers of blood cells; Dale & Hammond, 1988; Hammond, Price, Souza, & Dale, 1989).[3]

Moreover, menstrual cycle phase may be important in predicting responsivity to various treatments. For example, the menstrual cycle–related timing of breast cancer excision may affect the duration of the disease-free interval (Hrushesky, Bluming, Gruber, & Sothern, 1989), although the data are mixed. In one study (Senie, Rosen, Rhodes, & Lesser, 1991), excision during the postmenstrual (follicular) phase was associated with higher recurrence risk (43%) compared with that later in the cycle (29%). This tendency is supported by the results of another group (Badwe et al., 1991). Hence, the menstrual cycle may have much broader implications for health than mood and behavioral syndromes alone. It may also be an important variable in pharmacological research (Hamilton, 1991; Hamilton, in press; Jensvold et al., 1992).

Treatment

Despite limited understanding of the syndrome or syndromes, a number of treatments, mainly pharmacological, have been studied. At present, there is no one agreed-upon treatment (Severino & Moline, 1989), and a comprehensive review by Steinberg (1991) should be consulted for further information. Nondrug treatments—which are widely used but less well studied—are discussed in a later section.

Treatment trials for PMS are difficult to evaluate because of high rates of placebo responding, which range from 25% to 80% (Freeman, Rickels, & Sondheimer, 1992; Halbreich & Endicott, 1985; Mira, Vizzard, Macaskill, & Abraham, 1986), nonspecific responding, for which symptoms are known to diminish (often markedly) over the course of 1 or more months or charting in at least 15% of patients; and attrition, for which as many as 42% have dropped out of treatment trials (Harrison, Endicott, & Nee, 1990).

Numerous controlled clinical trials of progesterone treatment have shown that it is ineffective overall (Steinberg, 1991), although it is

---

[3] Also, in a series of studies, Parry et al. (1990) have demonstrated that women with confirmed PMS have abnormalities in melatonin secretion, a light-responsive hormone that can be used as a marker for circadian phase. Patients with PMS also benefit from chronobiological interventions, such as sleep deprivation (i.e., advancing the sleep–wake cycle; Parry & Wehr, 1987) and exposure to bright light (Parry et al., 1989).

possible that an unidentified subgroup of women may nonetheless be responsive. As examples, Sampson (1979) studied progesterone therapy (by suppository) in a double-blind, placebo-controlled cross-over trial and found no significant advantage of progesterone over placebo in reducing symptoms of PMS; however, 43% of the women found placebo to be more helpful than progesterone. More recently, a similarly designed and randomized large-scale study of progesterone therapy (by suppository) confirmed earlier findings (Freeman, Rickels, Sondheimer, & Polansky, 1990).

Only one study has documented the course of symptoms after 8 months of progesterone treatment, with the average follow-up occurring at 1 year (Freeman et al., 1992). In the responsive subgroup, some improvement gained during treatment with progesterone was maintained, but subjects remained moderately symptomatic. Only 17% of patients were still taking progesterone for premenstrual symptoms at follow-up, which suggests limited long-term utility even in the subgroup that initially appeared to be responsive.

Two controlled trials of alprazolam (a benzodiazepine) for treatment of LLPDD have demonstrated its efficacy compared with placebo (Harrison et al., 1990; Smith, Rinehart, Ruddock, & Schiff, 1987). Harrison et al. (1990) studied the use of alprazolam for 14–6 days before the menses. After a 1–2 month placebo washout, subjects were treated with placebo or active drug for three full cycles and were then crossed over. Harrison et al. (1990) found that 70% of the subjects rated the alprazolam cycles superior to the placebo cycles. The benefits of longer term treatment are unknown.

A more aggressive approach to treatment of severe and treatment-refractory PMS is to abolish the menstrual cycle, either by chemical (drug-induced) "ovariectomy" (Muse, Cetel, Futterman, & Yen, 1984) or by surgical ovariectomy (i.e., removal of the ovaries; Casper & Hearn, 1990; Casson, Hahn, Van Vugt, & Reid, 1990). Although these treatments appear to be dramatically effective, only 2–6-month follow-ups have been reported, and surgery is, of course, not a blind procedure.

Conclusions

The biomedical approach to PMS has merit. Beginning in the early 1980s, biomedically oriented researchers defined cutoff criteria for degree of symptomatic change, created a consensus diagnosis as a guide to research, intensively studied possible biological mechanisms, and proceeded rapidly to pharmacological treatment trials, as well as other dramatic interventions. The approach appears to be powerful and straightforward, as well as fast-paced and efficient. As we discuss in the next section, however, the biomedical approach to PMS is far from adequate, and findings presented so far may not be so clear-cut and compelling as they may, at first, appear to be.

Critique From the Health Psychology Perspective

Despite the obvious appeal of the biomedical model, psychological processes are known to contribute to symptom formation for both physical and mental symptoms (Pennebaker, 1982). In fact, there is some evidence that the relative contribution of contextual factors to perceptions of symptoms is greater for females than for males (Pennebaker & Roberts, 1992); if so, then psychological and contextual factors may be especially important in understanding women's symptomatic experiences, including those occurring premenstrually.

To the extent that the biomedical model is correct, the following predictions should hold for human menstrual cycle research: (a) Social effects on the cycle itself should be negligible; (b) the effect of expectations or awareness of a study's focus on menstrual symptoms should be negligible; (c) the effect of using the onset of menses as a "marker" for the attribution of symptoms should be negligible, such that hysterectomy (with intact ovarian functioning) should have little or no effect on symptoms; (d) cross-cultural, ethnic, or cohort variability in symptoms should be negligible, except to the extent that there may be genetic differences; (e) social or contextual variables, such as stress or family context, should have negligible effects on symptoms; and (f) multiple comparison groups should not be needed to determine cutoff criteria—with men, in particular, appearing to be superfluous. In contrast, to the extent that these effects are substantial rather than negligible, the health psychology perspective is supported. Each of these issues is considered in turn.

Social Regulation and Natural History

When one thinks of the menstrual cycle, one tends to envision the events shown in Figure 1 occurring repeatedly, month after month.

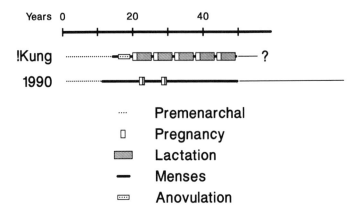

Figure 5. The top line indicates age in years. The middle line indicates reproductive-related life events for !Kung women, and the bottom line indicates such events for modern women in the 1990s in westernized industrial nations. Premenarche is indicated by dots; pregnancy by open rectangles; lactation by shaded rectangles; menses by bold solid lines; and anovulation by rectangles containing dots. From "The Evolution of Human Reproduction" by R. V. Short, 1976, *Proceedings of the Royal Society of London, 195,* p. 16. Copyright 1976 by The Royal Society. Adapted by permission.

As shown in Figure 5, however, the cycle has not always been so repetitive as might be imagined (Short, 1976). The average age of menarche (the onset of menstruation) is earlier in the U.S. at present than in other times, and more women live to the age of menopause (the end of menstruation), so that women menstruate over a longer period of time. Women are typically older at first pregnancy; their cycles are disrupted by an average of only two births and are only briefly, if ever, delayed by lactation. This means that a woman in American society can expect 400–500 menstrual cycles in her lifetime.

In marked contrast, women in other societies, such as the !Kung (a contemporary hunter–gatherer tribe of the Kalahari Desert in Africa), are likely to experience far fewer cycles because of the later onset of menarche, an earlier average age of first pregnancy, a three- to fourfold higher birth rate, and prolonged and repeated periods of anovulation associated with lactation (often accompanied by amenorrhea, or an absence of menses). This means that the number of menstrual cycles may be reduced by a factor of 10, to as few as 40 in a !Kung woman's lifetime. Repeated menstrual cycles have probably occurred commonly only recently.

Premenstrual symptoms or syndromes are obviously much less likely to be recognized—even if cyclic symptoms occur and are largely driven biologically—in societies in which menstruation occurs infrequently (Shostak, 1983). The natural history of menstruation challenges the biomedical model's fixed, acontextual notion of the cycle, as though it were driven purely by sex steroid hormone fluctuations. It clearly supports viewing menstrual-linked symptoms as a complex, biobehavioral phenomenon of relatively recent onset, one that is strongly influenced by social context, and includes decisions about child-bearing and lactation.

Studies of nonhuman animals have demonstrated the social regulation of fertility (e.g., McClintock, 1981). In rodents, this commonly takes the form of suppression of ovulation in nondominant, nonbreeding females. Social signals can also alter the neuroendocrine cycle itself, which leads to synchronization of the estrous cycle in the rat (the analogue of the human menstrual cycle); moreover, dominance may mediate ovarian synchrony within a group. Female rats living in isolation have longer and more irregular cycles, higher levels of certain sex steroid hormones (e.g., plasma estradiol and progesterone), and earlier reproductive senescence (the analogue of human menopause) (LeFevre & McClintock, 1991).

Synchrony in the onset of menses (i.e., in which individuals' dates of onset of menstruation shift progressively closer together) was first documented in humans by McClintock (1971). Although the finding of synchrony was once controversial, it has been replicated by several groups and is now well accepted. Recent data by Graham and McGrew (1992) show that menstrual synchrony depends on social interactions between individuals and not just on environmental factors. For example, cycles of close friends were more synchronized than those of neighbors or randomly paired individuals.[4] Social regulation of the human menstrual cycle further challenges the reified notion that the cycle is biologically autonomous. The social context

---

[4] It is not known whether something analogous to synchrony occurs for the presence or absence (or severity) of symptoms related to the cycle. For example, does menstrual-linked symptomatology become more similar in a group of women undergoing synchrony in the onset of menses? It is also unclear whether such synchrony is led by one woman, perhaps in relation to dominance status, or whether it is the result of mutual shifts in timing.

in which premenstrual symptoms occur is further discussed in the next three sections.

Attributional Biases and Effects of Expectations on Symptoms

From the standpoint of attributional research and theory, it is instructive to consider how one might attempt to maximize perceptions of a cyclic syndrome. Self-reports of premenstrual symptoms depend on recognition of two sets of information: (a) perceptions of symptoms and (b) perceptions of having a cycle. In lay experience, a correlation between these two sets of information would justify naming the symptoms after the menstrual cycle. Despite the fact that the observed information is only correlation (i.e., in timing), it is likely experienced as though the cycle were causal.

According to Ruble and Brooks-Gunn (1979), a social cognition analysis of research suggests that perceptions of a cycle are enhanced by *selectivity* because there is excess attention to confirmatory information, regardless of the frequency of nonassociation. Once a causal association is established, other kinds of attributional errors perpetuate these beliefs. For example, there may be *distortion of evidence* to heighten apparent self-consistency. Awareness of being in a menstrual cycle study could heighten *category accessibility*, thereby introducing bias into memory.

Expectations and culturally available stereotypes. To the extent that attributional biases and culturally available stereotypes help to shape one's symptomatic experiences, the mind can be said to play a role in PMS. In Western culture, women have long held unequal and devalued social roles. Menstruation is, to some extent, a symbol for womanhood (Delaney, Lupton, & Toth, 1988). Negative stereotypes about women and bleeding in general, and menstruation in particular, may contribute to symptom experiences premenstrually. Referring to menstruation as "the curse," for example, probably does not diminish symptom reports.

Koeske and Koeske (1975) found that college-age students tend to use information about premenstrual cycle phases in making attributions about negative, but not positive, mood symptoms. Bains and Slade (1988) also found that nonstudent, older women attributed negative moods occurring premenstrually to health-related factors, whereas positive moods were attributed to environmental events and aspects of life-style; hence, the findings of Koeske and Koeske (1975) can be generalized to a broader population.

Brooks-Gunn and Ruble (1980) developed a questionnaire to assess attitudes towards menstruation (the Menstrual Attitude Questionnaire [MAQ]).[5] Increasing evidence has linked premenstrual symptom reports with negative socialization about menstruation (Taylor, Woods, Lentz, Mitchell, & Lee, 1991).

Coyne (1983) found that women who anticipate premenstrual symptoms have elevated muscle tension, as assessed by electromyography (EMG). The relationship between expectancy and EMG was stronger than that between actual symptoms and EMG on the same day. Van der Akker and Steptoe (1989) also found that expectancies about perimenstrual symptoms are more important in explaining skin conductance level levels than actual symptom patterns.

Beliefs about whether one is premenstrual also have powerful effects on symptoms. In Ruble's (1977) classic experiment, simply leading college-student, nonpatient women to believe they were either earlier (intermenstrual, i.e., with a period expected in 7–10 days) or later (imminently premenstrual, i.e., with a period expected in 1–2 days) in their cycle than was actually estimated (subjects were tested 6–7 days before their periods were expected, i.e., when premenstrual but not immediately prior to the expected onset) resulted in nearly 10–30% change in symptoms. Even for physical symptoms such as water retention and pain, incorrectly believing oneself to be imminently premenstrual led to increases, and believing oneself to be in-

---

[5] Positive relationships between concurrent premenstrual well-being and MAQ predictability and between well-being and MAQ debilitation (based on a scale that assesses belief in cyclic variation rather than impairment per se) suggest a protective factor of what might be called "acceptance" of variability (Gallant, Hamilton, Popiel, Morokoff, & Chakraborty, 1991). Positive relationships between dysphoric moods, depression, and MAQ denial (on the basis of a scale that does not actually measure denial of symptoms, but rather negative assessments of having cyclic symptoms) suggest harmful effects of what could be termed a "rejection" factor. These findings suggest a response bias theory of premenstrual distress, such that one's responses to symptomatic changes may dampen or elevate the negative impact of symptoms (Hamilton & Gallant, 1990); this proposal is somewhat analogous to Nolen-Hoeksema's (1987) theory of sex differences in depression.

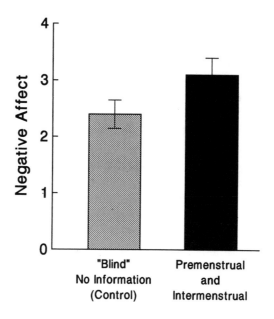

Figure 6. Negative affect ratings are shown for two groups: those given no information about cycle phase and those led to believe they were earlier (less imminently premenstrual) or later (more imminently premenstrual) in the cycle than they actually were. Experimental groups averaged almost 30% higher concurrent negative affect ratings than controls, although the direction of the effect did not vary as expected. From "Premenstrual Symptoms: A Reinterpretation" by D. N. Ruble, 1977, *Science, 197,* p. 292. Copyright 1977 by the American Association for the Advancement of Science. Adapted by permission.

termenstrual led to decreases in concurrent symptom reports. Figure 6 illustrates the finding for affective change.

Although the results of Ruble's (1977) study have not been precisely replicated in a nonstudent, symptomatic population (and indeed, it might be difficult to alter beliefs about cycle phase in a symptomatic population), these findings document a major flaw in the biomedical model's approach to LLPDD: It cannot be assumed that concurrent, daily self-reports are 100% reliable,[6] although proponents of the LLPDD diagnosis, prospective ratings, and the 30% change rule appear to do so. Klebanov and Jemmoff (1992) recently documented an expectancy effect similar to that observed by Ruble.

---

[6] Although some would speak this in terms of accuracy, we prefer to speak of reliability or meaningfulness.

Another flaw in the biomedical model is suggested, ironically, by a study done by one of the leading adherents of biologically-based theories. Schmidt et al. (1991) manipulated the endocrine environment of the cycle in symptomatic women in a blinded manner, such that women believed they were PM, but actually experienced the hormonal climate of the postmenstrual cycle phase. The active hormonal manipulation induced early-onset vaginal bleeding; there was also a placebo control group that did not have bleeding induced earlier than expected. The authors are silent on the women's expectations, e.g., it is unclear whether the women interpreted the early vaginal bleeding as real or artificial periods, or whether they expected symptoms to change accordingly. Half of the women with early induced bleeding were given an additional treatment that sustained a luteal-like hormonal profile. Women in all three groups experienced an increase in their usual (PM-like) symptoms, even those who were post-bleeding (i.e., whose expectations might have been to have decreased symptoms, at least if they believed they had a real period and could not feel premenstrual) and those who were not hormonally PM, as well as those on placebo (in whom one might have expected no change). The Schmidt et al. (1991) study has been criticized on the basis of the hormonal manipulation used, but it is also impossible to interpret in terms of expectancies, as it might appear either to support or undermine effects of expectations.[7]

A special case: Awareness effects. Several investigators have shown that knowing one is in a study of the menstrual cycle (category accessibility) can influence daily ratings in a fashion similar to that observed for retrospective reports (AuBuchon & Calhoun, 1985; Englander-Golden, Sonleiter, Whitmore, & Corbley, 1986; Olasov & Jackson, 1987). As shown in Figure 7, the increase in symptom ratings can be as great as 70–80%. This is potentially important for the LLPDD diagnosis because it is next to impossible to disguise the focus of health care and treatment among women seeking care for premenstrual symptoms.

---

[7] The agent used, RU-486, has been characterized as a progesterone receptor antagonist. However, MacDonald et al. (1992) argued that RU-486 could cause rather than ameliorate premenstruallike symptoms because it does not act solely as a progesterone receptor antagonist. For example, it can act as a glucocorticosteroid receptor antagonist as well (Bourgeois, Pfahl, & Baulieu, 1984), and it is known that glucocorticosteroid withdrawal can provoke premenstruallike symptoms. In addition, RU-486 can mimic progesterone (Chen, Huang, Mazella, & Tseng, 1989), but also cause regression of progesterone-producing tissue (the corpus luteum), eventuating progesterone withdrawal (Nieman et al., 1987). Alternatively, perhaps symptoms are related to some other cyclic process.

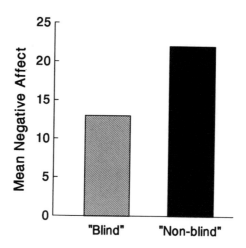

Figure 7. Negative affect ratings are shown for two groups: the open bar indicates those who were unaware of the menstrual focus of the study (blind), and the cross-hatched bar those who were aware of the study focus (non-blind). Awareness of the menstrual focus of the study increased concurrent negative affect ratings by about 76%. From "Menstrual Cycle Symptomatology: The Role of Social Expectancy and Experimental Demand Characteristics" by P. G. AuBuchon and K. S. Calhoun, 1985, *Psychosomatic Medicine, 47,* p. 40. Copyright 1985 by the American Psychosomatic Society. Adapted by permission.

One limitation of studies showing awareness effects is that they use primarily young, nonpatient, college students as subjects. Using several methodological refinements, however, Gallant, Hamilton, Popiel, Morokoff, and Chakraborty (1991) found that awareness of a study's menstrual focus had much less effect on an older, nonstudent population and also much less effect on women who met provisional criteria for LLPDD (Gallant, Popiel, Hoffman, Chakraborty, & Hamilton, 1992a). The latter finding may be due to a ceiling effect because menstruation may already be so highly salient in women with LLPDD.

However, other unexamined demand characteristics may be more problematic. For example, women who seek treatment may be motivated to report higher symptoms to qualify for treatment (distortion of evidence). As shown in Figure 8, measurement increase may also be introduced by using diaries that display an entire month, or several months, of ratings at one time to assess symptoms (Halbreich, Endicott, & Lesser, 1985; Severino & Moline, 1989).

Daily Ratings Form

Severity Ratings: 1 = Not at All, 2 = Minimal, 3 = Mild, 4 = Moderate, 5 = Severe, 6 = Extreme

Day of Week	Date	Menstruating?	Stay at Home, Avoid Social Activity
Mon	/	_____	1 2 3 4 5 6
Tues	/	_____	1 2 3 4 5 6
Wed	/	_____	1 2 3 4 5 6
Thrs	/	_____	1 2 3 4 5 6
Fri	/	_____	1 2 3 4 5 6
Sat	/	_____	1 2 3 4 5 6
Sun	/	_____	1 2 3 4 5 6
Mon	/	_____	1 2 3 4 5 6
Tues	/	_____	1 2 3 4 5 6
Wed	/	_____	1 2 3 4 5 6
Thrs	/	_____	1 2 3 4 5 6
Fri	/	_____	1 2 3 4 5 6
Sat	/	_____	1 2 3 4 5 6
Sun	/	_____	1 2 3 4 5 6

Figure 8.   This daily rating form displays 6 weeks of ratings (i.e., more than an entire month), which may introduce demand characteristics, for example, increasing symptom ratings premenstrually. From *The Clinical Diagnosis and Classification of Premenstrual Changes* by U. Halbreich, J. Endicott, and J. Lesser, 1985, p. 493. Copyright 1985 by the Canadian Psychiatric Association. Adapted by permission. The *Daily Rating Form* was developed by J. Endicott, S. Schact, and U. Halbreich, 1982, Research Assessment and Training Unit, 722 West 168th Street, New York, NY 10032.

A particularly problematic measure in this regard is the visual analogue scale used by Rubinow and colleagues at NIMH and adopted by other investigators on the basis of their research. The measure assesses mood using one of several bipolar scales (see Figure 3). As discussed earlier, in one of the often-used scales, one end is labeled *most happy ever* and the other is labeled *most depressed ever*. This scale assumes that happiness and depression are opposite sides of the same emotion, a suspect assumption given the relative independence of positive and negative emotions. Furthermore, it is not clear what ratings in the middle of the scale mean. Are they neutral (i.e., intended to reflect being neither depressed nor happy), or are they a rating of mixed or ambivalent emotions (i.e., both [or equally] depressed and happy)? Scrutiny of this measure is warranted because it has been used often in psychiatric PMS/LLPDD research, and ultimately, conclusions based on it are only as valid as the measure itself.

Importance of having a marker for cyclic syndromes: Hysterectomy. In applying social cognition theory to the menstrual cycle & Brooks-Gunn, 1979), it is important to have a cyclic marker (e.g., bleeding), especially one that is highly salient (e.g., having to do with one's core identity or sexuality and with one's well-being). One way to understand the effects of having a marker is to study what happens when it is removed.

Three groups of investigators have studied women before and after hysterectomy (removal of the uterus, with conservation of the ovaries) since the 1970s. Among women who were not selected because they had PMS, Osborn and Gath (1990) found that luteal phase, premenstruallike symptom ratings fell dramatically 6 months after surgery in the absence of menstruation. In the absence of a marker, the severity of psychological symptoms was reduced by an average of 59%, and the severity of physical symptoms was reduced by an average of 72%. These findings are consistent with those of an earlier study by Osborn (1981). In a much smaller study of women selected for having PMS (Backstrom, Boyle, & Baird, 1981), luteal phase, premenstruallike symptoms were also less severe.

It is likely that the timing of follow-up after surgery is important because symptoms may diminish gradually over time. Another group found that hysterectomized women demonstrated lower rates of late luteal phase, premenstruallike symptoms compared with controls (36% vs. about 72%), and that symptoms occurred on average about 2.5 days earlier than in controls (Metcalf et al., 1991). These data also suggest effects of expectations and the presence of a marker.

Finally, adherents of the biomedical model have presented data that suggest the importance of menstruation as a marker for recognizing symptoms. As noted earlier, the LLPDD diagnosis restricts attention to symptoms occurring premenstrually even though it is well known that symptoms can also be linked in timing, for example, with ovulation. That is, there are often two or more peaks in symptoms during the cycle, although only the one having an obvious marker is retrospectively recalled and reported (Rubinow et al., 1984, Figure 2, Patient 5). The LLPDD diagnosis may impede progress in understanding cyclic processes more generally by prematurely restricting the range of inquiry and thereby biasing it (Gallant & Hamilton, 1988).

Cognitive and attributional measures across the menstrual cycle. Given the considerable overlap between women with a lifetime history of affective disorder and those with PMS/LLPDD, it is not surprising that putative cognitive or attributional markers for depression have been examined in the latter group. For example, if certain types of attributions are related to depressive thinking (Abramson, Seligman, & Teasdale, 1978), then it is reasonable to hypothesize that PMS/LLPDD patients will be more similar to depressed patients than controls and that there may be a depressive shift in attributions premenstrually (Hamilton, Alagna, & Sharpe, 1985; McMillan & Pihl, 1987). Early findings are mixed (Trunnell, Turner, & Keye, 1988), providing only limited support for this hypothesis (O'Boyle, Severino, & Hurt, 1988). However, typical self-report measures may not be the best methods for assessing changes of interest. Cognitive measures are further discussed in the section on severity.

Cross-Cultural, Ethnic, or Cohort-Related Variability in Symptoms

Simple biomedical accounts of premenstrual changes would be weakened if symptomatology varied by culture. Predominant symptoms do appear to vary according to ethnic or cultural background or place of parent's origin. For example, Masin et al. (1988; cited in Severino & Moline, 1989, p. 27) studied women living in Australia whose mothers were originally from Australia, Italy, Greece, Turkey, or Vietnam and found that their predominant symptoms varied widely (these were irritability, tension, headache, breast pain, and abdominal pain, respectively).

In the U.S., there are Black–White differences in premenstrual symptoms. For example, Blacks report higher rates of food cravings

(Stout, Grady, & Steege, 1986); this may be due to ethnic (in the sense of cultural) differences. Studies such as these are limited by reliance on retrospective reports of symptoms. However, Woods, Most, and Dery (1982) more precisely estimated the prevalence of perimenstrual symptoms in a multiethnic study. Black women reported less severe cramping and premenstrual negative feelings but more weight gain, swelling, and headache compared with White women.

Biomedical models of PMS/LLPDD would also be weakened by large cohort effects on symptomatology. In describing PMS as a "Western culture-specific disorder," Johnson (1983) pointed out an apparent (although not well-documented) increase in rates of premenstrual symptoms, as well as attention to and societal concern about PMS in the 1970s and early 1980s; these changes coincided with dramatic changes in women's roles and status. According to Johnson, PMS serves as a means by which women negotiate access to power (i.e., the traditionally male world of work) without directly threatening gender roles or the status quo; it does so by retaining the stereotypical view of women as the weaker sex, although encapsulating and restricting expression of certain stereotypical behaviors to the premenstrual cycle phase.

Anthropological studies can also be examined to test specific hypotheses. For example, an obvious hypothesis is that cultures with positive images of menstruation (or relatively equal social roles; Zelman, 1977) will have relatively lower rates of premenstrual symptoms and that those with negative menstrual images that, for example, represent pollution or defilement (or less equal social roles) will have higher rates (Paige, 1973).

According to Shostak (1983), !Kung women and men hold almost equal positions in society, and menarche is celebrated. However, menstruation occurs infrequently, and it is seen as a "thing of no account." In a prospective study that documented normal endocrine functioning across the cycles, !Kung women had the usual mild fluctuations in symptoms seen in women in other societies, although the women themselves did not recognize the changes and were surprised when premenstrual symptoms were pointed out. Although this example lends support to the hypothesis that cultural factors can have a positive influence on premenstrual symptoms, effects of positive images or equal social roles are confounded by the low base rates of menstruation.[8]

Other Social or Contextual Effects on Symptom Severity: Stress and Family Relationships

Stress. There has been a great deal of controversy over the possible effects of daily stressor and cumulative life events on premenstrual symptoms. One problem is that ratings of stress and other

---

[8] Evidence of the negative influences of culture in the hypothesis is that menstruating women are considered unclean in Judaism. *Mikvah* is a practice consisting of ritual bathing at the end of menses. Contrary to the negative hypothesis, however, Siegel (1985) and Rothblum and Jackson (1990) found that women who engaged in Mikvah did not have higher rates of negative premenstrual symptoms compared with controls.

A clue to understanding these findings comes from contemporary study in India, another country with negative menstrual taboos. Despite the fact that as much as 75% of women in India follow pollution taboos associated with menstruation, they do not see menstruation as a negative event. Instead, a World Health Organization study (Snowden & Christian, 1983) found that the vast majority of women in India see menstruation as a positive event and would not voluntarily submit to drug-induced amenorrhea, as might result from OCs. Chandra and Chaturvedi (1989) suggested that Indian women, in fact, "gain a number of privileges during menstruation by not being allowed to cook or look after the household." That is, seemingly negative taboos are not all bad, and in fact may be advantageous. This reinterpretation may help to explain why women in India do not show higher rates of dysphoria premenstrually compared with women in the U.S.

The proposed reinterpretation is supported by ethnographic accounts of other cultures. Powers (1980) suggested that menstrual taboos restricting women have been misinterpreted by anthropologists educated in the Western tradition. For example, the Oglala (living in southwestern South Dakota) and the Navajo also celebrate menarche and attribute special powers to menstruating women. Similarly, Buckley (1988) suggested that scholars have misinterpreted Yurok (living today from northern California to Oregon) menstrual taboos as overly negative; original field notes can be reinterpreted as showing that menstruation provided spiritual potency and a special route to knowledge and wealth. If so, then isolation rituals per se can no longer be seen as automatically supporting a prediction of higher rates of premenstrual symptoms or syndromes. That is, researchers may need to understand better the meaning of supposed menstrual taboos to the women themselves before they can make informed predictions with regard to rates of PMS. It would be of interest to assess rates of premenstrual symptoms among the Oglala, Navajo, and Yurok, which are predicted to be relatively low.

symptoms may be confounded (with high ratings of one correlated with high ratings of the other). However, it is possible to separate these effects by using mood and physical symptom ratings as co-variates in analyses of stress effects. In a study of women with LLPDD (although they averaged only a 20% worsening in mood symptoms), multiple regression techniques were used to determine that daily stress accounted for 6% of the unique variance in physical symptoms and 10% in mood symptoms, whereas cycle phase accounted for 29% of the unique variance in physical symptoms but only 7% in mood (Beck et al., 1990). These investigators concluded that physical symptoms are more strongly influenced by cycle phase than mood symptoms and that daily stress is relatively unimportant in determining premenstrual symptoms.

However, it could also be argued that an effect accounting for 10% of the variance is not negligible, particularly not for mood changes. In the behavioral sciences, correlations are usually on the order of 0.30–0.35, which accounts for about 10% of the variance. What is most striking is that cycle phase is not, apparently, any more important than stress in determining affective symptoms in LLPDD patients. Particularly when a 30% change criterion is used to confirm symptoms and menstrual cycle phase accounts for less than 10% of the variance, it appears imprudent to discount effects of concurrent, daily stress. More important, 83% of the variance in affective symptoms remains to be accounted for.

Another study of confirmed LLPDD patients (Schmidt, Grover, Hoban, & Rubinow, 1990) found that patients and nonpatient female controls reported similar overall numbers of stressful events but that patients reported significantly greater numbers of negative events premenstrually. The latter finding is not supported by other evidence (Gallant et al., 1992b), however, and data remain mixed. In the study by Schmidt et al. (1990), patients rated events occurring premenstrually, compared with postmenstrually, as more unpleasant than did controls. Unfortunately, symptom ratings were not used as co-variates (although changes in mood ratings were said to be uncorrelated with changes in number of events or degree of unpleasantness), nor were multivariate techniques used.

In a much larger community-based study, both daily stressors and cumulative major life events were assessed (Woods, Most, & Long-necker, 1985). Daily stress early in the cycle, but not premenstrual, was correlated with higher premenstrual symptom ratings. Correlations between daily stressors and symptoms were higher than those between cumulative life events and symptoms. Earlier studies have been reviewed previously (Beck et al., 1990; Woods et al., 1985) but are of limited relevance to the present discussion because nonpatient groups were studied using retrospective methods.

A laboratory study documented effects of stress on EMG correlates of low back pain in PMS patients and nonpatient controls (Dickson-Parnell & Zeichner, 1988), although LLPDD criteria and prospective daily ratings were not used. Two subgroups of PMS patients were defined by whether they reported high or low levels of premenstrual low back pain. Stressors were neutral, cognitive, or emotional and personally relevant (having to do with anxiety-related experiences or premenstrual symptoms). As expected, the PMS subgroups differed in concurrent ratings of premenstrual–postmenstrual low back pain (with the high-pain subgroup averaging a 153% increase premenstrually and the low-pain subgroup 82%, compared with no increase for controls). Groups did not differ in EMG activity in response to neutral or cognitive stressors, but the PMS subgroups showed four- to ninefold increases in EMG activity in response to emotional stimuli during the premenstrual cycle phase compared with virtually no change for controls. Among nonpatient women, there is also evidence of shifts in the salience of emotionally toned, but not neutral, stimuli across the menstrual cycle, as evidenced by greater P3 (also known as P300) amplitude premenstrually (Johnston & Wang, 1991).

Severity of symptoms and family relationships.   The main LLPDD severity criterion relies on reports of disturbance that seriously interferes with work or with usual social activities or relationships with others. The validity of this criterion has been challenged because most women's reports of premenstrual impairment (e.g., of cognition) are not supported by objective measures (Richardson, 1992; Sommer, 1983, 1992). Indeed, there are several reports of the opposite: Women who report PMS typically underestimate their performance and in some cases actually perform better premenstrually than postmenstrually (Gallant (Alagna) & Hamilton, 1988; Hamilton, Alagna, & Sharpe, 1985). Such discrepancies are supported, in part, by physiological data. For example, women with PMS have demonstrated greater responsivity, as assessed by heart rate and skin conductance, postmenstrually compared with premenstrually (Kirsch & Geer,

1988), despite subjective reports suggesting the reverse.[9] Data on skin conductance level responsivity, however, are mixed (Woods, personal communication, University of Washington at Seattle, March 15, 1993).

Severino and Moline (1989) singled out the effects of PMS/LLPDD on interpersonal and family functioning as a particularly neglected area of research, and Burnett (1992) reviewed studies of social interactions and PMS. Recent research has focused on the impact of premenstrual symptoms on family members and the effect of marital dissatisfaction on the intensity of premenstrual symptoms. Despite anecdotal reports of disturbed parenting premenstrually, among mothers of preschoolers who were not selected for having premenstrual symptoms, greater task persistence and more positive mothering were observed during the premenstrual cycle phase (Fradkin & Firestone, 1986). These effects should be studied in LLPDD patients as well.

Among nonpatient women, moods in male partners have been shown to vary in accordance with the woman's menstrual cycle, with activation being highest when the female partner is premenstrual (LeFevre, Hedricks, Church, & McClintock, 1992). Male partners of women who report premenstrual distress report considerable personal distress as well (Brown & Zimmer, 1986). However, Mansfield, Hood, and Henderson (1989) found that social factors (day of the week) were more important than biological factors (menstrual cycle phase) in accounting for variance in ratings for couples.

One reason for distress may be that women tend to show an increased need for "personal space" premenstrually, as shown in Figure 9 (Gallant et al., 1991; Schecter, Bachmann, Vaitukaitis, Phillips, & Saperstein, 1989). Yet many women are either unable to find personal space, feel undeserving of it, or feel guilty about wanting it. This need, combined with the relatively high degree of assertiveness observed in some women premenstrually (Alagna & Hamilton, 1986) may precipitate interpersonal conflict. Furthermore, the stress of an unhappy relationship may exacerbate the intensity of premenstrual

---

[9] More recent findings concerning objective evidence of impairment are mixed, with some evidence suggesting that women with PMS may have difficulty learning new material that is independent of cycle phase and mood (Keenan, Stern, Janowsky, & Pedersen, 1992).

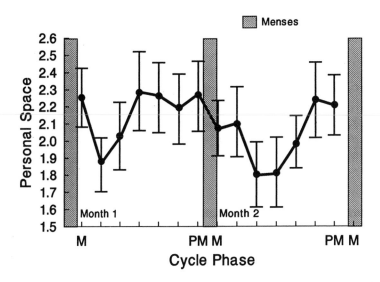

Figure 9.   Concurrent, daily ratings of need for personal space are shown for 2 months. Shaded areas indicate menstruation. M, menstruation; P, peri-ovulation; L, luteal; and PM, premenstrual. Ratings are higher around menstruation, including premenstrually, than postmenstrually, with especially low ratings around midcycle. From "Daily Moods and Symptoms: Effects of Awareness of Study Focus, Gender, Menstrual-Cycle Phase, and Day of the Week" by S. J. Gallant, J. A. Hamilton, D. A. Popiel, P. J. Morokoff, and P. K. Chakraborty, 1991, *Health Psychology, 10,* p. 185. Copyright 1991 by Erlbaum. Adapted by permission.

symptoms. Coughlin (1990) found a positive correlation between marital dissatisfaction and the intensity of premenstrual symptoms.

Some women may use the premenstruum as a time to express gender role–incongruent affects, such as anger (Hamilton, Parry, Alagna, Blumenthal, & Herz, 1984; Martin, 1992). Laws (1983) described PMS as a survival strategy for women that allows culturally unacceptable traits such as anger and aggression to be labeled as "sick." If such behaviors are attributed to a hormonal imbalance or to another biological cause, then the traits can be both expressed and simultaneously disowned, so that responsibility for one's actions is denied.

The ways that members of a couple understand premenstrual distress may be critically important both to their satisfaction with the relationship and to the woman's expression of premenstrual symptoms. If members of a couple attribute the woman's perceptions and feelings premenstrually to biological causes, then even a woman's legitimate concerns are likely to be discounted. This in turn could have cumulative negative effects on relationship satisfaction and stress.

Siegel (1986) offered an interesting model of marital dynamics associated with PMS that supports this notion, hypothesizing that the positive relationship between PMS and marital dissatisfaction reflects a chronic pattern of ineffective conflict resolution. Some women try to avoid conflict and deny problems at the cost of a buildup of emotional tension. Premenstrually, in the presence of additional symptoms, these avoided feelings and unresolved conflicts may gain awareness and be expressed behaviorally in ways that are labeled as being premenstrual rather than being recognized as legitimate complaints about the relationship or family life.

Multiple Comparison Groups in Determining Cutoff Criteria

In a "monolithic" view of the menstrual cycle as biologically autonomous, it would appear bizarre to use men as controls in menstrual cycle research. After all, the effects of interest are believed to result directly from the biology of the menstrual cycle, and because men do not menstruate, they appear irrelevant as controls. At most, one might consider studying patient and nonpatient female controls, although many biologically oriented studies do not even include the latter.

A more considered approach, however, would be to explore a broader universe of what one is controlling for. For example, women on OCs might be used to control for the effects of intact menstrual cycles (because OCs suppress endogenous hormonal fluctuations) and men might be used to control for the effects of gender and the passage of time (Gallant et al., 1992b; Wilcoxin, Schrader, & Sherif, 1976).

To establish empirically based cutoff criteria for defining symptomatic groups of women, Gallant et al. (1992b) studied women who met provisional criteria for LLPDD, women who did not report premenstrual symptomatology, women on OCs, and men, the latter being assigned to an arbitrary 28-day cycle. As shown in Figure 10, the 30% change criterion (for a single symptom) is inadequate to distinguish symptomatic from asymptomatic individuals. For exam-

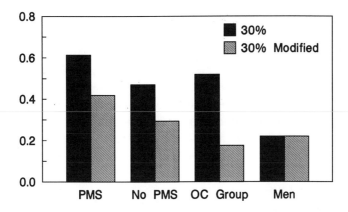

Figure 10.   Percantages of subjects meeting the 30% (filled bars) and modified 30% (shaded bars) change criteria for one affective symptom are shown for four groups: those who retrospectively met provisional criteria for LLPDD (PMS), those who retrospectively reported no PMS, those on OCs, and men. From "Daily Ratings of Premenstrual Symptoms: II. Differentiating Women With Severe Symptoms From Women With Normal Menstrual Cycles" by S. J. Gallant, D. A. Popiel, D. H. Hoffman, P. K. Chakraborty, and J. A. Hamilton, 1992, *Psychosomatic Medicine, 54,* p. 175. Copyright 1992 by the American Psychosomatic Society. Adapted by permission.

ple, the proportions of women who meet this criterion are similar across all three female groups—including women without endogenous cycles. It is also striking that the proportion of men who meet the modified 30% change criterion is not significantly different from that for the women. Other cutoff scores (e.g., 75% change) and numbers of symptoms (i.e., for which criteria for 5 items were met) also generally failed to distinguish groups.

Conclusions

Adherents of the biomedical model discounted, or ignored, possible expectancy and awareness effects in studies conducted in the early 1980s, moving quickly to intensive biological and treatment studies. As it turned out, this strategy was not particularly problematic when it came to awareness effects (arising from subjects' awareness of a study's focus) because these appear to be less important in symptomatic LLPDD populations than in less symptomatic college-age students.

Because biomedically oriented research also tends to overlook contextual effects, however, interventions aimed at the family (e.g., the couple) have been understudied. It appears that many women's premenstrual symptoms and syndromes may be highly interactive. Although dramatic interventions (e.g., surgical castration) may be effective, such remedies are extreme for many if not most women, because more modest and less costly interventions are also beneficial. For example, if simply removing the marker for menstruation (i.e., simple hysterectomy alone) can reduce symptoms by as much as 72%, then it may be unnecessary to offer hysterectomy combined with ovariectomy to some women with severe PMS (Casper & Hearn, 1990; Casson et al., 1990).

Moreover, dramatic interventions deserve scrutiny in view of the persistence of negative ideas about women and menstruation in Western culture and the apparent continuity in the social and medical construction of PMS (Rodin, 1992). For example, gynecological surgery for the treatment of mental disorders in women has a long history, dating back to Victorian times. Given concern about high rates of hysterectomy in the U.S. compared with other countries (Payer, 1988), there is a need for consensus guidelines for aggressive surgical treatments for PMS/LLPDD. In addition, the use of Valium-like drugs for the treatment of women's premenstrual symptoms remains a concern because women have been the primary recipients of psychotropic drugs in general, with some women feeling silenced by them (Russo, 1985).

Although early findings concerning the 30% change criterion deserve replication, they nonetheless suggest a "fatal flaw" in much of the recent, biomedically oriented research: The assumption that an arbitrary change criterion is sufficient to ensure selection of a well-defined symptomatic group appears unfounded. Instead, just as advocates of the 30% change criterion suggested discarding earlier research that defined groups by using retrospective reports, it could be argued that research relying on prospective measures and the 30% cutoff could be discarded as well (although our own view is relatively conservative on this issue). At best, a change of 30% is relatively small compared with other known psychosocial effects on symptoms, as illustrated in Figure 11.

The biomedically oriented approach has appeared to be both fast and efficient, but it has proven merely to be fast. In particular, genetic

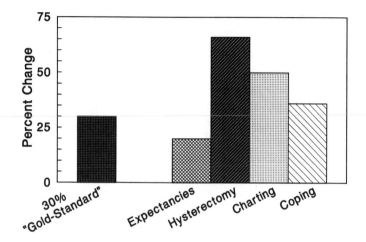

Figure 11. The proposed "gold standard" for defining PMS/LLPDD, the 30% change criteria, is compared with the degree of change known to accompany other psychosocial effects. The figure illustrates that the 30% change criterion is comparable with or dwarfed by other effects.

studies appear to be premature. Aggressive treatments that are now reported in the medical literature are likely to be overused despite qualifying statements made by the investigators (Roy, 1992, pp. 189); these treatments deserve special scrutiny and editorial commentary by interdisciplinary panels of experts, including health psychologists.

Clinical Advances in the Health Psychology of PMS/LLPDD: Recommendations for Clinical Practice and Research

Health psychologists will be increasingly involved in the clinical evaluation and psychological treatment of PMS/LLPDD. In this section, we examine advances with respect to clinical evaluations and nondrug treatments.

Clinical Evaluation

If prospective ratings cannot be used reliably as the "gold standard" for confirming "real" PMS/LLPDD, then what can? Some investigators have suggested that retrospective reports should be revisited (Graze et al., 1990; Hart, Coleman, & Russell, 1987; Warner et al., 1991). For example, women with a provisional diagnosis of LLPDD can be better discriminated from a control group of women by their self-esteem, patterns of coping with stress, and certain defenses than by degree of change in their premenstrual symptoms according to daily ratings (Gallant, Popiel, & Hoffman, in press). Hence, "there is value in retrospective reports . . . as a representation of the degree to which self-identification as suffering PMS is an important factor in one's identity" (Gallant et al., 1992b, p. 179).

Warren and Baker (1992) studied coping resources in women with PMS. LLPDD criteria were not used, but the women's PMS was said to be confirmed using concurrent ratings (i.e., by having higher ratings premenstrually than postmenstrually). High self-disclosure and stress monitoring showed a positive correlation with severe premenstrual symptoms, whereas social support showed a negative correlation. Findings such as these point to fruitful areas for future research.

Even if retrospective reports are revisited, findings using the LLPDD diagnosis and the 30% change confirmation criterion would not simply be discarded. Instead, such findings may need to be put into perspective. Even if the 30% change criterion is inadequate to distinguish groups, researchers may be no worse off than if they had merely relied on retrospective reports. Alternatively, the method may have increased the homogeneity of patient groups somewhat; next, however, we discuss possible dissociative processes that may be linked to menstrual cycles, confounding simple methods of assessment and potentially biasing research.

Are some dissociative processes to menstrual cycles linked?   It is possible that findings over the past decade have been skewed by the exclusion from research of nearly half of the women presenting for treatment. Some women have been labeled *false positives* (disconfirmed) and excluded from entry into research protocols, when in fact, their retrospective reports may be more meaningful, not less, than some of their concurrent reports (Hamilton & Gallant (Alagna), 1990). A crucial question for clinicians is why these women's global reports of having PMS/LLPDD are unconfirmed.

At least in part, discrepancies between some women's retrospective reports and various types of concurrent reports may be related to exacerbation of dissociative processing premenstrually (Hamilton & Gallant (Alagna), 1990). As shown earlier in Figure 4, for example, Jensvold and Putnam (1990) found that dissociative symptoms increased by nearly 30% in women with confirmed LLPDD. The possibility of a menstrual cycle–related effect on the patterning of PTSD and dissociative symptoms is interesting in view of the apparent increased prevalence rate of PTSD in women compared with men (Breslau et al., 1991).

Figure 12 shows a spontaneous, hand-written report from a woman who describes suffering from her usual PMS; yet her concurrent nu-

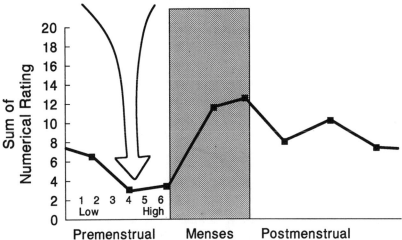

Figure 12. The sum of concurrent, daily ratings of negative symptoms (made on a six-point scale) is shown for one subject. The cross-hatched area designates menstruation. The statement appearing in the balloon was written by the subject spontaneously during the same premenstrual period when numerical ratings were otherwise low. From "Problematic Aspects of Diagnosing Premenstrual Phase Dysphoria: Recommendations for Psychological Research and Practice" by J. A. Hamilton and S. J. Gallant (Alagna), 1990, *Professional Psychology, 21*, p. 41. Copyright 1990 by the American Psychological Association. Adapted by permission.

merical self-ratings from the same time period revealed no increase in premenstrual symptoms. Clearly, she was using the two methods of self-reporting in different—and disassociated—ways (Hamilton & Gallant (Alagna), 1990). The biomedical database developed over the past decade has excluded this woman's experience from investigation, just as it has tended to exclude different patterns (Figure 3) and types of symptoms from study.

If dissociative symptoms are important in understanding the premenstrual experiences of a substantial subgroup of women (estimated to be from perhaps 15% to as much as 30–40%), then there may be implications for selection of measures for testing hypotheses as well. For example, the usual paper-and-pencil tests of possible menstrual-related shifts in attributions (Trunnell et al., 1988) may be unrevealing for those women who dissociate their reports depending on the type of measure used. For these women, free-associative or other spontaneous speech or writing techniques may be more useful than numerical rating scales (Dan, 1980; Hamilton & Gallant (Alagna), 1990).

Several lines of evidence suggest that trauma-related variables may be predictors of self-identified premenstrual distress (Hamilton & Jensvold, 1992; Paddison et al., 1990). For example, high rates of PTSD were observed in confirmed LLPDD patients, compared with controls, by Jensvold and Putnam (1990); however, the increased prevalence rate of PTSD in LLPDD patients is not explained simply by higher rates of exposure to trauma. Other studies have not reported unusually high rates of PTSD in PMS/LLPDD patients, but they did not specifically screen for it (Gise et al., 1990; Stout et al., 1986).

Although in need of replication, these data suggest potentially important new hypotheses. For example, is PTSD a risk factor for PMS/LLPDD, or conversely, is PMS/LLPDD a risk factor for development of PTSD? Or is a third variable (e.g., clinical depression, possibly when combined with trauma, or a biological vulnerability, such as preferential pathway for progesterone metabolism) related to both? Data on increased sensitivity to induction of paniclike attacks in PMS/LLPDD patients support further exploration of links to anxiety-related disorders such as PTSD. But there is considerable overlap between anxiety and depressive disorders, especially in women (Blazer et al., 1988).

For crime victims, there is some evidence that pretrauma depression may be a vulnerability factor in the development of PTSD, especially with high stress exposure during the crime (Resnick, Kilpatrick, Best, & Kramer, 1992). It is possible that milder forms of depression, such as that occurring premenstrually, might also be a risk factor for PTSD; Graze et al. (1990) showed that a history of premenstrual depressive symptoms predicts future risk of a major depressive disorder.

The possibility that dissociative processes are increased in some women premenstrually is especially interesting in view of the progesterone metabolite hypothesis. For example, some progesterone metabolites have effects like benzodiazepines, which are known to induce dissociativelike symptoms (Good, 1989). Although clinicians tend to think of dissociative processes as maladaptive, the processes probably exist on a continuum, with some types or degrees of dissociation being adaptive in certain situations (Hamilton, Haier, & Buchsbaum, 1984; Tellegen & Atkinson, 1974).

In the coming decade, it will be necessary to study the entire range of experiences that actually occur in relation to the menstrual cycle in a more systematic way. This means rethinking what groups must be studied and why. It is clear that three types of information have been considered important in classifying subjects in PMS/LLPDD studies: (a) retrospective reports, (b) prospective (concurrent daily) ratings, and (c) Axis I comorbidity. As shown in Figure 13, this conceptualization results in a 2 × 2 × 2 classification scheme (Hamilton, Gullion, & Yonkers, 1992; also in MacDonald et al., 1992), so that a balanced design would assess all eight subgroups. Yet the past decade of research has been dominated by studies using unbalanced designs, which are inadequate for testing many biologically based hypotheses. Most studies have used only two of the eight subgroups, which thereby focuses attention on Groups 2 (retrospective LLPDD, confirmed by prospective ratings, without Axis I comorbidity) and 8 (no retrospective LLPDD, no actual change on prospective ratings, and no comorbidity), whereas Group 4 is also conceptually of high interest. In addition, some biological theories should be tested using Group 6 (those who retrospectively deny premenstrual symptoms, yet show changes on daily ratings as great as those who retrospectively report them) as well as Group 2.

Recommendations for clinical evaluations.   It is impossible to do blind clinical assessments of symptomatic women who seek treatment. However, it is prudent to choose reasonably sound rating instruments and to attempt to minimize unwanted demand characteristics. Instead of choosing bipolar rating scales, we recommend that

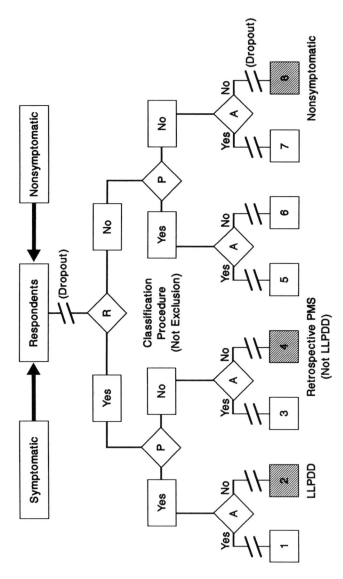

Figure 13. The figure demonstrates three types of information considered important in classifying women in PMS/LLPDD studies: R, retrospective reports; P, prospective, daily (concurrent) ratings; and A, clinical diagnostic assessment (e.g., by an interview schedule such as the SCID). This results in a 2 × 2 × 2 procedure, with eight cells of potential interest. From *Progesterone Metabolism/Action and Premenstrual Syndrome* by P. C. MacDonald, M. L. Casey, K. A. Yonkers, J. A. Hamilton, C. M. Gullion, S. Chantilis, and F. M. Rogerson, 1992, unpublished manuscript, University of Texas Southwestern Medical School, Dallas.

they be unipolar. In addition, the instrument should have statements to anchor the meaning in terms of symptom severity. Ratings should be displayed one day at a time and should be returned by mail at least once a week. Until better criteria for defining symptomatic groups are available, it is advisable to use the Mitchell et al. (1991) rating scale because population-based cutoff criteria are available.

Preliminary data suggest that nearly 50% of women who seek treatment for PMS/LLPDD will not be confirmed by the usual daily rating methods. A subgroup may fail to do so because of measurement error related to dissociative processes; although speculative, measurement may be enhanced by adding spontaneous speech or writing samples, as well as by direct observation or behavioral ratings. As in all clinical populations, a history of victimization should be explored.

Clinicians must remain clinically oriented, and we advise clinical researchers to do the same. This means that the clinician must pay attention to multiple sources of information about the patient and not just to numerical ratings. We advise the clinician to pay special attention to possible interactive, contextual effects on symptoms, for example, to external stressors and daily hassles, to ways of dealing with conflict in relationships, to attitudes toward menstruation and anger, to coping strategies, and to self-esteem. The final section has implications for evaluation as well as treatment.

Nondrug Treatments

Nondrug treatments are commonly used (Casson et al., 1990, pp. 99–100; Corney & Clare, 1989; Coyne, Woods, & Mitchell, 1985; Keye, 1988) and should be studied with at least the same frequency and intensity as biologically oriented treatments. Nondrug treatments include validation, education, charting of symptoms, life-style modification such as increased exercise, regulation of diet, stress management, relaxation training, participation in group counseling programs, family counseling, and psychotherapy.

An important study recently compared hormone therapy (dydrogesterone, a synthetic progestin), coping skills training in group sessions (based on rational–emotive therapy), and relaxation training (provided as audiotaped instructions using Benson's procedure) for the treatment of PMS (Morse, Dennerstein, Farrell, & Varnavides, 1991). Although the patients did not necessarily meet criteria for

LLPDD, negative moods dominated symptom reports, and 85% reported severe symptoms. Two months of daily ratings were used to confirm symptom reports, although exact criteria were not specified. The hormone and relaxation groups showed early benefits, but by 2 months the coping skills group showed changes in both psychological and physical symptoms. Treatments were maintained for 3 months, with follow-up after an additional 3 months. At follow-up, both the hormone and coping skills groups maintained improvements over the pretreatment baseline (26% vs. 43% improvement for psychological symptoms and 24% vs. 29% for physical symptoms, respectively). Only the coping skills training resulted in improvement in cognitive symptoms. In this study, relaxation was used for comparison purposes, but others have documented benefits of relaxation therapy for premenstrual symptoms (Goodale, Domar, & Benson, 1990), especially for severe symptoms.

Conclusions and Recommendations for Future Research

Biopsychosocial models of PMS facilitate adopting a contextual perspective that addresses the interrelationships of biological, psychological, and sociocultural factors in symptom experience. However, actually performing biopsychosocial research poses a special challenge for many who are unfamiliar with theories of women's development from a contextual perspective or who are uncomfortable with the designs, methods, and procedures for data analysis that are required. Many researchers are reductionists at heart and assume that complex phenomena are most appropriately understood by investigating component parts. Adopting a contextual perspective means abandoning simple cause-and-effect relationships and unidirectional models and embracing multicausality—which a priori places no greater emphasis on biological determinants than on psychosocial, relational, or cultural factors.

Ultimately, the goal should be to develop more complex models for research (Taylor et al., 1991; Ussher, 1992), thereby better apportioning variance among multiple factors, as demonstrated by investigators in related fields (Brooks-Gunn & Warren, 1989). The 30% change criterion is dwarfed by psychosocial effects on symptomatology, demonstrating that the mind does indeed play a powerful role in PMS/LLPDD.

REFERENCES

Abramson, L. Y., Seligman, M. E. P., & Teasdale, J. D. (1978). Learned help-lessness: Critique and reformulation. *Journal of Abnormal Psychology, 87,* 49–74.

Alagna, S. W., & Hamilton, J. A. (1986). Social stimulus perception and self-evaluation: Effects of menstrual cycle phase. *Psychology of Women Quarterly, 10,* 327–338.

Altschule, M. D., & Brem, J. (1963). Periodic psychosis of puberty. *American Journal of Psychiatry, 119,* 1176–1178.

American Psychiatric Association. (1987). *Diagnostic and statistical manual of mental disorders* (3rd ed., rev.). Washington, DC: Author.

American Psychiatric Association. (in press). *Diagnostic and statistical manual of mental disorders* (4th ed.). Washington, DC: Author.

AuBuchon, P. G., & Calhoun, K. S. (1985). Menstrual cycle symptomatology: The role of social expectancy and experimental demand characteristics. *Psychosomatic Medicine, 47,* 35–45.

Backstrom, C. T., Boyle, H., & Baird, D. T. (1981). Persistence of symptoms of premenstrual tension in hysterectomized women. *British Journal of Obstetrics and Gynecology, 88,* 530–536.

Badwe, R. A., Gregory, W. M., Chaudary, M. A., Richards, M. A., Bentley, A. E., & Rubens, R. D. (1991). Timing of surgery during the menstrual cycle and survival of premenopausal women with operable breast cancer. *Lancet, 337,* 1261–1264.

Bains, G. K., & Slade, P. (1988). Attributional patterns, moods, and the menstrual cycle. *Psychosomatic Medicine, 50,* 469–476.

Beck, L. E., Gevirtz, R., & Mortola, J. F. (1990). The predictive role of psychosocial stress on symptom severity in premenstrual syndrome. *Psychosomatic Medicine, 52,* 536–543.

Berlin, F. S., Bergey, G. K., & Money, J. (1982). Periodic psychosis of puberty: A case report. *American Journal of Psychiatry, 139,* 119–120.

Blazer, D., Swartz, M., Woodbury, M., Manton, K. G., Hughes, D., & George, L. K. (1988). Depressive symptoms and depressive diagnosis in a community population. *Archives of General Psychiatry, 45,* 1078–1084.

Blume, E. (1983). Methodological issues plague PMS research. *Journal of the American Medical Association, 249,* 2866.

Bourgeois, S., Pfahl, M., & Baulieu, E. E. (1984). DNA binding properties of glucocorticosteroid receptors bound to the steroid antagonist RU-486. *EMBO, 3,* 751–755.

Breslau, N., Davis, D. C., Andreski, P., & Peterson, E. (1991). Traumatic events and posttraumatic stress disorder in an urban population of young adults. *American Journal of Psychiatry, 48,* 216–222.

Brier, A., Charney, D. S., & Heninger, G. R. (1986). Agoraphobia with panic attacks. *Archives of General Psychiatry, 43,* 1029–1036.

Brooks-Gunn, J., & Ruble, D. N. (1980). The menstrual attitude questionnaire. *Psychosomatic Medicine, 42,* 503–511.

Brooks-Gunn, J., & Warren, M. P. (1989). Biological and social contributors to negative affect in young adolescent girls. *Child Development, 60,* 45–55.

Brown, M. A., & Zimmer, P. A. (1986, January/February). Personal and family impact of premenstrual symptoms. *Journal of Obstetrical and Gynecological Nursing,* 31–38.

Buckley, T. (1988). Menstruation and the power of Yurok women. In T. Buckley & A. Gottlieb (Eds.), *Blood magic: Explorations in the anthropology of menstruation* (pp. 187–209). Berkeley, CA: University of California Press.

Burnett, R. (1992). *Review on social interaction and the menstrual cycle.* Unpublished manuscript, Duke University, Department of Psychology: Social and Health Science, Durham, NC.

Cameron, O. G., Kuttesch, D., McPhee, K., & Curtis, G. C. (1988). Menstrual fluctuation in the symptoms of panic anxiety. *Journal of Affective Disorders, 15,* 169–174.

Casper, R. F., & Hearn, M. T. (1990). The effect of hysterectomy and bilateral oophorectomy in women with severe premenstrual syndrome. *American Journal of Obstetrics and Gynecology, 162,* 105–109.

Casson, P., Hahn, P. M., Van Vugt, D. A., & Reid, R. L. (1990). Lasting response to ovariectomy in severe intractable premenstrual syndrome. *American Journal of Obstetrics and Gynecology, 162,* 99–105.

Chandra, P. S., & Chaturvedi, S. K. (1989). Cultural variations of premenstrual experience. *International Journal of Social Psychiatry, 35,* 343–349.

Chen, G., Huang, J. R., Mazella, J., & Tseng, L. (1989). Long-term effects of progestin and RU-486 on prolactin production and synthesis in human endometrial stroma cells. *Human Reproduction, 4,* 355–358.

Chisholm, G., Jung, S. O. J., Cumming, C. E., Fox, E. E., & Cumming, D. C. (1990). Premenstrual anxiety and depression: Comparison of objective psychological tests with a retrospective questionnaire. *Acta Psychiatrica Scandinavica, 81,* 52–57.

Conrad, C. D., & Hamilton, J. A. (1986). Recurrent premenstrual decline in lithium concentration: Clinical correlates and treatment implications. *Journal of the American Academy of Child Psychiatry, 26,* 852–853.

Cook, B. L., Noyes, R., Garvey, M. J., Beach, V., Sobotka, J., & Chaudhry, D. (1990). Anxiety and the menstrual cycle in panic disorder. *Journal of Affective Disorders, 19,* 221–226.

Corney, R. H., & Clare, A. W. (1989). The treatment of premenstrual syndrome. *The Practitioner, 233,* 233–236.

Coughlin, P. C. (1990). Premenstrual syndrome: How marital satisfaction and role choice affect symptom severity. *Social Work, 35,* 351–355.

Coyne, C. (1983). Muscle tension and its relation to symptoms in the premenstruum. *Research in Nursing Health, 6,* 199–206.

Coyne, C. M., Woods, N. F., & Mitchell, E. S. (1985, November/December). Premenstrual tension syndrome. *Journal of Gynecologic and Neonatal Nursing,* 446–454.

Dale, D. C., & Hammond, W. P. (1988). Cyclic neutropenia: A clinical review. *Blood Review, 2,* 185–187.

Dalton, K., Dalton, M. E., & Guthrie, K. (1987). Incidence of the premenstrual syndrome in twins. *British Medical Journal, 295,* 1027–1028.

Dan, A. (1980). Free-associative versus self-report measures of emotional change over the menstrual cycle. In A. J. Dan, E. A. Graham, & C. P. Beecher (Eds.), *The menstrual cycle* (Vol. 1, pp. 115–120). New York: Springer.

DeJong, R., Rubinow, D. R., Roy-Byrne, P., Hoban, M. C., Grover, G. N., & Post, R. M. (1985). Premenstrual mood disorder and psychiatric illness. *American Journal of Psychiatry, 142,* 1359–1361.

Delaney, J., Lupton, M. J., & Toth, E. (1988). *The curse: A cultural history of menstruation* (rev. ed.). Chicago: University of Illinois Press. (Original work published in 1976)

Dickson-Parnell, B., & Zeichner, A. (1988). The premenstrual syndrome: Psychophysiologica concomitants of perceived stress and low back pain. *Pain, 34,* 161–169.

Dinnerstein, L., Morse, C., & Gotts, G. (1988). Perspective from a PMS clinic. In L. H. Gise, N. G. Kase, & R. L. Berkowitz (Eds.), *The premenstrual syndromes* (pp. 109–118). New York: Churchill Livingstone.

Eliasson, O., & DeGraff, A. C. (1987). A cautionary tale about the investigation of the effect of the menstrual cycle on asthma. *American Review of Respiratory Disease, 136,* 1515.

Eliasson, O., Scherzer, H. H., & DeGraff, A. C. (1986). Morbidity in asthma in relation to the menstrual cycle. *Journal of Allergy and Clinical Immunology, 77,* 87–94.

Endicott, J., & Halbreich, U. (1982). Prospective reports of premenstrual depressive changes: Factors affecting confirmation of ratings. *Psychopharmacology Bulletin, 18,* 109–112.

Endicott, J., Halbreich, U., Schacht, S., & Nee, J. (1981). Premenstrual changes and affective disorders. *Psychosomatic Medicine, 43,* 519–529.

Endicott, J., Schact, S., & Halbreich, U. (1982). *Daily rating form.* New York: Research Assessment and Training Unit, 722 West 168th Street, New York, NY 10032.

Endo, M., Daiguji, M., Asano, Y., Yamashita, I., & Takahashi, S. (1978). Periodic psychosis recurring in association with the menstrual cycle. *Journal of Clinical Psychiatry, 39,* 456–466.

Englander-Golden, P., Sonleiter, F. S., Whitmore, M. R., & Corbley, G. J. M. (1986). Social and menstrual cycles. In V. L. Olesen & N. F. Woods (Eds.), *Culture, society, and menstruation* (pp. 97–114). Washington, DC: Hemisphere.

Englander-Golden, P., Whitmore, M. R., & Dienstbier, R. A. (1978). Menstrual cycle as a focus of study and self-reports of moods and behavior. *Motivation and Emotion, 2,* 75–87.

Facchinetti, F., Romano, G., Fava, M., & Genazzani, A. R. (1992). Lactate infusion induces panic attacks in patients with premenstrual syndrome. *Psychosomatic Medicine, 54,* 288–296.

Fradkin, B., & Firestone, P. (1986). Premenstrual tension, expectancy, and mother–child relations. *Journal of Behavioral Medicine, 9,* 245–259.

Freeman, E. W., Rickels, K., & Sondheimer, S. J. (1992). Course of premenstrual syndrome symptom severity after treatment. *American Journal of Psychiatry, 149,* 531–533.

Freeman, E. W., Rickels, K., Sondheimer, S. J., & Polansky, M. (1990). Ineffectiveness of progesterone suppository treatment for premenstrual syndrome. *Journal of the American Medical Association, 264,* 349–353.

Freeman, E. W., Sondheimer, S. J., & Rickels, K. (1988). Effects of medical history factors on symptom severity in women meeting criteria for premenstrual syndrome. *Obstetrics and Gynecology, 72,* 236–239.

Gallant (Alagna), S. J., & Hamilton, J. A. (1988). On a premenstrual psychiatric diagnosis: What's in a name? *Professional Psychology, 19,* 271–278.

Gallant, S. J., Hamilton, J. A., Popiel, D. A., Morokoff, P. J., & Chakraborty, P. K. (1991). Daily moods and symptoms: Effects of awareness of study focus, gender, menstrual-cycle phase, and day of the week. *Health Psychology, 10,* 180–189.

Gallant, S. J., Popiel, D. A., & Hoffman, D. H. (in press). The role of psychological variables in the experience of premenstrual symptoms. *Proceedings of the Society for Menstrual Cycle Research.*

Gallant, S. J., Popiel, D. A., Hoffman, D. H., Chakraborty, P. K., & Hamilton, J. A. (1992a). Daily ratings of premenstrual symptoms: I. Awareness effects. *Psychosomatic Medicine, 54,* 149–166.

Gallant, S. J., Popiel, D. A., Hoffman, D. H., Chakraborty, P. K., & Hamilton, J. A. (1992b). Daily ratings of premenstrual symptoms: II. Differentiating women with severe symptoms from women with normal menstrual cycles. *Psychosomatic Medicine, 54,* 167–181.

Gibbs, C. J., Coutts, I. I., Lock, R., Finnegan, O. C., & White, R. J. (1984). The premenstrual exacerbation of asthma. *Thorax, 39,* 833–836.

Gise, L. H., Lebovits, A. H., Paddison, P. L., & Strain, J. J. (1990). Issues in the identification of premenstrual syndromes. *Journal of Nervous and Mental Disease, 178,* 228–234.

Gladis, M. M., & Walsh, B. T. (1987). Premenstrual exacerbation of binge eating in bulimia. *American Journal of Psychiatry, 144,* 1592–1595.

Glick, I. D., & Stewart, D. (1980). A new drug treatment for premenstrual exacerbation of schizophrenia. *Comprehensive Psychiatry, 21,* 281–287.

Goldstein, R., Duff, S., & Karsh, J. (1987). Functional assessment of symptoms of rheumatoid arthritis in relation to menstrual cycle phase. *Journal of Rheumatology, 14,* 395–396.

Good, M. I. (1989). Substance-induced dissociative disorders and psychiatric nosology. *Journal of Clinical Psychopharmacology, 9,* 88–93.

Goodale, I. L., Domar, A. C., & Benson, H. (1990). Alleviation of premenstrual syndrome with the relaxation response. *Obstetrics and Gynecology, 75,* 649–655.

Graham, C. A., & McGrew, W. C. (1992). Social factors and menstrual synchrony in a population of nurses. In A. J. Dan & L. L. Lewis (Eds.), *Menstrual health in women's lives* (pp. 246–253). Chicago: University of Illinois Press.

Graze, K. K., Nee, J., & Endicott, J. (1990). Premenstrual depression predicts future major depressive disorders. *Acta Psychiatrica Scandinavica, 81,* 201–205.

Halbreich, U., & Endicott, J. (1985). Methodological issues in studies of premenstrual changes. *Psychoneuroendocrinology, 10,* 15–32.

Halbreich, U., Endicott, J., & Lesser, J. (1985). The clinical diagnosis and classification of premenstrual changes. *Canadian Journal of Psychiatry, 30,* 489–497.

Halbreich, U., Endicott, J., Schacht, S., & Nee, J. (1982). The diversity of premenstrual changes as reflected in the premenstrual assessment form. *Acta Psychiatrica Scandinavica, 65,* 46–56.

Hamilton, J. (Ed.). (1991). Clinical pharmacology panel report. In S. J. Blumenthal, P. Barry, J. Hamilton, & B. Sherwin (Eds.), *Forging a women's health research agenda* (pp. 1–27). Washington, DC: National Women's Health Resource Center.

Hamilton, J. A. (in press). Sex and gender as critical variables in psychotropic research. In B. Brown, P. Rieker, & C. Willie (Eds.), *Racism and sexism and mental health,* Pittsburgh, PA: University of Pittsburgh Press.

Hamilton, J. A., Alagna, S. W., & Sharpe, K. (1985). Cognitive approaches to understanding and treating premenstrual depression. In O. J. Osofsky & S. J. Blumenthal (Eds.), *Premenstrual syndrome: Current findings and future directions* (pp. 66–83). Washington, DC: American Psychiatric Press.

Hamilton, J. A., & Gallant (Alagna), S. J. (1990). Problematic aspects of diagnosing premenstrual phase dysphoria: Recommendations for psychological research and practice. *Professional Psychology, 21,* 60–68.

Hamilton, J. A., Gallant (Alagna), S., & Lloyd, C. (1989). Evidence for a menstrual artifact in determining rates of depression. *Journal of Nervous and Mental Disease, 177,* 359–365.

Hamilton, J. A., Gullion, C., & Yonkers, K. (1992). *Proposal for PMS research.* Unpublished manuscript, University of Texas Southwestern Medical School, Dallas.

Hamilton, J. A., Haier, R. J., & Buchsbaum, M. S. (1984). Intrinsic enjoyment and boredom coping scales: Validation with personality, evoked potential and attention measures. *Personality and Individual Differences, 5,* 183–193.

Hamilton, J. A., & Jensvold, M. (1992). Personality, psychopathology and depressions in women. In L. Brown & M. Ballou (Eds.), *Personality and psychopathology: Feminist reappraisals* (pp. 116–143). New York: Guilford Press.

Hamilton, J. A., Parry, B. L., Alagna, S. W., Blumenthal, S., & Herz, E. (1984). Premenstrual mood changes: A guide to evaluation and treatment. *Psychiatric Annals, 14,* 426–435.

Hamilton, J. A., Parry, B. L., & Blumenthal, S. J. (1988). The menstrual cycle in context: I. Affective syndromes associated with reproductive hormonal changes. *Journal of Clinical Psychiatry, 49,* 474–480.

Hammond, W. P., Price, T. H., Souza, L. M., & Dale, D. C. (1989). Treatment of cyclic neutropenia with granulocyte colony stimulating factor. *New England Journal of Medicine, 320,* 1306–1311.

Harrison, W. M., Endicott, J., & Nee, J. (1990). Treatment of premenstrual dysphoria with alprazolam. *Archives of General Psychiatry, 47,* 270–275.

Harrison, W. M., Sandberg, D., Gorman, J. M., Fyer, M., Nee, J., Uy, J., & Endicott, J. (1989). Provocation of panic with carbon dioxide inhalation in patients with premenstrual dysphoria. *Psychiatry Research, 27,* 183–192.

Hart, W. G., Coleman, G. J., & Russell, J. W. (1987). Assessment of premenstrual symptomatology: A re-evaluation of the predictive validity of self-report. *Journal of Psychosomatic Research, 31,* 185–190.

Helzer, J. E., Robins, L. N., & McEvoy, L. (1987). Post-traumatic stress disorder in the general population. *New England Journal of Medicine, 317,* 1630–1634.

Hrushesky, W. J., Bluming, A. Z., Gruber, S. A., & Sothern, R. B. (1989). Menstrual influence on surgical cure of breast cancer. *Lancet, 2,* 949–952.

Janiger, O., Riffenburgh, R., & Karsh, R. (1972). Cross cultural study of premenstrual symptoms. *Psychosomatics, 13,* 226–235.

Jenner, F. A. (1968). Periodic psychoses in the light of biological rhythm research. *International Review of Neurobiology, 11,* 129–169.

Jensvold, M., & Putnam, F. (1990, March). *Postabuse syndromes in premenstrual syndrome patients and controls.* Paper presented at the National Conference of the Association of Women in Psychology, Tempe, AZ.

Jensvold, M. J., Reed, K., Jarrett, D. B., & Hamilton, J. A. (1992). Menstrual cycle–related depressive symptoms treated with variable antidepressant dosage: A case report and case series. *Journal of Women's Health, 1,* 109–115.

Johnson, T. M. (1983). Premenstrual syndrome as a Western culture–specific disorder. *Culture, Medicine, and Psychiatry, 11,* 337–356.

Johnston, V. S., & Wang, X. T. (1991). The relationship between menstrual phase and P3 component of ERPs. *Psychophysiology, 28,* 400–409.

Keenan, P. A., Stern, R. A., Janowsky, D. S., & Pedersen, C. A. (1992). Psychological aspects of premenstrual syndrome: I. Cognition and memory. *Psychoneuroendocrinology, 17,* 179–187.

Kendler, K. S., Silberg, J. L., Neale, M. C., Kessler, R. C., Heath, A. C., & Eaves, L. J. (1992). Genetic and environmental factors in the aetiology of menstrual, premenstrual and neurotic symptoms: A population-based twin study. *Psychological Medicine, 22,* 85–100.

Keye, W. R. (1988). Premenstrual symptoms: Evaluation and treatment. *Comprehensive Therapy, 14,* 19–26.

Kirsch, J. R., & Geer, J. H. (1988). Skin conductance and heart rate in women with premenstrual syndrome. *Psychosomatic Medicine, 50,* 175–182.

Klebanov, P. K., & Jemmott, J. B. (1992). Effects of expectations and bodily sensations on self-reports of premenstrual syndromes. *Psychology of Women Quarterly, 16,* 289–310.

Koeske, R. K., & Koeske, G. F. (1975). An attributional approach to moods and the menstrual cycle. *Journal of Personality and Social Psychology, 31,* 473–478.

Labbate, L. A., Shearer, G., & Waldrep, D. A. (1991). A case of recurrent premenstrual psychosis. *Amerian Journal of Psychiatry, 148,* 147.

Latman, N. S. (1983). Relation of menstrual cycle phase to symptoms of rheumatoid arthritis. *American Journal of Medicine, 74,* 957–960.

Laws, S. (1983). The sexual politics of pre-menstrual tension. *Women's Studies International Forum, 6,* 19–31.

LeFevre, J., Hedricks, C., Church, R. B., & McClintock, M. (1992). Psychological and social behavior of couples over a menstrual cycle: "On-the-spot" sampling from everyday life. In A. J. Dan & L. L. Lewis (Eds.), *Menstrual health in women's lives* (pp. 75–81). Chicago: University of Illinois Press.

LeFevre, J., & McClintock, M. (1991). Isolation accelerates reproductive senescence and alters its predictors in female rats. *Hormones and Behavior, 25,* 258–272.

Leon, G. R., Phelan, P. W., Kelly, J., & Patten, S. R. (1986). The symptoms of bulimia and the menstrual cycle. *Psychosomatic Medicine, 48,* 415–422.

Loewenstein, R. J., Hamilton, J., Alagna, S., Reid, N., & deVries, M. (1987). Experiential sampling in the study of multiple personality disorder. *American Journal of Psychiatry, 144,* 19–24.

Logue, C. M., & Moos, R. H. (1986). Perimenstrual symptoms: Prevalence and risk factors. *Psychosomatic Medicine, 48,* 388–414.

MacDonald, P. C., Casey, M. L., Yonkers, K. A., Hamilton, J. A., Gullion, C. M., Chantilis, S., & Rogerson, F. M. (1992). *Progesterone metabolism/action and premenstrual syndrome.* Unpublished manuscript, University of Texas Southwestern Medical School, Dallas.

MacDonald, P. C., Dombroski, R. A., & Casey, M. L. (1991). Recurrent secretion of progesterone in large amounts: An endocrine/metabolic disorder unique to young women? *Endocrine Review, 12,* 372–401.

MacGregor, E. A., Chia, H., Vohrah, C., & Wilkinson, M. (1990). Migraine and menstruation: A pilot study. *Cephalgia, 10,* 305–310.

Mansfield, P. K., Hood, K. E., & Henderson, J. (1989). Women and their husbands: Mood and arousal fluctuations across the menstrual cycle and days of the week. *Psychosomatic Medicine, 51,* 66–80.

Martin, E. (1992). *The woman in the body: A cultural analysis of reproduction* (rev. ed.). Boston: Beacon Press. (Original work published in 1987)

McClintock, M. K. (1971). Menstrual synchrony and suppression. *Nature, 229,* 244–245.

McClintock, M. K. (1981). Social control of the ovarian cycle and the function of estrus synchrony. *American Zoologist, 21,* 243–256.

McMillan, M. J., & Pihl, R. O. (1987). Premenstrual depression: A distinct entity. *Journal of Abnormal Psychology, 96,* 149–154.

Metcalf, M. G., Livesey, J. H., & Wells, J. E. (1989). Assessment of the significance and severity of premenstrual tension: II. Comparison of methods. *Journal of Psychosomatic Research, 33,* 281–292.

Metcalf, M. G., Livesey, J. H., Wells, J. E., Braiden, V., Hudson, S. M., & Bamber, L. (1991). Premenstrual syndrome in hysterectomized women: Mood and physical symptom cyclicity. *Journal of Psychosomatic Research*, 35, 555–567.

Mitchell, E. S., Woods, N. F., & Lentz, M. J. (1991). Recognizing PMS when you see it: Criteria for PMS sample selection. In D. L. Taylor & N. F. Woods (Eds.), *Menstruation, health, and illness* (pp. 89–102). Washington, DC: Hemisphere.

Mira, M., Vizzard, J., Macaskill, P., & Abraham, S. (1986). Placebo response in premenstrual syndrome sufferers. *Exerpta Medica, 707*, 204–212.

Monagle, L., Al-Gasser, N., Woods, N. F., & Dan, A. (1992, October). *Cross-cultural comparison of perimenstrual symptom prevalence.* Paper presented at the Reframing Women's Health Conference, Chicago, IL.

Moos, R. H. (1985). *Perimenstrual symptoms: A manual and overview of research with the Menstrual Distress Questionnaire.* Palo Alto, CA: Stanford University and Veterans Affairs Hospital.

Morley, A. (1970). Periodic diseases, physiological rhythms and feedback control: A hypothesis. *Australian Annals of Medicine, 3*, 244–249.

Morse, C. A., Dennerstein, L., Farrell, E., & Varnavides, K. (1991). A comparison of hormone therapy, coping skills training, and relaxation for the relief of premenstrual syndrome. *Journal of Behavioral Medicine, 14*, 469–489.

Mortola, J. F., Girton, L., & Yen, S. C. (1989). Depressive episodes in premenstrual syndrome. *American Journal of Obstetrics and Gynecology, 161*, 1682–1687.

Muse, K. N., Cetel, N. S., Futterman, L. A., & Yen, S. C. (1984). The premenstrual syndrome: Effects of "medical ovariectomy." *New England Journal of Medicine, 311*, 1345–1349.

Newmark, M. E., & Penry, J. K. (1980). Catamenial epilepsy: A review. *Epilepsia, 21*, 281–300.

Nieman, L. K., Choate, T. M., Chrousos, G. P., Healy, D. L., Morin, M., Renquist, D., Merriam, G. R., Spitz, I. M., Bardin, C. W., Baulieu, E. E., & Loriaux, D. L. (1987). The progesterone anatagonist RU 486. *New England Journal of Medicine, 316*, 187–191.

Nolen-Hoeksema, S. (1987). Sex differences in unipolar depression: Evidence and theory. *Psychological Bulletin, 101*, 259–282.

O'Boyle, M., Severino, S. K., & Hurt, S. W. (1988). Premenstrual syndrome and locus of control. *International Journal of Psychiatry in Medicine, 18*, 67–74.

Olasov, B., & Jackson, J. (1987). Effects of expectancies on women's reports of mood during the menstrual cycle. *Psychosomatic Medicine, 49*, 65–78.

Osborn, M. (1981). Physical and psychological determinants of premenstrual tension: Research issues and proposed methodology. *Journal of Psychosomatic Research, 25*, 363–367.

Osborn, M. F., & Gath, D. H. (1990). Psychological and physical determinants of premenstrual symptoms before and after hysterectomy. *Psychological Medicine, 20*, 565–572.

Paddison, P. L., Gise, L. H., Lebovits, A., Strain, J. J., Cirasole, D. M., & Levine, J. P. (1990). Sexual abuse and premenstrual syndrome: A comparison between a lower and higher socioeconomic group. *Psychosomatics, 3,* 265–272.

Paige, K. E. (July 1973). Women learn to sing the menstrual blues. *Psychology Today, 7,* 41–46.

Parlee, M. B. (1973). The premenstrual syndrome. *Psychological Bulletin, 80,* 454–465.

Parry, B. L., Berga, S. L., Kripke, D. F., Klauber, M. R., Laughlin, G. A., Yen, S. C., & Gillin, J. C. (1990). Altered waveform of plasma nocturnal melatonin secretion in premenstrual syndrome, *Archives of General Psychiatry, 47,* 1139–1146.

Parry, B. L., Berga, S. L., Mostofi, N., Sependa, P. A., Kripke, D. F., & Gillin, J. C. (1989). Morning versus evening bright light treatment of late luteal phase dysphoric disorder. *American Journal of Psychiatry, 146,* 1215–1217.

Parry, B. L., & Wehr, T. A. (1987). Therapeutic effect of sleep deprivation in patients with premenstrual syndrome. *American Journal of Psychiatry, 144,* 808–810.

Payer, L. (1988). *Medicine and culture.* New York: Penguin.

Pearlstein, T. B., Frank, E., Rivera-Tovar, A., Thoft, J. S., Jacobs, E., & Mieczkowski, T. A. (1990). Prevalence of Axis I and Axis II disorders in women with late luteal phase dysphoric disorder. *Journal of Affective Disorders, 20,* 129–134.

Pennebaker, J. W. (1982). *The psychology of physical symptoms.* New York: Springer-Verlag.

Pennebaker, J. W., & Roberts, T. (1992). Toward a his and hers theory of emotion: Gender differences in visceral perception. *Journal of Social and Clinical Psychology, 11,* 199–212.

Powers, M. N. (1980). Menstruation and reproduction: An Oglala case. In C. R. Stimpson & E. S. Person (Eds.), *Women: Sex and sexuality* (pp. 117–128). Chicago: University of Chicago Press.

Price, T. R. P. (1980). Temporal lobe epilepsy as a premenstrual behavioral syndrome. *Biological Psychiatry, 15,* 957–963.

Price, W. A., Torem, M. S., & DiMarzio, L. R. (1987). Premenstrual exacerbation of bulimia. *Psychosomatics, 28,* 378–379.

Ramcharan, S., Love, E. J., Fick, G. H., & Goldfien, A. (1992). The epidemiology of premenstrual symptoms in a population-based sample of 2650 urban women: Attributable risk and risk factors. *Journal of Clinical Epidemiology, 45,* 377–392.

Rapkin, A. J., Chang, L. C., & Reading, A. (1988). Comparison of retrospective and prospective assessment of premenstrual symptoms. *Psychological Reports, 62,* 55–60.

Rapkin, A. J., Chang, L. C., & Reading, A. (1989). Mood and cognitive style in premenstrual syndrome. *Obstetrics and Gynecology, 74,* 644–649.

Regier, D. A., Boyd, J. H., Burke, J. D., Rae, D. S., Myers, J. K., Kramer, M., Robins, L. N., George, L. K., Karno, M., & Locke, B. Z. (1988).

One-month prevalence of mental disorders in the United States. *Archives of General Psychiatry, 45,* 977–986.

Resnick, H. S., Kilpatrick, D. S., Best, C. L., & Kramer, T. L. (1992). Vulnerability-stress factors in development of posttraumatic stress disorder. *Journal of Nervous and Mental Disease, 180,* 424–430.

Richardson, T. E. (Ed.). (1992). *Cognition and the menstrual cycle.* New York: Springer-Verlag.

Rivera-Tovar, A. D., & Frank, E. (1990). Late luteal phase dysphoric disorder in young women. *American Journal of Psychiatry, 147,* 1634–1636.

Robins, L. N., Helzer, J. E., Weissman, M. M., Orvaschel, H., Gruenberg, E., Burke, J. D., & Regier, D. A. (1984). Lifetime prevalence of specific psychiatric disorders in three sites. *Archives of General Psychiatry, 41,* 949–958.

Rodin, M. (1992). The social construction of premenstrual syndrome. *Social Science and Medicine, 35,* 49–56.

Rothblum, B. O., & Jackson, J. (1990). Religious influence on menstrual attitudes and symptoms. *Women and Health, 16,* 63–77.

Rovner, S. (1986, February 19). New PMS theories discount hormones. *Washington Post Health,* pp. 5–6.

Rovner, S. (1987, May 12). A new manual for mental disorders. *Washington Post Health,* p. 8.

Roy, J. M. (1992). Surgical gynecology. In R. D. Apple (Ed.), *Women, health and medicine in America* (pp. 173–195). New Brunswick, NJ: Rutgers University Press.

Rubinow, D. R., & Roy-Byrne, P. (1984). Premenstrual syndrome: Overview from a methodological perspective. *American Journal of Psychiatry, 141,* 161–172.

Rubinow, D. R., Roy-Byrne, P., Hoban, M. C., Gold, P. W., & Post, R. M. (1984). Prospective assessment of menstrually related mood disorders. *American Journal of Psychiatry, 141,* 684–686.

Ruble, D. N. (1977). Premenstrual symptoms: A reinterpretation. *Science, 197,* 291–292.

Ruble, D. N., & Brooks-Gunn, J. (1979). Menstrual syndromes: A social cognition analysis. *Journal of Behavioral Medicine, 2,* 171–194.

Russo, N. F. (Ed.). (1985). *A woman's mental health agenda.* Washington, DC: American Psychological Association.

Sampson, G. (1979). Premenstrual syndrome: A double-blind controlled trial of progesterone and placebo. *British Journal of Psychiatry, 135,* 209–215.

Schacter, S. C. (1988). Hormonal considerations in women with seizures. *Archives of Neurology, 45,* 1267–1270.

Schechter, D., Bachmann, G. A., Vaitukaitis, J., Phillips, D., & Saperstein, D. (1989). Perimenstrual symptoms: Time course of symptom intensity in relation to endocrinologically defined segments of the menstrual cycle. *Psychosomatic Medicine, 51,* 173–194.

Schmidt, P. J., Grover, G. N., Hoban, M. C., & Rubinow, D. R. (1990). State-dependent alterations in the perceptions of life events in menstrual-related mood disorders. *American Journal of Psychiatry, 147,* 230–234.

Schmidt, P. J., Nieman, L. K., Grover, G. N., Muller, K. L., Merriam, G. R., & Rubinow, D. R. (1991). Lack of effect of induced menses on symptoms in women with premenstrual syndrome. *New England Journal of Medicine, 324,* 1174–1179.

Senie, R. T., Rosen, P. P., Rhodes, P., & Lesser, M. L. (1991). Timing of breast cancer excision during the menstrual cycle influences duration of disease-free survival. *Annals of Internal Medicine, 115,* 337–342.

Severino, S. K., Hurt, S. H., & Shindledecker, R. D. (1989). Spectral analysis of cyclic symptoms in late luteal phase dysphoric disorder. *American Journal of Psychiatry, 146,* 1155–1160.

Severino, S. K., & Moline, M. L. (1989). *Premenstrual syndrome: A clinician's guide.* New York: Guilford Press.

Short, R. V. (1976). The evolution of human reproduction. *Proceedings of the Royal Society of London, 195,* 3–24.

Shostak, M. (1983). *Nisa: The life and world of a !Kung woman.* New York: Random House. (Original work published in 1981)

Siegel, J. P. (1986). Marital dynamics of women with premenstrual tension syndrome. *Family System Medicine, 4,* 358–365.

Siegel, S. J. (1985). The effect of culture on how women experience menstruation: Jewish women and Mikvah. *Women and Health, 10,* 63–74.

Smith, S., Rinehart, J. S., Ruddock, V. E., & Schiff, I. (1987). Treatment of premenstrual syndromes with alprazolam: Results of a double-blind, placebo-controlled, randomized cross-over clinical trial. *Obstetrics and Gynecology, 70,* 37–42.

Snowden, R., & Christian, B. (Eds.). (1983). *Patterns and perceptions of menstruation: A World Health Organization international collaborative study.* New York: St. Martin's Press.

Sommer, S. (1983). How does menstruation affect cognitive competence and psychophysiological response? *Women and Health, 8,* 53–90.

Sommer, S. (1992). Cognitive performance and the menstrual cycle. In T. E. Richardson (Ed.), *Cognition and the menstrual cycle* (pp. 39–66). New York: Springer-Verlag.

Stein, M. D., Schmidt, P. J., Rubinow, D. R., & Uhde, T. W. (1989). Panic disorder and the menstrual cycle: Panic disordered patients, healthy control subjects, and patients with premenstrual syndrome. *American Journal of Psychiatry, 146,* 1299–1306.

Steinberg, S. (1991). The treatment of late luteal phase dysphoric disorder. *Life Sciences, 49,* 767–802.

Stout, A. L., Grady, T. A., & Steege, J. F. (1986). Premenstrual symptoms in Black and White community samples. *American Journal of Psychiatry, 143,* 1436–1439.

Stout, A. L., Steege, J. F., Blazer, D. G., & George, L. K. (1986). Comparison of lifetime psychiatric diagnoses in premenstrual syndrome clinic and community samples. *Journal of Nervous and Mental Disease, 174,* 517–522.

Taylor, D., Woods, N. F., Lentz, M. J., Mitchell, E. S., & Lee, K. A. (1991). Perimenstrual negative affect: Development and testing of an explanatory model. In D. L. Taylor & N. F. Woods (Eds.), *Menstruation, health, and illness* (pp. 103–118). Washington, DC: Hemisphere.

Teja, J. S. (1976). Periodic psychosis of puberty: A longitudinal case study. *Journal of Nervous and Mental Disease, 162,* 52–57.

Tellegen, A., & Atkinson, G. (1974). Openness to absorbing and self-altering experiences ("absorption"), a trait related to hypnotic-susceptibility. *Journal of Abnormal Psychology, 83,* 266–268.

Trunnell, E. P., Turner, C. W., & Keye, W. R. (1988). A comparison of psychological and hormonal factors in women with and without premenstrual syndrome. *Journal of Abnormal Psychology, 97,* 429–436.

Ussher, J. M. (1992). The demise of dissent and the rise of cognition in menstrual-cycle research. In T. E. Richardson (Ed.), *Cognition and the menstrual cycle* (pp. 132–173). New York: Springer-Verlag.

van den Akker, O. B. A., Stein, G. S., Neale, M. C., & Murray, R. M. (1987). Genetic and environmental variation in menstrual cycle: Histories of two British twin samples. *Acta Geneticae et Medicae Gemellologiae, 36,* 541–548.

van den Akker, O., & Steptoe, A. (1989). Psychophysiological response in women reporting severe premenstrual symptoms. *Psychosomatic Medicine, 51,* 319–328.

Warner, P., Bancroft, J., Dixson, A., & Hampson, M. (1991). The relationship between perimenstrual depressive mood and depressive illness. *Journal of Affective Disorders, 23,* 9–23.

Warren, C. J., & Baker, S. (1992). Coping resources of women with premenstrual syndrome. *Archives of Psychiatric Nursing, 6,* 48–53.

Wilcoxin, L. A., Schrader, S. L., & Sherif, C. W. (1976). Daily self-reports on activities, life events, moods, and somatic changes during the menstrual cycle. *Psychosomatic Medicine, 38,* 399–417.

Williams, E. Y., & Weekes, L. R. (1952). Premenstrual tension associated with psychotic episodes. *Journal of Nervous and Mental Disease, 116,* 321–329.

Wilson, J. D., Braunwald, E., Isselbacher, K. J., Petersdorf, R. G., Martin, J. B., Fauci, A. S., & Root, R. K. (Eds.). (1991). *Harrison's principles of internal medicine* (12th ed.). New York: McGraw-Hill.

Woods, N. F. (1987). Premenstrual symptoms: Another look. *Public Health Reports,* Suppl., pp. 106–113.

Woods, N., Most, A., & Dery, G. (1982). Estimating the prevalence of perimenstrual symptoms. *Research in Nursing Health, 5,* 81–91.

Woods, N. F., Most, A., & Longnecker, G. D. (1985). Major life events, daily stressors, and perimenstrual symptoms. *Nursing Research, 34,* 263–267.

Yonkers, K. A., & White, K. (1992). Premenstrual exacerbation of depression: One process or two? *Journal of Clinical Psychiatry, 53,* 289–292.

Zelman, E. C. (1977). Reproduction, ritual, and power. *American Ethnologist, 4,* 714–733.

Author Index

439

Subject Index

About the Editors

Robert J. Gatchel received his BA in psychology from the State University of New York at Stony Brook in 1969 and his PhD in clinical psychology from the University of Wisconsin in 1973. Dr. Gatchel is currently Professor of Psychiatry and Rehabilitation Science at the University of Texas Southwestern Medical Center at Dallas. He is a diplomate of the American Board of Professional Psychology and is on the Board of Directors of the American Board of Health Psychology. He has conducted extensive research on the psychophysiology of stress and emotion; clinical applications of biofeedback; and the etiology, assessment, and treatment of chronic pain behavior. Dr. Gatchel is also the recipient of a Research Scientist Development Award from the National Institutes of Health. He has published over 100 scientific articles and has authored or edited eight other books, including *An Introduction to Health Psychology* (with A. Baum and D. Krantz) and *Functional Restoration for Spinal Disorders: A Sports Medicine Approach* (with T. Mayer). He is on the editorial board of numerous journals and is a member or fellow of the American Psychological Association, the Academy of Behavioral Medicine Research, the Society for Psychophysiological Research, and the International Society for the Study of the Lumbar Spine.

Edward B. Blanchard is Distinguished Professor of Psychology at the State University of New York at Albany and codirector of the Center for Stress and Anxiety Disorders. He received his PhD from Stanford University in 1969. His primary research and clinical interests have been in the fields of behavioral medicine and health psychology, with a particular focus on evaluating nondrug treatments of psychophysiological disorders. He is past president of Division 38 (Health Psychology) of the American Psychological Association and past editor of the journals *Behavior Therapy* and *Biofeedback and Self-Regulation*. Dr. Blanchard is also a diplomate in clinical psychology of the American Board of Professional Psychology.